MEDICAL RECORDS FOR THE SOUTH WALES COALFIELD, *c.*1890–1948

Medical Records for the South Wales Coalfield, *c.*1890–1948:

AN ANNOTATED GUIDE TO THE SOUTH WALES COALFIELD COLLECTION

ANNE BORSAY AND SARA KNIGHT

UNIVERSITY OF WALES PRESS
CARDIFF
2007

British Library Cataloguing-in-Publication Data
A catalogue record for this book is available from the British Library.

ISBN 978–0–7083–2047–1

wellcometrust

Typeset by Columns Design Ltd, Reading
Printed in Great Britain by Cambridge Printing, Cambridge

Contents

CONTENTS

Illustrations

Acknowledgements

This book is the product of a project to identify medical records in the South Wales Coalfield Collection (SWCC), which was funded by a Research Resources in Medical History Award from the Wellcome Trust (Grant number: 074808/Z/04/Z). We are grateful to the Trust for its generous support. The project was a collaborative venture between the School of Health Science (SHS) and the Library and Information Services (LIS) at Swansea University. We are grateful for the administrative assistance received from SHS and for the enthusiastic engagement of staff from LIS. Chris West and Sara Marsh made an invaluable contribution to the management of the project, Pam Beardsmore to catalogue enhancement and Alex Roberts to web-page development. Dr Ian Glen kindly translated Welsh-language documents. However, particular thanks are due to Elisabeth Bennett, the University Archivist, Siân Williams, the Librarian of the South Wales Miners' Library, and Sue Thomas, the Archive and Library Assistant. Without their consistent assistance and support, the project would have been impossible. Dr Jo Melling of the Centre for Medical History at the University of Exeter has offered helpful advice as our external adviser, and we thank Sarah Lewis, the staff of the University of Wales Press, and their anonymous referee for the careful and efficient way in which they have processed the volume. Finally, we are indebted to the South Wales Coalfield Collection at the University of Wales Swansea for permission to use all the illustrations, except the photograph of the Ton Co-operative Society's weighing scales which is reproduced by kind permission of Averyweigh-Tronix. Every effort has been made to trace copyright ownership. If we have inadvertently made use without permission of any materials in which you believe that you may have rights, we ask you to contact us as soon as possible.

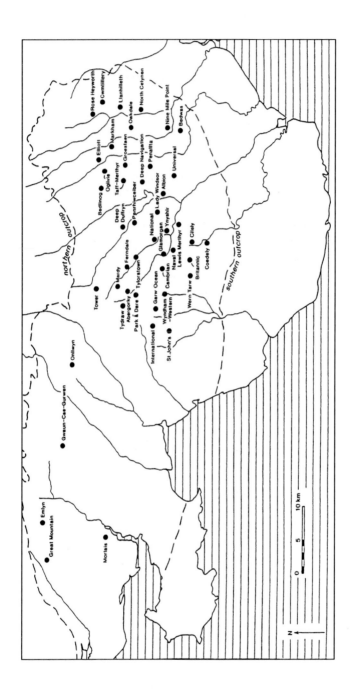

Map 1: Major Collieries on the South Wales Coalfield

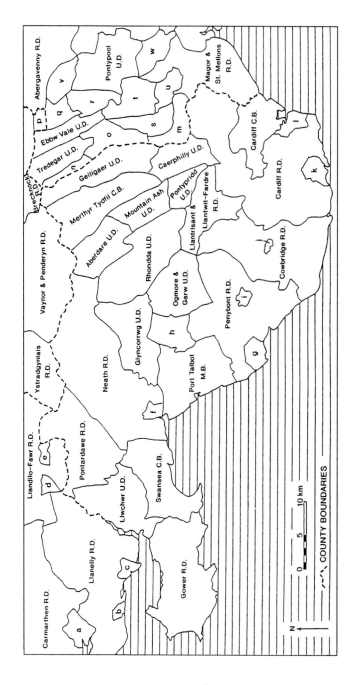

Map 2: Local Government Areas in South Wales, 1937

xi

Abbreviations

AGM	Annual General Meeting
ARP	Air Raid Precautions
BL	British Library
BMA	British Medical Association
BMJ	British Medical Journal
CAS	Carmarthenshire Archive Service
CWS	Co-operative Wholesale Society
DAC	Disablement Advisory Committee
DP	Data Protection
DWRGWU	Dock, Wharf, Riverside and General Workers' Union
ENT	Ear, Nose and Throat
Exec	Executive
GP	General Practitioner
GlamRO	Glamorgan Record Office
GwRO	Gwent Record Office
ILP	Independent Labour Party
MFGB	Miners' Federation of Great Britain
MOH	Medical Officer of Health
MO	Medical Officer
MRC	Medical Research Council
NCB	National Coal Board
NHI	National Health Insurance
NHS	National Health Service

NI	National Insurance
NLW	National Library of Wales
NSA	National Sound Archive
NSSAW	National Screen and Sound Archive of Wales
NUM	National Union of Mineworkers
PAC	Public Assistance Committee
PQ	Parliamentary Questions
RDC	Rural District Council
ROF	Royal Ordnance Factory
SW	South Wales
SWMF	South Wales Miners' Federation
TB	Tuberculosis
TGWU	Transport and General Workers' Union
TNA	The National Archives
TUC	Trades Union Congress
UAB	Unemployment Assistance Benefit
ud	undated
UDC	Urban District Council
VD	Venereal Disease
wef	with effect from
WGAS	West Glamorgan Archive Service
WL	Wellcome Library for the History and Understanding of Medicine
WWI	First World War
WWII	Second World War

Introduction

The South Wales Coalfield Collection

The South Wales Coalfield Collection (SWCC) is part of the Library and Information Services at Swansea University. It consists of the South Wales Coalfield Archive, based in the Library and Information Centre on the main Singleton Campus, and the South Wales Miners' Library, based on the Hendrefoelan Campus approximately two miles away. Archive collections have been deposited in the library since the 1950s and the holdings are particularly strong in relation to the industrial history of southwest Wales. However, the SWCC has its origins in a project funded by the Social Science Research Council (SSRC) and conducted from the History and Economic History Departments of the then University College of Swansea between 1971 and 1974. The aim of the project was to preserve oral and written evidence of coal miners and coal mining in south Wales at a time when the industry had started to decline and these records were in danger of being lost (Francis, 1976). Such was the success of the first project that it was followed by a second SSRC-funded project from 1979 to 1982. Substantial deposits have since been made to create a unique collection of international significance that is one of the largest of its kind in the UK.

The SWCC is unusual in that it contains a variety of media. Over 700 linear metres of documents are held, which include books, periodicals, pamphlets, and newspaper cuttings as well as records of the Miners' Federation and the National Union of Mineworkers (South Wales Area), miners' lodges and institutes, and the personal papers of miners. The collection also incorporates more than 4,000 photographs, 600 hours of oral history interviews, 200 hours of video footage, over 100 posters and 42 trade union banners. Therefore, the SWCC provides an invaluable resource for investigating the distinctive history of the South Wales Coalfield during the nineteenth and twentieth centuries. It is the

1

purpose of this guide to identify records within the collection for the medical history of the region.

The historiography of the coalfield

The South Wales Coalfield industrialized rapidly. Between 1854 and 1874, coal production climbed dramatically from 8.5 million tons to 16.5 million tons, and achieved its maximum output in 1913 with a haul of 57 million tons (C. Williams, 1998). Although coal was central to this thriving regional economy, iron and steel (B. Davies, 1983; Strange, 1983), copper and tin (Toomey, 1985; Rees, 2000; O. S. Jones, 1987) also played a vital role in its development. So too did the docks along the south Wales coast from which the products of local industries were exported (Daunton, 1977). Such rapid economic growth attracted workers looking for jobs that were relatively well paid and secure. Migration into the area was thus heavy, with an influx of population from England and the rest of Europe as well as from other parts of Wales (D. G. Evans, 2000; J. Williams, 1988). But in the aftermath of the First World War, the heavy industries went into sharp decline. Wartime demands brought a brief respite at the beginning of the Second World War. However, when coal was nationalized in 1947, production in south Wales was down to 21 million tons compared with 35 million tons in 1939 (C. Williams, 1998).

Early twentieth-century historians of Wales largely ignored this industrial heritage and concentrated their attention on the nation's more distant rural past (Adamson, 1999). Consequently, initial histories of the coalfield were penned by trade unionists celebrating the achievements of organized labour from socialist or communist perspectives; Ness Edwards (1926), for instance, was a miners' agent and later a Labour MP, whilst Robin Page Arnot was a veteran campaigner and leading Communist (1967, 1975). In the hands of Hywel Francis and David Smith (1980), the trade union history of south Wales acquired new sophistication. As part of the project that led to the South Wales Coalfield Collection, it was based on a careful review of primary sources that acknowledged internal conflicts and the significance of local society. During the intervening years, the labour history of the region has blossomed, not least through a rich strand of comparative analysis that embraces coalfields across the UK and internationally (see, for example, Berger, Croll and LaPorte (eds), 2005). Furthermore, political history has broadened to include communism, fascism and Labour as well as Liberal representation in local as well as central government (Francis, 1984; Morgan, 1981; C. Williams, 1996). What has been less satisfactory is the coverage of social history.

Although the economic history of the coalfield was being written from the 1950s (see, for example, John, 1950), the sub-discipline of social history that emerged in the following decade was slow to take root in Wales (Jordanova, 2000). Needless to say, there are now social histories addressing themes like popular culture (Smith and Williams, 1980), religion (Pope, 1998) and gender (John (ed.), 1991; Aaron et al. (eds), 1994; Beddoe, 2000). Moreover, studies of women's history have ventured into employment (Beddoe, 1989; Beddoe, 2000), childbirth (A. S. Williams, 1997), diet (White and Williams, 1997) and cleanliness (Evans and Jones, 1994; Salway, 2005): themes of central importance to health. However, comparatively little work has been published on the social history of medicine per se. More than three decades ago, John Cule compiled a list of sources on *Wales and Medicine* (1980). *Llafur*, the journal of the Society for the Study of Welsh Labour History, has periodically carried articles on occupational health (see, for example, Earwicker, 1981). Institutional histories have been written for the Cardiff Royal Infirmary (Aldis, 1984), the Swansea General and Eye Hospital (T. G. Davies, 1988), Morriston Hospital in Swansea (D. G. Williams, 1993), Nevill Hall Hospital in Abergavenny (G. Jones, 1998) and the County Infirmary, Carmarthen (Bolwell and Evans, 2005). And mental illness – the subject of a detailed monograph of the Denbigh Asylum (Michael, 2003) – has generated a number of articles on the Welsh scenario (see, for example, K. Davies, 1996), though little of specific relevance to the coalfield (T. G. Davies, 1995–6). Two collections of essays on the medical history of Wales have appeared in which there are chapters on south Wales (Borsay (ed.), 2003; Michael and Webster (eds), 2006). However, it was not until the publication of Steven Thompson's *Unemployment, Poverty and Health in Interwar South Wales* (2006) that the coalfield acquired a major academic study of its medical past.

3

Given the consequences of industrialization for the health of the population, this lacuna is surprising. It is, of course, important not to exaggerate the impact. Neither mining nor the other heavy industries were confined to the Valleys but spread west into Carmarthenshire where the environment remained comparatively rural. Furthermore, to the north and east, the coalfield was bordered by countryside and so industrial families were never a great distance from the pastoral ideal. Nevertheless, industrialization did transform the physical landscape, in the process creating hazards for occupational and community health that were compounded by the volatilities of the capitalist economy.

The occupational profile of the coalfield not only exposed workers to industrial diseases and injuries but also polluted the environment in ways that jeopardized the health of the community as a whole. Population growth aggravated these poor living conditions by exerting pressure on the housing stock. And low wages and unemployment exacerbated social deprivation. Under these circumstances, the incidence of infectious diseases, and of illness and disability, was high (Morgan, 1981; Thompson, 2006), babies and young children being particularly vulnerable (Tew, 1998). Where a male breadwinner was incapacitated, the effect was to plunge the family further into poverty, but women were often pivotal to the functioning of the household and thus their poor health – whether due to dangerous employment or domestic drudgery – was similarly disruptive (Beddoe, 1991; D. Jones, 1991). Since the expansion of the coalfield coincided with an increasingly collective stance on the part of the state, public sector solutions were put forward in response to its health care problems – some from central government; others from local government, frequently operating in partnership with the voluntary sector. However, self help and mutual aid remained key players (Finlayson, 1994; Kidd, 1999). Therefore, friendly societies and co-operative societies, trades unions and welfare institutes participated in a mixed economy of provision where workers and employers sponsored services and in return were allowed to engage in their management (Francis and Smith, 1980; Nash, Davies and Thomas, 1995).

How to use this guide

This guide has been prepared to encourage research into the neglected medical past of the South Wales Coalfield. The entries have been divided into two main sections: occupational health and community health. Within occupational health, there are four subsections: mining diseases and injuries; non-mining diseases and injuries; safety and welfare; and accidents. Within community health, there are nine subsections: infectious diseases; illness and disability; housing and sanitation; food and nutrition; women's health; children's health; health care personnel (doctors, nurses, dentists, pharmacists); health insurance and medical aid; and medical institutions (hospitals, asylums, sanatoria, convalescent homes).

Each section consists of a short introduction and a table of annotated references. The introduction briefly outlines the theme and draws attention to material in the collection of particular relevance. The table gives the SWCC reference code for each item, the collection in which it is held, the dates covered, a description of the content, the media (for example, document, audio tape, transcript of audio tape, photograph, banner), and whether the location is the South Wales Coalfield Archive or the South Wales Miners' Library. If usage raises a data protection (DP) issue this is also indicated. Items are listed in order of their reference code, unless they are still to be catalogued in which case they are placed at the beginning of the sequence. To avoid the unnecessary duplication of entries, material has been allocated to the subsection that best reflects its preponderance of interest. However, some overlap is inevitable. Items dealing with workmen's compensation, for instance, are to be found in the tables for mining and non-mining diseases and injuries, disability, accidents, and health insurance and medical aid.

Medical Records for the South Wales Coalfield complements the online catalogue for the SWCC, which is accessible via the Coalfield Web Materials page (http://www.agor.org.uk/cwm) and includes subject headings at item level for medicine and health; the web page also offers an introduction to the occupational and community health of the coalfield with illustrations, short bibliographies and internet links to related sites. A database containing all the annotated records from which this guide was prepared is also available on CD-ROM at the South Wales Coalfield Archive (archives@swan.ac.uk) and the South Wales Miners' Library (miners@swan.ac.uk). The archivist and the librarian welcome enquiries and offer comprehensive advice and support. Appendix A explains how to consult the SWCC. Appendix B looks beyond the collection to explore sources for the medical history of the coalfield in the British Library, the National Archives, the Wellcome Library for the History and Understanding of Medicine, the National Library of Wales, and the local record offices and libraries of the south Wales region. Appendix C lists the contact details for these repositories. Finally, there is a bibliography of printed and web resources, and indexes of names, places, organisations, and subjects. Original spellings are retained in the tables and given in parenthesis in the indexes.

Occupational Health

~ 1 ~
Mining Diseases and Injuries

From the later nineteenth century, increasing concern about occupational diseases and injuries generated pressure for improvements in the design of workshops. Legislation ensued. In 1879, for example, 'Occupations Injurious to Health' were officially recognized by the Chief Inspector of Factories. In 1891 special rules to safeguard workers in dangerous jobs were issued, although there was no power to impose these regulations on employers. In 1893 women factory inspectors were appointed, to be followed by the first medical inspector in 1898. And in 1901 and 1937 the Factory and Workshops Acts required the provision of adequate means of ventilation.

However, the landmark legislation for occupational health was the Workmen's Compensation Act of 1897. The outcome of trade union influence, the Act established the right to some degree of financial compensation in the event of injury at work – almost irrespective of any direct culpability. Initially, workmen's compensation applied to employment 'in or about a railway, factory, mine, quarry, or engineering work' and in buildings over 30 ft high that were being constructed, repaired or demolished using scaffolding or mechanical power. In 1906, however, new legislation began the process of listing diseases that were eligible for compensation.

Founded in 1898, the South Wales Miners' Federation (SWMF) played a crucial part in applying this legislation to the mining industry, acting in concert with the Miners' Federation of Great Britain. Thus by 1916 the schedule of diseases that qualified for compensation had been amended to include conditions that affected coal miners: ankylostomiasis (miners' worm disease); miners' nystagmus; Weil's disease (leptospirosis); subcutaneous cellulitis of the hand (beat hand); subcutaneous cellulitis over the patella (beat knee); acute bursitis over the elbow (beat elbow);

9

inflammation of the synovial lining of the wrist joint and the tendon sheaths (beat wrist); ulceration of the skin, or any dermatitis produced by dust or liquids; ulceration of the mucous membrane of the nose or mouth by dust; and glanders, an equine disease that also affected humans. In 1934 legislation, especially for colliers, ensured that coal companies had workmen's compensation insurance.

Miners' diseases were related to the environment in which men worked as well as directly to the physical act of mining. Ankylostomiasis (or 'miners' anaemia') was spread by poor hygiene underground. The difficulty of providing water closets underground was a particular problem for which resolutions were sought. In 1909, for example, Henry Kenwood published an article called 'Sanitation of mines in respect to human dejecta' in the *Journal of the Royal Sanitary Institute* (XXX, 10), which showed a design for a 'Tram fitted as Colliery Commode', and another 'Plan of Suggested Closet Convenience' for use in the pits (SWCC: MNA/PP/55/8).

Weil's Disease, an infection caused by contact with rats' urine, was also a potentially serious health hazard for miners. Conditions underground were an ideal habitat for rats and mice, with access to water and to food from men and pit ponies. Underground water sources were especially vulnerable to contamination, and were dangerous to anyone drinking or coming into contact with them. Surface water near the mines could likewise become polluted in this way. Dogs were used to help with rat catching, to reduce the number of rodents living in and around the collieries. Other common conditions caused by adverse working conditions were dermatitis and miners' furunculosis (boils), associated with working underground in wet conditions and high temperatures (SWCC: MNA/NUM/2/5).

The zoonotic disease 'glanders' (which can be transmitted from equines to humans) was common until the early twentieth century, and is fatal. It was another potential health hazard to miners dealing with pit ponies, and could appear either as a respiratory disease or skin lesions. In 1894 the Board of Agriculture implemented an order relating to glanders, which gave instructions about how to deal with suspected cases. No vaccine has ever been discovered, but a 'mallein' test was used in diagnosis, which involved a skin test with concentrate from cultures or extracts of the glanders bacillus. In 1902 a departmental committee appointed by the board concluded that mallein testing was effective in the prevention and treatment of glanders. In 1910 – the year in which a collier died from blood poisoning following infection by glanders – a report to the secretary of state on *An Outbreak of Glanders among the Horses, and the alleged General Insanitary Condition of the Collieries, belonging to the Ebbw Vale Steel, Iron and Coal Co Ltd., in the County of Monmouth* was published (SWCC:MNA/PP/55/8). Pit ponies were among the working horses subsequently tested for glanders before they were taken underground. By the 1930s, the disease was in decline and had been eradicated from Britain and much of Europe through statutory testing, the slaughter of infected animals and import restrictions.

Nystagmus – an eye disease that causes oscillation of the eyeballs – was aggravated by poor underground lighting. It had been listed in 1906, and in a 1913 report by the Departmental Committee on Compensation for Industrial Diseases it was renamed 'miner's nystagmus'. Research into nystagmus continued in the 1920s and 1930s. In 1922, for example, the first report of the Miners' Nystagmus Committee was published by the Medical Research Council: a study of the psycho-neurotic symptoms associated with the condition by the famous psychoanalyst and anthropologist, W. H. R. Rivers (SWCC: RE748 GRE). In 1924 Dr Frederick Robson concluded, on the basis of investigations in the South Wales Coalfield, that Monmouthshire had the biggest increase in cases between 1901 and 1919 (SWCC: RE748 ROB). And in 1930 Ivor J. Lane published his observations on the relationship between miners' nystagmus and the mine environment, based on a paper that he presented to the South Wales Institute of Engineers (SWCC: RE748 LAN). Although research into the disease continued into the second half of the twentieth century, its incidence decreased with the introduction of better safety lamps and more efficient lighting.

Injuries and disease caused by overuse of the joints were also common in mining. Beat hand, beat knee, beat elbow and beat wrist were frequently cited in claims for workmen's compensation. In 1924 the Medical Research Council published a *Report on Miners' 'Beat Knee', 'Beat Hand', and 'Beat Elbow'* by E. L. Collis and T. L. Llewellyn, which contained details of the incidence and

11

clinical configurations of these diseases, and an explanation of the meaning of 'beat' (SWML: no reference code).

The lung disease, silicosis, appeared in workmen's compensation legislation from 1918, though not in relation to the coal mining industry. In 1928, however, coal miners were included in the Various Industries (Silicosis) Scheme, whereby the claimant had to prove that he had been working in silica rock containing 50 per cent or more free silica, had been 'blasting, drilling, dressing or handling such rocks', and had already been totally disabled by silicosis. In 1931 the clause relating to rock containing 50 per cent or more free silica was removed from the scheme, and a Special Medical Board for Silicosis was introduced, along with provision for partial disablement and for widows. In 1934 the scheme was extended to include colliery workers in any underground occupation, and five years later the period of claim was extended to 'within 5 years of working underground'. It was intended to celebrate these achievements on May Day 1939 when the SWMF planned a Silicosis Pageant in the Amman Valley depicting the 'enormous struggle' against unemployment, inadequate pensions and the ravages of lung disease. However, the event was cancelled due to bad weather (SWCC: Special Collections).

All the previous schemes were amended in 1943 to provide full compensation for those suffering from 'Pneumokoniosis of coalworkers' (including silicosis and all the various forms found in the Welsh coalfield). This new definition was a result of investigations undertaken by the Medical Research Council and published in 1942. The report by Dr Philip D'Arcy Hart and Dr Edward Aslett renamed the condition 'pneumoconiosis' rather than 'silicosis' after it was established that coal trimmers, who did not work underground but were exposed to coal dust, exhibited similar results in tests on their lungs. The Medical Research Council's Pneumoconiosis Research Unit was founded in 1945. Initial staff appointments to the unit were made by Dr Charles Fletcher, who was responsible for dividing pneumoconiosis into two categories: 'simple' (PNC – Pneumoconiosis) and 'complicated' (PMF – Progressive Massive Fibrosis). The unit began work at Curran's Steel Works in Cardiff, but a few years later moved to Llandough Hospital on the outskirts of the city, where doctors such as Archie Cochrane became widely known for their work. The official opening ceremony at Llandough Hospital took place on 28 October 1950.

Reference Code	Collection	Dates	Description	Media	Location	DP
	Chronic Pulmonary Disease in South Wales Coalminers (3 volumes)	1942–45	Medical Research Council. Vol. I, *Medical Studies*. Vol. II, *Environmental Studies*. Vol. III, *Experimental Studies* (London: HMSO, 1942–45). Includes photos and statistics. Silicosis and pneumoconiosis.	Document	SWML	
	Report on Miners' 'Beat Knee', 'Beat Hand', and 'Beat Elbow' (pamphlet)	1924	Medical Research Council. E. L. Collis and T. L. Llewellyn (London: HMSO), Special Report Series No. 89. Contents: Incidence of diseases in UK and Belgium, clinical aspects, description of diseases and meaning of 'beat', treatments, photos, statistics, 1906 Workmen's Compensation Act.	Document	SWML	
AUD/45	Dr Anne Cockroft	1970–82	Pneumoconiosis Unit (MRC). NCB involvement. Compensation. Bronchitis, emphysema, fibrosis. Post-mortems. Genetic predisposition theory. Prevention of diseases. Asbestosis.	Audio tape	SWML	Y
AUD/56	Haydn Mainwaring	1910–80	Workmen's Compensation Secretary for 33 years. Applications from 1948 relating to dust in lungs. Supplementary allowances for the totally disabled. Sending of doctors' certificates to Compensation Secretary. Reforms to compensation and NHS from 1948 – abuse of scheme and absenteeism. Workmen's Compensation; cases and earnings formulae. Indemnity Society agents and pressurization of men and wives to settle compensation cases. Proof of silica in rocks. Proof of dust and silica in lungs pre-1943 Pneumoconiosis Act. Pneumoconiosis and surface workers. Fines for employing pneumoconiotic workers. Nystagmus symptoms, lighting and lamps. Visits to compensation doctor at colliery office. Pneumoconiosis certification and surface work.	Audio tape	SWML	Y

Reference Code	Collection	Dates	Description	Media	Location	DP
AUD/164	John Evans (Maerdy Community Study)	1930–c.1960	Pneumoconiosis and silicosis. Compensation. Colleagues suffering or died from dust-related disease. Own experiences of pneumoconiosis and medical check and X-ray by Dr Cochrane. Re-entry to mining in WWII for miners with medical certificates.	Transcript of audio	SWML	Y
AUD/170	Lee Hutchinson	1875–c.1960	1942 reference to pit work, skin complaint (psoriasis), working in water and heat, visit to doctors.	Transcript of audio	SWML	Y
AUD/174	George Baker	1930–c.1974	Nystagmus and Workmen's Compensation.	Transcript of audio	SWML	Y
AUD/192	Mr and Mrs Fred Morris (Maerdy)	1900–c.1973	Surface workers suffering from bad bronchitis and dust on lung.	Transcript of audio	SWML	Y
AUD/195, 196	Will 'Box' Thomas (Maerdy)	1900–c.1973	Work as Lodge official, and efforts to encourage dust suppression. Reference to pneumoconiosis.	Transcript of audio	SWML	Y
AUD/215	Walter Powell	c.1900–74	Nystagmus caused by bad lighting. Dust, pneumoconiosis, silicosis. Workmen's Compensation.	Transcript of audio	SWML	Y
AUD/300	Percy James Matthews	1898–c.1973	Work-related injuries, septic knees, back injury (visit for X-ray and compensation claim), pneumo-silicosis.	Transcript of audio	SWML	Y
AUD/336	Harold Finch (permission needed for use)	1920–c.1973	SWMF Compensation Secretary. Advised NUM regarding pneumoconiosis. Dr Harper and pneumoconiosis. History of legislation, silicosis and pneumoconiosis. Industrial Injuries Scheme. Llandough Hospital research unit.	Transcript of audio	SWML	Y
AUD/374	Dr Thomas	1900–1960s	Silicosis and pneumoconiosis. Nutritional factors in resistance to dust diseases. Coal dust type and relation to X-ray quality and affect on compensation claims (anthracite harder, more opaque in X-rays; steam coal less dense). Clinical description of lung damage.	Audio tape	SWML	Y

Reference Code	Collection	Dates	Description	Media	Location	DP
AUD/382	D. C. Davies	1930–c.1976	Treatments at Llandough Hospital. Doctors' opinions on dust in lungs. Pneumoconiosis and anthracosis, legislation 1943, and compensation problems. Compensation panels. Disablement benefit. Suspension from work of men on compensation. Widows of pneumoconiosis victims and effect on them. Accidents and disease amongst pit workers and effects on them and families. Work as Lodge Compensation Secretary. Compensation – silicosis only; campaign to include other chest diseases (e.g. bronchitis, emphysema).	Transcript of audio	SWML	Y
AUD/481	Mrs Bessie Webb and Mrs Hannah Katie Evans	1920–75	TB and silicosis of family members.	Audio tape	SWML	Y
AUD/488	Mrs Exon	1910–1975	Silicosis; father's illness, compensation, masks.	Audio tape	SWML	Y
HD661.TRA	TUC Annual Reports of Proceedings (incomplete set)	1904–85	Workmen's Compensation including silicosis.	Document	SWML	
HD9550 EBB	The Ebbw Vale Works Magazine, Vol. 3, No. 9	1923	Article: 'Health and Welfare in the Coal Mining Industry', by Edgar Collis, Welsh National School of Medicine. Article and letter relating to nystagmus.	Document	SWML	
HD9550 EBB	The Ebbw Vale Works Magazine, Vol. 7, No. 27	1928	Article: 'The Advantages of Exercise'. Health hints to miners – reference to eyesight (nystagmus), beat hand, rheumatism, bronchitis, lumbago and sciatica (from wet clothing).	Document	SWML	
HD9552.3 MIN	The Miner, Vol. I, No. I	1944	Articles: 'Dust Suppression', re silicosis and pneumoconiosis; 'Pneumoconiosis – Treatment and Rehabilitation' and 'Periodical Examinations Recommended'.	Document	SWML	
HD9552.3 MIN	The Miner, Vol. I, No. 3	1944	Safety Department article: 'The Coal Mines (South Wales) (Pneumoconiosis) Order 1943'.	Document	SWML	

Reference Code	Collection	Dates	Description	Media	Location	DP
HD9552.3 MIN	*The Miner*, Vol. I, No. 4	1945	Letter: disabled miners (references to silicosis and pneumoconiosis).	Document	SWML	
HD9552.3 MIN	*The Miner*, Vol. I, No. 7/8	1945	Article: Workmen's Compensation, mobile X-ray unit in South Wales for Medical Board examinations, and pneumoconiosis.	Document	SWML	
HD9552.3 MIN	*The Miner*, Vol. I, No. 9/10	1945	NUM Annual Conference report, with reference to pneumoconiosis in Wales.	Document	SWML	
HD9552.3 MIN	*The Miner*, Vol. II, No. 7	1946	Articles: 'Removing a Pestilence – Silicosis and Pneumoconiosis dust suppression'. Pneumoconiosis 1946 Regulation details from General and Compensation Secretaries.	Document	SWML	
HD9552.3 MIN	*The Miner*, Vol. II, No. 9	1946	Report, NUM Annual Conference, references to industrial diseases.	Document	SWML	
HD9552.3 MIN	*The Miner*, Vol. II, No. 11	1946	Article: 'New Industries in South Wales', reference factories for disabled workers (and silicosis and pneumoconiosis cases).	Document	SWML	
HD9552.3 MIN	*The Miner*, Vol. II, No. 12	1946	Editorial: Miners' Medical Service, refers to pneumoconiosis, Llandough Hospital, rehabilitation, training, aftercare, research, Pneumoconiosis Dust Committee (South Wales). Article: 'Factories in South Wales for Disabled Persons'; Disabled Persons' Employment Act, numbers of disabled people, training centres, workers and jobs at other establishments, sheltered employment, Grenfell Scheme (south Wales miners with silicosis or pneumoconiosis).	Document	SWML	
HD9552.3 MIN	*The Miner*, Vol. III, No. 1/2	1946	Article: 'Dust Consolidation on Mine Roadways', dust, silicosis, pneumoconiosis.	Document	SWML	

Reference Code	Collection	Dates	Description	Media	Location	DP
HD9552.3 MIN	*The Miner*, Vol. III, No. 3	1947	Review of NUM Conference – Safety Regulations, Health and Welfare (including pneumoconiosis). Article: 'Organisation of Pneumokoniosis Research in South Wales under the Medical Research Council', reference Llandough Hospital, Drs D'Arcy Hart and Aslett.	Document	SWML	
HD9552.3 MIN	*The Miner*, Vol. III, No. 4/5	1947	Report re Pneumoconiosis Conference, Cardiff.	Document	SWML	
HD9552.3 MIN	*The Miner*, Vol. III, No. 8/9	1947	Article: 'Greetings to Welsh Miners from Australian Miners', refers to dust hazard and compensation.	Document	SWML	
HV686.R3	Reports of the MOH, and School MO, Rhondda UDC	1945	Reports of the MOH including reference to silicosis and pneumoconiosis.	Document	SWML	
MNA/1/16/3	Forest of Dean District Welfare Association (committee minutes)	1929–35	Applications: neurasthenia, sciatica, artificial eye, silicosis, gastric ulcer, spectacles.	Document	Archives	Y
MNA/COL/2/1	Clydach Merthyr Colliery (arbitration meeting minutes)	1942–7	Rough minutes of arbitration meetings held to resolve disputes: Compensation cases. Rehabilitation and light work. Pneumoconiosis. Disabled workman (partial deafness). Rheumatism.	Document	Archives	Y
MNA/COL/2/4–38	Clydach Merthyr Colliery (Manager's carbon-copy correspondence books)	1937–48	House coal for pneumoconiotic men. Workmen's Compensation. Beat elbow and knee. Hernia. Silicosis and pneumoconiosis. Nystagmus. Inquests.	Document	Archives	Y
MNA/COL/2/54	Clydach Merthyr Colliery (Manager's correspondence)	1938–9	Silicosis and dust respirators. Beat knee.	Document	Archives	Y
MNA/COL/2/55	Clydach Merthyr Colliery (Manager's correspondence)	1940–1	Workmen's Compensation. Reports re medical examinations of workmen. Beat knee. Silicosis. Hernia.	Document	Archives	Y

Reference Code	Collection	Dates	Description	Media	Location	DP
MNA/COL/2/56	Clydach Merthyr Colliery (compensation correspondence to Manager)	1938-45	Details of medical examinations of injured workmen, e.g. fibrositis, dermatitis, fractures, nystagmus, burns, beat knee, amputations, silicosis, 'hysterical blindness'.	Document	Archives	Y
MNA/COL/2/60	Clydach Merthyr Colliery (NCB circulars, memoranda etc.)	1947-50	Papers relating to employment of workmen with pneumoconiosis.	Document	Archives	Y
MNA/I/4/C5	Bargoed and District Workmen's Library and Institute	1922-4	Book of counterfoils – Workmen's Compensation Act 1906, Powell Duffryn Steam Coal Co. Ltd. Claims for compensation and notices of injury. Including name, address, occupation, cause of injury, date of accident, amount claimed. Including nystagmus and beat elbow.	Document	Archives	Y
MNA/NUM/1/1	Records of the Miners' Federation of Great Britain (Minute books of MFGB Executive Committee, and Annual and Special Conferences)	1903 and 1905	1903: Disease: ankylostomiasis ('worm disease' or 'miners' anaemia'); reference to Cornwall tin miners; case at Glasgow Infirmary; full text of speech by Dr Court. Sanitation; Scottish mines and south Wales. 1905: Workmen's conditions re nystagmus or 'night blindness'. Worm disease. Workmen's Compensation Act lung diseases. Ventilation. Compensation Amendment Bill.	Document	Archives and SWML	
MNA/NUM/1/1	Records of the Miners' Federation of Great Britain (Minute books of Executive Committee, and Annual and Special Conferences)	1921-30	1921-2: Workmen's Compensation. Coal Dust experiments. 1923-4: Nystagmus: connection with lamps; report and Home Office Order 1922. Workmen's Compensation Act. 1925-26: Nystagmus, Home Office Scheme. Miners' beat knee and beat elbow. Compensation cases including silicosis. 1927-30: Miners' beat knee and beat elbow. Silicosis. Various Industries (Silicosis) Scheme 1928.	Document	Archives and SWML	

Reference Code	Collection	Dates	Description	Media	Location	DP
MNA/NUM/1/1	Records of the Miners' Federation of Great Britain (Minute books of MFGB Executive Committee, and Annual and Special Conferences)	1931–40	1931–3: Silicosis; draft schemes, report, discussion. Workmen's Compensation – anthracosis. Industrial diseases; anthracosis, silicosis. Workmen's Compensation; silicosis, nystagmus, boils (furunculosis). 1934: Nystagmus; medical examination for, compensation, conference discussion. Occupational diseases – international table of diseases. Silicosis; Medical Arrangements Scheme, research, regulations re compensation. High temperature in mines and effect on workers. 1935–6: Medical referees. Nystagmus. Silicosis, and 1931 Scheme. Workmen's Compensation – skin disease. 1937–40: Silicosis and Asbestosis Fund.	Document	Archives and SWML	
MNA/NUM/1/1	Records of the Miners' Federation of Great Britain (Minute books of MFGB Executive Committee, and Annual and Special Conferences)	1943–4	1943: Coal Mining (Training and Medical Examination) Order 1943. Medical certificates and payment by workers. Rehabilitation centres. Pneumoconiosis schemes and Workmen's Compensation. 1944: Mines Medical Service and functions of doctors. Pneumoconiosis Compensation Scheme. Rehabilitation, incapacity by illness or industrial disease.	Document	Archives and SWML	
MNA/NUM/1/1–2	Records of the Miners' Federation of Great Britain/NUM (Minute books of Executive Committee, and Annual and Special Conferences)	1902–48	General themes include disease. 1947: Pneumoconiosis. Industrial diseases extension of schedule.	Document	Archives and SWML	
MNA/NUM/1/2	Records of the Miners' Federation of Great Britain/NUM (Minute books of NUM National Executive Committee, and Annual and Special Conferences)	1945–6	Workmen's Compensation, emphysema, dermatitis. Disability through use of air picks and boring machines.	Document	Archives and SWML	

Reference Code	Collection	Dates	Description	Media	Location	DP
MNA/NUM/2/5	Lancashire and Cheshire Miners' Federation (reports on skin diseases case)	1935	Pamphlet (8 pages); case at Parsonage Pit, Wigan Coal Corporation. References to mine conditions, medical examination of miners, water analysis. To urge government to include the skin diseases in Schedule of Workmen's Compensation Act. Four photographs of skin disease cases.	Document	Archives	
MNA/NUM/2/6	Yorkshire Area NUM: *Industrial Injuries* Quiz (National Ins Industrial Injuries Act, 1946)	1948	Pamphlet (56 pages). Questions and Answers re the 1946 Act. Appendix 'List of Prescribed Diseases'. Re insurance pneumoconiosis, silicosis, byssinosis – regulations being prepared under Sect. 57 of N. I. (Industrial Injuries) Act, 1946. Points of action for accidents.	Document	Archives	
MNA/NUM/3/1/1	Minutes of the SWMF Exec Council, and Annual and Special Conferences: Records of the SWMF/NUM	1907–40	Nystagmus (and Home Office Scheme 1925). Industrial diseases. Coal dust. Rock analysis. Partially disabled. Medical examinations of workmen. Medical attention underground. Silicosis. Tetanus. Fibrosis of lungs. Anthracosis.	Document	Archives and SWML	
MNA/NUM/3/10/20	Records of the NUM (South Wales Area)	1907	Pamphlet: SWMF Workmen's Compensation Act, 1906: Explanatory notes. Injuries and diseases including ankylostomiasis, nystagmus, beat hand, knee, and elbow, inflammation of synovial lining of wrist joint. Persons entitled to Compensation, injuries and diseases, notice of accidents and claims, amounts, calculation methods, prospective loss, light employment, medical referees, contracting out, recording of agreements.	Document	Archives	

Reference Code	Collection	Dates	Description	Media	Location	DP
MNA/NUM/3/3/2	Correspondence (bound volume of circulars)	1916–27	1920 conference on Amendments to Coal Mines Act including lamps, Coroners at Inquests, gas testers, Compensation (inclusion of miners' phthisis, rheumatism, yellow jaundice), reference medical examination of workmen and doctors' notes. Workmen's Compensation Acts references. Nystagmus: correspondence including 1926 MFGB letter, collecting evidence.	Document	Archives	
MNA/NUM/3/3/3	Correspondence (bound volume of circulars)	1927–35	Compensation: SWMF manifesto, 1927 TUC and Labour Party booklet re Consolidating Bill, 1928 – gas poisoning in mines (scheduled) and inclusion of carbon monoxide poisoning (not scheduled). Stone dusting and health issues. 1928 letter: spirochaetal or infectious jaundice, requesting details of cases. SWMF statistics including accidents. 1932 conference references to silicosis, inspection of mines, lighting of mines (nystagmus). 1935 May Day Demonstrations referring to Workmen's Compensation amendments, Silicosis Order, anthracosis and compensation.	Document	Archives	
MNA/NUM/3/3/14	Correspondence with SWMF No. 1 Area (File 1)	1931–42	Two medical cases detailed. Workmen's Compensation, Notice forms and medical certificates. Amputated finger case. 1933 Medical report from Cefn Coed Hospital (Swansea) relating to nystagmus case and anxiety neurosis (report by Medical Superintendent of Swansea County Borough Mental Hospital).	Document	Archives	Y

Reference Code	Collection	Dates	Description	Media	Location	DP
MNA/NUM/3/3/14	Correspondence with SWMF No. 1 Area (File 2)	1931–42	Lists of compensation cases including silicosis, nystagmus, injuries, hernia. Epilepsy case. Medical Boards. Compensation calculations. Notes for Amendment of Silicosis Scheme re coal mines (suggestions of Judge Rowlands). Partial compensation payment calculations. Letter to doctor re certificates. Insurance. Heart specialists recommended. Expenses to attend treatment and X-ray. Compensation case details including court dates, disputed cases. New Silicosis Order 1934. 2 post-mortem reports (septic poisoning and heart failure). Support for scheduling of anthracosis as industrial disease.	Document	Archives	Y
MNA/NUM/3/3/14	Correspondence with SWMF No. 1 Area (File 3)	1931–42	Compensation cases, lists, letters, including many silicosis, nystagmus, hernia, injuries, accidents. Lodge Compensation Secretaries. Members funds for artificial limbs and surgical appliances, request for money by injured man. Medical certificates.	Document	Archives	Y
MNA/NUM/3/3/14	Correspondence with SWMF No. 1 Area (Files 4 and 5)	1931–42	File 4: 1933: Compensation cases, refers to pneumoconiosis cases, doctors' reports, letters. Dr Harper – writing BMJ article and examination of 60–70 cases (surface workers). File 5: Memo: disabled workmen on light employment (wages and conditions).	Document	Archives	Y
MNA/NUM/3/3/14	Correspondence with SWMF No. 1 Area (File 11)	1931–42	Compensation cases, silicosis, Medical Board. Flyer re SWMF meeting re government Medical Research Council, Silicosis Investigation 1938. Refusal of certificates for silicosis cases. Accidents.	Document	Archives	Y
MNA/NUM/3/3/14	Correspondence with SWMF No. 1 Area (Files 12 and 13)	1931–42	File 12: 1937: Compensation cases. Nystagmus cases doctors' reports (e.g. fracture). Silicosis investigation at Wernos. Silicosis Relief Committee. File 13: 1939 cutting from the *Lancet* 'Irradiation and Miners', p. 1281, 16/12/1939.	Document	Archives	Y

Reference Code	Collection	Dates	Description	Media	Location	DP
MNA/NUM/3/3/14	Correspondence with SWMF No. 1 Area (Files 14 and 15)	1931–42	File 14: Compensation cases. Correspondence with Medical Defence Union regarding payment of fees to doctor for silicosis cases. File 15: 1940; Compensation. New Act and Supplementary Allowances.	Document	Archives	Y
MNA/NUM/3/3/14	Correspondence with SWMF No. 1 Area (Files 16 and 17)	1931–42	File 16: 1941: Compensation cases. File 17: 1942. Compensation cases. Ammanford, Llandebie and District Trades Council and Local Labour Party Statement of Accounts and Reports 1941–42. Silicosis Research Committee of Amalgamated Anthracite Collieries.	Document	Archives	Y
MNA/NUM/3/3/18	Correspondence with SWMF No. 5 Area	1934–41	Silicosis and support for compulsory risk reduction by mine owners. Expenses to attend medical referee.	Document	Archives	
MNA/NUM/3/3/21	Correspondence with SWMF No. 8 Area	1934–42	Partial Compensation and house coal. Compensation – resumption of employment, and refusal to re-employ due to nystagmus.	Document	Archives	
MNA/NUM/3/3/23	Correspondence with lodges (Files 2–8)	1934–42	Commuted nystagmus case and employment. Silicosis references; Compensation case, conference.	Document	Archives	Y
MNA/NUM/3/3/33/1	Great Mountain Lodge (correspondence)	1934–41	Llanelly Medical Scheme and eye specialist, nystagmus. Compensation officer. Dust at screens and health, excessive dust complaints. Inspection report. Silicosis cases, medical examinations, post-mortems, numbers, silicosis and TB.	Document	Archives	
MNA/NUM/3/3/33/4	Gwaun-Cae-Gurwen Lodge (correspondence)	1934–42	1934: Silicosis Orders references, possible one-day strike because of shortcomings (on Annual Conference Agenda). Notification of accident, Federation Compensation Scheme correspondence and details. 1936 reference to Dust Summonses to Gwaun-cae-gurwen Collieries. 1939 reference to X-ray scheme for silicosis at collieries and cost.	Document	Archives	

23

Reference Code	Collection	Dates	Description	Media	Location	DP
MNA/NUM/3/4/43	Compensation claims arising out of the liquidation of the Ebbw Vale and Subsidiary Cos. (SWMF/NUM miscellaneous office papers and reports)	1936–40	1937: List of Workmen's Compensation claims, Ebbw Vale, name and address, age, date of accident, injury, amounts. Including nystagmus, fractures, amputations, loss of eye, crush injuries. Correspondence re compensation cases. (Ebbw Vale in liquidation)	Document	Archives	Y
MNA/NUM/3/4/45	SWMF/NUM Miscellaneous office papers and reports (May Day Pageants 1938–9; Inter-colliery Sports 1939; wartime film scenarios)	1938–54	May Day Pageant Pontypool script 1939, refers to miners' deaths by silicosis. Dulais Valley Pageant of History script refers to silicosis. SWMF form re silicosis cases for 1937. 1938 letter re questions for Silicosis Pageant (1939). Committee report list of events for 1939 including portrayal of struggle with silicosis.	Document	Archives	
MNA/NUM/3/4/48	Mines Inspectorate (SWMF/NUM miscellaneous office papers and reports)	1943–47	1943: notes relating to meeting of Joint Pneumoconiosis Sub-Committee. 1943 letter; pneumoconiosis and silicosis.	Document	Archives	
MNA/NUM/3/5/1	SWMF: Compensation Records (book)	1937–40	Details of miners, collieries, injuries, court decisions, awards, comments, operations. Injuries; fatal, heart, stomach, lungs, eyes, Weil's disease, skin, VD, cancer, septicaemia.	Document	Archives	Y
MNA/NUM/3/5/2	SWMF: Compensation Records (register of industrial diseases cases)	1934–40	Details of miners, collieries, injuries, court decisions, awards, comments, operations. Disablement caused by; silicosis, nystagmus, dermatitis, hernia, Weil's Disease, beat knee, hand, wrist, and elbow, dyspepsia and jaundice, water rash, fractured skull.	Document	Archives	Y
MNA/NUM/3/5/3	SWMF: Compensation Records (register of fatal accidents)	1934–41	Details of miners, collieries, injuries, court decisions, awards, comments, operations. Cause of death; lung and heart problems, shock, septicaemia, suicide, hernia, suffocation, crush injuries, drowning, gassed, burns, meningitis, electric shock, cancer.	Document	Archives	Y

Reference Code	Collection	Dates	Description	Media	Location	DP
MNA/NUM/3/5/8	SWMF: Compensation Records (certified silicosis case papers)	1941–45	Certificates of Suspension for silicosis, asbestosis, pneumoconiosis or any of those accompanied by TB. Certificates of SWMF Lodge Compensation Secretaries. Medical Board certificates. Correspondence from collieries, insurance companies, solicitors. Correspondence from Silicosis and Asbestosis Medical Expenses Fund. Certificates refer to Workmen's Compensation Acts 1925 to 1943, Silicosis and Asbestosis (Medical Arrangements) Scheme 1931 to 1943. Personal and claim details on certificates.	Document	Archives	Y
MNA/NUM/3/5/9	SWMF/NUM: Compensation Records	1946–60	Pneumoconiosis claims.	Document	Archives	Y
MNA/NUM/3/5/10	SWMF: Compensation Records (annual reports of silicosis cases)	1935–40	Numbers of death and disablement cases, applications to Medical Board, certificates granted or refused, Compensation paid, costs.	Document	Archives	Y
MNA/NUM/3/5/10	SWMF: Compensation Records (annual reports of silicosis cases)	1938–39	Pamphlet: Silicosis in the South Wales Coalfield Parts I and II, by T. David Jones (Prof. of Mining), 1938, 30 pages and illustrations; SWMF Annual Conference 1939 Agenda, including compensation, safety, dust absorbers, lamps, miscellaneous (respirators). 1938: Letter from P. D'Arcy Hart, Medical Research Council, with attached article from University College Hospital Magazine, 'Economics of Fractures', by Prof. R. S. Pilcher, fracture clinics.	Document	Archives	
MNA/NUM/3/5/11	SWMF: Compensation Records (Annual Reports of Fatal Accidents)	1936–9	Reports from each area: numbers of amounts paid, and details re where compensation not paid. Details re causes of death, and collieries. Includes nystagmus, silicosis, beat knee, wrist, elbow, and hand, and suicide.	Document	Archives	Y

Reference Code	Collection	Dates	Description	Media	Location	DP
MNA/NUM/3/5/13	SWMF: Compensation Records (general correspondence)	1931–35	Correspondence: Tirbach Colliery silicosis cases. Nystagmus compensation and re-employment, details from each SWMF Area for Home Office Enquiry into nystagmus 1934/5. Letters: calculation of compensation. Letter from South Africa; silicosis and TB.	Document	Archives	Y
MNA/NUM/3/5/14	SWMF: Compensation Records (Compensation Secretary's correspondence)	1936–7	1936–7: Silicosis. Partially disabled and light employment. 1938: Correspondence; Royal Commission on Workmen's Compensation, and Medical Research Council Committee on Industrial Pulmonary Disease. Silicosis, anthracosis, bronchitis, hernia, beat knee. Deafness and use of coal-cutting machinery. 1939: Silicosis. Weil's Disease, BMJ article by Swansea doctor, reference to coalfield. Silicosis Pageant (May Day) historical background and banners. Royal Commission on Workmen's Compensation questionnaire. MFGB Pamphlet. 1940: Medical Research Council notes re industrial hygiene. Industrial Health Research Board projects. British Rhondda Colliery shock cases (explosion). 1941: Silicosis.	Document	Archives	Y
MNA/NUM/3/5/15	SWMF: Compensation Records (Compensation Secretary's correspondence: Area No. 4)	1934–41	Silicosis. Nystagmus. 1934 paper: 'Fighting eye disease', nystagmus case. Employer's liability for dentures and artificial limbs.	Document	Archives	Y
MNA/NUM/3/5/16	SWMF: Compensation Records (Compensation Secretary's correspondence: Area No. 5)	1934–41	Silicosis. Nystagmus. SWMF Agents' Report Area 6 (1935) including deaths, compensation claims, silicosis, and nystagmus.	Document	Archives	Y
MNA/NUM/3/5/17	SWMF: Compensation Records (Compensation Secretary's correspondence: Area No. 6)	1934–41	Detailed case notes for each colliery. Silicosis, nystagmus, hernia, synovitis of knee.	Document	Archives	Y

Reference Code	Collection	Dates	Description	Media	Location	DP
MNA/NUM/3/5/18	SWMF: Compensation Records (Compensation Secretary's correspondence: Area No. 8)	1934–41	Silicosis, ulcer, hernia, nystagmus. Dermatitis case detailed papers. Death certificate relating to beat hand (subcutaneous cellulitis). Silicosis investigation notices and letters to collieries and miners. 1913 papers re nystagmus case at Blaina: doctor's certificate and report, County Court notices, certificate of disablement.	Document	Archives	Y
MNA/NUM/3/5/20	SWMF: Compensation Records	1936	Correspondence and press cuttings: Silicosis Distress Fund. Articles by Louise Morgan – News Chronicle January 1936. Western Mail article 31/1/36. Letters in response.	Document	Archives	
MNA/NUM/3/5/22	SWMF: Compensation Records	1943–47	1946: tables of deaths from silicosis and pneumoconiosis, and accidents, with pit and compensation details. Doctor's report on suicide case.	Document	Archives	Y
MNA/NUM/3/5/24	SWMF: Compensation Records	1925–34	Correspondence and law papers about disputed compensation cases. Silicosis and accident claims. Transcript of County Court case. Court of Appeal Judgement Notes. Solicitors' correspondence. Colliery visit report. Worker's statement.	Document	Archives	Y
MNA/NUM/3/5/25	SWMF: Compensation Records	1920–35	1934: Compensation Department letter: nystagmus and Home Secretary's inquiry. Letter: 1931 Amended Act. Copy Central Compensation Department first report. Transcript of recruitment publicity for SWMF with reference to accidents, diseases and compensation. 1934 Silicosis New Orders.	Document	Archives	Y
MNA/NUM/3/5/26	SWMF: Compensation Records	1934	Report on first year of SWMF Central Compensation Department. Notes on Workmen's Compensation, National Health Insurance Bill 1935, Accidents and Industrial Diseases in Mines, Amount of compensation in cases of death, silicosis (and preventive measures), unsuccessful cases.	Document	Archives	Y

Reference Code	Collection	Dates	Description	Media	Location	DP
MNA/NUM/3/5/27	SWMF: Compensation Records	1938–40	Reports of Area Compensation Secretaries. Statistical tables from SWMF Areas re disputed compensation cases. Include personal details, colliery, insurance company, dispute details, costs, remarks. Reference to injuries, nystagmus and silicosis.	Document	Archives	Y
MNA/NUM/3/5/28	SWMF: Compensation Records	1936–41	Monthly SWMF Agents' reports Area No. 6. Includes many detailed references to compensation claims, accidents, safety and silicosis.	Document	Archives	Y
MNA/NUM/3/6/23	Records of the SWMF/NUM (S Wales Area) (Conciliation Board minutes)	1944	Pneumoconiosis Joint Committee. Notice to terminate compensation men's contracts. Payment of wages to workmen who attend at rehabilitation or other centres for re-examination.	Document	Archives	
MNA/NUM/3/8/17	Area No. 2 Council Minutes (register of ordinary accident cases)	1934–52	Silicosis. Pneumoconiosis. Nystagmus. Hernias. Weil's disease and rat infestations. Compensation. Colliery examiners. Workmen's Examiner's Reports. Dust analysis. X-ray levy for doctors' fees and prices. Compensation centralization scheme.	Document	Archives	Y
MNA/NUM/3/8/17	Area No. 2 correspondence re silicosis (district, area and combine records)	1924–49	1931 Report for guidance of Federation officials regarding silicosis cases. 1935 House of Lords transcript relating to Silicosis Compensation. Correspondence and reports on rock analyses. SWMF correspondence. Doctors' reports, four X-ray photographs of lungs. 1930 case details relating to deceased miner. SWMF charts of cases and Compensation. Forms relating to Various Industries (Silicosis) Scheme 1931 and Amendments Scheme 1934. Employment Exchange correspondence. Home Office correspondence. 1949 NUM (SW) letter outlining silicosis legislation.	Document	Archives	Y

Reference Code	Collection	Dates	Description	Media	Location	DP
MNA/NUM/3/8/17	Area No. 2 correspondence re pneumoconiosis (district, area and combine records)	1924–52	Report relating to National Insurance (Industrial Injuries) Act 1946 and pneumoconiosis. Reference to Welsh Pneumoconiosis Research Unit. Industrial Disablement Benefit. Compensation and appeals. Reports: Health of Coal Mine Workers in South Wales; Dust in Coal Mines; Pneumoconiosis and Re-Employment of Workmen. 1952 NUM (SW) Pneumoconiosis Conference, Porthcawl, detailed report. Refers to Pneumoconiosis Research Unit, Socialist Medical Association (including report), Dr Cochrane, industrial health and hygiene.	Document	Archives	Y
MNA/NUM/3/8/17	Area No. 2 correspondence re pneumoconiosis (district, area and combine records)	1934–53	Correspondence re rock analyses. Collieries' annual returns of cases. NUM summaries of cases. West Wales case data for MP. Accident data. Medical Examination Boards. Details of Coal Mining Industry (Pneumoconiosis) Compensation Scheme 1943. Correspondence re dust suppression.	Document	Archives	Y
MNA/NUM/3/8/17	Area No. 2 correspondence re pneumoconiosis (district, area and combine records)	1943–52	Numbers of silicosis cases in South Wales. Report on Powell Duffryn Associated Collieries. SWMF Compensation Policy Committee, and Safety Committee agendas and minutes. Report of 1947 Cardiff Conference on Pneumoconiosis in Coal Mines (refers to Llandough Hospital). Report of Pneumoconiosis Research Unit recent finds. Report re pneumoconiosis cases (medical examinations) for National Joint Pneumoconiosis Committee. Memo: principles governing selection of diseases for insurance under National Insurance (Industrial Injuries) Act 1946. Notes of meeting of Pneumoconiosis Sub-Committee at Coal Owners' Association. Reports on dust suppression.	Document	Archives	

Reference Code	Collection	Dates	Description	Media	Location	DP
MNA/NUM/L/1	Abercrave Lodge (annual and general meetings minutes)	1935-57	Compensation: silicosis, industrial diseases, beat knee and hand, nystagmus. Deaths by silicosis. Medical examinations and boards including silicosis and dust inhalation. Silicosis and pneumoconiosis.	Document	Archives	
MNA/NUM/L/1/9	Abercrave Lodge (NUM (SW Area) notice of increase in weekly contributions; with attached statistics)	c.1948	Compensation, including costs comparisons 1934/46. Numbers of silicosis and pneumoconiosis certifications. Chart of payments to Medical Board 1936-46. Sample expenditure on three lodges for silicosis and pneumoconiosis. Compensation costs 1925, 1939, 1947.	Document	Archives	
MNA/NUM/L/3/7	Abergorki Lodge (Lodge Secretary's correspondence book)	1917-18	Nystagmus case, light work, pay. Exhumation of soldier's body (ex-miner) re inquiry into his death.	Document	Archives	
MNA/NUM/L/3/12	Abergorki Lodge (Lodge Secretary's correspondence book)	1924-25	Compensation cases. Light work. Nystagmus cases.	Document	Archives	Y
MNA/NUM/L/3/16	Abergorki Lodge (Lodge Secretary's correspondence book)	1930-31	Compensation cases. Light work. Nystagmus case.	Document	Archives	Y
MNA/NUM/L/3/18	Abergorki Lodge (correspondence re compensation cases)	1926-39	Doctor's examination. Compensation rates. Partial compensation, light work. Member's death, Medical Silicosis Board notified. Hernia operation. Nystagmus cases.	Document	Archives	Y
MNA/NUM/L/6/1	Abertridwr Lodge (meetings minutes, balance sheet, membership lists)	1925-59	Silicosis and medical examinations. Compensation case and partial disablement. Meeting regarding diseases and compensation (silicosis, asbestosis, and silicosis and TB).	Document	Archives	
MNA/NUM/L/8/45 and 46	Ammanford Lodge (SWMF circulars and printed material)	1931-34	Information leaflets. Item 45: Industrial Diseases (March 1931). Item 46: Compensation Insurance Fund (December 1934).	Document	Archives	
MNA/NUM/L/10/1 and 3	Bedwas Lodge (annual, general and committee meetings minutes)	1925-33 1940-2	(1) 1925-33: Silicosis cases. Sick workmen and pay. (3) 1940-2: Silicosis cases.	Document	Archives	

Reference Code	Collection	Dates	Media	Location	DP
MNA/NUM/L/10/5	Bedwas Lodge (annual, general and committee meetings minutes)	1944–1946	Document	Archives	
MNA/NUM/L/13/1	Blaengwrach Lodge (annual and committee meetings Minute book)	1946–8	Document	Archives	
MNA/NUM/L/13/12	Blaengwrach Lodge	c.1940–61	Document	Archives	Y
MNA/NUM/L/29/1	Duffryn Rhondda Lodge	1940–67	Document	Archives	Y
MNA/NUM/L/29/2	Duffryn Rhondda Lodge	1948–67	Document	Archives	Y
MNA/NUM/L/29/3	Duffryn Rhondda Lodge	1948–67	Document	Archives	Y
MNA/NUM/L/34/1	Fforchaman Lodge (annual, general and committee minutes)	1938–40	Document	Archives	Y

Description column:

MNA/NUM/L/10/5 — Compensation cases. Reference to death certificate for silicosis and TB.

MNA/NUM/L/13/1 — Doctor of MRC to address Dulais Valley Group of Lodges Conference 1947. Employment of silicotics and pneumoconiotics at colliery in order of seniority, but withdrawn first if general withdrawals.

MNA/NUM/L/13/12 — Lists of workmen at Blaengwrach Collieries; notices of disability. Names, dates (including date of birth), addresses. Some state disability e.g. pneumoconiosis, illness, injury.

MNA/NUM/L/29/1 — Register of members, with details of pneumoconiotic condition and retirement and redundancy dates. Includes personal details and date of certification.

MNA/NUM/L/29/2 — Record of pneumoconiosis cases, includes personal details, percentage of disease, if deceased. NUM Record of Re-Assessment of pneumoconiosis cases. Answers to questionnaire from Cardiff relating to statistics.

MNA/NUM/L/29/3 — Record of pneumoconiosis progressions, including personal details, date of certification, and progression graphs.

MNA/NUM/L/34/1 — References to Medical Boards. Silicosis compensation claims. Various references to full and part-compensation. Beat knee and compensation. Nystagmus cases.

Reference Code	Collection	Dates	Description	Media	Location	DP
MNA/NUM/L/34/6	Fforchaman Lodge (annual, general and committee minutes)	1947-9	1946 National Injuries Act, old and new cases of compensation. Area conference, Dr Fletcher stated cost of further pneumoconiosis experiments could not be borne by them and asked Union to finance it, Union agreed. New Compensation zones 1947. Nystagmus case, recovery and employment. Brief references to compensation cases including dermatitis and pneumoconiosis. Reference to Medical Board reports (brief), e.g. if certified or not, pneumoconiosis and nystagmus (names and addresses), if 'Early stages' or 'Totally Disabled'.	Document	Archives	Y
MNA/NUM/L/35/1	Fochriw No. 1 and Nantwen Lodges (Minute books)	1917-34	Workmen's Compensation Act and consideration of industrial disease cases.	Document	Archives	
MNA/NUM/L/39/8	Gellyceidrim Lodge (book recording notices of injury and claims for compensation)	1916-22	Personal details, date of injury and cause, date of claim and amount. Injuries including wounds, bruising, fractures, amputations, dislocations, hernia rupture, head injuries, septic wound, cellulitis, nystagmus.	Document	Archives	Y
MNA/NUM/L/39/12 and 13	Gellyceidrim Lodge (Lodge Secretary's carbon-copy letter book)	1927-31	Compensation cases, including silicosis.	Document	Archives	Y
MNA/NUM/L/39/14	Gellyceidrim Lodge (general correspondence to Lodge Secretary)	1925-31	Solicitors' letters: Compensation cases, e.g. silicosis (few details).	Document	Archives	Y

Reference Code	Collection	Dates	Description	Media	Location	DP
MNA/NUM/L/43/A1	Graig Merthyr Lodge (general and committee minutes)	1937–40	References to Dr Harper: Silicosis X-ray contribution scheme 1937, assistance in diagnosis of silicosis and other chest diseases, placed before meeting, weekly contributions from all workmen, Area delegate to support scheme. Doctor unsatisfied at response to scheme, unable to continue, decision to ascertain lodges contributing, 1937. Compensation case references (brief). Silicosis and 'dread results' in south Wales especially anthracite area. Fatalities and silicosis deaths reports. Reference to report of Royal Commission on Safety in Mines' visit; unsupported roof, packing, nystagmus and silicosis 1937.	Document	Archives	Y
MNA/NUM/L/43/A8	Graig Merthyr Lodge (general and committee minutes)	1948	Factories for disabled, pressure to have factories built, Tumble and Ponthenry factories to take 50% men and women. Under new scheme, Insurance certified men to continue working unless they have TB. Men with 50% assessment at work in mines – MPs and Dr Fletcher to discuss. Compensation zoning, delays in payment, cases. Employment of pneumoconiotic men. Application to go to Dr Harper re chest sickness. Re 'Harper's list' being approved, and case going to specialist, Dr Cellan Jones. Pneumoconiosis circular; new procedures. Pneumoconiosis cases and admission to Llandough Hospital research department, patients invited, covered financially.	Document	Archives	Y
MNA/NUM/L/52/2	Morlais Lodge (Lodge Secretary's carbon-copy letter book)	1931–3	Medical examinations (travel expenses). Miners' nystagmus and compensation. Compensation cases. Doctor's certificate and report re collier.	Document	Archives	

33

Reference Code	Collection	Dates	Description	Media	Location	DP
MNA/NUM/L/58/1	Norchard and Princess Royal Lodges (minute-book of Norchard Lodge Pit Head Committee meetings)	1942-9	1947: complaint regarding lack of respirators, enquiry for dust suppression and men with chest trouble certified in recent years. Zoning of south Wales for Compensation, new Industrial Injuries Bill. X-ray treatment and loss of bonus for attending hospital. Harold Finch (Compensation Secretary) to visit Forest of Dean to discuss new Industries Bill. 1948 reference to report on X-ray situation, Joint representation to County Health Department to include Norchard Lodge.	Document	Archives	
MNA/NUM/L/60/A1	Onllwyn Central Washery Lodge (minute-book of general and committee Meetings (also reports of Dulais Group meetings))	1942-50	Discussion relating to X-rays – Dr Harper, expenses and loss of time waiting. Industrial dermatitis case, examination by specialist, contact with contaminated water, dust and liquid. Register of disabled men. Pneumoconiosis cases, and levy of each worker each time person goes for examination. Compensation cases. Lump sum settlements.	Document	Archives	
MNA/NUM/L/62/A3	Park and Dare Lodge (minute book for Annual, General and Committee Meetings; also special and colliery workers meetings and subscribers to Pentwyn Cottage Hospital 1943)	1941-3	Part-silicosis cases. Reference to Buergars disease scheduling in category of industrial disease.	Document	Archives	
MNA/NUM/L/63/C32	Penallta Lodge (Lodge Secretary's correspondence and papers)	1949-55	Correspondence with the Socialist Medical Association, regarding industrial diseases.	Document	Archives	
MNA/NUM/L/68/C/9	Saron Lodge (correspondence and miscellaneous material)	1948-66	Circulars, including reference to industrial disease.	Document	Archives	
MNA/NUM/L/74/D/20	Windsor Lodge	1944-62	Certificates of compensation for pneumoconiosis (sample); also certificates of disallowance of disablement claims (sample).	Document	Archives	Y

Reference Code	Collection	Dates	Description	Media	Location	DP
MNA/POL/2/3	Aberdare Trades and Labour Council (annual and monthly meetings minutes)	1944–52	Reference to pneumoconiotic miners.	Document	Archives	
MNA/POL/3/3	Ammanford, Llandebie and District Trades and Labour Council (annual, general and Executive Council minutes)	1941–8	Pneumoconiosis Research talk by Dr Fletcher of Medical Research Council: 'Dust in the Lung'. Pneumoconiosis cases and unemployment. 1943: new Order relating to pneumoconiosis. Factory for disabled miners. Disabled Persons Act and disabled workers.	Document	Archives	
MNA/POL/3/3/1	Ammanford, Llandebie and District Trades and Labour Council (annual, general and Executive Council minutes)	1938–41	1939: TUC circular re Workmen's Compensation Conference in Swansea, pressing for changes in law. 1940 Workmen's Compensation Conference in Cardiff. 1940: effort to interest King Edward Memorial Association in silicosis as for TB. Refers to letter to MP to hasten report of Ammanford Silicosis Inquiry.	Document	Archives	
MNA/POL/21/1–2	South Wales Fabian Society (Regional Council minutes including minutes of South Wales Fabian Societies' conference 1942)	1942–59	Brief references to Health Survey circular, pneumoconiosis, health centre, medical services.	Document	Archives	
MNA/POL/24/2	Ynyshir Ward Committee minutes	1947–51	Council employee and silicosis compensation claim. Pneumoconiosis cases and light work.	Document	Archives	
MNA/PP/9/44	H. W. Currie	1938–47	County Court memos certifying HWC partially disabled by pneumoconiosis, and financial settlement with NCB Powell Dyffryn Unit.	Document	Archives	Y
MNA/PP/15/2 and 11	John Davies (Gwaun-Cae-Gurwen)	Inter-war period	John Davies's essay relating to East Pit, Gwaun-Cae-Gurwen Collieries. Paragraph referring to pneumoconiosis.	Document	Archives	

Reference Code	Collection	Dates	Description	Media	Location	DP
MNA/PP/16/50/10	S. O. Davies	1948	Constituency correspondence; doctors' certificates; Pneumoconiosis Compensation Scheme benefit; Workmen's Compensation; Ministry of Supply Depot closure, impact on disabled workforce.	Document	Archives	Y
MNA/PP/16/50/2	S. O. Davies	1940	Constituency correspondence; benefits problem of nystagmus sufferer.	Document	Archives	Y
MNA/PP/16/50/7/2	S. O. Davies	1945	Constituency correspondence; Ministry of NI letter regarding case of Indemnity Society and workman (pneumoconiosis); two medical certificates for miners.	Document	Archives	Y
MNA/PP/16/50/8 and 9	S. O. Davies	1946–7	Constituency correspondence: (8) 1946; doctor's report on miner; NUM letter re death of silicosis and nystagmus sufferer, Compensation claim; doctors' certificates. (9) 1947; NUM letter, Pneumoconiosis Benefit Scheme.	Document	Archives	Y
MNA/PP/16/7/1	S. O. Davies	1915–17	Newspaper cuttings relating to 'Combing Out' – miners called before Medical Board and passed into Army when should be exempt. Controversy of passing nystagmus sufferers so that colliery owners could repudiate compensation obligations.	Document	Archives	
MNA/PP/16/80	S. O. Davies	1930–1	Papers relating to Silicosis and Asbestosis (Medical Arrangements) and Various Industries (Silicosis) Draft Schemes: drafts, reports, comments and proposed amendments (SWMF and government correspondence). Tredegar Valley District – list of silicosis deaths, disability and compensation.	Document	Archives	Y

Reference Code	Collection	Dates	Description	Media	Location	DP
MNA/PP/16/85	S. O. Davies	1940s	NUM South Wales Compensation Department report on pneumoconiosis. Correspondence: compensation, e.g. for eye injury and pneumoconiosis. X-ray report and letters re miner's lung (silicosis). Notes on Miners' Medical Service. SWMF agendas including dust in mines, medical certificates, coal for injured, trainees' medical examinations.	Document	Archives	Y
MNA/PP/16/9/1	S. O. Davies	Late 1940s–early 1950s	Questions and Answers 'Compensation and Social Insurance' by Head of Compensation Department reference to Industrial Injuries Act. Article: government plan to build light factories to employ silicosis sufferers.	Document	Archives	
MNA/PP/28/20	James Evans (Tumble)	1931–43	1931 and 1937: SWMF Conciliation Board Agreement for Coal Trade of Monmouthshire and South Wales, Compensation and Insurance. 1943 SWMF Executive Council minutes referring to Pneumoconiosis Benefit Scheme.	Document	Archives	
MNA/PP/28/24	James Evans (Tumble)	1937–42	Insurance details for SWMF employees, and Monmouthshire and South Wales Coal Mining Industry. 1942 SWMF proposals for annual conference agenda, including Workmen's Compensation, dust, silicosis.	Document	Archives	
MNA/PP/28/28	James Evans (Tumble)	1952	NUM (SW) Executive Council minutes: Mineworkers' Industrial Diseases Scheme re deceased miner. Pneumoconiosis Conference. National Insurance Industrial Injuries and Workmen's Compensation Acts. Pneumoconiosis workers.	Document	Archives	Y
MNA/PP/28/36	James Evans (Tumble)	1930s–1950s	Undated election SWMF leaflets; refers to silicosis and compensation benefit.	Document	Archives	
MNA/PP/28/40 and 42	James Evans (Tumble)	1939–44	SWMF Annual Conferences; 1944 address by A. Horner – refers to Compensation Department and pneumoconiosis.	Document	Archives	

Reference Code	Collection	Dates	Description	Media	Location	DP
MNA/PP/28/47–49	James Evans (Tumble)	1942–46	1942: MFGB Executive Committee Meeting minutes – Workmen's Compensation, Pneumoconiosis Schemes, part-disabled unemployed, dependants' allowances, disability payments. 1946 NUM National Exec Meeting minutes – Workmen's Compensation Sub-Committee minutes.	Document	Archives	
MNA/PP/34/4	Harold Finch	1936	Amalgamated Anthracite Collieries Ltd meeting minutes 24 June 1936, regarding silicosis. Included company representatives, SWMF and doctors. Report: Silicosis: Research and Preventive Measures at Amalgamated Anthracite Collieries.	Document	Archives	
MNA/PP/34/5	Harold Finch	1936	Statements by workmen employed at Great Mountain Colliery, suffering from silicosis. Suggestions regarding silicosis and its prevention.	Document	Archives	Y
MNA/PP/34/6–8	Harold Finch	1937	Special silicosis investigations; Saron Slant, Carmarthenshire; Tirbach Slant, Glamorganshire; Pontyberem Glynhebog Slant, Carmarthenshire. Detailed reports including occupational histories and statements from silicosis sufferers. Table of case numbers. Dust and ventilation. Effect on horses.	Document	Archives	Y
MNA/PP/34/9–10	Harold Finch	1936–7	Meeting at Pontyberem regarding silicosis at Glynhebog Colliery. Silicotic workers' statements. Interview with colliery officials. Meeting at Gwaun-Cae-Gurwen, 4 December 1936 about pits – East, Maerdy and Steer. Silicotic workers' statements.	Document	Archives	Y
MNA/PP/41/2	David Harris (Glais) (exercise books containing bilingual manuscript reminiscences)	1970s	(Written in 1970s, refers to early–mid C 19th) health; silicosis, pneumoconiosis, beat knee and elbow, nystagmus. Swansea Pneumoconiosis Board.	Document	Archives	Y
MNA/PP/46/40	Arthur Horner	1936	Open letter to Bedwas workmen from Ness Edwards, SWMF: refers to silicosis and Compensation.	Document	Archives	

38

Reference Code	Collection	Dates	Description	Media	Location	DP
MNA/PP/46/45	Arthur Horner	1945	Transcript of BBC talk on the mining situation. Refers to miners' diseases and silicosis.	Document	Archives	
MNA/PP/46/54	Arthur Horner	1924	*Colliery Workers' Magazine* Vol. II, No. 10: The Workers' Charter (housing, industrial accidents and diseases). Reports of District Meetings (Compensation cases).	Document	Archives	
MNA/PP/46/58	Arthur Horner	1936	*The Miners' Monthly*, Vol. III, No. 9. Commission on Safety in Mines: silicosis, respiratory diseases, ventilation and dust, hand, knee, elbow and wrist inflammation.	Document	Archives	
MNA/PP/46/59	Arthur Horner	1936	*The Miners' Monthly*, Vol. III, No. 10. Nystagmus victim, court case and Workmen's Compensation.	Document	Archives	
MNA/PP/46/61–63	Arthur Horner	1940–3	Speeches by Arthur Horner at SWMF Annual Conference: 1940, 1942, 1943: refers to compensation (pneumoconiosis chest problems and dust).	Document	Archives	
MNA/PP/46/67	Arthur Horner	c.1935	Proposed British Mineworkers' Union Constitution: refers to diseases, Compensation and legislation. Schedule of industrial diseases – silicosis, phthisis and others.	Document	Archives	
MNA/PP/50/2	W. R. James (Trelewis) (SWMF Executive Council minutes)	1935	Anthracosis – scheduling as industrial disease and extension of Silicosis Order. Nystagmus case. Compensation claims and cases. Silicosis cases and Medical Board.	Document	Archives	Y
MNA/PP/50/3	W. R. James (Trelewis) (Taff Merthyr Lodge minute book)	1946–52	Nystagmus compensation and death by silicosis. Cardiff and District Hospital Society, and Pneumoconiosis Clinic at Royal Infirmary.	Document	Archives	

Reference Code	Collection	Dates	Description	Media	Location	DP
MNA/PP/55/5	J. D. Jenkins (MOH, Rhondda UDC) (Correspondence and papers re Silicosis Scheme)	1929–37	Sandstone Industries (Silicosis) Scheme 1929. Letters from TB physician re examination of patients (with details, opinions and decisions). Details of scheme centres in UK and examinations for new employees. Correspondence re length of time to contract silicosis.	Document	Archives	Y
MNA/PP/55/8	J. D. Jenkins (MOH, Rhondda UDC)	1910–37	1910: Report to Secretary of State: *An Outbreak of Glanders among the Horses, and the alleged General Insanitary Condition of the Collieries, belonging to the Ebbw Vale Steel, Iron and Coal Co. Ltd, in the County of Monmouth*, by J. S. Martin and D. Rocyn Jones. Reference to collier's death by blood poisoning following glanders infection. Details of other deaths, typhoid and ankylostomiasis. *Statutory Rules and Orders 1912, No 497*, re testing horses for glanders before being taken underground.	Document	Archives	Y
MNA/PP/67/17	W. Eddie Jones	1932	Surgical intervention and lack of facilities, no surgeons for chest surgery. Dust and miners.	Document	Archives	
MNA/PP/73/7	James Lewis (Maesteg)	1933–46	Pamphlet: 1944 SWMF *Case for an Increase in the Workers' Contribution to 1/- per week*, re Workmen's Compensation, pneumoconiosis and safety.	Document	Archives	
MNA/PP/82/1	D. Morgan (general correspondence, letters and circulars re Rhymney Workingmen's Medical Aid Fund)	1946–9	Silicosis and Asbestosis (Medical Arrangements) Scheme 1931/1946 re X-ray of man.	Document	Archives	Y
MNA/PP/86/3	W. J. Nind	1936–7	Bedwas Navigation Colliery Co – analysis of accidents Jan–Mar 1937, including industrial diseases (beat knee, hand, elbow and wrist), fatalities. Report including details of ages, shifts, occupations, areas of pit. Handwritten version including personal details.	Document	Archives	Y

Reference Code	Collection	Dates	Description	Media	Location	DP
MNA/PP/87/1–2	Charles Parker (transcripts of interviews with miners and their wives)	1961	Inter-war period: Husband's death, pit accident, silicosis. Miners with lung diseases, accidents. Mine ventilation, dust. Lamps and blindness. Pneumoconiosis.	Document	Archives	Y
MNA/PP/111/1	Bryn Thomas ('Llandybie Over the Ages')	Early 1900s	Miners, lamps and prevalence of nystagmus.	Document	Archives	
MNA/PP/114/2	Evan Thomas (Cwmgorse)	1932–47	Lists of partial and full silicosis and pneumoconiosis men, including names, some ages, dates certified, remarks, e.g. if still working, nystagmus.	Document	Archives	Y
MNA/PP/118/52	John Thomas (Aberavon)	1924	Ness Edwards, *The Industrial Revolution in South Wales*: working conditions: illness, lung disease.	Document	Archives	
MNA/PP/122/1	Wilfred Timbrell (Tumble)	1896–1960s	Memoirs of Tumble: workmen's conditions, coal dust and pneumoconiosis. Work above ground, avoiding dust problems.	Document	Archives	
MNA/PP/127/C19	D. J. Williams	1920s–1940s	Memo on need for new industries to provide employment for men suspended from Mining Industry on account of silicosis and pneumoconiosis prepared by Amalgamated Anthracite Combine Committee. 1944 Ministry of Fuel and Power Report of the Advisory Committee on Treatment and Rehabilitation of Miners in Wales Region suffering from Pneumoconiosis. 1945 Report by Working Party, Provision of Employment in South Wales for Persons suspended from Mining Industry on account of Silicosis and Pneumoconiosis. 1945 Board of Trade, Provision of Employment in South Wales for Persons Suspended from the Mining Industry on Account of Silicosis and Pneumoconiosis. Summary of results of investigation and recommendations. Conference Report 1945 Swansea, Establishment of New Industries to provide Employment for men suspended from the	Document	Archives	Y

Reference Code	Collection	Dates	Description	Media	Location	DP
			Mining Industry on account of Silicosis and Pneumoconiosis. Interim reports of deputation appointed at Swansea Conference for the establishment of such new industries. 1946 correspondence; disabled miners, silicosis and pneumoconiosis; proposed new factory in Tumble Employment Exchange area; new factory at Cross Hands. 1947 correspondence; recruitment and employment of miners disabled by silicosis and pneumoconiosis. 1945 NUM (South Wales Area Council) Enquiry into the incidence of silicosis and pneumoconiosis in the South Wales Area, and the after employment of these disabled men. SWMF notepaper, written notes on silicosis problem, prevention, compensation. Tables for silicosis and pneumoconiosis cases of disablement and death 1931-44 (South Wales and Anthracite only), Summary of allcases certified at Amalgamated Anthracite Collieries 1929-45 including compensation, deaths, disabled, commuted. 1945 correspondence; light employment. Disabled Persons (Employment) Act 1944, employment of ex-miners affected by pneumoconiosis or silicosis, notes for guidance 1948, Ministry of Labour and National Service. Letter from Ministry, Ness Edwards. Silicosis and pneumoconiosis statement of cases 1937-44. Questions to Ness Edwards; employment of disabled miners			Y
MNA/PP/132/8	James Winstone	1916	SWMF Annual meeting Eastern Valley District pamphlet minutes 1916. Claims for nystagmus. Compensation case.	Document	Archives	
MNA/PP/132/9	James Winstone (scrapbook of newspaper cuttings and handwritten notes)	1912	Labour statistics relating to deaths and lead poisoning. Medical and compensation cases including nystagmus.	Document	Archives	

Reference Code	Collection	Dates	Description	Media	Location	DP
MNB/COL/17/C25A and C25G	Morlais Colliery (Secretarial Dept circulars)	1928-37	(C25A) Reference to Workmen's Compensation Act 1925 and Various Industries (Silicosis) Scheme 1928. (C25G) Workmen's Compensation Department Committee and nystagmus.	Document	Archives	
MNB/COL/17/C6B	Morlais Colliery (Board of Conciliation circulars)	1925-42	Cases commuted (accidents). Details include name, age, address, nature of injury, amount of compensation, date recorded in court. Injuries include nystagmus and arthritis.	Document	Archives	Y
MNB/COL/17/C6B and C	Morlais Colliery (Board of Conciliation circulars)	1928-38	Cases commuted 1928-31 (monthly): accident date, personal details, injury, commutation amount, date recorded in Court. Nystagmus, arthritis, spine, eyes, head, ulcers, silicosis, deafness.	Document	Archives	Y
MNB/COL/17/C8A	Morlais Colliery (Monmouthshire and S Wales Employers' Mutual Indemnity Society circulars)	1916-38	1924: circular relating to Workmen's Compensation Acts – Partially Incapacitated Workmen – Unable to Obtain Employment. 1924 Commutation of nystagmus cases. 1924: General Summary of Assets and Liabilities, and Balance Sheet.Reference to Workmen's Compensation Act 1906, nystagmus and other industrial diseases, forms for new employees. Instructions about completion of Register for Protection of Members for accidents. Men on light work and War Bonus. 1916: Disease List, Workmen's Compensation Act. Ordinary and Extraordinary Accident Funds Balance Sheets. List of collieries and members registered with Society. 1917: Certificate of Protection. 1917: Compensation awards, nystagmus, beat knee, beat elbow. AGM Agenda and report to directors 1917.	Document	Archives	

43

Reference Code	Collection	Dates	Description	Media	Location	DP
MNB/COL/17/C8B	Morlais Colliery (Monmouthshire and South Wales Employers' Mutual Indemnity Society circulars)	1916–38	Statistics to Home Secretary for accidents, industrial diseases and compensation; nystagmus, beat hand, knee and elbow, lead poisoning. 1929 circular; Workmen's Compensation Act and silicosis (claims for silicosis or silicosis and TB). Extraordinary Accident Class 1930. 1931 statistics for accidents and compensation: nystagmus, beat hand, knee, and elbow, inflammation of wrist joint, lead poisoning, dermatitis, silicosis. Silicosis and Mark IV Respirators. Employers' Liability Policy notice to members re provisions of Workmen's Compensation (Coal Mines) Act 1934.	Document	Archives	
MNB/COL/17/C8C	Morlais Colliery (Monmouthshire and South Wales Employers' Mutual Indemnity Society circulars)	1916–38	Ordinary and Extraordinary Account Funds. 1925 circular – nystagmus cases, safety lamps. List of nystagmus cases commuted 1924, including personal details, amount of settlement, court settlement date. Compensation costs, old and new Acts. Statistics sent to Home Secretary; accidents and disablement and compensation. Reports to AGMs, solicitor and directors, including Workmen's Compensation, silicosis and nystagmus. Insurance schedules. Statistics including accidents and injuries. Compensation cost statement. Summary of assets and liabilities. 1925 circular, Workmen's Compensation Acts 1906–23, fatal cases. Register for Protection of Members.	Document	Archives	Y
MNB/I/13/1	Yniscedwyn Sick Fund (general and committee minute book)	1930–58	Reference to individual claimants. Silicosis claims.	Document	Archives	
MNB/NUM/1/A7	Area Safety Committee (Swansea District minutes of meetings)	1945–63	1945: Minutes of Safety Committee NUM SW. Refers to Pneumoconiosis Committee on Dust Suppression. 1946, 1949 and 1956 minutes.	Document	Archives	

Reference Code	Collection	Dates	Description	Media	Location	DP
MNB/NUM/1/D66	Amalgamated Anthracite Collieries (correspondence with colliery managements)	1943–4	Amalgamated Anthracite Collieries Health Measures (1944), agreed measures. 1941 Neath County Council Workmen's Compensation case, silicosis.	Document	Archives	Y
MNB/NUM/1/D48–49	Abercrave and International Colliery (correspondence with colliery managements)	1943–54	1943–44: 1943 Workmen's Compensation, silicosis case, under Silicosis and Asbestosis (Medical Arrangements) Schemes 1931–43. Papers and correspondence for miners' nystagmus case.1944–54: Workmen's Compensation case Neath County Council papers, nystagmus.	Document	Archives	Y
MNB/NUM/1/D388	Yniscedwyn Colliery (correspondence with colliery managements)	1942–53	Workmen's Compensation cases, Neath County Council papers: 1943 Yniscedwyn Colliery, nystagmus; 1942 nystagmus; 1940 injuries; 1943 beat elbow. 1944 letter to Dr Stubbins MOH (Neath, Swansea); proposed Electro-Massage Treatment Centre for miners' chest problems, e.g. silicosis and pneumoconiosis.	Document	Archives	Y
MNB/NUM/1/D504	NUM rehabilitation and compensation circulars (correspondence with Lodge Secretaries)	1947–59	Compensation Department NUM (SW) 1947 from H. Finch, relating to pneumoconiosis and fatal accidents.	Document	Archives	Y
MNB/NUM/2/25	SWMF/NUM circulars and papers	1935–77	SWMF and NUM circulars and papers relating to nystagmus, 1935.	Document	Archives	Y
MNB/NUM/D/412	Abercrave (correspondence with Lodge Secretaries)	1943–65	References to pneumoconiosis.	Document	Archives	Y
MNB/NUM/D/499	Yniscedwyn (correspondence with Lodge Secretaries)	1943–62	Pneumoconiosis and water infusion.	Document	Archives	Y

Reference Code	Collection	Dates	Description	Media	Location	DP
MNB/NUM/L/1/6	Abercynon Lodge (Lodge Secretary's carbon-copy letter book)	1938	Certifying surgeon's fees. Compensation cases, e.g. silicosis, nystagmus, beat elbow, eczema, accidents. Light employment and Compensation cases. Lump sum and Compensation. Compensation Conference in Cardiff.	Document	Archives	
MNB/NUM/L/12/1	Hendreladis / Yniscedwyn Lodge	1946–52	Lodge Committee Expenditure Book: including expenses for Compensation (for attending Court), mine inspections, and attending Silicosis Board.	Document	Archives	
MNB/NUM/L/13/B4	Maerdy Lodge	1931	Handwritten note on back of 1929 handbill – written by medical referee (doctor) for collier with astigmatism (previously diagnosed as nystagmus), and fitness for work. Refers to Workmen's Compensation Act 1926, Certificate under Section 19.	Document	Archives	Y
MNB/NUM/L/15/E1	Mountain Lodge (minutes of Safety Committee meeting)	1945	Pneumoconiosis Committee. Dust problems, and ventilation.	Document	Archives	
MNB/NUM/L/2/11	Ammanford No. 2 Lodge (medical reports on compensation claimants)	1926	Copy letters from doctor relating to injured and sick miners – unfit for work or fit for light work. Including nystagmus, eye and ear problems, fractures, beat knee, septicaemia, arthritis, epilepsy. Doctors' letters to solicitors regarding miners' compensation claims. Discuss hearing and eye problems, neurasthenia, hypertropic astigmatism, nystagmus, septicaemia, arthritis, epilepsy.	Document	Archives	Y
MNB/NUM/L/2/1–4	Ammanford No.2 Lodge (minute books)	1924–34	Medical Board volunteers' payment for attendance at Broughton Hospital, London, relating to Silicosis Investigation run by Dr Haslett. Silicosis Inquiry and Inspection Report. Silicosis examinations for compensation and silicotic men.	Document	Archives	

Reference Code	Collection	Dates	Description	Media	Location	DP
MNB/NUM/L/2/8	Ammanford No. 2 Lodge (Lodge balance sheet for 1938)	1939	Refund – Loss of Work relating to Silicosis Investigation. Payments, compensation, members before Silicosis Board, and medical referees. Silicosis investigations.	Document	Archives	
MNB/NUM/L/9/1	Ffaldau Lodge (minute book)	1939–41	Silicosis: case inquest, Compensation, examination of men. Medical support for court case. Compensation, various cases.	Document	Archives	
MNB/POL/1/12	Ammanford Trades and Labour Council (balance sheet and annual report)	1948	Lecture: 'Further Researches re Dust in the Lung'. Radiologists' visit with mobile X-ray unit (Welsh National Memorial Hospital).	Document	Archives	
MNB/PP/10/F26	S. O. Davies	1925–30	MFGB 'Silicosis Among Coalminers, Case submitted to the TUC', pamphlet 1930. Case details, expert's examination – Dr Scholberg (Cardiff Royal Infirmary). Compensation, 1925 Act and Various Industries (Silicosis) Scheme 1928. Rock sampling. History of subject since 1926.	Document	Archives	
MNB/PP/12/A19 and A20	William Henry Davies (Penclawdd)	1911–36	Workmen's Compensation Act 1925 Copy Certificate (completed 1936), for miners' nystagmus, and neurosis.	Document	Archives	Y
MNB/PP/22/1	Harold Finch (minute book, Miners' Group)	1942–6	Workmen's Compensation 1942 Bill, rates details. Pneumoconiosis to replace silicosis in schedule. Benefit scheme, rejected cases. Supplementary benefit, disablement. Part-compensation. National Insurance Industrial Injuries Bill 1946. 'Roof Support' and 'Dust Suppression' films to be shown.	Document	Archives	
MNB/PP/34/A6	Berwyn Howells	1944	Lists of compensation cases. Name, date of birth, date of accident, nature of injury, Compensation rate, outstanding liability. Injuries – fracture, amputated limb, wound, eye injury, crush, hernia, head injury, nystagmus, silicosis.	Document	Archives	Y
MNB/PP/72/26	Alistair Wilson (compensation case examination cards and notes)	1939–42	Handwritten notes for compensation cases. 1939 totals; beat knee, elbow and hand, nystagmus and tenosynovitis.	Document	Archives	Y

Reference Code	Collection	Dates	Description	Media	Location	DP
MNB/PP/7228	Alistair Wilson	1933	Enid M. Williams MD, *The Health of Old and Retired Coalminers in South Wales*, Cardiff: University of Wales Press Board.	Document	Archives	Y
MNB/PP/7229	Alistair Wilson (HMSO Booklet)	1942	Medical Research Council, *Chronic Pulmonary Diseases in South Wales Coalminers*. Medical Studies- Report by Committee, Medical Survey by P. D'Arcy Hart and E. A. Aslett, pathological report. Including X-ray photos, and photos of cross-sections of lungs.	Document	Archives	
MNB/PP/7230	Alistair Wilson (HMSO Booklet)	1955	Medical Research Council, Special Report Series No. 290. *Lung Function in Coalworkers' Pneumoconiosis*, by J. C. Gilson and P. Hugh-Jones. Includes photographs.	Document	Archives	Y
MNC/COP/1/6	Aberdare Co-operative Society (minute book)	1945-8	Convalescent Fund, silicosis and pneumoconiosis.	Document	Archives	Y
MNC/NUM/23/39	NUM South Wales Area	1934-1960s	NCB Compensation for pneumoconiosis claim form (ud) for widow or dependent (blank).	Document	Archives	Y
MNC/NUM/5/228	Cambrian Lodge (correspondence and papers)	1938-41	SWMF Conference agendas 1940 and 1941, including compensation (references that neurasthenia, rheumatism, dermatitis and boils should be scheduled as industrial diseases), dust menace, silicosis.	Document	Archives	
MNC/NUM/L/18/1	Gwaun-Cae-Gurwen Lodge	1948-c.1969	Record of pneumoconiosis cases, 1948 to c.1969. A re-assessment of pneumoconiosis cases giving names and percentage to which disease has affected victim.	Document	Archives	Y
MNC/NUM/L/18/2	Gwaun-Cae-Gurwen Lodge	1896-1969	Miscellaneous correspondence and papers including reference to pneumoconiosis.	Document	Archives	Y

Reference Code	Collection	Dates	Description	Media	Location	DP
MNC/NUM/L/29/22	Pentremawr Lodge	1936–53	Silicosis compensation correspondence and report. Correspondence and report; Compensation case, one of first cases of silicosis to be contested at Pentremawr Colliery.	Document	Archives	Y
MNC/NUM/L/34/23	Treharris/Deep Navigation Lodge	1948–84	Record of reassessment of pneumoconiosis cases, names and assessment ratings.	Document	Archives	Y
MNC/NUM/L/34/25	Treharris/Deep Navigation Lodge	1946–71	Miscellaneous correspondence and reports, references to pneumoconiosis and compensation.	Document	Archives	Y
MNC/PP/15/10	Dr Gwent Jones (newspaper cuttings)	c.1938–c.1948	'South Wales Research Unit, New attack on dust diseases in mines', Medical Research Council special report, 'Chronic Pulmonary Disease in South Wales Coalminers' (Llandough Unit). 'New Methods to Combat Industrial Diseases' (silicosis, pneumoconiosis, dust). Committee on Miners' Lung Diseases, pneumoconiosis and compensation. 'To Prevent Disease in Coal Pits' (pneumoconiosis). Miners' Welfare Investigations, Medical Research Council report 1937–8, Ammanford, chronic pulmonary diseases. 'What Science is Doing for the Miner – Precautions Against Accidents and Silicosis', by Prof. Granville Poole. Copy of *Welsh Cutter*, published by Ministry of Fuel and Power, 05/8/1946, including: 'Scourge of the Welsh has been Vanquished. Deadly Dust Cloud is Lifting from Pits', dust suppression and water infusion; miners' health.	Document	Archives	
MNC/PP/15/1–2	Dr Gwent Jones	1943	A Survey of Silicosis in Wales. To the Chairman and Council of the New Wales Union. Historical survey, silicosis, treatment. Handwritten drafts and notebooks.	Document	Archives	

Reference Code	Collection	Dates	Description	Media	Location	DP
MNC/PP/15/3	Dr Gwent Jones (correspondence)	1942–4	1942 correspondence between Gwent Jones and Committee, pointing out that much work done previously, e.g. Royal Commission on Safety in Mines, 1935–9. 1942–4: Letters: South Wales and Monmouthshire Council of Social Service re Gwent Jones's silicosis pamphlet, reference to diet, and survey of expenditure on food during Depression years. University College of South Wales and Monmouth, research on coal dust in Department of Mining, Mines Medical Service.	Document	Archives	Y
MNC/PP/15/4	Dr Gwent Jones	1942	Minutes of meeting at Ammanford Welfare Rooms, HM Inspector of Mines and question of silicosis and dust at the collieries. Silicosis, and dust elimination techniques.	Document	Archives	
MNC/PP/15/5	Dr Gwent Jones	1944	MFGB Minutes of Executive Committee Meeting 7 January 1944. Refers to pneumoconiosis and details of silicosis and pneumoconiosis schemes.	Document	Archives	
MNC/PP/15/6	Dr Gwent Jones	1943	SWMF, minutes of Executive Council Meeting 30 November 1943. Reference to booklet on silicosis by Dr Rocyn Jones. Letter from Home Office in effect of Compensation (Temporary Increases) Act on pre-1924 cases.	Document	Archives	
MNC/PP/15/8	Dr Gwent Jones	1940–4	The Coal Mines (South Wales) (Pneumoconiosis) Order 1943. Emergency Powers (Defence), Coal Mines (South Wales), Statutory Rules and Order 1943, No. 1696.	Document	Archives	
MNC/PP/15/9	Dr Gwent Jones	1942–50	Copies of articles referring to dust, silicosis, and pneumoconiosis. Pamphlet: 'Silicosis: Terror Disease of Welsh miners', Dr D.J. Davies, reprint from *The Welsh Nationalist* (3 copies). Silicosis	Document	Archives	

Reference Code	Collection	Dates	Description	Media	Location	DP
			and compensation. 'Medical Notes on Pneumoconiosis', Ministry of National Insurance, 1950. 'Industrial Pulmonary Fibrosis with Special Reference to Silicosis in Wales', T. W. Davies (TB physician, Swansea Union Area, Welsh National Memorial Association), reprint from *Public Health* Nos 5 and 6, Vol. LV, February and March 1942. Silicosis, Compensation, dust and rehabilitation. 'The Reduction of Dust at the Coal Face – A new method of applying water to allay dust as adopted at Amalgamated Anthracite Collieries Ltd, East Pit, Gwaun-Cae-Gurwen', by Dan Jones. (Reprint from *The Colliery Guardian*, 19 February, 1943.			
MNC/PP/26/4	Lance Rogers	1934	Court of Appeal Judgement 1934, Griffiths v The Powell Duffryn Steam Coal Co. Re Silicosis, Compensation, Medical Board, Silicosis and Asbestosis (Medical Arrangements) Scheme 1931.	Document	Archives	Y
MNC/PP/26/5	Lance Rogers	1935	House of Lords Judgement 1935, Tirbach Appeal Cases. Morgan (and Hutchings) and Amalgamated Anthracite Collieries Ltd. Re silicosis, Workmen's Compensation Act 1925, Various Diseases (Silicosis) Scheme 1931.	Document	Archives	Y
MNC/PP/26/7	Lance Rogers	1935	Court of Appeal Judgement 1935. Workmen's Compensation Act 1925. Arbitration between Edward Weeks and Powell Duffryn Steam Coal Co Ltd. Reference nystagmus (disabled by), medical referee and certifying surgeon's certificates, Workmen's Compensation.	Document	Archives	Y
MNC/PP/26/8	Lance Rogers	1935	Court of Appeal Judgement 1935. Workmen's Compensation Act 1925 and the Various Industries (Silicosis) Scheme 1930-4. Wragg v Samuel Fox and Co Ltd. Reference silicosis, compensation, dust of silica rock.	Document	Archives	Y

Reference Code	Collection	Dates	Description	Media	Location	DP
MNC/PP/35/1	Anon	1945	NUM (South Wales Area Council) Report on Incidence of the Diseases of Silicosis and Pneumoconiosis and Preventive Measures adopted to Combat the Diseases in South Wales, 1945.	Document	Archives	Y
MNC/PP/35/1	Anon	1938	Report of Investigation into Conditions of Employment at Powell Duffryn Collieries within the Frank Hann Group and into the Administration of the SWMF Lodges within the same Group. References to compensation.	Document	Archives	Y
MNC/PP/35/1	Anon	c.1930s	Correspondence relating to silicosis cases, 1930s, personal details. Silicosis and TB case. Rock sample results re silica. Cases listed under Various Industries (Silicosis) Scheme 1928. Silicosis and Asbestosis (Medical Arrangements) Scheme 1931.	Document	Archives	Y
MNC/PP/35/1	Anon (Envelope II)	c.1930s	MFGB 1933 Minutes: nystagmus compensation case. 1934 MFGB Minutes: Compensation and silicosis.	Document	Archives	Y
MNC/PP/35/1	Anon	c.1930s	Leaflet: 'The Prevention of Silicosis, The New Improved 'Hay Dust Trap' (Inventor Capt. P. S. Hay OBE of Mines Dept).' Dust suppression. Copy Medical Board certificate. Statistics on silicosis and pneumoconiosis cases. Compensation.	Document	Archives	Y
RC73 PNE	Institute of Occupational Medicine	1975	Four pamphlets. Reports: Fifth radiological survey of Oakdale Colliery. Pneumoconiosis Field Research: Environmental conditions at Oakdale Colliery Pentremawr/Cynheidre 3 Colliery, and Deep Navigation Colliery.	Document	SWML	
RC773 COL	Milroy Lectures (1915). 'Industrial Pneumoconiosis, with special reference to Dust-phthisis, by Edgar L. Collis HM Medical Inspector of Factories'	1919	Pamphlet: Reprint from *Public Health* the official organ of the Society of MOHs. Includes photos. Refers to report of Royal Commission on Metalliferous Mines and Quarries. Asthma. Bronchitis. Pneumonia. Dust-phthisis or pulmonary silicosis. Characteristics of silica.	Document	SWML	

Reference Code	Collection	Dates	Description	Media	Location	DP
RC773 FLE	'Pneumoconiosis of Coal Miners', by CM Fletcher, Director of Pneumoconiosis Research Unit, Medical Research Council	1948	Pamphlet: Reprint from BMJ 29 May-5 Jun 1948, Vol. I, pp.1015–1065. Dust suppression. Certification rates. Post-mining employment. Radiological progression. Progressive massive fibrosis. Prevention. Therapy. History of the disease.	Document	SWML	
RC773 GRE	NCB	1948-9	Pamphlet: *Employment of Pneumoconiosis Cases* (1948). The sampling of air-borne dusts (1949). Copy of form Industrial Injuries (Prescribed Diseases) Regulations, 1948.	Document	SWML	
RC773 GRE	Disabled Persons (Employment) Act 1944	1944	Pamphlet: *Disabled Persons (Employment) Act 1944.* *Employment of ex-miners affected by pneumokoniosis or silicosis.* 1 page; Introduction, Nature of the Diseases, Unsuitable Work.	Document	SWML	
RC773 GRE	Ministry of Fuel and Power. Digest of Pneumoconiosis Statistics.	1952–75	Pamphlets: Pneumoconiosis in the Mining and Quarrying Industries. Contents: Boards held under National Insurance (Industrial Injuries) Act 1946, Certificates of disablement or death under Workmen's Compensation Acts 1925–45, Employment of persons suffering from pneumoconiosis.	Document	SWML	
RC773 GRE	Home Office Memorandum	1932	Pamphlet: *Memorandum on the Industrial Diseases of Silicosis and Asbestosis* (London, HMSO, 1932). Including silicosis, dust, ventilation and compensation.	Document	SWML	
RC773 GRE	Home Office Memo on the Industrial Diseases of Silicosis and Asbestosis	1932	Pamphlet: *Origin and development of silicosis.* Industries and processes in which silicosis occurs. Prevention; dust suppression, exhaust ventilation, medical examinations. Provision for compensation. Medical arrangements for examination and certification of cases. Asbestosis.	Document	SWML	
RC773 HAR	'Silicosis and South Wales Colliers', by Archibald Harper.	1934	Pamphlet: Reprint from BMJ 19 May 1934. Three stages, diagnosis, X-rays, own observations of cases.	Document	SWML	

Reference Code	Collection	Dates	Description	Media	Location	DP
RC773 HAR	'Chronic Pulmonary Disease in South Wales Coal Mines: An Eye-Witness Account of the MRC Surveys (1937–1942)'	1998	Article by P. D'Arcy Hart. Edited and annotated by E. M. Tansey, *Society for the Social History of Medicine*, 1998, Vol. 11, No. 3, 459–68.	Document	SWML	
RC773 JEN	'The South Wales Institute of Engineers. Medico-Mining Aspects of Pneumokoniosis in South Wales'	1948	Pamphlet, T. H. Jenkins, B.Sc. (Hons) (Wales), MB, BS (Lond). Excerpt from Proceedings, Vol. LXIV, No. 2, with Discussion. (Cardiff: The Institute, 1948). Includes photos.	Document	SWML	
RC773 JON	Monmouthshire County Council, 'Silicosis in Monmouthshire', Report of Gwyn Rocyn Jones, County Pathologist.	1943	Life expectancy. Risk amongst miners, borers, colliers, hauliers, repairers and labourers, fireman. Relation to other diseases. Disease types. Observations on diagnosis. Treatment; medical facilities, hospital treatment and rehabilitation, domiciliary supervision, employment.	Document	SWML	
RC773 JON	Monmouthshire County Council, 'Silicosis in Monmouthshire', Report of Gwyn Rocyn Jones, County Pathologist.	1943	Autopsies, causes of death of suspected silicosis cases. Silicosis and TB, silicosis and emphysema, bronchiectasis, pneumonia in relation to silicosis, relationship between silicosis and cancer, and cardiovascular disease associated with diseases of miners.	Document	SWML	
RC773 MEI	'History of Lung Diseases of Coal Miners in Great Britain: Part III, 1920–1952'	1952	Pamphlet: Andrew Meiklejohn. (London: BMA, 1952). Reprint from *British Journal of Industrial Medicine*, Vol. 9, 1952, p. 208.	Document	SWML	
RC773 MIN	MFGB. Silicosis among Coalminers. Case submitted to TUC.	1930	Memo on Silicosis among Coalminers. History since 1926.The Various Industries (Silicosis) Scheme 1928 (1/2/1929). 50% free Silica Clause. Details of cases from South Wales, North Staffordshire, Somerset, North Wales, Durham (personal and medical details from doctors).	Document	SWML	Y

Reference Code	Collection	Dates	Description	Media	Location	DP
RC773 ORE	The 1st Sir Julius Wernher Memorial Lecture of the Institute of Mining and Metallurgy	1947	Delivered at The Royal Institute, London, 15 April 1947. 'The History and Prevention of Silicosis, with Special Reference to the Witwatersrand', by A. J. Orenstein. Silicosis in South Africa.	Document	SWML	
RC773 POW	The King Edward VII Welsh National Memorial Association (for the Prevention, Treatment, and Abolition of Tuberculosis in Wales and Monmouthshire) Report	1940	Treatment and cost. Nature of silicosis. Pathology. Relationship between silicosis and TB. Silicosis in south Wales coalfield. Diagnosis and prognosis. Complications and sequelae. Compensation. Medical examinations and certificates. Prevention. Non-compensateable industrial fibrosis (including anthracosis).	Document	SWML	
RC773 REP	International Conference on Silicosis held at Johannesburg (Home Office Report)	1931	International Conference on Silicosis held at Johannesburg, August 1930 (including account of steps taken in regard to the disease in South Africa) by E. L. Middleton MD, HM Medical Inspector of Factories. Including silicosis, pneumoconiosis, dust, ventilation, and compensation.	Document	SWML	
RC773 ROL	'The Role of Periodic Examination in the Prevention of Coalworkers' Pneumoconiosis'	1951	Article by A. L. Cochrane, C. M. Fletcher, J. C. Gilson, P. Hugh-Jones (Pneumoconiosis Research Unit, MRC, Llandough Hosp, Cardiff), *British Journal of Industrial Medicine*, 1951, 8, 53.	Document	SWML	
RC773 SOU	SWMF Anthracite District. The Prevention of Silicosis and Anthracosis	c.1930s	Pamphlet: *Methods of Preventing Miners' Silicosis and some other Lung Diseases in the Anthracite District*, by J. H. Davies. 8 point conclusion re dust prevention and ventilation.	Document	SWML	
RC773 Tre	'A Study of the Efficiency of Groups of Ex-miners Disabled by Pneumoconiosis Employed in Light Industries in South Wales'		By J. A. P. Treasure, from Pneumoconiosis Research Unit of MRC. *British Journal of Social Medicine* (1949), 3, 127–38. Data and results.	Document	SWML	

Reference Code	Collection	Dates	Description	Media	Location	DP
RC927 RHE	*Rheumatism and the Miners*	1950	Pamphlets: National Miners' Welfare Joint Council. *Rheumatism and the Miners*: Interim Report (1), and First results (2), on a survey of rheumatic complaints conducted from an experimental treatment clinic at Walkden in Lancashire.	Document	SWML	
RE748 CAM	*Miners' Nystagmus*	1952	Pamphlet: Dorothy R. Campbell, W. J. Wellwood Ferguson, R. C. Browne and A. Smith. Medical Memorandum 7, NCB, London, 1952.	Document	SWML	
RE748 GRE	*First Report of the Miners' Nystagmus Committee*	1922	Medical Research Council. (London: HMSO, 1922). Contents: general report on miners' nystagmus; report on psycho-neurotic symptoms Associated with miners' nystagmus, by W. H. R. Rivers. Committee: J. S. Haldane, E. L. Collis, T. L. Llewellyn, G. H. Pooley, W. H. R. Rivers.	Document	SWML	
RE748 LAN	*Observations on Miners' Nystagmus and Mine Environment*	1930	Pamphlet: Ivor J. Lane. (Cardiff: The Institute, 1930). To be read before the South Wales Institute of Engineers, Cardiff, 29 May 1930.	Document	SWML	
RE748 NYS	*Nystagmus in Otherwise Normal Coal Miners*	1953	NCB Medical Service Research Report 2 (London: NCB, 1953).	Document	SWML	
RE748 PER	*A Neglected Factor in the Aetiology of Miners' Nystagmus*	ud	Pamphlet: by A. S. Percival.	Document	SWML	
RE748 Rob	*Coal Miners' Nystagmus*	1924	By Frederick Robson, MD (Cardiff: The Institute, Park Place, 1924).	Document	SWML	
RE748 ROC	'An Investigation of Miners' Nystagmus'	1931	Pamphlet: W. J. Roche. Reprinted from *The British Journal of Ophthalmology*, April 1931 (London: George Pulman and Sons Ltd, 1931).	Document	SWML	

Reference Code	Collection	Dates	Description	Media	Location	DP
RE748 SMI	*The Binocular Vision of Miners with Nystagmus*	1953	NCB Medical Service Research Report 1. By Arthur Smith and R. C. Browne (London: NCB, 1953).	Document	SWML	
TN295 COL	*The Coal Miner: His Health, Diseases and General Welfare*	c.1924	Pamphlet: occupational diseases; nystagmus, beat knee, hand and elbow, parasitic diseases (e.g. ankylostomiasis).	Document	SWML	
	Scrapbooks of newspaper cuttings (dark blue 'Cathedral' news cuttings book)	1950–79	Asbestos cancer. Mass X-rays and TB in pit areas. Mass radiography unit, X-rays of miners and ex-miners. Dust, accidents, fatalities, disease. Farmers' lung.	Document	SWML	
	Scrapbooks of newspaper cuttings (labelled scrapbook (green): 'Cuttings Book, 1945–1947')	1945–7	'Aluminium Therapy of Silicosis' (BMJ 1946). Industrial diseases, occupational ophthalmology. Skin problems e.g. miners' furunculosis, dermatitis caused by working in wet places, infection (article, *Mining Journal*, 1945). Silicosis and pneumoconiosis. Suicide case.	Document	SWML	
	Scrapbooks of newspaper cuttings (light blue book: 'Pneumoconiosis Research Unit, Press Cuttings, 1948-52')	1948–52	1943 Order under Workmen's Compensation Act, Medical Board enabled to certify men suffering from pneumoconiosis as well as silicosis. Dr Charles M. Fletcher set up clinic at Cardiff, where men suffering from the disease kept under observation. Five doctors working with him. Death of female sand blaster, foundry (West Bromwich), from silicosis 1948. New factories, employment of disabled miners. 1929 legislation, silicosis contracted in coal mines qualification for Workmen's Compensation. 1931–43 cases resembling silicosis turned down by Silicosis Medical Board. 1945 Workmen's Compensation (Pneumoconiosis) Act. 1956 loose article re MRC unit. Envelope – Reviews of Drs Hugh-Jones's and Fletcher's 'Social	Document	SWML	

Reference Code	Collection	Dates	Description	Media	Location	DP
			Consequences of Pneumoconiosis among Coalminers in South Wales. Medical Research Council Memo 25'. Silicosis, TB, dust and suppression, compensation, pneumoconiosis.			
	Scrapbooks of newspaper cuttings (unlabelled green scrapbook)	1946–8	Dust, disease, silicosis, pneumoconiosis. MRC. Non-notifiable complaints e.g. rheumatism, bronchial disorders, stomach complaints – record-keeping.	Document	SWML	

~ 2 ~

Non-mining Diseases and Injuries

Coal mining was only one of several industries in south Wales with a big workforce; the docks, along with the metal industries – tinplate production, copper, iron and steel – also employed large numbers of workers. Although the docks were perilous environments where accidents were not unusual, the Factory and Workshop Acts ignored ships, wharves and quays. The early workmen's compensation schemes were similarly indifferent to dock workers. Yet the cargoes that they unloaded and the conditions in which they laboured exposed them to a host of work-related illnesses, which included skin problems, nose bleeds and blood poisoning, chest complaints, burns, vomiting and blindness.

In the tinplate industry, health was especially threatened by the 'flux' and poisonous fumes, which – made worse by ineffective ventilation – caused lung problems and asthma as well as general debility and exhaustion. In addition, there were not always adequate sanitary facilities for women workers. Concerns were expressed from the 1890s by the Tinplate Workers' Union. However, it was not until 1907 – following a Home Office Committee on Industrial Diseases – that the factory inspectors agreed that the more hazardous machinery should be covered and that there should be sufficient exhaust draft to carry away all fumes and dust (SWCC: AUD/222; MNA/PP/118/1). In the same year, a special report on the risks of contracting plumbism from coating metals with lead and/or tin suggested that workers under the age of sixteen should not be employed in the tinning process and that women should be excluded from certain activities (SWCC: MNA/PP/118/11). The recommendations on ventilation were reiterated in a 1912 report by the factory inspectorate, which also voiced anxieties about excessive weight-carrying, the splashing of molten metal, zinc chloride and grease, dangerous machinery, fumes, dust and high temperatures (SWCC: MNA/PP/118/12). Despite trade union pressure for more efficient factory inspections, the ventilation of tinhouses was slow to improve.

The other metal industries brought about similar health problems. Workers in the copper industry were thus exposed to lead and zinc poisoning, and their teeth became black and rotten. In the iron and steel industries, the high temperatures associated with handling molten metals led to dehydration and tiredness; and in 1918 the Home Office commissioned a report from the Industrial Fatigue Research Board, which led to the replacement of the twelve-hour shift with an eight-hour one to help alleviate the dangers of tiredness. Renamed the Industrial Health Research Board in 1928, this board was the outcome of worries about the health of women munitions workers at Royal Ordinance Factories during the First World War; in 1916 the toxic jaundice that they suffered as a result of filling shells with tri-nitro-toluene (TNT) became a notifiable disease.

By the Second World War, the board was investigating the accident and sickness records of munitions workers: a shift in focus indicative of a more psychological approach to occupational health (SWCC: AUD/488; MNA/PP/16/50/5–6). It was matched by a growing commitment to the well-being of employees. During the 1920s, for example, the Industrial Welfare Society sought to increase the number of workplace welfare schemes (SWCC: MNA/COP/7/1–13); in 1935 the Association of Industrial Medical Officers was founded; and, during the 1940s, larger factories began to appoint their own occupational health staff of medical officers, nurses and first-aiders.

Reference Code	Collection	Dates	Description	Media	Location	DP
AUD/222	Dick Cook	c.1910–74	Work injuries; foot (hammer toe), cuts, blindness, concussion. Hospital treatments; Neath and Cardiff. Tin workers health and safety; heat protection, dehydration, burns, injuries, death. Workmen's Compensation and NI.	Transcript of audio	SWML	Y
AUD/342	Mrs Nancy Davies (Seven Sisters)	1910–c.1974	Women's work at ROF Bridgend – accidents especially on night shifts and wet weather which caused explosions.	Transcript of audio	SWML	Y
AUD/344	Mr W. Knipe	1905–c.1973	Work as policeman during Tonypandy Riots 1910. Casualties of fighting, deaths of 2 policemen. Own injuries, head and teeth. Dr Llewellyn at Llwynypia attendance of over 500 casualties.	Transcript of audio	SWML	Y
AUD/481	Mrs Bessie Webb and Mrs Hannah Katie Evans	1920–75	Work at tin works; conditions, clothing, accident. Sister's work at Bridgend munitions factory. TB and silicosis of family members.	Audio tape	SWML	Y
AUD/488	Mrs Exon	1910–75	Munitions factory Bridgend; working with detonators, face shields, safety overalls and shoes.	Audio tape	SWML	Y
HD6661.TRA	TUC Annual Reports of Proceedings (Missing: 1906–8, 1910–14, 1917–18, 1920, 1922, 1929, 1931, 1940–1, 1945)	1904–85	1924: Manor House Hospital ('Labour Hospital'), Industrial Orthopaedic Society. Safety and welfare – mines, building, vehicles. Unhealthy offices. Workmen's Compensation including silicosis. Building Industry Safety Regulations. Coal Trimmers Compensation Deputations to Minister of Health. Factory inspection.	Document	SWML	
MNA/COP/5/1/1-14	Pembroke Dock Co-op Society (general and committee meetings minutes)	1888–1951	Assistance to members for medical treatment. Staff sickness and injuries. Victoria Nurses Home Committee. Medicine chest for Workmen's Compensation Act.	Document	Archives	
MNA/COP/5/1/16	Pembroke Dock Co-op Society	1898–1931	Manager's Instruction Book: References to staff providing medical certificates when off sick.	Document	Archives	

Reference Code	Collection	Dates	Description	Media	Location	DP
MNA/COP/5/2/1–4	Pembroke Dock Co-op Society – Kilgetty Branch (committee minutes)	1919–51	Staff injury, accidents and sick leave.	Document	Archives	
MNA/COP/7/1–13	Ton Co-op Society (general and committee minutes)	1884–1927	Employees: sickness; diphtheria case; welfare scheme; butchery overalls. Accidents. Smoking ban (bakery). Industrial Welfare Society. Public Health Regulations. Factory and Workshops Act re staff welfare provisions.	Document	Archives	
MNA/COP/7/14–15	Ton Co-op Society (Board Meetings minutes)	1928–48	Accidents (staff and other) and compensation. Staff illness including work-related dermatitis.	Document	Archives	
MNA/J/19/C3	Lily of the Valley Lodge of the Unity of Oddfellows, Ystrad Rhondda	1899–1950	Health certificates: 1899: 2 doctors' certificates – unable to work (no illness details). 1930: 8 doctors' certificates including 3 from Mid-Rhondda Medical Aid Society, some have illness details.	Document	Archives	Y
MNA/NUM/3/5/14	SWMF: Compensation Records (Compensation Secretary's correspondence)	1938	Public Health Department Cardiff booklet re Cardiff Municipal Accident Service (talk to Cardiff Medical Society); fracture clinic, rehabilitation of disabled workmen.	Document	Archives	Y
MNA/NUM/2/89	Abercynon Lodge (explanatory leaflet on the work of the Cardiff and District Hospital Society)	1942	Benefits. Contributions. Dependants. Privileges. Surgical appliances. Reciprocity between contributory schemes. Municipal hospitals. Hospital vouchers. Non-contributors. Cases where responsibility not accepted, e.g. TB, mental cases, infectious diseases, incurable.	Document	Archives	
MNA/NUM/L/43/A8	Graig Merthyr Lodge (general and committee minutes)	1948	Factories for disabled, pressure to have factories built, Tumble and Ponthenry factories to take 50% men and women. Under new scheme, insurance certified men continue work unless have TB.	Document	Archives	Y
MNA/POL/2/3	Aberdare Trades and Labour Council (annual and monthly meetings minutes)	1944–52	Reference to working conditions at Trecynon Dairies.	Document	Archives	

Reference Code	Collection	Dates	Description	Media	Location	DP
MNA/POL/24/2	Ynyshir Ward Committee minutes	1947–51	Council employee silicosis compensation claim. Public institutions: institution staff and abuse of sick payment benefits.	Document	Archives	
MNA/POL/3/3/1	Ammanford, Llandebie and District Trades and Labour Council (annual, general and Executive Council minutes)	1938–41	1939 TUC circular re Workmen's Compensation Conference in Swansea, pressing for changes in law. 1940 Women's Compensation Conference in Cardiff. 1941 campaign for establishment of light industries in area for injured workers.	Document	Archives	
MNA/POL/6/1	Caerphilly Labour Party (Executive Committee minutes)	1938–41	County council work: Extension of Isolation Hospital, staff working conditions and houses. Employee medical examinations.	Document	Archives	
MNA/POL/8/1	Ebbw Vale Branch Iron and Steel Trades and Labour Council (cash book)	1899–1919	Receipts and expenditure re compensation cases and secretary, artificial limbs, Porthcawl Rest, Hereford Eye Hospital, Cardiff and Bristol Infirmaries, Nursing Association.	Document	Archives	
MNA/PP/118/1	John Thomas (Aberavon) Annual Trade Conference Minutes of Dock, Wharf, Riverside and General Workers' Union (Tinplate Section)	1907–17 (1910–11 missing)	1907: sanitary conditions of tinhouses – gave evidence to Committee on Industrial Diseases (Home Office). Questions re injurious effect of flux and dust from pink meal and lack of ventilation. Tried to get men affected into New Workmen's Compensation Act. Visited Swansea for inspection, case strengthened. 1908: resolution to see Inspector of Factories to secure improved ventilation in tinhouses and see what is nature of material in which tinhousemen have to work. 1909: lighting, ventilation and sanitation. Circular to branches asking details of complaints and suggestions to go to HM Factory Inspector. Deputation to Home Secretary to get improvements and urging appointment of additional factory inspectors. 1913: ventilation in Tinhouses. Report of Factory Inspector and doctor, should be sufficient exhaust draft to carry all fumes and dust away, all rubbing and dusting machines should be covered. Home Office wanted measures to reduce health danger. Employers criticized report. 1916: ventilation, better ventilation of tinhouses, suggestions by Home	Document	Archives	

Reference Code	Collection	Dates	Description	Media	Location	DP
			Office and Factory Inspectors not happened due to war. Efforts being made to see that women introduced to Finishing Department, provision made for ventilation and other matters connected with employment of women	Document	Archives	
MNA/PP/118/11	John Thomas (Aberavon) (circulars and other papers re DWRGWU.)	1899–1916	1901: form of rules re DWRGWU Tinplate Section Special Fund. Refers to permanent disability (accident – £20 disablement grant) and funeral benefit. 1912: London Dock Strike, letter to workmen – cause of distress, starvation, appeal for funds. 1906 poster: 'Flux' fumes dangerous, poisonous, inducing pulmonary distress/disease. Poor ventilation, hardship, endangers health. Sanitary decencies not observed for both sexes. Adequate inspection to prevent infringement of clauses re child, youth, women workers. 1906 poster as above: refers to Meeting of Tinplate Trade (Wales, Monmouthshire, and Gloucestershire) to request government to include tin and blackplate manufacturing under 'unhealthy' clauses and afford more inspection to tinplate works. 1906 poster for DWRGWU Tinplate Section re conference held in Swansea on 21 April1906. Resolution to include tinplate trade in 'dangerous occupations' under Factories Act. 1912 DWRGWU Tinplate Section poster re National Insurance Act and Insurance Cards. Notification of Insurance Scheme Proposals	Document	Archives	
MNA/PP/118/12	John Thomas (Aberavon) (*The Dockers' Record* (24 monthly reports of the DWRGWU))	1901–16	August 1915: appeal for Lydney Medical Aid; appointment of additional Factory Inspectors, Trade union urges Home Office re more efficient factory inspections, calls attention to unhealthy conditions in galvanizing and tinplate industries, need for proper sanitation and ventilation. February 1907: letter from Ben Tillett to Home Office re health problems of members – skin troubles, blood poison, loss of limbs. Spathic and calcined ores causing burns, nose/throat bleeding,	Document	Archives	

Reference Code	Collection	Dates	Description	Media	Location	DP
			vomiting, prostration, total incapacity, sight loss. Use of bran for tinplate cleaning, dust arising including influx fumes.			
			Copper work, diseases as of lead poisoning, and zincs. Diseases develop over slow and long periods. Disease of jaw and teeth with black and rotten teeth. Drug cargoes – diseases, chest troubles, sight loss. Tinplate trade flux, use of flux instead of palm oil – pulmonary complaints, poisonous fumes, heavy vapours. Colic, lung problems, asthma, high mortality, exhaustion, illness. Pitch, patent fuel cause sight loss, skin troubles. Bilge water emits worst of gases and smells and poisonous. Lead handling – poisoning. Guano cargoes – dangerous fumes. Some special woods poisonous when handled. Grain cargoes cause nose bleeds, lime and sulphur used to cleanse grain have noxious fumes. Oxen tread on wheat and their excreta add to ferment. Frequent chest complaints esp. asthma. June 1911: Factory Inspectors – more needed and information to be given re numbers of accidents, disabilities, injuries, deaths, diseases to dock workers. Factory Acts in docks. Feb 1907: Sick Benefit Society meeting, letter re Compensation Act, need to include all dangerous trades and occupational disease. June 1911: Swansea spelter workers demand increase in Factory Inspectors, protest re conduct of authorized medical men giving evidence as government experts for employers, data collected for Home Office experts – dangerous and unhealthy occupations in lead, pitch, flux, arsenic. Roll of Honour – members elected to public bodies – Board of Guardians, Hospital Trustees. May 1907: reference industrial diseases, Special Committee appointed by House of Commons, occupations with bad health effect, e.g. grain discharging, iron ore, hides, fuel work, night soil men.			

Reference Code	Collection	Dates	Description	Media	Location	DP
			August 1906: Inspector of Docks, Wharves, and Factories, Congress instructs Parliamentary Committee to prepare Bill re inspections under Factories' Act, and qualifications of inspectors. Ventilation and flux poisoning; Home Office interest, questions in Parliament. References including tinplate trade in 'dangerous occupations'. 1906: details re own insurance scheme. Various items re insurance scheme and benefits. December 1909: 2 serious accidents, Home Office involved, view of getting more efficient inspection of gear, June 1911: refers to accidents and claiming comp, National Insurance, Invalidity and Unemployment Insurance. Reports of Legal Department, Compensation for injuries, case lists, amounts. Points made at conference 1904 re health and safety, decrease in work hours, legislation for injured workers, appointment of inspectors under Factory and Workshops' Act, laws re proper compensation, full wages during disablement. March 1913: Factories Act and Compensation Act references. Article re night work of boys in factories – conditions re sleep and rest, meals, travel time, recreation. Sept 1915: Swansea District compensation case, member suffering from plumbism – commuted claim but now also gets compensation. February 1907: most not covered under Workmen's Compensation Act. Dock Regulations – structural defects in ships a danger. Safety re docks, wharves and quays, registered for inspection? Subject to Factory Act? December 1912: tinplate industry investigation by HM Medical Inspector of Factories and HM Inspector of Factories. Reports that health of workers in tinning and finishing of plates injured by fumes and dust. Recommendations re efficient exhaust provision, washing of walls, employment of under-16s			

66

Reference Code	Collection	Dates	Description	Media	Location	DP
MNA/PP/118/14	John Thomas (Aberavon) (correspondence, circulars, agendas and other papers re South Wales, Monmouthshire and Gloucs Tinplate Workers' Union)	1888–99	Tinplate Workers' Union meeting agendas: 1894: proposal that General Council attract attention of HM Inspector of Factories re unsanitary conditions; 1891: accidents, causes to be investigated, whether compensateable or not; 1891: fund for relief of workmen who had had accident. 1899: letter to workmen from Tinhousemen's Association, refers to Accident and Funeral Funds; 1889: questionnaire for Annual Council Meeting, 'How many Sets at your Tinhouse working through flux'?	Document	Archives	
MNA/PP/118/24	John Thomas (Aberavon) (minutes of TGWU Tinplate Section Annual Conference)	1925	Swansea Conference, TGWU Area 4, 9 May 1925 (Tinplate Section): Payment of permanent disablement grants (2 men, names and amounts). Sickness grants and funeral benefits. Working conditions in Finishing Department of tinplate trade, need for new legislation re buildings and better sanitary and hygienic conditions. Elimination of dust and noxious fumes. Stringent exercise of powers, Factory and Workshop Acts.	Document	Archives	Y
MNA/PP/118/25	John Thomas (Aberavon) (minutes of TGWU Tinplate Section Annual Conference)	1930	Swansea Conference, TGWU Area 4, 20 April 1929 (Tinplate Section): Refers to payment to Convalescent Home of the union. Sickness and funeral benefit payments.	Document	Archives	
MNA/PP/118/33	John Thomas (Aberavon) (correspondence and papers re tinplate union affairs)	1893–1928	Card 'Welsh Artizans' Utd Association' (ud) refers to Benefits including Workmen's Compensation Act, and permanent disability.	Document	Archives	
MNA/PP/118/50	John Thomas (Aberavon) (*Ironworkers' Journal*)	1900	The Ironworkers' Journal June 1900: Workmen's Compensation Act and casual labour; housing of the working classes; fatal accident and Workmen's Compensation case.	Document	Archives	
MNA/PP/118/51	John Thomas (Aberavon) (annual report and balance sheet for Port Talbot Steel Works' Relief Fund)	1917	Expenditure on sickness and distress, and surgical instrument fund in local hospital.	Document	Archives	

Reference Code	Collection	Dates	Description	Media	Location	DP
MNA/PP/118/52	John Thomas (Aberavon) (Ness Edwards, *The Industrial Revolution in South Wales*)	1924	Working conditions: accidents, safety, illness, ventilation, injuries, lung disease.	Document	Archives	
MNA/PP/124/1	W. S. Watkins (Neath)	1920s	Brief notes re interview. Copper refinery works and 'terrible conditions' and dermatitis. Father's blindness re cataracts from copper and no Workmen's Compensation. 1921: Provident fund for staff set up. 1935: silicosis case.	Document	Archives	
MNA/PP/16/2	S. O. Davies	1948–51	Letter to Prime Minister relating to unemployment, disabled workers, Remploy factories, numbers of unemployed registered disabled persons.	Document	Archives	
MNA/PP/16/11/1–34	S. O. Davies	1944–8	Parliamentary debates (Hansard). 17 October 44 – Written answers re British Army – vaccinations, sickness (hospital cases).	Document	Archives	
MNA/PP/16/12	S. O. Davies	1930s–1940s	May Day resolution re Compensation Bill. Notes re Industrial Injuries Bill. Disablement Employment Act; reference to 1943 report Committee on the Rehabilitation and Resettlement of Disabled Persons.	Document	Archives	
MNA/PP/16/50/10	S. O. Davies	1948	Constituency correspondence: doctors' certificates; war pensions and disablement and discharge; TB pension; Workmen's Compensation; Ministry of Supply Depot closure, impact on disabled workforce.	Document	Archives	Y
MNA/PP/16/50/2	S. O. Davies	1940	Constituency correspondence re compensation re worker at Royal Ordnance Factory, ill workers at Royal Ordnance Factory (ROF), compensation for government contract workers.	Document	Archives	Y
MNA/PP/16/50/5	S. O. Davies	1943	Constituency correspondence; women workers at ROF, illness and absence, and neurasthenia of workers.	Document	Archives	Y

68

Reference Code	Collection	Dates	Description	Media	Location	DP
MNA/PP/16/50/6	S. O. Davies	1944	Constituency correspondence; Workmen's Compensation – heart, lungs, dermatitis, ROF worker (lost fingers), copy Treasury memo Scheme of Compensation no. 133 (injury to workmen in government establishments).	Document	Archives	Y
MNA/PP/16/50/7/1 and 2	S. O. Davies	1945	Constituency correspondence: (1) ROF worker compensation for lost finger; Workmen's Compensation for factory worker's hand injury; letters re RAF aircraftman with 2nd-degree burns; specialist nerve operation for wounded soldier; pension claims for dependants of servicemen, and disabled/sick war veterans (both world wars). (2) ROF compensation claims (e.g. dermatitis).	Document	Archives	Y
MNA/PP/16/50/8	S. O. Davies	1946	Constituency correspondence; ROF compensation claim.	Document	Archives	Y
MNA/PP/16/50/9	S. O. Davies	1947	Constituency correspondence: compensation claim for accident at government hostel; death of government worker; new tenure and sick pay conditions for teachers.	Document	Archives	Y
MNA/PP/16/51	S. O. Davies	1945	Correspondence re ROF compensation claim for dermatitis.	Document	Archives	Y
MNA/PP/16/59	S. O. Davies	1962–3	Correspondence re closure of Remploy factory at Merthyr (orthopaedic footwear). Letters from local hospitals and people. Majority of employees disabled – concerns re redundancies.	Document	Archives	
MNA/PP/16/81	S. O. Davies	1967	Bill – National Insurance (Industrial Injuries) (Amendment) Act 1967; Drafts, Bill, and Act (10 May 1967)	Document	Archives	
MNA/PP/34/11	Harold Finch	1939	Royal Commission on Workmen's Compensation minutes, 27–28 April 1939. Paper no. 7 Memo of Evidence by the Board of Trade 18 May 1939 and 1 June 1939.	Document	Archives	

Reference Code	Collection	Dates	Description	Media	Location	DP
MNA/PP/55/5	J. D. Jenkins (MOH, Rhondda UDC), correspondence and papers re Silicosis Scheme	1929–37	Sandstone Industries (Silicosis) Scheme 1929. Letters from TB physician re examination of patients (with details, opinions and decisions). Details of scheme centres in UK and examinations for new employees. Correspondence re length of time to contract silicosis.	Document	Archives	Y
MNA/PP/6/1/1–2	E. M. Collins	1930s?	Taff Vale Railway Co. book of regulations (undated); includes items re illness and disability, workplace safety, no smoking, Accident Fund, Code of Byelaws for passengers. 1933: newspaper cutting commenting on these regulations.	Document	Archives	
MNA/PP/67/25	W. Eddie Jones	1935	1935 statement by man sent to Pontypool Labour Exchange to Shobden Hardening Centre. Harsh conditions, contracted muscular rheumatism and under doctor's treatment for 5 weeks. Trainees unable to afford medical services there.	Document	Archives	
MNA/PP/91/2	William Picton (Maerdy)	1936	Report on visit to Treglog and Cynarth Instructional Centres for Unemployed, Brechfa, (Carmarthenshire); by unemployed workers' representatives. Refers to conditions, drainage, first aid, hygiene.	Document	Archives	
MNA/TUG/1/A2	Coaltrimmers' Union (Cardiff, Penarth and Barry Branch), annual, general, committee, and Executive Committee minutes	1890–95	Accident pay claims references, injury, compensation. Members' sickness and arrears. Applications for benefits. 1895: letter from Whitehall re insertion into Factories and Workshops Bill clause re ventilation of holds and bunkers on ships. Newspaper cuttings re fire on ship, spontaneous combustion whilst taking in coal cargo. 1895: Cardiff, 5 men, serious injuries and burns, sent to Hamadryad Hospital. 1895: minutes, resolution re escape holes to prevent disasters, to recover men or let them escape, if taken ill in hot weather, gas explosion, fire, collision. Many 1895 newspaper cuttings	Document	Archives	

Reference Code	Collection	Dates	Description	Media	Location	DP
			re ventilation of coal cargoes. Union rules re contributions and benefits. Safety of coaltrimmers, 1894 newspaper cutting, Cardiff, re escape holes in decks of vessels. 1895 poster for Cardiff meeting re manholes cut in cover of water ballast tank. 1894: balance sheet – accident pay, doctors' fees. 1895: letter from Marine Department, Board of Trade inquiries and meeting re ventilation of coal-carrying vessels whilst being loaded. Swansea docks explosion on steamer, newspaper cutting, 2 deaths, 2 injuries. 1895: Union memo, inspector sent from London to report.			
MNA/TUG/5/1	South Wales and Monmouthshire Enginemen, Stokers, and Craftsmen's Association, Quarterly report of the Association	1906	Section re compensation, fatal accident case and widow's claim, court case. Claim details for another fatal accident, fall. TUC delegate's report reference to Helping the Blind (League of Blind), and Workmen's Compensation Amendment Bill.	Document	Archives	
MNA/TUG/6/1	Tin and Sheet Millmen's Association, monthly report books; minutes of Executive Council meetings, balance sheets, contributions etc.	1905	Numbers of members on sick list, and deaths. Distress grants paid per branch, amounts and illness. Wattstown Disaster (explosion). Workmen's Compensation Act Amendment Bill. Compensation case, cost of doctors. Accident levy for member. Compensation cases references.	Document	Archives	
MNA/TUG/7/1/B/70	Iron and Steel Trades Confederation, general office correspondence files and papers	1945	DAC Memo No 5 Quota and Designated Employment Schemes 1944. Disabled Persons (Employment) Act 1944, Registration (1945 pamphlet from Ministry of Labour and National Service). Disablement Advisory Committees – required under Disabled Persons (Employment) Act 1944. Copy of Act, Memo (No. 23) for Disablement Advisory Committees, DAC Memo No 2 Applications for Entry of Name in (or Removal of Names from) Register of Disabled Persons 1944.	Document	Archives	

Reference Code	Collection	Dates	Description	Media	Location	DP
MNA/TUG/7/1/C/1–2	Iron and Steel Trades Confederation, reports, circulars, minutes and papers	1934–48	1934: Workmen's Compensation Act 1925, letter reporting accidents. 1936: Act, hernia cases letter. 1939: Workmen's Compensation Acts, industrial diseases, letter re certifying surgeon's certificates. 1946: letter re supplementary clothing coupons 1946–7.	Document	Archives	
MNA/TUG/7/1/C/1–2	Iron and Steel Trades Confederation, reports, circulars, minutes and papers	1934–48	1943: Memo re Workmen's Compensation (Temporary Increases) Act 1943. Memo re supplementary clothes coupons. 1944: Workmen's Compensation Act – industrial diseases (date of disablement). Workmen's Compensation (calculations). Memo re legal services, accidents at work and Compensation. 1948: Letter re accidents caused by explosion of live shells. Letter re convalescent home facilities for women members. Letter re NHI Act 1946, sickness benefit. Letter re reporting of accidents.	Document	Archives	
MNA/TUG/9/1	Amalgamated Engineering Union, minute book	1922–6	References to Sick Steward's reports. Accident case, no dependents to claim sick benefit, visit to hospital by Sick Steward. Hospital passes for Sick Steward.	Document	Archives	
MNA/TUG/9/5	Amalgamated Engineering Union, Superannuation Benefit and Benevolent Fund Book	1920–49	Benevolent Fund: names, dates, grant amounts, illness (including heart disease, cerebral haemorrhage, bronchitis, TB, cancer, gangrenous foot, gastric ulcers, senility/dementia, pneumonia, and lost in action during wartime).	Document	Archives	Y
MNA/TUG/10/1	Amalgamated Society of Engineers (minute book)	1917–22	References: Sick Steward's reports. Sick Benefit cases. Sick member needing specialist doctor. Government scheme for training disabled sailors and soldiers	Document	Archives	
MNB/COL/17/C27	Morlais Colliery, Solicitor's Dept circulars	1935–42	Re Factories Act 1937, including health and safety. Liability for wages during illness, and health benefit. Workmen's Compensation (Supplementary Allowances) Act 1940.	Document	Archives	

Reference Code	Collection	Dates	Description	Media	Location	DP
MNB/POL/5/1–2	National Council of Labour Colleges, lists of classes	1943–4	Class entitled 'Workmen's Compensation Law'.	Document	Archives	
MNB/POL/6/A30	Newport Constituency Labour Party, miscellaneous letters and papers	1918–76	1948 copy PQ 137/3/48, Question to Minister of Labour re disabled ex-servicemen in Newport and work in new factory. Reply re disabled unemployed in area.	Document	Archives	
MNB/POL/6/A8	Newport Constituency Labour Party, Executive and General Committee minutes, and Health Committee report	1938–44	Workmen's Compensation conference. Disabled servicemen and marriage allowances. Sick pay at town council. Double Summer-Time and its effect on health of workers.	Document	Archives	Y
MNB/PP/10/H31	S. O. Davies	1937–47	Report of Inter-departmental Committee on Rehabilitation and Resettlement of Disabled Persons 1943 (TB, orthopaedic, medical rehabilitation, Emergency Hospital Scheme, cardiac cases, blind, deaf, neuroses and psychoses, industrial diseases, artificial limbs, disabled. Copies: Workmen's Compensation Bill 1937; Workmen's Compensation (Supplementary Allowances) Bill 1940; Disabled Persons (Employment) Act 1944. Summary of Provisions of National Assistance Bill 1947. National Assistance Bill Financial Memorandum 1947 (terminate exist poor law, provision for disabled).	Document	Archives	
MNB/PP/12/C2/1–15	William Henry Davies (Penclawdd), Annual reports: MOH, Gower Rural Sanitary Authority	1895–97, 1899, 1900, 1902–11	1907: Local Government Board requiring inspection of all Workshops and Factories under Workshop and Factories Act, comments re being agricultural area with some collieries, so difficulty in doing so.	Document	Archives	
MNB/PP/64/K1	J. S. Williams (Dowlais), miscellaneous printed material, press-cuttings and circulars	c.1924–37	1934 Parliamentary papers: Questions for Oral Answer, and not for Oral Answer, medical fitness of army officers, lavatory facilities in army quarters, Poor Law Medical Officers (Durham) loss of medical benefit.	Document	Archives	

Reference Code	Collection	Dates	Description	Media	Location	DP
MNB/PP/72/26	Alistair Wilson, compensation case examination cards and notes	1939-42	Cards re Examination of Young Persons – Factories Act 1937.	Document	Archives	Y
MNB/TUG/2/1	British Iron, Steel and Kindred Trades Association	1892-7	1892-4: funeral levy, benefits, obituaries (inc. names and cause of death, and family members' deaths), Employers' Liability Bill 1894 details. Compensation case relating to accident and death, details (knocked down by crane), at Briton Ferry. Accident at Flemington, lost hand. 1895-7: funeral levy, obituaries, causes of death (men and family members). Accident claims and grants. Workmen's Compensation Act 1897, details and schedules.	Document	Archives	
MNC/COP/1/1	Aberdare Co-operative Society, minute book	1929-32	Injured employee and compensation. Staff accidents at work (1 fatal). Staff member on compensation – doctor's examination. Staff sickness and pay. Medical examination of new employees. Medical certificates for staff. Staff member sent to Pontsarn Sanatorium.	Document	Archives	
MNC/COP/1/3 and 6	Aberdare Co-operative Society, minute book	1937-48	(3) Staff sickness, sick pay, compensation. Staff member sent to Roden House. Sanitary inspection notice re temperature at Miskin Branch. Convalescent Benefit and ticket applications. (6) Staff sickness, compensation, medical examinations, certificates, Employees Sickness Scheme. Roden Convalescent Home, employees granted stays. Sick pay – ex-servicemen. Employee's wife – Diphtheria. Staff member – dermatitis. Employee's typhoid contact. Employment of disabled.	Document	Archives	
MNC/COP/15/2	Penarth Co-op Society, minute book	1937-9	Staff accidents, Compensation, sick pay, medical fees. Dispute between Insurance Society and employee's doctor relating to fitness of person to return to work. Milk department employee's 'rash' on hands.	Document	Archives	
MNC/COP/16/1	Penygraig Co-op Society, minute book	1912-16	Accidents, compensation claim. 1913 Convalescent Fund set up, and Convalescent Home (1915). Reference to doctor's report on staff member tested for TB.	Document	Archives	

Reference Code	Collection	Dates	Description	Media	Location	DP
MNC/COP/27/1	People's Yearbooks, Annual of the Co-operative Wholesale Society Ltd	1920	Industrial accidents and diseases, statistics of deaths and disability. Photograph of women workers at 'Drug Room at Pelaw'. Labour Legislation 1919, including employment and training of disabled men. National Scheme for Employment of Disabled Ex-Service Men, CWS statistics.	Document	Archives	
MNC/COP/3/1, 3 and 4	Abersychan Co-op Society, minute Book	1908–49	(1) Staff sickness and injury absences. Insurance re ptomaine poisoning risks. Workmen's Compensation Insurance. (3) Staff sick pay allowance. Reference to appointment of Sick Visitors. (4) Disablement Advisory Committee of Co-operative Society (re Disabled Persons (Employment) Act 1945). References to staff sick pay, absence, medical examinations and operation.	Document	Archives	
MNC/COP/6/5	Blaenavon Co-op Society, minute Book,	1937–54	Staff accidents. HM Factory Inspector letter re fencing of machine. Sanitary Inspector's letter re heating of shops.	Document	Archives	
MNC/ISTC/3/1	National Union of Blastfurnacemen, Ore Miners, Coke Workers and Kindred Trades, Delegate Board minutes	1922–31	1931: Compensation cases (Dowlais and Cardiff). Notice re cases of Workmen's Compensation – National Executive Committee to submit amendments to Compensation Acts to General Council of TUC. Reports re Convalescent Home Benefit Fund, national convalescent benefit, disablement benefit, compensation. Medical certificate example and details (for convalescent homes). 1923: accident and compensation – 3 deaths from injuries. Sick, disablement and funeral Benefits. Cleveland Convalescent Home Fund details. 1923: Workmen's Compensation Act varies 1906 Act (details) – War Addition Acts repealed. Every factory to have certain first-aid boxes or cupboards unless in an ambulance room with arrangements for immediate treatment. Orthopaedic Society subscriptions. Accidents and compensation cases. Total disablement benefit rule of union to be	Document	Archives	

Reference Code	Collection	Dates	Description	Media	Location	DP
			rescinded. Welfare committees set up. Gas poisoning case and compensation. Sunderland Eye Infirmary donations. Convalescent homes section re Durham Coke Workers' Association efforts to establish as industrial diseases afflictions which coke oven and by products workers susceptible to. Reference to gassing. Compensation cases re Ebbw Vale and Dowlais (4 fatal) 1930.			
RC773 GRE	Home Office Memo on the Industrial Diseases of Silicosis and Asbestosis (pamphlet)	1932	*Origin and development of silicosis.* Industries and processes in which silicosis occurs. Prevention; dust suppression, exhaust ventilation, medical examinations. Provision for compensation. Medical arrangements for examination and certification of cases. Asbestosis.	Document	SWML	
RC773 GRE	Ministry of Fuel and Power. Digest of Pneumoconiosis Statistics (pamphlets)	1952–75	*Pneumoconiosis in the Mining and Quarrying Industries.* Contents inc: Boards held under National Insurance (Industrial Injuries) Act 1946, certificates of disablement or death under Workmen's Compensation Acts 1925–45, employment of persons suffering from pneumoconiosis.	Document	SWML	
RC773 GRE	Home Office Memorandum (pamphlet)	1932	*Memorandum on the Industrial Diseases of Silicosis and Asbestosis* (London, HMSO, 1932). Including silicosis, dust, ventilation, compensation.	Document	SWML	
RC773 Ind	Symposium Report	1945	*Industry Tuberculosis and Compensation, A Symposium* (National Tuberculosis Association), New York, 1945).	Document	SWML	
	Scrapbooks of newspaper cuttings, light blue book: 'Pneumoconiosis Research Unit, Press Cuttings, 1948–52'.	1948–52	Death of female sand-blaster – foundry (West Bromwich) from silicosis, 1948. Dust in cotton mills.	Document	SWML	

~ 3 ~
Safety and Welfare

Safety and welfare was an issue for all workplaces on the South Wales Coalfield, whether their business was in the industrial or the service sector. Trade unions campaigned vigorously for improvements, gradually winning concessions from employers who came to appreciate the advantages of a less hazardous working environment and additional benefits for staff. The problems faced by the South Wales Miners' Federation were most acute. Like other coalfields, South Wales experienced recurring difficulties with pit ventilation, firedamp and gas that several Royal Commissions attempted to tackle. In 1911, for instance, the Third Report of the Royal Commission on Mines laid down recommendations for percentages of gas in working areas, for adequate ventilation to remove firedamp and for robust procedures to communicate threats from gas and to withdraw men from dangerous places.

When, for whatever reason, accidents occurred, specialist safety equipment (for example; breathing apparatus, stretchers, helmets, ambulances) was used by pit rescue teams (SWCC: PHO/COL/68; PHO/COL/104) who honed their skills by competing regularly for prizes at local events that were reported in periodicals like *The Ebbw Vale Works Magazine* (SWCC: HD9550 EBB). In 1911, a Departmental Committee reported on the organization of rescue and aid in the case of mining accidents and its requirements were set out in a draft order to be issued under the Miners' Accidents (Rescue and Aid) Act of 1910. The Report recommended the number of rescue brigades to be kept in each mine according to the number of miners employed, the size of the brigades, their knowledge and training, and the equipment that they should possess. Fifteen years later, the recommendations were strengthened when another Departmental Committee suggested that mine owners retain the choice between two alternative types of rescue brigade: a specified proportion of trained men; or a rescue corps of permanent, highly trained staff in constant attendance at central rescue stations. Rescue stations were to operate within a 15-mile radius, and the grouping of mines was not to be limited to those in the same ownership. Rescue brigades and the number of men to act within rescue corps were to be reduced to enable training to be more efficient. A condition of acceptance for rescue work was to be a minimum of two years' underground experience, and recommendations were made in respect of age, fitness, medical examination, training, and the management of rescue stations.

First aid was taught to many other members of the workforce and to the local community, in evening classes and lectures held by the British Red Cross Society and the St John Ambulance, as well as in workplace schemes. Carrying the ambulance, or first aid, box underground was recognized as an important responsibility, and on occasions additional payment was received for assuming it. If a colliery had an ambulance room, it was usually situated near the pithead, or within the pithead baths accommodation. Accidents were reported there, and treatment for minor injuries undertaken by personnel with first-aid training, or a nurse or doctor employed or subsidized by the colliery. In 1914, Glamorgan County Council, the British Red Cross Society and Heriot-Watt College, Edinburgh successfully campaigned for their first-aid certificates to be approved by the Secretary of State for the purposes of the Coal Mines Act. An appendix set out the subjects to be added to the St John's and St. Andrew's courses for the certificate to win the kitemark.

Safety lamps were a vital part of the miners' equipment, as poor underground lighting was responsible for the prevalence of 'miners' nystagmus', and other serious eye complaints and even blindness (see Chapter 1, 'Mining Diseases'). Miners received extra pay for carrying safety lamps. In a report of 1912, recommendations were made that safety lamps be subjected to various tests, and conform to a standard specification. Safety lamp manufacturers were to possess a certificate from the Home Office for their product. There were a variety of designs and fuelling methods, such as electricity, sodium vapour and oil. Even electric lamps could be dangerous; one containing sulphuric acid, for instance, blinded a miner (SWCC: AUD/323). Although open flame lamps could cause burns, some areas continued to use them where there was considered to be little risk of gas explosions.

Indeed, a 1906 photograph, in which a pit pony is hauling a tram of coal, shows one miner holding a candle and another holding an oil lamp whilst smoking; they were at a lamp station, an area known to be free of gas, where safety lamps were relit (SWCC: PHO/COL/113).

Miners' welfare provisions included not only welfare institutes, but also pithead baths and canteens. Workplace canteens became more widespread as the links between nutrition, fitness to work and increased productivity were better understood (see Chapter 8, 'Food and Nutrition'). Pithead baths came to play a key role in the lives of many miners and their families. The majority of miners' homes did not have separate bathrooms, so bathing had to take place in a tin bath in front of the living-room fire. This adversely affected the health of those women who had constantly to prepare the baths for the men in their family (see Chapter 9, 'Women's Health'). There was also the persistent danger of children falling into the hot water and being scalded or even killed (SWCC: MNC/PP/11/1). The drying of washed pit clothing in front of the fireplace also caused a continuous damp atmosphere in the house. Pithead baths supplied not only bathing facilities for miners but drying rooms for their pit clothing too. Men were thus able to return home in clean, dry clothing and did not contaminate public transport with their coal-covered clothing. Allowances of soap and towels were made for use in the baths, miners receiving additional soap rations during wartime. In 1913, a Departmental Committee reporting on the provision of washing and drying accommodation under section 77 of the 1911 Coal Mines Act made various recommendations in respect of the structure, fittings, ventilation and temperature of washing and drying facilities. It suggested that, on the joint representation of owners and workmen, the Inspector of Mines for the division could vary the regulations. 'Baths committees', with three representatives each for the owner and for the workers, were to be set up to manage the accommodation and facilities. In 1924, the provision of pithead baths was made compulsory, but some collieries were slow to build them, and in south Wales a campaign was started by miners' wives in support of baths (SWCC: MNC/PP/11/1).

The general welfare of miners was financed by an official Welfare Fund, which in 1933 was investigated by a Departmental Committee of Inquiry. The fund had previously been financed by a levy of 1*d*. per ton on all coal raised in Great Britain, and was administered by the Central Miners' Welfare Committee and district committees. It provided for recreation, as well as health, convalescent treatment, hospitals, ambulance schemes and nursing services. Pithead baths and canteens were also part of the brief. The committee decided that the fund should retain its original purpose, and that the construction of more pithead baths and canteens should be a priority. Reductions in the levy were discussed, along with the merging of funds into a central account. However, the Miners' Welfare Committee was to have discretion in each locality, spending sums proportionate to contributions.

Reference Code	Collection	Dates	Description	Media	Location	DP
	The Welsh Housing and Development Year Book	1920-2	1921: pithead baths.	Document	SWML	
AUD/170	Lee Hutchinson	1875–c.1960	Bathing at home after work. Drying clothes, working in water. 1942 work in pit, skin complaint (psoriasis), working in water and heat, visit to doctor.	Transcript of audio	SWML	Y
AUD/188	W. C. Davies	1920s–1930s	Work as Safety Inspector. Lack of pithead baths. 1929 gas explosion – Milfrain Pit, details re first aid. Safety conditions and inspections. 1930s flood Levenstone Drift, drownings and rescue attempt. Ventilation and gas. Men smoking underground.	Transcript of audio	SWML	Y
AUD/192	Mr and Mrs Fred Morris (Maerdy)	1900– c.1973	Miners bathing at home – details of preparation and washing.	Transcript of audio	SWML	Y
AUD/215	Walter Powell	c.1900–1974	Baths (at home and at pit). Work conditions in pits. Mines Inspectors.	Transcript of audio	SWML	Y
AUD/221	Jim Evans	c.1910s– c.1930s	Pit baths, Wales and Nottinghamshire bathing habits. Gyms.	Transcript of audio	SWML	Y
AUD/239	Albert Davies (Blaenavon)	1910– c.1973	Safety Inspector, details of job. Lack of pithead baths. Milfren explosion. Gas in mines. Comparison of mine safety in south Wales and Newcastle areas. Gas explosion at Six Bells, possible causes and details of scene underground.	Transcript of audio	SWML	Y
AUD/303	Mr B. Edwards (Tonypandy)	1898– c.1973	Ambulance work, no ambulance men in colliery, used own equipment. Ambulance classes formed. Joined ambulance proper 1910. Injuries, e.g. cuts, breaks. Serious accidents, officials would compel men to work. Riots – injuries and death. Treatment of men at surgery. Pit explosion 1905, 35 deaths, gas/fire, 77 horses killed, recovering bodies. Safety lamp use.	Transcript of audio	SWML	Y

Reference Code	Collection	Dates	Description	Media	Location	DP
AUD/310, 311	Abel Morgan	1878–c.1972	Colliery first aider and Pit Baths Superintendent. Pit baths and ambulance room. Details of some accidents, e.g. crush injury (graphic), groin injury.	Transcript of audio	SWML	Y
AUD/323	W. H. Taylor (Blaenavon)	1903–1930s	Pit fireman and first-aider. Examinations – gas test. Lamps underground; open light causing death by burns, Oldham electric lamps contained sulphuric acid and blinding miner. Milfraen Pit accident and explosion. Stretcher bearers. First aid; details of some cases, lack of facilities, introduction of rescue brigades (W. H. Taylor a member). Explosive fumes and carbon monoxide caused headaches.	Transcript of audio	SWML	Y
AUD/461	Mrs Alexander	c.1910–c.1950	Bathing of miners – father and brothers.	Audio tape	SWML	Y
AUD/481	Mrs Bessie Webb and Mrs Hannah Katie Evans	1920–75	Miners bathing at home. Work at tin works; conditions, clothing, accident.	Audio tape	SWML	Y
AUD/488	Mrs Exon	1910–75	Munitions factory Bridgend; working with detonators, face shields, safety overalls and shoes. Bathing and cleaning house.	Audio tape	SWML	Y
AUD/56	Haydn Mainwaring	1910–80	Pit accidents attended, organizing help, loss of pay, negligence, safety improvements. First aid boxes. Nystagmus (own); symptoms, lighting and lamps.	Audio tape	SWML	Y
FX3263.5 SEC	The Second Industrial Survey of South Wales (3 volumes)	1937	Part 1, Industries. Part 2, Facilities. Part 3, Development. Part 2 reference to pithead baths. Miners' Welfare Fund.	Document	SWML	
HD661.TRA	TUC Annual Reports of Proceedings (incomplete)	1904–85	1924: Mines – gas poisoning, safety, mining disaster (Pouthenry Colliery, near Llanelly). Safety and welfare – mines, building, vehicles. Unhealthy offices. Building industry safety regulations. Coal trimmers, Workmen's Compensation. Deputations to Minister of Health. Factory inspection.	Document	SWML	

Reference Code	Collection	Dates	Description	Media	Location	DP
HD7269 M62 Oce	*After Ten Years: A Report of Miners' Welfare Work in the South Wales Coalfield 1921–1931* (pamphlet)	1931	(Ocean Collieries, Treorchy: The Ocean Area Recreation Union). St Athan's Holiday Camp (children) and Miners' Welfare Camp. Pithead baths, First aid room, canteens. Ambulance class for boys. Pit welfare work: health, disablement and old age.	Document	SWML	
HD7269.M62.OTH	*The Other Side of the Miner's Life: A Sketch of Welfare Work in the Mining Industry* (pamphlet)	1936	Issued by Philip Gee (Lincoln's Inn) with the authority of The Mining Association of Great Britain. Contents: recreation facilities; colliery canteens; welfare centres; convalescent homes; pithead baths; Miners' Welfare Fund; research – Safety in Mines Research Board.	Document	SWML	
HD9550 EBB	*The Ebbw Vale Works Magazine* (Vol. 3, No. 9)	Dec 1923	Article: 'Health and Welfare in the Coal Mining Industry', by Edgar Collis, Welsh National School of Medicine. Ambulance and fire brigade competition results.	Document	SWML	
HD9550 EBB	*The Ebbw Vale Works Magazine* (Vol. 5, No. 19)	June 1926	Notes and photograph relating to Celynen North Collieries' Ambulance Team.	Document	SWML	
HD9550 EBB	*The Ebbw Vale Works Magazine* (Vol. 7, No. 26)	Mar 1928	Health hints to miners by Industrial Health Education Council – references to first aid, wounds, contaminated water, accidents.	Document	SWML	
HD9550 EBB	*The Ebbw Vale Works Magazine* (Vol. 7, No. 27)	June 1928	Article: 'The Advantages of Exercise'. Health hints to miners – refers to eyesight (nystagmus), beat hand, rheumatism, bronchitis, lumbago and sciatica (re wet clothing).	Document	SWML	
HD9550 EBB	*The Ebbw Vale Works Magazine* (Vol. 3, No. 10)	Mar 1924	Article: 'Handkerchief Respirators – A Warning', by member of Monmouthshire Collieries Rescue Association. Reference to respiratory appliances, ambulance men, rescue stations.	Document	SWML	
HD9550 EBB	*The Ebbw Vale Works Magazine* (Vol. 8, Nos 30–2)	Mar–Sept 1929	Article: 'Are Factors of Safety Scientific?', reference to geological factors in safety.	Document	SWML	
HD9550 EBB	*The Ebbw Vale Works Magazine* (Vol. 9, No. 34)	Apr 1930	Notes relating to first aid and ambulance work.	Document	SWML	

Reference Code	Collection	Dates	Description	Media	Location	DP
HD9550 EBB	*The Ebbw Vale Works Magazine* (Vol. 9, No. 36)	Oct 1930	Notes relating to ambulance teams and divisions.	Document	SWML	
HD9550 EBB	*The Ebbw Vale Works Magazine* (Vol. 4, Nos 13–14)	Dec 1924–Mar 1925	1924 – Results of ambulance and fire brigade competitions. 1925 – 2 Photographs of Ambulance Team and Instructor. Article: 'The Art of Keeping Fit', personal health, hygiene and exercise.	Document	SWML	
HD9550 EBB	*The Ebbw Vale Works Magazine* (Vol. 10, No. 40)	Oct 1931	Article: 'Abertillery Ambulance Division'; history, staff, Aberbeeg Hospital. First aid and home nursing classes. Ambulance and fire brigade competition results.	Document	SWML	
HD9550 EBB	*The Ebbw Vale Works Magazine* (Vol. 10, No. 39)	Jul 1931	Article: Abertillery Pithead Baths opening and speeches, and plans of baths. Notes on Cwm Ambulance and Nursing Divisions awards evening.	Document	SWML	
HD9550 EBB	*The Ebbw Vale Works Magazine* (Vol. 10, No. 38)	Apr 1931	Article: 'Massage and Manipulations', 3 pages and photographs about physiotherapy, remedial gym, electrical treatments. Details and photograph of opening of new Abertillery Ambulance Hall. Notes regarding new pithead baths, Rose Heyworth Colliery.	Document	SWML	
HD9550 EBB	*The Ebbw Vale Works Magazine* (Vol. 10, No. 37)	Jan 1931	Results of ambulance and fire brigade competitions, including photographs (8 pages).	Document	SWML	
HD9550 EBB	*The Ebbw Vale Works Magazine* (Vol. 6, No. 21)	Dec 1926	Ambulance brigade competition results. Article: 'Welfare Conference at Oxford'. Industrial Welfare Society; advice on individuals' rights.	Document	SWML	
HD9550 EBB	*The Ebbw Vale Works Magazine* (Vol. 4, No. 16)	Sept 1925	Notes about S. John Ambulance class and Ebbw Vale Workmen's Medical Society. Article: 'Colds', prevention and cause.	Document	SWML	
HD9552.3 MIN	*The Miner* (Vol. I, No. 3)	Dec 1944	Safety Department article: 'The Coal Mines (South Wales) (Pneumoconiosis) Order 1943'. Letter about the Coal Mines Act – health and safety issues. Letter relating to dust suppression and ventilation.	Document	SWML	

84

Reference Code	Collection	Dates	Description	Media	Location	DP
HD9552.3 MIN	*The Miner* (Vol. I, No. 5)	Feb 1945	Articles: 'Labour Safety in Soviet Mines'; and 'Ventilation'. Letter 'Dust Suppression and Costs'.	Document	SWML	
HD9552.3 MIN	*The Miner* (Vol. I, No. 7/8)	Apr/May 1945	Summary of SWMF Conference, including safety, Red Cross penny-a-week fund. Summary of Annual Report of HM Inspector of Mines.	Document	SWML	
HD9552.3 MIN	*The Miner* (Vol. I, No. 9/10)	June/July 1945	Article: 'Welfare Activities in Mining Communities, South Wales Coalfield', refers to pithead baths, canteens, St John Ambulance, hospitals, convalescence, rehabilitation. Report of Technical Advisory Committee on Coal Mining referring to ventilation, health and safety.	Document	SWML	
HD9552.3 MIN	*The Miner* (Vol. I, No. 11/12)	Aug/Sept 1945	Articles: 'Outdoor Welfare in the South Wales Coalfield'; 'Colliery Canteens, Food Supplies and Permits'; 'Mining Enters a New Era', health and safety conditions, ventilation, canteens and baths, garden villages.	Document	SWML	
HD9552.3 MIN	*The Miner* (Vol. II, No. 1/2)	Oct/Nov 1945	Editor's notes: 'Miners' Welfare Fund'. Articles: 'Pit Welfare', referring to pithead baths and canteens; and 'First Aid and Ambulance Work in the Mines'.	Document	SWML	
HD9552.3 MIN	*The Miner* (Vol. II, No. 9)	July 1946	Report relating to NUM Annual Conference, reference to safety. Letter re Workmen's Safety Inspections.	Document	SWML	
HD9552.3 MIN	*The Miner* (Vol. II, No. 11)	Sept 1946	Article: 'Dutch Miners' – sick and injured miners, medical service, safety clothing, compensation, pithead baths.	Document	SWML	
HD9552.3 MIN	*The Miner* (Vol. III, No. 3)	Jan 1947	Review of NUM Conference – Safety Regulations, Health and Welfare (including pneumoconiosis). Tables for Disabled Persons (Employment) Act (1946 figs), and Government Vocational and Disabled Training Schemes 1946. Pithead baths programme, and towels.	Document	SWML	

Reference Code	Collection	Dates	Description	Media	Location	DP
HD9552.3 MIN	The Miner (Vol. III, No. 3)	Jan 1947	Article: 'Miners' Welfare', including canteens, pithead baths, clinics, nurse, welfare.	Document	SWML	
HV686.R3	Reports of the MOH, and School MO, Rhondda UDC (reports of the Medical Officer of Health)	1925	Ambulance facilities; Porth and District Hospital use of own ambulances; accident cases, St John Ambulance and British Red Cross Society ambulances also used.	Document	SWML	
MNA/COL/2/1	Clydach Merthyr Colliery (rough minutes of arbitration meetings held to resolve disputes)	1942–7	Rehabilitation and light work. Safety lamps. Night shift health – sleep, clothes drying. Ventilation. Canteens. Ambulance services.	Document	Archives	Y
MNA/COL/2/4–38	Clydach Merthyr Colliery (Manager's carbon-copy correspondence books)	1937–48	Clothing coupons. Protective clothing. Safety boots and lamps. Red Cross fund. Safety classes. Ambulance and first aid. Safety inspections.	Document	Archives	Y
MNA/COL/2/54	Clydach Merthyr Colliery (Manager's correspondence)	1938–9	Royal Commission on Safety in Coal Mines Report. Ambulance and first aid. Safety in Mines lecture. Silicosis and dust respirators.	Document	Archives	Y
MNA/COL/2/55	Clydach Merthyr Colliery (Manager's correspondence)	1940–1	Safety lamps. Safety inspections. Safety classes. First aid. Ambulances. Red Cross fund.	Document	Archives	Y
MNA/COL/63	Clydach Merthyr Colliery (NCB Group Safety Officer's Reports)	1950–60	NCB Group Safety Officer's Reports for Clydach Merthyr and Abergelli Collieries.	Document	Archives	Y
MNA/COP/7/1–13	Ton Co-op Society (general and committee Minutes)	1884–1927	Employees: welfare scheme; butchery overalls. Smoking ban (bakery). Industrial Welfare Society. Public health regulations. Factory and Workshops Act in relation to staff welfare provisions.	Document	Archives	
MNA/II/16/1	Forest of Dean District Welfare Association (committee minutes)	1921–4	Provision of ambulance classes and competitions. Public Health and Safety division. Meetings with Industrial Welfare Society. St John Ambulance Association, Forest of Dean Centre, grants, visit relating to establishment of a sick room, stores.	Document	Archives	

Reference Code	Collection	Dates	Description	Media	Location	DP
MNA/NUM/1/1	Records of the Miners' Federation of Great Britain (minute books of MFGB Executive Committee, and annual and special conferences)	1903–44	1903: Coal Mines (Regulation) Bill. Mines Inspectors. 1905: Safety. Ventilation. Mining Inspectors. 1921–2: Visit to Industrial Orthopaedic Society, Manor House Hospital (London). Employment. Hours and conditions. Pithead baths. Safety appliances. Coal dust experiments. Safety Lamps Bill. 1923–4: Nystagmus: connection with lamps; report and Home Office Order 1922. Rescue aid regulations. Safety in mines. Safety appliances. Miners' lamps – testing for firedamp. 1925–6: water dangers in mines (floods). Miners' Welfare Fund and Committee. Royal Commission on Mining Subsidence. Mines Inspectors. Miners' lamps. 1935–6: Automatic firedamp alarms. Pithead baths. Rehabilitation of Persons Injured by Accidents, Home Office Inquiry. 1943: Coal Mining (Training and Medical Examination) Order 1943. Rehabilitation and centres. Pithead baths. Rationing; food, clothes, work clothes, boots. 1944: Fire and Rescue Brigade Men. District Safety Boards – Workmen's Inspectors. Mines medical service, function of doctors. Protective clothing and boots. Rehabilitation and incapacity by illness or industrial disease.	Document	Archives and SWML	
MNA/NUM/1/1–2	Records of the Miners' Federation of Great Britain/NUM (minute books of Executive Committee, and annual and special conferences)	1902–1948	General themes include; Inspectors, safety in mines, Improved Mines Act 1908. (1/2) 1945–6: Safety and health: dust suppression, medical service at mines, first aid rooms, compulsory medical examinations. Sanitation. Ventilation. 1947: Fatal Accident Scheme. Miners Accident Benevolent Fund. Re-employment of injured miners. Provision- disabled foreign workers. First aid service. Pithead baths. 1948: Employment of disabled miners. Sanitary arrangements at collieries. Rationing – industrial soap for miners.	Document	Archives and SWML	

Reference Code	Collection	Dates	Description	Media	Location	DP
MNA/NUM/3/1/1	Minutes of the SWMF Exec Council, and Annual and Special Conferences (records of the SWMF/NUM (South Wales Area))	1907–40	Industrial diseases. Coal dust. Rock analysis. Partially disabled. Medical examinations of workmen. Medical attention underground. Ventilation. Dust absorbers. Gas masks and detector lamps (1939). St John Ambulance Association. Medical examinations – general (and military – 1917). Mines Inspection. Colliery Examiners' Association. Safety apparatus. Ambulances. First aid. Rescue work. Protective equipment and clothing. Royal Commission on Safety (1937). Safety lamps. Safety in mines research (1927). Explosions and gas. Pithead baths. Clothes and boots for miners.	Document	Archives and SWML	
MNA/NUM/3/3/1	Correspondence (bound volume of circulars)	1899–1915	1914 conference, safety. Safety lamps: Arbitration re extra pay, design. Miners' Eight Hours' Bill Manifesto including safety.	Document	Archives	
MNA/NUM/3/3/14	Correspondence with SWMF No. 1 Area (Files 16 and 17)	1931–42	File 17: 1941–2, Clothing coupons for workmen.	Document	Archives	Y
MNA/NUM/3/3/18	Correspondence with SWMF No. 5 Area	1934–41	Pithead baths, procedure for application to build. Mines Inspector. Silicosis and support for compulsory risk reduction by mine owners. Carrying of 2 safety lamps. Ambulance agreement and payment for carrying ambulance box. Automatic gas detectors.	Document	Archives	
MNA/NUM/3/3/2	Correspondence (bound volume of circulars)	1916–27	Coal-cutting machinery safety. Firedamp, coal dust. Ambulance men and cars. Silica dust, siliceous rock. Water Dangers Committee. Coal dust explosions and using closed trams. Ambulances and first aid. 1916: contributions to motor ambulance cars for Army in France, to be used for colliery ambulance work after War. Contributions to St John Ambulance Association. 1918: conference references to cage safety catches, motor ambulances. Colliery stoppage Inquiry (gas). Colliery ventilation. 1919 Report: Amendments to Coal Mines Act – Safety, Lamps, Ambulance. Maximum working temperature and	Document	Archives	

Reference Code	Collection	Dates	Description	Media	Location	DP
			absence of regulation. Safety oil lamps: gas dangers, objections to Amended Order to the Hailwood Lamps and Modifications (1918) 1919 Government Committee of Inquiry. 1920: Labour Party Conference – pithead baths. Mine Safety booklet 1924. 1926 Questionnaire – collieries paying extra for using lamps, and Royal Commission on Mining Industry references to safety lamps. Report of Coal Industry Commission including pithead baths.			
MNA/NUM/3/3/21	Correspondence with SWMF No. 8 Area (correspondence)	1934–42	Partial compensation and house coal. Letter concerning patent for safety equipment.	Document	Archives	
MNA/NUM/3/3/23	Correspondence with lodges (Files 2–8))	1934–42	First-aiders' reports relating to accidents. Ambulance men's pay, boxes, First aid. Safety helmets, refusal to wear until supplied free. Pithead baths application.	Document	Archives	Y
MNA/NUM/3/3/3	Correspondence (bound volume of circulars)	1927–35	Conference references: Distress Fund, electric lamps, pithead baths, safety, stone dusting.	Document	Archives	
MNA/NUM/3/3/33/1	Great Mountain Lodge (correspondence)	1934–41	Examination of collieries and Safety Committee. Dust at screens and health, excessive dust complaints. Inspection report. Pithead bath attendants.	Document	Archives	Y
MNA/NUM/3/3/33/2	Great Western Lodge (correspondence)	1934–42	Damaged lamps. Introduction of detector lamps. Safety Committee. Gas detectors. House coal to compensation men. Safety Committee report 1939. Mine Inspection report 1939.	Document	Archives	
MNA/NUM/3/3/33/3	Groesfaen Lodge (correspondence)	1934–40	Gas detectors. Safety in mines. Questionnaire re Firedamp Detector Regulations; flame safety lamps, automatic detectors, Thornton detectors.	Document	Archives	
MNA/NUM/3/3/33/4	Gwaun-Cae-Gurwen Lodge (correspondence)	1934–42	Proposed pithead baths, site, ballot to install. 1936 reference to dust summonses to Gwaun-Cae-Gurwen Collieries.	Document	Archives	

Reference Code	Collection	Dates	Description	Media	Location	DP
MNA/NUM/3/3/44/8	Ystalfera Lodge (correspondence with lodges)	1937–9	1938: copy of Colliery Examination report. 1937: correspondence relating to safety, workman charged with sleeping (breach of Mines Act Regulations). 1937: letter – grading of ambulance men	Document	Archives	Y
MNA/NUM/3/4/48	Mines Inspectorate (SWMF/NUM miscellaneous office papers and reports)	1943–7	1946: letter regarding division of South Wales Mines and Quarries Inspection Division, as per recommendation of Royal Commission on Safety in Coal Mines 1935–8. 1947: letter from HM Divisional Inspector about South Wales Mines Inspectorate Division, fatal accidents, firedamp, explosion. 1948: Safety in mines pamphlet, NCB, representative of HM Divisional Inspector of Mines. Various correspondence from Mines Inspectorate regarding accidents.	Document	Archives	
MNA/NUM/3/5/10	SWMF: Compensation Records (annual reports of silicosis cases)	1938–9	SWMF Annual Conference 1939 Agenda, including safety, dust absorbers, lamps, respirators.	Document	Archives	
MNA/NUM/3/5/14	SWMF: Compensation Records (Compensation Secretary's correspondence)	1936–7	1936–7: Miners' safety classes. Ambulance conveyance scheme. 1940: Medical Research Council notes concerning industrial hygiene. Industrial Health Research Board projects.	Document	Archives	Y
MNA/NUM/3/5/15	SWMF: Compensation Records (Compensation Secretary's correspondence: Area No. 4)	1934–41	House coal and compensation. Examiners' report relating to conditions and safety, Clydach Vale Mine.	Document	Archives	Y
MNA/NUM/3/5/22	SWMF: Compensation Records (correspondence re Fatal Accidents Scheme)	1943–7	1943 minutes of SWMF Safety Committee.	Document	Archives	Y
MNA/NUM/3/5/28	SWMF: Compensation Records (monthly SWMF Agents' reports Area No. 6)	1936–41	Includes many detailed references to compensation claims, accidents, safety and silicosis.	Document	Archives	Y

Reference Code	Collection	Dates	Description	Media	Location	DP
MNA/NUM/3/6/42	Records of the SWMF/NUM (S Wales Area) (Joint standing Disputes Committee minutes)	1919	Extra payment for carrying safety lamps.	Document	Archives	
MNA/NUM/3/7/1 and 2	Minutes of Enquiry into disaster at Universal Colliery, Senghenydd, 14/10/1913, Vols. 1 and 2 (pit disaster records)	1914	Vol. 1 Minutes of Court Proceedings. Vol. 2: Reports on Causes and Circumstances, by HM Chief Inspector of Mines and Chair of South Wales and Monmouthshire Coalowners' Association, and President of MFGB. References to dust, firedamp, gas.	Document	Archives	
MNA/NUM/3/8/17	Area No. 2 Council Minutes (register of ordinary accident cases)	1934–52	Colliery examiners. Workmen's Examiner's Reports. Safety, health and welfare. Dust analysis. Clothing, boot, food and soap coupons for miners. Iron rations. Protective clothing and boots. Safety lectures. Dust suppression. Colliery canteens. Provision of soap and towels.	Document	Archives	Y
MNA/NUM/3/8/17	Area No. 2 Papers re wage levels (register of ordinary accident cases)	1915–48	NCB (South Western Division) Safety in Mines booklet May 1948; Report of the HM Divisional Inspector of Mines, references to fatalities and accidents.	Document	Archives	
MNA/NUM/3/9/6, 7 and 8	Petition pleadings and County Court proceedings (legal papers)	1934	6: 11 June 1934, Petition pleadings: T. Morgan and Amalgamated Anthracite Collieries Ltd. re compensation. 7: 21 August 1935, transcript of County Court proceedings: W. H. May and W. H. Hannaford, breach of safety provisions. 8: High Court Order May and Hannaford.	Document	Archives	Y
MNA/NUM/L/1	Abercrave Lodge (annual and general meetings minutes)	1935–57	References to health and safety. Dust on screens. Ambulance Committee. Pit ventilation.	Document	Archives	

Reference Code	Collection	Dates	Description	Media	Location	DP
MNA/NUM/L/10/1, 3 and 5	Bedwas Lodge (annual, general and committee meetings minutes)	1925–46	(1) 1925–33: Gas cases underground. Fatal accidents. Mines Examiners' reports. Ambulance car for hospital. Bedwas Ambulance Brigade appeal. Surface lavatories. Safety lamps. Ambulance boxes and men. (3) 1940–2: Claims for surgical boot, abdominal belt, truss, artificial limb repairs, gold injections treatment, artificial eye, dental repairs. Ambulance boxes – pilfering from. Airs raids safety. Pit baths safety. 1942: coupons for clothing and towels. (5) 1944–6: Pithead baths: skin disease, refusal of certifying surgeon to issue certificate (dermatitis), disinfectant foot baths requested, maintenance, foot powder, fumigation. Protective clothing and clothing coupons. Dust suppression, ventilation. Ambulance men.	Document	Archives	
MNA/NUM/L/13/1	Blaengwrach Lodge (annual and committee meetings minute book)	1946–8	Ambulance boxes and holding of certificates. Reference to oil lamps. Safety Board Inspector. Water and dust suppression, men unable to work as water unavailable. Safety regulations and search for contraband underground. Reference to supplies of 'dust bags'. Reduced coupon value for safety boots. House coal agreements for injured, ill and their dependants.	Document	Archives	
MNA/NUM/L/2/16	Abercyn Lodge (financial records)	1943	Balance sheet for Workmen's Motor-Ambulance Car account, December 1943.	Document	Archives	
MNA/NUM/L/ 20/121	Cambrian Lodge (Lodge Secretary's correspondence)	1939–40	Pit inspection reports.	Document	Archives	
MNA/NUM/L/ 24/31, 39 and 40	Cross Hands Lodge (Lodge Secretary's correspondence and papers)	1943–52	(31) Clothing coupons. (39) Mine inspection report, 29 March 1943. (40) Plan of first-aid arrangements, Cross Hands Colliery, January 1947.	Document	Archives	
MNA/NUM/L/26/1, 12 and 13	Cwmdu Lodge	1925–c.1935	Rules: Items 1 and 13 – Maesteg District Artificial Limb Fund, (1925 and c.1935); Item 12 – Lodge Ambulance Transport Fund (c.1935);	Document	Archives	

Reference Code	Collection	Dates	Description	Media	Location	DP
MNA/NUM/LJ/3/1	Abergorki Lodge (annual, general and committee meetings minute book)	1913–15	Safety lamps.	Document	Archives	
MNA/NUM/LJ/7	Abergorki Lodge (Lodge Secretary's correspondence book)	1917–1918	Safety lamps, complaints about condition, and new.	Document	Archives	
MNA/NUM/LJ/31/51	Elliot Lodge (Lodge Secretary's correspondence and papers)	1943–5	Mine inspection reports (2 items).	Document	Archives	
MNA/NUM/LJ/33/39	Ferndale Lodge (Lodge Secretary's correspondence and papers)	1931	Ferndale Lodge Hospital and Conveyance Fund rules.	Document	Archives	
MNA/NUM/LJ/34/1	Fforchaman Lodge (annual, general and committee minutes)	1938–1940	Proposed pithead baths. Talk relating to safety (Safety in Mines Commission) by D. Grenfel MP.	Document	Archives	Y
MNA/NUM/LJ/34/6	Fforchaman Lodge (annual, general and committee minutes)	1947–9	1948: Health Conference, Cardiff. Ambulance equipment and stretchers in one area, to be remedied. Pithead baths proposed. First aid boxes, and pilfering. Employment of Dust Suppression Officer. Soap for compensation men.	Document	Archives	Y
MNA/NUM/LJ/35/1	Fochriw No. 1 and Nantwen Lodges (minute books)	1917–34	Meeting with blind inventor of improved Safety Shot Firing. Demand for pithead baths. Grant to Ambulance Brigade.	Document	Archives	
MNA/NUM/LJ/41/46	Glyncorrwg Lodge (South Pit) (financial records)	1930–49	Account book containing: Glyncorrwg Ambulance accounts, 1930–8, and contribution accounts, 1942–9.	Document	Archives	
MNA/NUM/LJ/43/A1	Graig Merthyr Lodge (general and committee minutes)	1939–40	Dust problems. Mines Examiner report references. Disapproval of conveniences available for treatment of accident cases, 1939, ambulance facilities, telephone in one place.	Document	Archives	Y

Reference Code	Collection	Dates	Description	Media	Location	DP
MNA/NUM/L 43/A1	Graig Merthyr Lodge (general and committee minutes)	1937–40	Vote for installation of pithead baths (in favour) and application to Miners' Welfare Committee to build them. Safety lamps and new lighting order, 1939.	Document	Archives	Y
MNA/NUM/L 43/A8	Graig Merthyr Lodge (general and committee minutes)	1948	Mine inspections and reports. Dust suppression and ventilation. Soap supply to sick. Boot vouchers. Pithead baths, pressing for them to be built. Oil lamps, payment and safety. Reference to safety and dangers of smoking, men warned about searches and prosecutions.	Document	Archives	Y
MNA/NUM/L 48/C/45	Lewis Merthyr Lodge (Lodge Secretary's correspondence and papers)	1933	Pit inspection report.	Document	Archives	
MNA/NUM/L 49/D/1	Llanhilleth Lodge (safety reports)	1941–8	Pit inspection reports.	Document	Archives	
MNA/NUM/L 50/C/4	Maerdy Lodge (Lodge Secretary's correspondence and papers)	1924	Pit inspection report book.	Document	Archives	
MNA/NUM/L/58/1	Norchard and Princess Royal Lodges (minute book of Norchard Lodge Pit Head Committee meetings)	1942–9	Safety boots and permits for needy cases, supply shortage, 1944. Sanitary arrangements at pithead, company given 7 days to resolve, 1944. 1945: circular referring to safety boots and protective clothing for Safety Workers. New pithead baths at Easton and Northern. Ambulance room lighting and heating. Clothing coupons. Rehabilitation centres. Pit inspections. Contributions for Safety inspectors. Pithead baths, new works during War.	Document	Archives	
MNA/NUM/L 59/D/31	Oakdale Navigation Lodge (Lodge Secretary's correspondence and papers)	c.1930	Register of workmen prepared to use and contribute towards new pithead baths.	Document	Archives	Y

Reference Code	Collection	Dates	Description	Media	Location	DP
MNA/NUM/L/59/F/4	Oakdale Navigation Lodge (material re MFGB, SWMF, NUM)	c.1923–1941	Circulars and letters from SWMF including safety in mines.	Document	Archives	
MNA/NUM/L/59/A/3	Oakdale Navigation Lodge (minute books)	1919–20	Minute book for annual, general, special and committee meetings, (attached notices and agendas; also recommendations for pithead baths, 1919).	Document	Archives	
MNA/NUM/L/6/1	Abertridwr Lodge (meetings minutes, balance sheet, membership lists)	1925–59	St John Ambulance Corps levy. Improved safety lamps for examiners. Safety conferences.	Document	Archives	
MNA/NUM/L/60/A1	Onllwyn Central Washery Lodge (minute book of general and committee meetings (also reports of Dulais Group meetings))	1942–50	1947: safety boot vouchers, soap rations. Coupons, iron rations. Inspection regarding dust problems. Central Washery Ambulance Fund closure and contributions to Blaendulais Ambulance Car Association. Rules – ambulance workings. 1946: investigations – use of ambulance cars under new health scheme.	Document	Archives	
MNA/NUM/L/63/C/44	Penallta Lodge (Lodge Secretary's correspondence and papers)	1919–65	Miscellaneous papers, including hospital, ambulance and Welfare papers, 1927–54.	Document	Archives	
MNA/NUM/L/68/C8	Saron Lodge (correspondence and miscellaneous material)	1948	Pit inspection report.	Document	Archives	
MNA/NUM/L/9/1	Bargoed Housecoal Lodge (lodge committee minutes)	1947–50	Pithead baths. Cardiff District Hospital Fund. Nominations for Boards (including Safety, and Welfare). Ambulance box payment.	Document	Archives	
MNA/POL/2/1 and 2	Aberdare Trades and Labour Council (annual and monthly meeting minutes)	1925–35	(1) 1925–35: 1930s. St John Ambulance and collieries. Doctor's examination of men at pithead. District Council Health and Medical Committee; reference to workplace visits. (2) 1935–44: Complaint re lack of medical attention to injured miner from Nantymelyn Colliery, taken to general hospital where he died.	Document	Archives	

Reference Code	Collection	Dates	Description	Media	Location	DP
MNA/PP/11/15	Bryn Davies	1942	Order of the Hospital of St John 1942 income and expenditure statement. Ogmore Vale, Bridgend and District. Lists subscriptions and donations, cost of badges and meetings.	Document	Archives	
MNA/PP/111/1	Bryn Thomas ('Llandybie Over the Ages')	Early 1900s	Work in pits, references to pithead baths, and lamps (prevalence of nystagmus).	Document	Archives	
MNA/PP/118/107	John Thomas (Aberavon) ((D5) South Wales Labour Annual)	1902	Page on first aid advice.	Document	Archives	
MNA/PP/118/12	John Thomas (Aberavon) ('The Dockers' Record' (24 monthly reports of the DWRGWU))	1901–16	Points made at conference 1904 regarding health and safety, decrease in work hours, legislation for injured workers, appointment of inspectors under Factory and Workshops' Act, laws relating to proper compensation, full wages during disablement. February 1907 (Ben Tillett letter): Most not covered under Workmen's Compensation Act. Dock regulations – structural defects in ships a danger. Safety relating to docks, wharves and quays; queries whether docks registered for inspection or subject to Factory Act.	Document	Archives	
MNA/PP/118/52	John Thomas (Aberavon) (Ness Edwards, The Industrial Revolution in South Wales)	1924	Working conditions: safety, ventilation.	Document	Archives	
MNA/PP/122/1	Wilfred Timbrell (Tumble) (memoirs of Tumble)	1896–c1960s	Working conditions and lack of safety regulations. First aid classes, Drefach Council School, c.1910, attended by village men, St John Ambulance Association section formed.	Document	Archives	
MNA/PP/132/8	James Winstone	1916	SWMF Annual meeting Eastern Valley District pamphlet minutes 1916. Electric lamps Varteg colliery, gas danger. Blaenavon and electric lamps.	Document	Archives	Y

Reference Code	Collection	Dates	Description	Media	Location	DP
MNA/PP/15/2, 11	John Davies (Gwaun Cae Gurwen)	Inter-war period	JD's essay re East Pit, Gwaun-Cae-Gurwen Collieries. References to pit safety, lack of first aid equipment, ambulance room or attendant, yard uncovered and open to elements, ventilation deteriorated, work conditions.	Document	Archives	
MNA/PP/16/77	S. O. Davies	1924-5	Notebook containing notes relating to pithead baths.	Document	Archives	
MNA/PP/22/1	D. L. Evans (Abercrave)	1902	Western Division Special Rules: safety rules; safety lamps; use of explosives; abstract of Coal Mines Regulation Act 1887 – accidents and deaths, sanitation, ventilation, lamps, dangerous places, mine examination, clay and ironstone mines – water, refuges, ambulances.	Document	Archives	
MNA/PP/28/10	James Evans (Tumble)	1937	Letters regarding light employment of workers certified suffering from disease or after accident. Conciliation Board Agreement for the Coal Trade of Monmouth and South Wales – references to hours, mealtimes, holidays, rescue and aid services.	Document	Archives	
MNA/PP/28/20	James Evans (Tumble)	1931-43	1931 and 1937: SWMF Conciliation Board Agreement for Coal Trade of Monmouthshire and South Wales, references to fire brigades, rescue and aid services. 1943: SWMF Executive Council minutes reference to safety.	Document	Archives	
MNA/PP/28/24	James Evans (Tumble)	1937-42	1939: SWMF Safety Committee report. 1942: SWMF proposals for annual conference agenda – including dust, food and clothing rations, and safety.	Document	Archives	
MNA/PP/28/25	James Evans (Tumble)	1908-37	Correspondence regarding slant and drift winding enginemen and safety. Letter relating to Commission on Safety in Mines.	Document	Archives	Y

Reference Code	Collection	Dates	Description	Media	Location	DP
MNA/PP/28/26	James Evans (Tumble)	1937–1950s	1937: MFGB Executive Committee minutes relating to firedamp detector regulations. 1937: Mines Department Circular 92, safety of electrical apparatus underground. 1937 Royal Commission on Safety in Coal Mines booklet. Memo of MFGB evidence relating to shaft accidents. Accidents at Mines details – Coal Mines Act. 1938 Statutory Rules and Orders 797 Coal Mines and firefighting.	Document	Archives	
MNA/PP/28/36	James Evans (Tumble)	1930s–1950s	Undated election SWMF leaflets; references to 'dust menace' and extractors, safety and health of mines, ventilation.	Document	Archives	
MNA/PP/28/40 and 42	James Evans (Tumble)	1939–44	SWMF Annual Conferences; 1939: address by Arthur Horner – refers to safety and compensation; 1944: address by Arthur Horner – refers to safety in mines, Royal Commission on Safety in Mines, HM Inspectors, water dangers.	Document	Archives	
MNA/PP/28/9	James Evans (Tumble)	1939	Letter regarding bad condition of East Pit colliery train, inspected by SWMF officials after complaint by workmen.	Document	Archives	
MNA/PP/34/3	Harold Finch	1930	Risca Colliery Pithead Baths, Bather's Handbook; instructions how to use baths, management, features, ground plan, First Aid and ambulance room, drinking water facilities, smoking.	Document	Archives	
MNA/PP/41/1, 4, 5, 6	David Harris (Glais) (exercise books containing bilingual manuscript reminiscences)	1970s, ref C19th	Pithead baths and bathing at home. Gas incidents underground, and using safety lamp. Bathing in house, and landladies having to bathe lodging miners. Photograph of miners with lamp (naked light). Pithead baths, clothes lockers, home bathing. Pit ambulance room and doctor.	Document	Archives	Y
MNA/PP/46/40	Arthur Horner (open letter to Bedwas workmen from Ness Edwards, SWMF)	1936	Open letter: references to safety in mines.	Document	Archives	

Reference Code	Collection	Dates	Description	Media	Location	DP
MNA/PP/46/58 and 59	Arthur Horner, *The Miners Monthly* (SWMF)	1936	Vol. III, 9: Commission on Safety in Mines: ventilation and dust, high work temperatures, automatic gas detectors and firedamp. Vol. III, 10: Royal Commission on Safety in Mines; accidents, electricity dangers.	Document	Archives	
MNA/PP/46/61-63	Arthur Horner (speeches by Arthur Horner at SWMF Annual Conference)	1940-3	1940, 1942, 1943: References to safety.	Document	Archives	
MNA/PP/47/6	Noel Hutton (Bedwas), The Colliery Guardian'	1906	1905 Coalmines Inspection Reports, including accidents. Reports books and forms including safety lamps, ventilation, gas, dangerous conditions. Explosives in coalmines including safety issues.	Document	Archives	
MNA/PP/50/3	W. R. James (Trelewis) (Taff Merthyr Lodge minute book)	1946-52	Mines examinations; ventilation, safety appliances. Canteen and pithead baths. Ambulance Fund account and St John Ambulance Corp. Safety equipment. Safety lamps.	Document	Archives	
MNA/PP/50/5	W. R. James (Trelewis) (Inspection report, Taff Merthyr Colliery, Trelewis)	1948	References to ventilation, and first aid appliances.	Document	Archives	
MNA/PP/55/3	J. D. Jenkins (MOH, Rhondda UDC)	1910	Correspondence and papers between MOH and designer relating to water heating apparatus, and new apparatus for heating water for baths. Includes hand drawing and letter from the designer.	Document	Archives	
MNA/PP/55/6	J. D. Jenkins (MOH, Rhondda UDC) (Mines inspector's test, plans and letter re abandoned mines)	1918-19	Letter from Health Department, Rhondda UDC, inspection of Gelligaled Colliery, and plan of mine. 1918 and 1919: notices to local authority of discontinuance or abandonment of mine.	Document	Archives	

Reference Code	Collection	Dates	Description	Media	Location	DP
MNA/PP/55/8	J. D. Jenkins (MOH, Rhondda UDC) (miscellaneous printed material)	1910–37	Shorthand notes relating to 'Sanitation of Mines'. 1913: letter to Council Surveyor from Colliery Company; provision of water closets at pits, and drainage problems, request to discharge into culvert leading to river. 1930: Bather's Handbook: instructions on use, plan of baths, clothes drying, first aid and ambulance room. Poster, abstract of Coal Mines Act 1911: section 'Health' with references to baths, and dust suppression; sections on 'Accidents', and 'Safety Lamps'. Plan of 'Tram fitted as Colliery Commode', and 'Plan of Suggested Closet Convenience' for use underground. Article: 'Sanitation of Mines in Respect to Human Dejecta', by Henry Kenwood, *Journal of The Royal Sanitary Inst*, Vol. XXX, 10' (1909).	Document	Archives	Y
MNA/PP/63/6	I. G. Jones (Cwmtwrch)	1941	Desk diary, including fatal accident (crush) details, inquest and inspection. Ventilation problems and questions. Visit of Minister of Supply to ambulance room. Visits of Inspectors.	Document	Archives	
MNA/PP/73/4	James Lewis (Maesteg) (Lodge account book (Maesteg Deep Lodge))	1919–47	List of recipients of Iron Ration Coupons 1944-6. Issue of towels 1943-4. Miners' Safety Certificates issued 1946.	Document	Archives	
MNA/PP/73/6	James Lewis (Maesteg)	1930–47	Papers relating to James Lewis's tenure of office as secretary of Llynfi Sundries Lodge; iron rRations (clothing). Dust suppression. Light work and incapacitated miners. Pithead baths and supply of towels.	Document	Archives	
MNA/PP/73/7	James Lewis (Maesteg) (miscellaneous pamphlets and printed material)	1933–46	Pamphlet: 1944 SWMF 'Case for an Increase in the Workers' Contribution to 1/- per week', refers to safety. 1946–7: Clothes Rationing 'The fifth Iron Ration for workers in certain very heavy industries' for Works Clothing Committees (extra clothes).	Document	Archives	
MNA/PP/8/8–9	W. H. Crews	1926–1950s	NCB training syllabus; including welfare, social services, psychology of dealing with conflict, safety, environmental conditions underground, welfare and medical officers.	Document	Archives	

Reference Code	Collection	Dates	Description	Media	Location	DP
MNA/PP/81/19/1	Abel Morgan	1931	Lady Windsor Colliery Pithead Baths, Bather's Handbook. Opening ceremony 28 January 1931. Instruction on using baths, clothing, towels, soap, lockers. Funded by Mining Industry Act 1926, levy paid to Miners' Welfare Fund. Maps of baths, features, First aid room.	Document	Archives	
MNA/PP/81/28 and 29	Abel Morgan	1936–7	Ocean Area Recreation Union, Pithead Baths Competition. Reports of Inspector of Lady Windsor Pithead Baths, 1936–7. References to cleanliness, facilities, healthiness, buildings.	Document	Archives	
MNA/PP/86/3	W. J. Nind (analysis of underground accidents)	1936–7	Pamphlet: 'An Analysis of Underground Haulage Accidents in South Wales', 1936, by South Wales and Monmouthshire Safety in Mines Research Committee.	Document	Archives	
MNA/PP/87/1	Charles Parker (transcripts of interviews with miners and their wives)	1961	(Refers to interwar period) Mine ventilation, dust. Bathing. Lamps.	Document	Archives	Y
MNA/PP/9/6 and 7	H. W. Currie	1937–8	Newspaper cuttings relating to mine safety, accidents, and ARP safety.	Document	Archives	
MNA/PP/91/22	William Picton (Maerdy)	c.1966 ref C19th–C20th.	Handwritten short history of Maerdy. First aid and ambulance classes from 1877. St John Ambulance Association Division formed 1906. Rhondda Fach Corps 1907, Dr S. Glanville Morris Chief Surgeon, T. E. Richards Chief Superintendent, Maerdy No. 1 Squad prizes.	Document	Archives	
MNA/PP/93/28	Leo Price	1933	SWMF Rules 1933. Reference to Inspection of Mines on behalf of Workmen (Coal Mines Act 1911).	Document	Archives	

Reference Code	Collection	Dates	Description	Media	Location	DP
MNA/TUG/1/A2	Coaltrimmers' Union (Cardiff, Penarth and Barry Branch) (annual, general, committee, and Exec Committee minutes)	1890–5	Safety of coaltrimmers, 1894 newspaper cutting, Cardiff, escape holes in decks of vessels. 1895: poster for Cardiff meeting, manholes cut in cover of water ballast tank. 1895: minutes, resolution that escape holes to be used to prevent disasters, recover men or let them escape, if taken ill in hot weather, gas explosion, fire, collision. Many 1895 newspaper cuttings about ventilation of coal cargoes. 1895: letter from Whitehall relating to insertion into Factories and Workshops Bill a clause concerning ventilation of holds and bunkers on ships.	Document	Archives	
MNA/TUG/3/0/1	National Association of Colliery Overmen, Deputies and Shotfirers (minute book of conference and committees of General Federation of Colliery Firemen of GB)	1910–25	1910: Rescue and Ambulance Bill. 1914: Senghenydd Disaster Enquiry, Firemen's Certificates (and other years), Gas testing, ventilation, dust. 1915: Workmen's Inspections, District Mining Safety Boards. 1916: Safety in mines. Testing of eyesight and hearing for members (clause of Mines Act). Safety lamps.1923: Rescue appliances. 1925: First aid. 1916: Llanhilleth Colliery Enquiry relating to gas build-up. Safety shotfiring appliance (blind inventor).	Document	Archives	
MNB/COL/11/E1–2	Fernhill Colliery (contract books)	1942–53	Conciliation Board Agreements for the Coal Trade of Monmouthshire and South Wales, Schedule II relating to principles for periodical ascertainments; including contributions to fire brigades, rescue and aid services, Miners' Welfare levy.	Document	Archives	
MNB/COL/17/B7–25	Morlais Colliery (files of invoices)	1932–7	Requests for payment – Swansea District Collieries Rescue Association, and Industrial Welfare Society. 1936: invoice for mine dusts tests. 1937: invoice for smoke helmet apparatus.	Document	Archives	
MNB/COL/17/C12	Morlais Colliery (Home Office (Mines Dept) circulars)	1916–42	Reference to return of forms relating to ventilation, coal-cutting machines, pithead baths, safety lamps, rescue brigades and appliances, non-fatal accidents. 1925: Working Committee of Safety in Mines Research Board investigation into effect of machine work on accidents at coalface.	Document	Archives	

Reference Code	Collection	Dates	Description	Media	Location	DP
MNB/COL/17/C17A and B	Morlais Colliery (Miners' Assoc of GB circulars)	1921–44	1931: letter relating to lighting in mines and safety lamps.	Document	Archives	
MNB/COL/17/C23	Morlais Colliery (railway circulars)	1926–41	Copy Statutory Rules and Orders 1931, No. 945, Railway Safety: prevention of accidents, rules.	Document	Archives	
c	Morlais Colliery (Secretarial Dept Circulars)	1928–30	Coal Mines General Regulations (First-Aid) 1930. Cost sheets – 1930, including fire brigade, rescue and aid services. 1928: reference to Rescue Regulations.	Document	Archives	
MNB/COL/17/C25B, 5C, 5D, 5E, 5F, 5G, 5H	Morlais Colliery (Secretarial Dept circulars)	1925–42	(5B) 1925–7: Reference to pay for Safety Men. (5C) 1937: 2 pamphlets: Instructions and Advice Relative to the New Conciliation Board Agreement. Including references to pay for carrying ambulance boxes. (5D) 1939–42: Reference to fire prevention (business premises) (2) 1941: Safety lamps. Safety in Mines Research Board. (5E) 1934–42: Safety lamps. 1939: Regulation firedamp detectors. Clothes rations. Protective clothing, ARP workers. Extra protective clothing coupons. Miners' protective boots, clogs, gloves. Fire prevention. Safety Board and examination of mines. (5F) 1939–41: Payment to workmen for ambulance, first aid services, carrying first aid box. First aid certificates. ARP ambulance and first aid services. Safety classes. 1938: Deputies and Shotfirers (Safety Lamps) Order. (5G) 1931–7: Safety conferences. Protective equipment for mineworkers. 1936: Smoke abatement, reference to leaflet, 'Ravages of Smoke'. Underground lighting. (5H) 1934–8: 1938 reference to Mark IV dust respirator. Pay for carrying first aid boxes and ambulance duties.	Document	Archives	
MNB/COL/17/C27	Morlais Colliery (Solicitors Dept circulars)	1935–42	Reference to Factories Act 1937, including health and safety.	Document	Archives	

Reference Code	Collection	Dates	Description	Media	Location	DP
MNB/COL/17/C32A, 2B, and 2C	Morlais Colliery (miscellaneous memoranda, resolutions, agreements etc.)	1915–42	2A: Reports (Monmouthshire and South Wales Coal Owners' Association) 1941–2; Coal Dust Research Committee (suppression of dust, removal of dust clouds, dust reduction), and General Research Committee (sodium vapour lamps). 2B: Agreement relating to payment for ambulance and first aid services (refers to first aid certificates, and carrying first aid boxes). 2C: 1934 Cost sheet including fire brigade, rescue and aid services.	Document	Archives	
MNB/COL/17/C33A	Morlais Colliery (welfare and safety circulars)	1922–79	Miners' Welfare Fund correspondence relating to pithead baths, and washing and drying of clothes. Poster, 'Exhibition of Progress and Research in Mine Safety'. Publicity for pamphlet concerning Protective Equipment for Mineworkers. List of safety in mines classes 1939-40.	Document	Archives	
MNB/COL/17/C6A	Morlais Colliery (Board of Conciliation circulars)	1925–42	Pay for ambulance and first aid services.	Document	Archives	
MNB/COL/17/C8B	Morlais Colliery (Monmouthshire and South Wales Employers' Mutual Indemnity Society circulars)	1916–38	Silicosis and Mark IV respirators.	Document	Archives	
MNB/COL/17/F1-4	Morlais Colliery (Colliery workmen's contract book)	1926–42	Including Memo of Agreement, with references to fire brigades, rescue and aid services.	Document	Archives	
MNB/COL/18/1	Pentremawr Colliery (Special Rules to be observed at Pentremawr Colliery (bilingual English and Welsh))	1889	Safety rules: ventilation, gas, dangerous places, firedamp, safety lamps. Rules including: certificate of vaccinations as age proof; intoxication; travelling safely in pits; tram riding; smoking; illness. Abstract, Coal Mines Act 1887: reference to safety.	Document	Archives	

Reference Code	Collection	Dates	Description	Media	Location	DP
MNB/I/12/1–3	Pontygwaith Division, St John Ambulance Brigade (minute books, correspondence and bills/receipts)	1939–60	1939–49: minute book including administration details, references to Medical Home Comfort Fund and Scheme. 1944: letter relating to examination arrangements. Bills and receipts for first aid classes.	Document	Archives	
MNB/NUM/1/A/7	Swansea District Area Safety Committee (committee minutes)	1945–63	1945: Minutes of Safety Committee NUM SW. Reference to Pneumoconiosis Committee on Dust Suppression. 1946, 1949 and 1956 minutes. Describes complaints against named collieries, details of problems, visits and reports by committee inspectors.	Document	Archives	Y
MNB/NUM/1/D/123	Cefn Coed (correspondence with colliery managements)	1944–53	Safety.	Document	Archives	
MNB/NUM/1/D/16	General correspondence and papers re union elections and ballots (District Officer's correspondence and papers)	1941–68	Safety.	Document	Archives	
MNB/NUM/1/D/200	Ffaldau (correspondence with colliery managements)	1940–70	Clothing and sick pay.	Document	Archives	Y
MNB/NUM/1/D/412	Brynteg (correspondence with Lodge Secretaries)	1942–54	Disablement benefit and pithead baths.	Document	Archives	Y
MNB/NUM/1/D/45	Abercrave Colliery (correspondence with colliery managements)	1948–57	Reference to medical services and safety.	Document	Archives	
MNB/NUM/1/D/455	Graignedd (correspondence with Lodge Secretaries)	1949	Ambulance box.	Document	Archives	
MNB/NUM/L/1/1	Abercyn Lodge (minute book)	1939–41	Safety lamps and payment.	Document	Archives	

105

Reference Code	Collection	Dates	Description	Media	Location	DP
MNB/NUM/L/12/1	Hendreladis / Yniscedwyn Lodge (Lodge Committee expenditure book)	1946–52	Expenses: Mine Inspections.	Document	Archives	
MNB/NUM/L/15/A3	Mountain Lodge (SWMF and Conciliation Board circulars and awards)	1942–4	Pamphlet – 'Joint Recommendations for Continuity of Work During Air Raids', reference to first aid stations, treatment and training, and places of shelter.	Document	Archives	
MNB/NUM/L/2/1–4	Ammanford No. 2 Lodge (minute Books)	1924–34	Pithead baths.	Document	Archives	
MNB/NUM/L/2/6	Ammanford No. 2 Lodge (minute book – committee meeting)	1927	3d. levy to St John Ambulance.	Document	Archives	
MNB/NUM/L/3/1	Blaenserchan Lodge (account book)	1918–63	Expenditure: accompanying Mines Inspector, donations for nursing staff and Porthcawl Rest, deputation visiting scene of accident and inspecting scenes of accidents, safety class, Safety Board Exam.	Document	Archives	
MNB/NUM/L/5/7	Cambrian Lodge (circular)	1937	Circular (Board of Conciliation for the Coal Trade of Monmouthshire and South Wales): 'Safety Classes for Boys Employed in Mines' – importance of attendance at these classes.	Document	Archives	
MNB/NUM/L/7/1	Daren Lodge (general account book)	1943–60	Expenditure: Mine Inspections, National Safety Board Inspector.	Document	Archives	
MNB/NUM/L/9/1	Ffaldau Lodge (minute book)	1939–41	Copy of Mine Inspection, ventilation and firedamp.	Document	Archives	
MNB/NUM/L/9/1	Ffaldau Lodge (minute book)	1939–41	Ambulance men.	Document	Archives	
MNB/POL/6/A8	Newport Constituency Labour Party (Executive and General Committee minutes, and Health Committee report)	1938–44	Council conference including safety in mines. Sanitary and health requirements. Disablement allowances conference. First aid posts and ambulances.	Document	Archives	Y

Reference Code	Collection	Dates	Description	Media	Location	DP
MNB/PP/11/A17	W. A. Davies (Ystalfera) (colliery management papers)	Ud	Cwmgorse Colliery: diagram of safety device ('Gripper') for steel arches.	Document	Archives	
MNB/PP/11/B1	W. A. Davies (Ystalfera) (National Association of Colliery Managers conference papers)	1936	NACM Conference address by J. E. Lambert (ICI Ltd.) – 'The Safe Use of Explosives'. Refers to accidents and roof falls.	Document	Archives	
MNB/PP/12/C/2/1–15	William Henry Davies (Penclawdd) (Annual reports: MOH, Gower Rural Sanitary Authority)	1895-7, 1899, 1900, 1902–11	1907: Local Government Board requiring inspection of all workshops and factories under Workshop and Factories Act, comments re being agricultural area with some collieries.	Document	Archives	
MNB/PP/22/1	Harold Finch (minute book, Miners' Group)	1942–6	Safety Stemming Plug Co. Law Reform (Contributory Negligence) Bill 1945.	Document	Archives	
MNB/PP/59/14	Phillip Weekes (correspondence to Colliery Managers at Tredegar Iron and Coal Co. Ltd.)	1946	Safety of cage rope. Mines Inspector visit. General safety and tidiness. Ventilation and dust suppression. Fatality.	Document	Archives	
MNB/PP/70/1	Ken Williams (Onllwyn)	1936	Rules for Onllwyn No. 3 workmen's Ambulance Fund. 14 rules, including ambulance car and its use.	Document	Archives	
MNB/PP/72/12	Alistair Wilson (pamphlet (a))	1899	The Miners' Dictionary, 1899, Ammanford, T. E. Davies, including advertisements for safety lamps and safety equipment.	Document	Archives	
MNC/ISTC/3/1	National Union of Blastfurnacemen, Ore Miners, Coke Workers and Kindred Trades. (Delegate Board minutes)	1922–31	Every factory to have certain first aid boxes or cupboards unless in an ambulance room with arrangements for immediate treatment.	Document	Archives	
MNC/NUM/5/182	NUM South Wales Area (SWMF Eastern Valleys District monthly meeting minutes (D2/F53))	1915	Pithead baths. Electric lamps. Ambulance convoys, wounded soldiers scheme.	Document	Archives	

Reference Code	Collection	Dates	Description	Media	Location	DP
MNC/NUM/5/228	Cambrian Lodge (correspondence and papers)	1938-41	SWMF Conference agendas 1940 and 1941 including ambulance men, dust menace, pithead baths attendants, safety.	Document	Archives	
MNC/NUM/L/26/5 and 6	Pantyffyn Lodge	1938-47	Correspondence and papers, including references to health and safety of mineworkers and working conditions.	Document	Archives	Y
MNC/NUM/L/32/7	Tondu Artisans' Lodge	1938-63	Hospital and ambulance fund donations account book.	Document	Archives	Y
MNC/PP/11/1	G. James	c.1920s	1914: Treharris Baths Pithead Scheme details, Ocean Coal Co. pithead baths, women not in favour and men not using.	Document	Archives	
MNC/PP/11/1	G. James (newspaper cuttings)	c.1910–1920s	Reference to pithead baths and damp, grimy clothes, and travel to/from work in bad weather. Treherbert Colliers veto pit baths, 1930s. Reference to pamphlet 'Baths for Miners: a woman's plea…' re clause in Coal Mines Bill making baths compulsory, less dirt, immorality, disease, work.	Document	Archives	
MNC/PP/11/1	G. James (newspaper cuttings)	c.1910–1920s	Coroner's letter relating to children scalded or killed falling into baths prepared for miners. Mr M. Roberts-Jones (Coroner, South Monmouthshire), inquests into scalded children, and baths for miners. 1926: owners' support for pithead baths. Home drudgery, south Wales campaign case for pithead baths. Women's Labour League prominent in campaign. Campaign of Miners' Wives, Cardiff Conference re pithead baths. *South Wales Daily News* support for campaign. 1912: miners' living conditions, pithead baths, damp clothes drying in houses, overwork and drudgery of women. Good health helps to prevent accidents at work, e.g. firedamp explosions detection. Article: 'Pithead Baths, A Woman's Point of View', 1924 Act made compulsory, South Wales progress. Domestic burden on women. Men drank more at pub if bathed at home; no room due to drying clothes.	Document	Archives	

Reference Code	Collection	Dates	Description	Media	Location	DP
MNC/PP/15/10	Dr Gwent Jones (newspaper cuttings)	c.1938–c.1948	Could ride in public transport if cleaner. 'Baths at the Pits – What the Wives can do' (by Vernon Hartshorn), Cardiff conference, pithead baths and housing with bathrooms. 1914: Women's Advocacy, Pithead Baths Campaign launch. Cardiff conference of women and SWMF. Address by Dr R. Owen Morris on hygienic reforms. Copy of 'Welsh Cutter' published by Ministry of Fuel and Power, 05 August 1946, including: 'Scourge of the Welsh has been Vanquished. Deadly Dust Cloud is Lifting from Pits', re dust suppression and water infusion; training centres for safety in mines; miners' health.	Document	Archives	
MNC/PP/15/5	Dr Gwent Jones (MFGB Executive Committee minutes)	1944	MFGB Minutes of Executive Committee Meeting 07 January 1944. Refers to Mines Medical Service, details including first aid and ambulance work.	Document	Archives	
MNC/PP/26/10	Lance Rogers	1939	House of Lords Judgement 1939. Caswell v Powell Duffryn Associated Collieries Ltd. Caswell killed underground. Mother suing under Fatal Accidents Act to recover damages on ground that death caused by breach of statutory duty. Safety of machine.	Document	Archives	Y
MNC/PP/35/1	Anon (Envelope II)	c.1930s	MFGB Report on Explosion at Garswood Colliery nr Wigan 12 November 1932, reference to ventilation, gas, rescue. 1934: Mines Department letter; firedamp detectors, safety lamps.	Document	Archives	Y
MNC/PP/35/1	Anon (Envelope XIV, XV)	c.1940s	Pamphlet, clothes rationing 1945-6: 'The Fourth Iron Ration for workers in certain very heavy industries' (1946). Instructions and Guide for Works Clothing Committees.	Document	Archives	

Reference Code	Collection	Dates	Description	Media	Location	DP
MNC/PP/35/1	Anon	c.1930s–1938	1938: Inquiry into Conditions of Employment at Powell Duffryn Collieries and the Conditions of the Federation Organisation in relation thereto. Refers to safety (brief). Report; Investigation in D. A. Hann Group, working conditions, Compensation, safety.	Document	Archives	Y
MNC/PP/35/1	Anon	1938	Report of Investigation into Conditions of Employment at Powell Duffryn Collieries within the Frank Hann Group and into the administration of the SWMF lodges within the same group. References to safety, ventilation, water, accidents, examination of mines.	Document	Archives	Y
PHO/COL/100–103	Colliery photographs	c.1920 and ud	6 formal photographs of members of rescue team wearing their breathing apparatus and displaying their working tools.	Photographs	Archives	
PHO/COL/104	Colliery photographs	1914	Photograph of members of Hills Plymouth Collieries Rescue Brigade. Members wearing their breathing apparatus, and equipment displayed. Abercynon Collieries Rescue Association vehicle in background.	Photographs	Archives	
PHO/COL/105	Colliery photographs	c.1913	Formal photograph of members of colliery rescue team wearing breathing apparatus and masks. Rhymney Valley Rescue Station vehicle in background.	Photographs	Archives	
PHO/COL/106	Colliery photographs	ud	Photograph of members of Swansea District Collieries Rescue Association wearing breathing apparatus. Rescue Association vehicle in background.	Photographs	Archives	
PHO/COL/113	Colliery photographs	1906	Photograph of a pit pony hauling a tram of coal with a shaft and gun linkage. One miner holds candle and another holds an oil lamp and is smoking. He is at a lamp station, an area known to be gas free where safety lamps are relit.	Photographs	Archives	

Reference Code	Collection	Dates	Description	Media	Location	DP
PHO/COL/16	Colliery photographs	c.1920	Two formal photographs of members of Brynmenin Collieries Rescue Association. Members in front of rescue vehicle and wearing safety uniforms.	Photographs	Archives	
PHO/COL/25	Colliery photographs	1916	Formal photograph of miners at Cawdor Colliery. Group of miners and colliers' boys sitting on the ground holding their safety lamps.	Photographs	Archives	
PHO/COL/28	Colliery photographs	1932	Formal photograph of Clydach Merthyr Colliery Ambulance Division, group outside colliery.	Photographs	Archives	
PHO/COL/47	Colliery photographs	c.1900	Formal photograph of miners, workmen and officials of Garngoch 3 Colliery. Workers (most holding safety lamps) outside colliery.	Photographs	Archives	
PHO/COL/49	Colliery photographs	1916	Formal photograph of people who attended Glamorgan Colliery ambulance and home nursing classes.	Photographs	Archives	
PHO/COL/66	Colliery photographs	c.1900	Formal photograph of members of Mynydd Newydd Colliery rescue team, wearing their breathing apparatus.	Photographs	Archives	
PHO/COL/68	Colliery photographs	1910	Photograph of assistant instructor, superintendent and members of Nantwen 2 Bedlinog Rescue Brigade. Members wearing their breathing apparatus. Equipment displayed, and Abercynon Collieries Rescue Association vehicle in background.	Photographs	Archives	
PHO/COL/97	Colliery photographs	1931	Formal photograph of members of Wyndham Colliery rescue team wearing their breathing apparatus.	Photographs	Archives	
PHO/PC/7/6	Personal collections (David Rhys Grenfell MP)	ud	Photograph of a colliery rescue team with all their kit.	Photographs	Archives	
RC773 CHU	Articles from *Colliery Engineering*, by C. S. Chubb (Articles)	1941–2	All entitled 'Dust and Disease'. Subtitles include: Dust measurement; Dust prevention; Air cleaning (respirators, water, filters, ventilation).	Document	SWML	

Reference Code	Collection	Dates	Description	Media	Location	DP
TN295 COL	*The Coal Miner: His Health, Diseases and General Welfare* (pamphlet)	c.1924	Exposure to mine dust and stone dusting, accidents (first Aid, rescue). Social environment; miners' welfare.	Document	SWML	
TN295 COL	*The Coal Miner: His Health, Diseases and General Welfare* (pamphlet)	c.1924	Reprint from *Journal of Industrial Hygiene*, by E. L. Collis (Welsh National School of Medicine). Physiological needs; food, drink, salt. Physiologic reactions in coal mines; rhythm and method in work, pithead baths, alcoholism. Health-related adverts (4).	Document	SWML	
TN295 GRE	*Protective Equipment for Mineworkers* (pamphlet)	1937	Issued by the Safety in Mines Research Board. 20 pages. Includes photographs. Reference to hard hats, gloves, safety boots, goggles and other equipment.	Document	SWML	
TN63 HOM	Reports of Inspectors of Mines for Cardiff and Swansea Districts (Mines and Quarries)	1906–12	Details of accidents, fatalities, prosecutions. Safety lamps. Ambulance services and first aid (1908 photo of ambulance litters). Rescue stations. Nursing injured (1908). Coal dust. Ventilation and water spraying. Safety issues and Inspections.	Document	SWML	
	Scrapbooks of newspaper cuttings (unlabelled scrapbook (green))	1946–8	Colliery medical treatment centres. Safety aids. Employment of disabled miners. Mine rescue stations. Safety lamps. Rehabilitation of injured miners. Pithead baths. First aid.	Document	SWML	

~ 4 ~
Accidents

Although the numerous mining disasters that took place in the South Wales Coalfield were well publicized, accidents – minor and serious – also happened regularly on a smaller scale, to individuals or small groups of men. The causes of accidents underground were various and included explosions, roof falls, faulty machinery (for example, trams, cages and drills), electric shock, drowning, and being injured by pit ponies. The Workmen's Compensation Act of 1897 covered only occupational accidents, whilst the following Act of 1906 included industrial diseases (see Chapter 1, 'Mining Diseases'). In 1909 a Royal Commission, drawing on a committee of mining engineers, reported on the 'causes of and means of preventing accidents from falls of ground, underground haulage, and in shafts'. Moreover, a further seven official reports were published between 1912 and 1915, inquiring 'into the causes and means of prevention of coal dust explosions in mines'. Irrespective of their explanation, all accidents had to be logged at the surface and the Miners' Federation membership cards often carried reminders printed on the back page, stressing the importance of registering accidents (SWCC: MNA/NUM/L/3/24; MNA/PP/40/2–3). These records, kept by colliery managers, were then used to decide if compensation claims were eligible.

The Factory and Workshop Acts of 1901 and 1937 provided some protection for employees outside mining, regulating health and safety for specified industries and types of workplace as well as providing factory inspectors to enforce the legislation. Nevertheless, these industries were accident-ridden. Dock workers, for example, were subject to life-threatening situations not only on the dockside but also on board ships and in their holds. During the 1890s, the Coaltrimmers' Union highlighted safety issues around escape holes in the decks of vessels. In 1895, spontaneous combustion occurred on a ship in Cardiff whilst it was taking in a cargo of coal. Five men were seriously burned. The same year saw the Marine Department at the Board of Trade inquiring into the ventilation of coal-carrying ships when loading, after an explosion on a steamer at Swansea docks killed two men and injured two others (SWCC: MNA/TUG/1/A2). Subsequently, a clause was inserted into the Factories and Workshops Bill to address the ventilation of holds and bunkers on ships. But as Ben Tillett – the leading trade unionist and socialist – noted in 1907, most of the dangers relating to dock work were not covered by existing laws, notably docks, wharves, quays and structural defects in ships (SWCC: MNA/PP/118/12).

Iron and steel workers – employed in hot and ill-ventilated surroundings, and handling extremely hot metal – also suffered serious, and sometimes fatal, accidents that were often due to burns or scalds. Tin workers faced similar hazards. And women in the Royal Ordnance Factories during the Second World War similarly confronted danger when working with live ammunition, especially if the weather was damp (SWCC: AUD/342). However, employees in lighter occupations were also imperilled, Co-operative Society staff falling victim to accidents and even deaths at work (SWCC: MNC/COP/1/1).

In 1948, the Workmen's Compensation Acts were replaced by an Industrial Injuries Act, which not only made it easier for workers to obtain financial compensation for occupational injuries and diseases but also increased the level of benefit that they received.

Reference Code	Collection	Dates	Description	Media	Location	DP
	Gomer Evans (Pamphlet Box 6)	1924–39	Pamphlet: *Pageant of South Wales, May Day 1939*, SWMF; including play script with representations of mining accident and disease.	Document	SWML	
	Gomer Evans (Pamphlet Box 7)	1926–56	*The Coal Crisis: Facts from the Samuel Commission, 1925–26*, Labour Research Dept 1926; section on accidents in mines, including compensation cases, and causes of accidents below ground.	Document	SWML	
AUD/56	Haydn Mainwaring	1910–80	Work as Compensation Secretary for 33 years. Fatal accidents – Committees of Inquiry, payments for widows. Experiences of tribunals. Workmen's Compensation; cases and earnings formulae. Indemnity Society agents and pressurizing men and wives to settle compensation cases. Pit accidents attended, organizing help, loss of pay, negligence, safety improvements.	Audio tape	SWML	Y
AUD/81	Bryn Thomas	1900–c.1950	Details of death of man crushed between trucks in mine.	Transcript of audio	SWML	Y
AUD/164	John Evans (Maerdy Community Study)	1930–c.1960	Reference to minor accidents underground.	Transcript of audio	SWML	Y
AUD/165	Trevor Davies	1916–c.1960	Mining accident, fractured collar bone and face injury. 1931 accident, struck by stone and blinded for 2 years, no compensation. 1947: accident, split vertebra from roof fall, compensation from old scheme. Injured spine again later and compensation from new scheme.	Transcript of audio	SWML	Y
AUD/174	George Baker	1930–c.1974	Reference to pit accident.	Transcript of audio	SWML	Y

Reference Code	Collection	Dates	Description	Media	Location	DP
AUD/182	Arthur Morgan	1912– c.1960	Father's mining accident – lost leg (home amputation), made own artificial leg (also made them for others), no compensation except voluntary colliery sick fund. Details of drownings in sump at Maerdy Pit.	Transcript of audio	SWML	Y
AUD/185	Mr Reg Fine (Maerdy Community Study)	1920–c.1950	Reference to fatal pit accident of father, and compensation.	Transcript of audio	SWML	Y
AUD/188	W. C. Davies	1920s–1930s	1929: gas explosion – Milfrain pit, details re first aid. 1930s: flood Levenstone Drift, drownings and rescue attempt.	Transcript of audio	SWML	Y
AUD/212	Edgar Evans	c.1910–73	Father's fatal accident in mines.	Transcript of audio	SWML	Y
AUD/215	Walter Powell	c.1900–74	Own head injury. Death of boy in pit, crushed by tram. Deaths on public trains of men commuting to work. Accidents; cuts, stitches in head, ankle injury. Grandfather killed in pit, broken leg.	Transcript of audio	SWML	Y
AUD/217	Mr O. Edwards	1903–c.1973	Six Bells disaster, and compensation. Ambulance man at colliery. Incident of unconscious collier (gassed). Pneumoconiosis. Compensation. Pit explosion and disasters.	Transcript of audio	SWML	Y
AUD/222	Dick Cook	c.1910–74	Work injuries; foot (hammer toe), cuts, blindness, concussion. Hospital treatments; Neath and Cardiff. Tin workers health and safety; heat protection, dehydration, burns, injuries, death. Workmen's Compensation and NI. Lodge Compensation Secretary.	Transcript of audio	SWML	Y
AUD/239	Albert Davies (Blaenavon)	1910–c.1973	Milfren explosion. Gas in mines. Comparison of mine safety in south Wales and Newcastle areas. Gas explosion at Six Bells, possible causes and details of scene underground.	Transcript of audio	SWML	Y

116

Reference Code	Collection	Dates	Description	Media	Location	DP
AUD/254	George Hughes	1883– c.1930	Wife's first husband's death in pit (decapitated). Details of George Hughes' accident and rescue in pit, leg smashed by girder. Near miss re falling stone. Reference to other accidents; near drowning, deaths from crushing.	Transcript of audio	SWML	Y
AUD/300	Percy James Matthews	1898–c.1973	Work-related injuries including septic knees and back injury (visit for X-ray and compensation claim). Pit safety, accidents, working conditions, explosion.	Transcript of audio	SWML	Y
AUD/301	Jim Minton	1882– c.1973	Father's head injury. Reference to mining accidents and fatalities. Finger injury working on tramlines, went septic and doctor was to amputate, details of self-cure with herbal remedy.	Transcript of audio	SWML	Y
AUD/302	Harry Howells	1910–c.1973	Father's accident in pit as boy (broken back), no village doctor, another had to visit. Own pit work, conditions, e.g. dust, ventilation, lighting. Appointment as Compensation Secretary for lodge.	Transcript of audio	SWML	Y
AUD/303	Mr B. Edwards (Tonypandy)	1898–c.1973	Own accident and compensation. Horse injured Mr Edwards's ankle, taken to Cardiff Royal Infirmary, examined by specialist, compensation and sick fund money. Serious accidents, officials would compel men to work. Riots – injuries and death. Treatment of men at surgery. Pit explosion 1905, 35 deaths, gas/fire, 77 horses killed, recovering bodies.	Transcript of audio	SWML	Y
AUD/310, 311	Abel Morgan	1878– c.1973	Details of some accidents, e.g. crush injury (graphic), groin injury.	Transcript of audio	SWML	Y
AUD/323	W. H. Taylor (Blaenavon)	1903–1930s	Explosive fumes and carbon monoxide caused headaches. Details of 3 near-miss accidents. Pit fireman and first-aider. Examinations and testing for gas. Lamps underground; open light causing death by	Transcript of audio	SWML	Y

117

Reference Code	Collection	Dates	Description	Media	Location	DP
AUD/342	Mrs Nancy Davies (Seven Sisters)	1910– c.1974	burns, Oldham electric lamps contained sulphuric acid which blinded a miner. Milfraen Pit accident and explosion. Big Pit fire. Crush accidents. Stretcher bearers.	Transcript of audio	SWML	Y
AUD/374	Dr Thomas	1900–1960s	Mother-in-law's work at ROF Bridgend – accidents especially on night shifts, and wet weather which caused explosions.	Audio tape	SWML	Y
AUD/382	D. C. Davies	1930– c.1976	Back injuries and strains, slipped discs, osteo-arthritis, sciatica re miners, due to working in small spaces. Pit accidents, description of tending to a trapped miner, and camaraderie of other miners. Accidents and disease amongst pit workers and effects on them and families. Work as Lodge Compensation Secretary.	Transcript of audio	SWML	Y
AUD/391	Mrs Gwen Netherway	1914–50	Father injured – accident underground; fracture and dislocation of spine, leading to paralysis.	Audio tape	SWML	Y
AUD/481	Mrs Bessie Webb and Mrs Hannah Katie Evans	1920–75	Father's mining accident and compensation. Work at tin works; accident.	Audio tape	SWML	Y
AUD/658	H. Davies	1897– c.1977	Accidents and compensation, court cases – mine owners' legal counsel. Colliery company agents pressurized workmen and widows to take lump sums rather than compensation, paid less than worth. Many eye problems in district. Medical referees. Own fractured spine.	Transcript of audio	SWML	Y
BAN/24	Wernos Lodge Banner	c.1945	Slogan: 'An Injury To One Is The Concern Of All'. Slogan from the Amerian 'Wobblie', early C20th Marxist and syndicalist labour movement.	Banner	SWML	
HD6661.TRA	TUC Annual Reports of Proceedings (incomplete)	1904–85	1924: Mines – gas poisoning, safety, mining disaster (Ponthenry Colliery, near Llanelly). Workmen's Compensation.	Document	SWML	
HD9550 EBB	The Ebbw Vale Works Magazine (Vol. 7, No. 26)	Mar 1928	Health hints to miners by Industrial Health Education Council first aid, wounds, contaminated water, accidents.	Document	SWML	

Reference Code	Collection	Dates	Description	Media	Location	DP
HD9550 EBB	*The Ebbw Vale Works Magazine* (Vol. 7, No. 28)	Sept 1928	Article: 'Mining Accidents – Their Cause and Prevention'. Article: awards of Edward Medal to two men at Victoria Blast Furnaces for rescue of men overcome by poison gas.	Document	SWML	
HD9552.3 MIN	*The Miner* (Vol. I, No. 7/8)	Apr/May 1945	Notes re lump sum settlements and accidents.	Document	SWML	
HD9552.3 MIN	*The Miner* (Vol. IV, No. 1/2)	Nov/Dec 1947	Report of compensation case relating to accident which caused cancer. Report of damages at Common Law relating to fatal injuries incurred at pit, and part-severed arm.	Document	SWML	
HV686.R3	Reports of the MOH, and School MO, Rhondda UDC (reports of the Medical Officer of Health)	1914–47	Colliery fatalities. Inquests. Police court proceedings. Administration. Factory and Workshop Act. 1930: District Coroners' death statistics (including colliery accidents, suicide, heart disease, burns or scalds, run over or knocked down by motor vehicles).	Document	SWML	
MNA/COL/2/1	Clydach Merthyr Colliery	1942–7	Rough minutes of arbitration meetings held to resolve disputes: including compensation cases and fatal accidents.	Document	Archives	Y
MNA/COL/2/4–38	Clydach Merthyr Colliery (Manager's carbon-copy correspondence books)	1937–48	Amputees and artificial limbs. Orthopaedic treatment. Burns. Dental treatment and dentures. Inquests. Reference to medical examinations of workers. Accidents, injuries.	Document	Archives	Y
MNA/COL/2/54	Clydach Merthyr Colliery (Manager's correspondence)	1938–9	Accidents. Burns.	Document	Archives	Y
MNA/COL/2/55	Clydach Merthyr Colliery (Manager's correspondence)	1940–1	Accidents. Workmen's Compensation. Amputee and artificial limb.	Document	Archives	Y
MNA/COL/2/61–62	Clydach Merthyr Colliery	1934–61	Notices of accidents and monthly returns; Clydach Merthyr and Abergelli Collieries: Accident report forms including details of person, accident, injuries, doctor's name.	Document	Archives	Y

Reference Code	Collection	Dates	Description	Media	Location	DP
MNA/COP/1/19	Aberdare and District Co-op Society Ltd (resolution book)	1897–9	Reference to doctor's certificate for staff member. Staff illness, accidents and wages.	Document	Archives	
MNA/COP/5/1/1–14	Pembroke Dock Co-op Society (general and committee meeting minutes)	1888–1951	Staff sickness and injuries.	Document	Archives	
MNA/COP/5/2/1–4	Pembroke Dock Co-op Society – Kilgetty Branch (committee minutes)	1919–51	Staff injury, accidents, sick leave.	Document	Archives	
MNA/COP/7/1–13	Ton Co-op Society (general and committee minutes)	1884–1927	Employees: Accidents.	Document	Archives	
MNA/COP/7/14–15	Ton Co-op Society (board meetings minutes)	1928–48	Accidents (staff and other) and compensation.	Document	Archives	
MNA/J/4/C5	Bargoed and District Workmen's Library and Institute	1922–4	Book of counterfoils – Workmen's Compensation Act 1906, Powell Duffryn Steam Coal Co. Ltd. Claims for compensation and notices of injury. Including name, address, occupation, cause of injury, date of accident, amount claimed. Injuries including nystagmus, fall, fracture, beat elbow.	Document	Archives	Y
MNA/NUM/1/1	Records of the Miners' Federation of Great Britain (minute books of Executive Committee, and annual and special conferences)	1905–10	1905: Workmen's Compensation Act and safety. Accidents and inquiries. Ventilation. Compensation Amendment Bill. 1906–10: Workmen's Compensation Bill – Contracting Out Clause. Explosion in South Wales. 1925–6: Water dangers in mines (floods). Miners' Welfare Fund and Committee. Royal Commission on Mining Subsidence. Accident and disaster. Miners' beat knee and beat elbow. Compensation cases including silicosis. 1935–6: Rehabilitation of persons injured by accidents, Home Office inquiry.	Document	Archives and SWML	

Reference Code	Collection	Dates	Description	Media	Location	DP
MNA/NUM/1/1–2	Records of the Miners' Federation of Great Britain/NUM (minute books of MFGB/NUM Executive Committee, and annual and special conferences)	1902–48	General themes: Explosions, disasters and Inquiries. Compensation cases, legal appeals. Workmen's Compensation Act and Amendments. Disasters: Royal Commission 1906; other countries. Accidents. Insurance and compensation laws. Inspectors. Safety in mines. Improved Mines Act 1908.	Document	Archives and SWML	
MNA/NUM/1/2	Records of the Miners' Federation of Great Britain/NUM (minute books of NUM National Executive Committee, and annual and special conferences)	1947	Fatal Accident Scheme. Miners' Accident Benevolent Fund. Re-employment of injured miners.	Document	Archives and SWML	
MNA/NUM/1/9	Records of the MFGB/NUM (MFGB annual balance sheet)	1941	Distress and Disaster Funds: colliery disasters.	Document	Archives	
MNA/NUM/2/6	Yorkshire Area NUM	1948	*Industrial Injuries Quiz* (National Insurance Industrial Injuries Act, 1946); Pamphlet (56 pages). Questions and answers re the 1946 Act. Points of action re accidents.	Document	Archives	
MNA/NUM/3/1/1	Minutes of the SWMF Executive Council, and annual and special conferences	1907–40	References to accidents, fatalities, explosions and gas.	Document	Archives and SWML	
MNA/NUM/3/2/30	Account book: compensation expenses (financial records)	1943–7	Account book: compensation expenses	Document	Archives	Y
MNA/NUM/3/3/1	Correspondence (bound volume of circulars)	1899–1915	Royal Commission on Accidents 1908. Memo of Agreement relating to accidents. 1913 Senghenydd Colliery Disaster. Compensation: forms, questionnaires, conferences, contract-out schemes, Friendly Societies, 1906 explanatory booklets (English and Welsh).	Document	Archives	

Reference Code	Collection	Dates	Description	Media	Location	DP
MNA/NUM/3/3/2	Correspondence (bound volume of circulars)	1916–27	Accident cases. Workmen's Compensation Acts references. Statistics of UK accidents and deaths in coal mines. System of compensation for injuries. 1920: conference reference to Amendments to Coal Mines Act including coroners at inquests. Compensation: conferences, widows and dependents. Coal dust explosions and using closed trams.	Document	Archives	
MNA/NUM/3/3/3	Correspondence (bound volume of circulars)	1927–35	Compensation: SWMF manifesto, 1927 TUC and Labour Party booklet on Consolidating Bill. SWMF statistics including accidents.	Document	Archives	
MNA/NUM/3/3/14	Correspondence with SWMF No. 1 Area (Files 1–5)	1931–42	File 1: Two medical cases detailed. Workmen's Compensation, notice forms and medical certificates. Case re amputated finger. File 2: Expenses to attend treatment and X-ray. Compensation case details including court dates, disputed cases. Lists of compensation cases including injuries. Medical boards. Compensation calculations. Partial compensation payment calculations. Letter to doctor regarding certificates. File 3: Compensation cases, lists, letters, including injuries, accidents (including fatal). Lodge compensation secretaries. Members funds for artificial limbs and surgical appliances, request for money by injured man. Medical certificates. File 4: 1935: Compensation cases, doctors' reports, letters. Dr. Harper – reference to BMJ article and examination of 60–70 cases (surface workers). File 5: Memo relating to disabled workmen on light employment (wages and conditions).	Document	Archives	Y
MNA/NUM/3/3/14	Correspondence with SWMF No. 1 Area (Files 11–17)	1931–42	File 11: Compensation cases. Accidents. Correspondence with Indemnity Society (on behalf of Amalgamated Anthracite Collieries Ltd). File 12: 1937: Compensation cases. Doctors' reports (e.g. leg fracture), File 13: 1939 cutting from *The Lancet* 'Irradiation and Miners', p.1281, 16 December 1939. File 14: Compensation cases.	Document	Archives	Y

122

Reference Code	Collection	Dates	Description	Media	Location	DP
MNA/NUM/3/3/23	Correspondence with lodges (correspondence (Files 2-8))	1934–42	File 15: 1940: Compensation. New Act and supplementary allowances. File 16: 1941: Compensation cases. File 17: 1942: Compensation cases. Compensation case, conference. Fatal accident.	Document	Archives	Y
MNA/NUM/3/3/33/4	Gwaun-Cae-Gurwen Lodge (correspondence)	1934–42	Notification of accident, Federation Compensation Scheme correspondence and details.	Document	Archives	Y
MNA/NUM/3/3/48 and 49	Solicitor's correspondence (correspondence)	1922–50	48: Correspondence (and legal papers, bills of costs etc.) with Morgan, Bruce and Nicholas, SWMF solicitors, Pontypridd (1926–39), 49: Ditto for cases in Areas 1–6 (1922–50).	Document	Archives	Y
MNA/NUM/3/3/50 and 51	Solicitor's correspondence (correspondence)	1904–1950	50: Correspondence (and legal papers, bills of costs etc.) with T. S. Edwards and Sons, Newport (1930–6). 51: Ditto for cases in Areas 7–8 (1904–50).	Document	Archives	Y
MNA/NUM/3/3/52	Solicitor's correspondence (correspondence)	1933–9	Correspondence (and legal papers, bills of costs etc) with Randall, Saunders and Randall, Llanelly and Swansea.	Document	Archives	Y
MNA/NUM/3/3/53	Solicitor's correspondence (correspondence)	1934–6	Correspondence (and legal papers, bills of costs etc.) with E. Roberts, Bargoed.	Document	Archives	Y
MNA/NUM/3/3/54	Solicitor's correspondence (correspondence)	1934–6	Correspondence (and legal papers, bills of costs etc.) with John Jenkins, Swansea.	Document	Archives	Y
MNA/NUM/3/3/55	Solicitor's correspondence (correspondence)	1934–7	Correspondence (and legal papers, bills of costs etc.) with T. J. M. B. Parker, Port Talbot.	Document	Archives	Y

Reference Code	Collection	Dates	Description	Media	Location	DP
MNA/NUM/3/4/43	Compensation claims arising out of the liquidation of the Ebbw Vale and Subsidiary Cos. (SWMF/NUM misc office papers and reports)	1936–40	1937: List of Workmen's Compensation claims, Ebbw Vale, name and address, age, date of accident, injury, amounts. Including nystagmus, fractures, amputations, loss of eye, crush injuries. Correspondence re compensation cases. (Ebbw Vale in liquidation)	Document	Archives	Y
MNA/NUM/3/4/45	SWMF/NUM Misc. office papers and reports (May Day Pageants 1938–9; Inter-colliery Sports 1939; wartime film scenarios)	1938–54	May Day Pageant Pontypool script 1939, reference to miners' deaths by roof fall, explosions and silicosis. Dulais Valley Pageant of History script references to accidents.	Document	Archives	
MNA/NUM/3/4/48	Mines Inspectorate (SWMF/NUM misc. office papers and reports)	1943–7	1947: letter from HM Divisional Inspector regarding South Wales Mines Inspectorate Division, fatal accidents, firedamp, explosion. 1944: letter; fatal accidents under Coal Mines Act, Swansea Division. 1943: letter; fatal accidents.	Document	Archives	
MNA/NUM/3/5/1	SWMF: Compensation Records (compensation book)	1937–40	Details of miners, collieries, injuries, court decisions, awards, comments, operations. Injuries; fatal, limbs and extremities, heart, stomach, lungs, eyes, Weil's disease, skin, head, skeletal, spine, gassed, strain, amputation, septicaemia.	Document	Archives	Y
MNA/NUM/3/5/3	SWMF: Compensation Records (register of fatal accidents)	1934–41	Details of miners, collieries, injuries, court decisions, awards, comments, operations. Causes of death including shock, septicaemia, suffocation, crush injuries, drowning, gassed, burns, electric shock.	Document	Archives	Y
MNA/NUM/3/5/4	SWMF: Compensation Records (register of ordinary accident Cases)	1934–7	Accident details; miners, collieries, injuries, court decisions, awards, comments, operations.	Document	Archives	Y

Reference Code	Collection	Dates	Description	Media	Location	DP
MNA/NUM/3/5/5	SWMF: Compensation Records (register of ordinary accident Cases)	1938–41	Accident details; miners, collieries, injuries, court decisions, awards, costs, disputes, comments. Injuries; severed femoral artery, pleurisy, Weil's Disease, acid burns, insect sting, rupture, abscess, broken dentures.	Document	Archives	Y
MNA/NUM/3/5/7	SWMF: Compensation Records (card index to compensation cases)	1948–9	Details on cards including personal details, doctor's name, colliery, other benefits received, employment details, compensation application details, X-rays, medical examinations, dates of disablement, disputed cases, claim amount, benefits claimed, details of death.	Document	Archives	Y
MNA/NUM/3/5/10	SWMF: Compensation Records (annual reports of silicosis cases)	1935–40	Numbers of death and disablement cases, applications to Medical Board, certificates granted or refused, compensation paid, costs. Numbers of fatal accidents and amounts of compensation paid.	Document	Archives	Y
MNA/NUM/3/5/11	SWMF: Compensation Records (annual reports of fatal accidents)	1936–9	Reports from each area; numbers of amounts paid, and details relating to compensation not paid. Details relating to causes of death and collieries.	Document	Archives	Y
MNA/NUM/3/5/14	SWMF: Compensation Records (Compensation Secretary's correspondence)	1936–41	1938: Correspondence relating to Royal Commission on Workmen's Compensation. Accidents. Public Health Department Cardiff booklet about the Cardiff Municipal Accident Service (talk to Cardiff Medical Society); including fracture clinic, rehabilitation of disabled workmen. 1939: Accidents. Royal Commission on Workmen's Compensation questionnaire. MFGB Pamphlet. Local classes on Workmen's Compensation Law. 1940: Workmen's Compensation (Supplementary Allowances) Act 1940. British Rhondda Colliery shock cases (explosion). Accidents. 1936–41: Accidents. Partially disabled and light employment. Cardiff Medical Society reference to discussion 'The return to work of the Injured Colliery Workman'.	Document	Archives	Y

Reference Code	Collection	Dates	Description	Media	Location	DP
MNA/NUM/3/5/15	SWMF: Compensation Records (Compensation Secretary's correspondence: Area No. 4)	1934–41	1939: Miners' Women's Federation – talk relating to Workmen's Compensation. Cambrian Lodge unused certificates for Workmen's Compensation, notice of injury caused by industrial disease, and claim for compensation. Accidents. Employer's liability for dentures and artificial limbs. House coal and compensation.	Document	Archives	
MNA/NUM/3/5/16	SWMF: Compensation Records (Compensation Secretary's correspondence: Area No. 5)	1934–41	Accidents. Conference of Compensation Secretaries, Abercynon 1940. Registration card, Workmen's Compensation – Deep Duffryn Colliery. SWMF Agents' Report Area 6 (1935) accidents, deaths, compensation claims.	Document	Archives	Y
MNA/NUM/3/5/17	SWMF: Compensation Records (Compensation Secretary's correspondence: Area No. 6)	1934–41	Detailed case notes for each colliery, including accidents (e.g. back injury, and loss of eye).	Document	Archives	Y
MNA/NUM/3/5/18	SWMF: Compensation Records (Compensation Secretary's correspondence: Area No. 8)	1934–41	References to accidents.	Document	Archives	Y
MNA/NUM/3/5/22	SWMF: Compensation Records (correspondence re Fatal Accidents Scheme)	1943–7	1943: minutes of SWMF Safety Committee. 1946: tables of deaths including from accidents, with pit and compensation details.	Document	Archives	Y
MNA/NUM/3/5/24	SWMF: Compensation Records (Correspondence and law papers re disputed compensation cases)	1925–34	Silicosis and accident claims. Transcript of County Court case. Court of Appeal Judgement notes. Solicitors' correspondence. Colliery visit report. Worker's statement.	Document	Archives	Y
MNA/NUM/3/5/28	SWMF: Compensation Records (monthly SWMF agents' reports Area No. 6)	1936–1941	Include many detailed references to compensation claims, accidents, safety.	Document	Archives	Y

Reference Code	Collection	Dates	Description	Media	Location	DP
MNA/NUM/3/6	SWMF: Compensation Records (register of ordinary accident cases)	1941-5	Accident details; miners, collieries, injuries, court decisions, awards, costs, disputes, comments.	Document	Archives	Y
MNA/NUM/3/6/33	Records of the SWMF/NUM (South Wales Area) [Joint Standing Disputes Committee minutes)	1918	Accidents – slight and sympathetic stoppages. Fatal accidents and wage loss. House coal to men in receipt of compensation. Attendance at medical examinations and subsequent loss of wages.	Document	Archives	
MNA/NUM/3/6/53	Records of the SWMF/NUM (South Wales Area) [Joint Standing Disputes Committee minutes)	1922-3	Reinstatement of collier recovering from an accident.	Document	Archives	
MNA/NUM/3/7/1 and 2	Minutes of Enquiry into disaster at Universal Colliery, Senghenydd, 14/10/1913, Vols. 1 and 2 (pit disaster records)	1914	Vol. 1- Minutes of court proceedings. Vol. 2- Reports on causes and circumstances by HM Chief Inspector of Mines and Chair of South Wales and Monmouthshire Coalowners' Association, and President of MFGB.	Document	Archives	
MNA/NUM/3/7/3	Pit Disaster Records	1914	(Proceedings of the Inquest into the Universal Colliery explosion, Senghenydd) Includes list of the dead and cause of death (by doctor who examined them), including suffocation, burns, shock, injuries, wounds.	Document	Archives	
MNA/NUM/3/7/4, 7, 11 and 12	Pit Disaster Records	1913-27	(4) and (7) Bank book, and correspondence relating to Senghenydd Explosion Relief Trust Fund 1930 (opened 1914, closed 1919). (11) 1927 Marine Colliery Explosion Inquest, Coroner's summing up. (12) 'In Memoriam' card, 52 miners killed at Marine Colliery (Ebbw Vale) 1 March 1927.	Document	Archives	

Reference Code	Collection	Dates	Description	Media	Location	DP
MNA/NUM/3/7/6	Pit Disaster Records	1914–38	Senghenydd Relief Fund Minute Book, reference to accidents and relief for dependants, case details and decisions, grants for children in ill health.	Document	Archives	Y
MNA/NUM/3/7/8	Pit disaster records (press cuttings re Senghenydd explosion)	1913	Pit disaster, fires, explosions, rescue attempts. St John Ambulance, injured taken to King Edward VII Hospital Cardiff. Cuttings from *Western Mail, South Wales Daily News*, and *The Mining Journal*.	Document	Archives	
MNA/NUM/3/7/9	Pit disaster records (proceedings of Coroner's Inquiry into Trimsaran Colliery Disaster)	1923	Inquiry proceedings. 10 deaths. Accident caused by shackle breaking between carriages.	Document	Archives	
MNA/NUM/3/7/10	Pit Disaster Records (statement of claim for damages: Margaret Davies against the Trimsaran Co. Ltd)	1923	High Court of Justice Statement of Claim 1923, by widow and children – husband killed at Caeduan Slant at Trimsaran, Carmarthenshire. Particulars of defendants' breaches of statutory duty and negligence.	Document	Archives	Y
MNA/NUM/3/7/13 and 14	Pit Disaster Records	1927–9	(13) 1927: 'In Loving Memory' card for 3,589 miners killed in colliery disasters in north and south Wales and Monmouth between 1837–1927. (14) 'In Loving Memory' card 8 men killed by explosion of gas at Milfraen Colliery Blaenavon 10 July 29.	Document	Archives	
MNA/NUM/3/8/12	Swansea District/Area (district, area and combine records)	1946–72	Compensation papers, report on Gellyceidrim Colliery, 1946, and related correspondence 1946–59. Compensation Agents' reports 1954–72 with claim statistics 1946–59.	Document	Archives	Y
MNA/NUM/3/8/17	Area No. 2 Council Minutes (register of ordinary accident cases)	1934–52	Compensation centralization scheme. Accidents. Compensation.	Document	Archives	Y
MNA/NUM/3/8/17	Area No. 2 Papers re wage levels (register of ordinary accident cases)	1915–48	NCB (South Western Division) Safety in Mines booklet, May 1948; Report of the HM Divisional Inspector of Mines, relating to fatalities and accidents.	Document	Archives	

Reference Code	Collection	Dates	Description	Media	Location	DP
MNA/NUM/3/8/19	Area No. 4, SWMF (district, area and combine records)	1938–41	Report on compensation work, 1941.	Document	Archives	Y
MNA/NUM/3/9/1	Petition pleadings and County Court proceedings (legal papers)	1903–5	Petition, pleadings etc. in House of Lords: John Catterall and Cross, Tetley and Co. re compensation for injury at Bamfurlong Colliery, Lancashire (and covering letter from solicitor).	Document	Archives	
MNA/NUM/3/9/6, 7 and 8	Petition pleadings and County Court proceedings (legal papers)	1934	(6) 11/6/1934, Petition pleadings: T Morgan and Amalgamated Anthracite Collieries Ltd re compensation. (7) 21 August 1935, transcript of County Court proceedings: W. H. May and W. H. Hannaford re breach of safety provisions. (8) High Court Order May and Hannaford.	Document	Archives	Y
MNA/NUM/3/10/8	Records of the NUM (South Wales Area)	1908	1908 MFGB Reports of Inquiries into cause of explosions 1890–1908.	Document	Archives	
MNA/NUM/3/10/21	Records of the NUM (South Wales Area) (printed material, pamphlet)	1923	SWMF, *Notes on the Workmen's Compensation Act, 1923.* Scope of Act, accidents, fatal and near-fatal cases, medical referees, industrial diseases, payments and lump sums, partial incapacity, table of payments. 1923: SWMF notes on Workmen's Compensation Act.	Document	Archives	
MNA/NUM/E/1–145	Records of the NUM (South Wales Area)	1899–1960	Compensation case papers and correspondence (colliery and lodge).	Document	Archives	Y
MNA/NUM/L/1	Abercrave Lodge (annual and general meetings minutes)	1935–57	Compensation, including accidents. Fatal accidents and collections for dependants.	Document	Archives	
MNA/NUM/L/10/1	Bedwas Lodge (annual, general and committee meeting minutes)	1925–33	1932: pit explosion, Llynipia. Gas cases underground. Fatal accidents.	Document	Archives	
MNA/NUM/L/10/5	Bedwas Lodge (annual, general and committee meeting minutes)	1944–6	Compensation cases. Injury to workman.	Document	Archives	

Reference Code	Collection	Dates	Description	Media	Location	DP
MNA/NUM/L/11/28	Blaenavon Lodge [Lodge Secretary's correspondence and papers]	1906–7	Book recording notices of accidents and claims for compensation.	Document	Archives	
MNA/NUM/L/13/12	Blaengwrach Lodge	c.1940–61	Lists of workmen at Blaengwrach Collieries; notices of disability. Names, dates (including dates of birth), addresses. Some state disability, e.g. injury.	Document	Archives	Y
MNA/NUM/L 19/121–187	Caerau Lodge (compensation records)	1902–47	Books recording notices of injury and claims for compensation.	Document	Archives	Y
MNA/NUM/L 2/33–34	Abercynon Lodge (compensation correspondence and papers)	1918–21	33: Copy legal opinion (1918), Benjamin Thomas and The Naval Colliery Company re compensation payments to workmen in light employment. 34: Copy letter (1921) from Morgan, Bruce and Nicholas re compensation payments to workmen in light employment	Document	Archives	Y
MNA/NUM/L 2/35–36	Abercynon Lodge (compensation correspondence and papers)	1929–33	35: Letter from Morgan, Bruce and Nicholas to D. L. Davies (Agent, Pontypridd District) re compensation claim made on behalf of William Thomas (1929). 36: Certificate (1933) of medical referee on Edward Williams, under Workmen's Compensation Act 1925.	Document	Archives	Y
MNA/NUM/L 2/37–38	Abercynon Lodge (compensation correspondence and papers)	1937–42	37: Letters (1937–8) from D. E. Thomas (agent, No. 5 area SWMF) to T. Lewis (Lodge Secretary) re compensation claims (5 items). 38: Compensation correspondence file (1940–2) of T. Lewis, Lodge Secretary (103 items).	Document	Archives	Y
MNA/NUM/L 2/39–41	Abercynon Lodge (compensation correspondence and papers)	1906–47	39: Draft letter and notes re compensation claim of David Thomas (1943). 40: Correspondence file of Lodge Compensation Secretary (1945–7). 41: Thomas Richards, 'diadau Eglurhaol' (pamphlet re 1906 Compensation Act).	Document	Archives	Y

Reference Code	Collection	Dates	Description	Media	Location	DP
MNA/NUM/L/3/1	Abergorki Lodge (annual, general and committee meeting minute book)	1913–15	Compensation cases (brief details). Dispute relating to doctor forcing men to work, and Compensation Committee. Senghenydd Pit disaster. Reports of examiners, details.	Document	Archives	
MNA/NUM/L/3/7	Abergorki Lodge (Lodge Secretary's correspondence book)	1917–18	Compensation case – amputated arm and 'hook' replacement. Exhumation of soldier's body (ex-miner) regarding inquiry into his death. Colliery accidents, pay, compensation. Fatal accident, and dependant. Light employment.	Document	Archives	
MNA/NUM/L/3/12	Abergorki Lodge (Lodge Secretary's correspondence book)	1924–5	Compensation cases. Injury – loss of eye. Fatal accident. Light work. Loss of arm.	Document	Archives	Y
MNA/NUM/L/3/16	Abergorki Lodge (Lodge Secretary's correspondence book)	1930–1	Compensation cases. Accidents including fatal. Operation at Llwynypia Hospital. Light work.	Document	Archives	Y
MNA/NUM/L/3/18	Abergorki Lodge (correspondence re compensation cases	1926–39	Doctor's examination. Compensation rates. Partial compensation, light work. Crush and spinal injuries. Copies of two doctors' reports for leg fractures. Reference to loss of eye.	Document	Archives	Y
MNA/NUM/L/3/24	Abergorki Lodge (membership cards)	1929–41	On back of cards – reference to Compensation Act 1923, reporting of injuries and compensation entitlements.	Document	Archives	
MNA/NUM/L/3/25	Abergorki Lodge (medical certificates)	1934–6	Three doctors' notes (brief) certifying men unable to work; septic hand, injured hand, fractured leg.	Document	Archives	Y
MNA/NUM/L/20/127–129	Cambrian Lodge (compensation material)	1940–7	Compensation secretary's carbon-copy letter books.	Document	Archives	Y
MNA/NUM/L/20/130–132	Cambrian Lodge (compensation material)	1937–45	Books recording notices of injury and claims for compensation.	Document	Archives	Y
MNA/NUM/L/23/131–144	Coegnant Lodge (Lodge Secretary's correspondence and papers)	1908–34	Workmen's compensation book.	Document	Archives	

Reference Code	Collection	Dates	Description	Media	Location	DP
MNA/NUM/J/24/28	Cross Hands Lodge (Lodge Secretary's correspondence and papers)	1939–61	General and compensation correspondence.	Document	Archives	Y
MNA/NUM/J/24/41	Cross Hands Lodge (Lodge Secretary's correspondence and papers)	c.1946–57	Register of compensation cases.	Document	Archives	Y
MNA/NUM/J/31/29 and 33	Elliot Lodge (Lodge Secretary's correspondence and papers)	1931–48	General and compensation correspondence. Item 29: 1931–48, Item 33: 1943–7.	Document	Archives	Y
MNA/NUM/J/31/41-43	Elliot Lodge (Lodge Secretary's correspondence and papers)	1939–48	Items 41–2 (1945–8): Compensation books (notices of injury and claims for compensation). Item 43: Register of compensation cases (1945–c.1948).	Document	Archives	Y
MNA/NUM/J/31/44	Elliot Lodge (Lodge Secretary's correspondence and papers)	c.1940–c.1949	Notebook including compensation case notes c.1948.	Document	Archives	Y
MNA/NUM/J/33/61–63	Ferndale Lodge (compensation papers)	c.1932–58	Compensation case record books.	Document	Archives	Y
MNA/NUM/J/33/64	Ferndale Lodge (compensation papers)	c.1948–55	Compensation case files.	Document	Archives	Y
MNA/NUM/J/33/65	Ferndale Lodge (compensation papers)	1938–43	Register of disputed compensation cases.	Document	Archives	Y
MNA/NUM/J/33/66	Ferndale Lodge (compensation papers)	1947–59	Book recording notices of accidents and claims for compensation.	Document	Archives	Y
MNA/NUM/J/33/67	Ferndale Lodge (compensation papers)	1936	Medical reports on injured workmen.	Document	Archives	Y
MNA/NUM/J/33/69	Ferndale Lodge (compensation papers)	c.1936–54	General compensation correspondence and papers.	Document	Archives	Y

Reference Code	Collection	Dates	Description	Media	Location	DP
MNA/NUM/L/33/70	Ferndale Lodge (compensation papers)	1928–44	Book containing accident and compensation records for Ferndale Collieries (1928–37), and register of hospital entrance (1936–44).	Document	Archives	Y
MNA/NUM/L/39/8	Gellyceidrim Lodge (book recording notices of injury and claims for compensation)	1916–22	Personal details, date of injury and cause, date of claim and amount. Injuries including wounds, bruising, fractures, amputations, dislocations, hernia rupture, head injuries, septic wound, cellulitis, nystagmus.	Document	Archives	Y
MNA/NUM/L/39/12 and 13	Gellyceidrim Lodge (Lodge Secretary's carbon-copy letter book)	1927–31	Compensation cases and accidents.	Document	Archives	Y
MNA/NUM/L/45/6	Gwaun-Cae-Gurwen Lodge (funeral and house coal agreement)	c.1944	Funeral and house coal agreement for partial compensation men.	Document	Archives	Y
MNA/NUM/L/47/C/41	Lady Windsor Lodge (lodge correspondence and papers)	1946–52	Compensation correspondence.	Document	Archives	Y
MNA/NUM/L/47/C/42–44	Lady Windsor Lodge (lodge correspondence and papers)	1903–45	Four registers of non-fatal accidents.	Document	Archives	Y
MNA/NUM/L/47/C/45–50	Lady Windsor Lodge (lodge correspondence and papers)	1928–48	Six books recording notification of injury and claims for compensation.	Document	Archives	Y
MNA/NUM/L/52/2	Morlais Lodge (Lodge Secretary's carbon-copy letter book)	1931–33	References to doctors' certificate relating to accident and disagreement with company doctor. Doctor's certificate and report details relating to collier. Accident – roof fall. Fatal accident and widow's lump sum compensation agreement. Compensation cases.	Document	Archives	Y
MNA/NUM/L/52/3	Morlais Lodge (Lodge Secretary's carbon-copy letter book)	1933–4	Injury case. Doctor's certificates. Compensation cases. Medical examination arrangements and vouchers.	Document	Archives	

Reference Code	Collection	Dates	Description	Media	Location	DP
MNA/NUM/LJ57/B/47	Nine Mile Point Lodge (Lodge Secretary's correspondence and papers)	1940–59	Compensation data and correspondence.	Document	Archives	Y
MNA/NUM/LJ57/B/59	Nine Mile Point Lodge (Lodge Secretary's correspondence and papers)	1946	Rough draft of report relating to shot firing accident, Nine Mile Point Colliery.	Document	Archives	
MNA/NUM/LJ59/D/5	Oakdale Navigation Lodge (Lodge Secretary's correspondence and papers)	1927–53	Compensation claims and related correspondence.	Document	Archives	Y
MNA/NUM/LJ59/D/6	Oakdale Navigation Lodge (Lodge Secretary's correspondence and papers)	1937–67	Accident reports, pit investigations and related correspondence.	Document	Archives	Y
MNA/NUM/LJ 59/D/32	Oakdale Navigation Lodge (Lodge Secretary's correspondence and papers)	c.1936–64	Newspaper cuttings, including reference to colliery disasters.	Document	Archives	
MNA/NUM/LJ62/A3	Park and Dare Lodge (minute book for annual, general and committee meetings; also special and colliery workers meetings and subscribers to Pentwyn Cottage Hospital, 1943)	1941–3	Cost of conveying body to Pentwyn Hospital for post-mortem. Establishment of fund for travel expenses for medical attention. Injury case, complaint regarding availability of ambulance facilities. Fatal injury and funeral. Loss of teeth in accident, possible compensation claim for loss of earnings, referred to Compensation Secretary. Complaint about lack of medical attention to injured worker. Lack of facilities for reporting accidents during early morning.	Document	Archives	
MNA/NUM/LJ63/30 and 31	Penallta Lodge (Lodge Secretary's correspondence and papers)	c.1930–c.1960	Two boxes containing compensation case files.	Document	Archives	Y

Reference Code	Collection	Dates	Description	Media	Location	DP
MNA/NUM/L/68/7	Saron Lodge (correspondence and miscellaneous Material)	1947–57	Letters to Lodge Secretary, including compensation.	Document	Archives	Y
MNA/NUM/L/70/C18	Trelewis Drift Lodge (Lodge Secretary's correspondence and papers)	1900	Court of Appeal Judgement re Workmen's Compensation Act, 1897.	Document	Archives	
MNA/NUM/L/70/D26	Trelewis Drift Lodge (Dowlais District correspondence)	1923–4	General correspondence of S. O. Davies as Miners' Agent of Dowlais District SWMF, relating to compensation.	Document	Archives	Y
MNA/NUM/L/70/C7	Trelewis Drift Lodge (Lodge Secretary's correspondence and papers)	1944–9	Book recording accidents and claims for compensation.	Document	Archives	Y
MNA/NUM/L/70/C8–14	Trelewis Drift Lodge (Lodge Secretary's Correspondence and Papers)	1921–33	Papers relating to insurance claims, awards, hearings, appeals.	Document	Archives	Y
MNA/NUM/L/71/B17–20	Tylorstown Lodge (financial records and agreements)	1924–9	Four books recording claims for compensation and notices of injury.	Document	Archives	Y
MNA/NUM/L/74/D19	Windsor Lodge (miscellaneous)	1941–61	Correspondence regarding compensation cases (sample of 15 cases).	Document	Archives	Y
MNA/NUM/L/74/D20	Windsor Lodge (miscellaneous)	1944–62	Certificates of disallowance of disablement claims (sample).	Document	Archives	Y
MNA/POL/3/3/1	Ammanford, Llandebie and District Trades and Labour Council (annual, general and Executive Council minutes)	1938–41	1939: TUC circular for Workmen's Compensation Conference Swansea, pressing for changes in law. 1940: Workmen's Compensation Conference Cardiff.	Document	Archives	

Reference Code	Collection	Dates	Description	Media	Location	DP
MNA/POL/8/1	Ebbw Vale Branch Iron and Steel Trades and Labour Council (cash book)	1899–1919	Receipts and expenditure for compensation cases and Secretary, and artificial limbs.	Document	Archives	
MNA/PP/10/15/1	Brin Daniels (Ammanford)	c.1926	Pantyffynn Colliery Price List; abstract of 1912 Minimum Wage Act, including instructions to compensation claimants, reporting injuries, light employment for injured. Copy of solicitor's letter (1917) relating to chief points of Compensation Act.	Document	Archives	
MNA/PP/12/9	Mrs Beatrice Davies (née Phippen), Ystrad Rhondda	1922	Labour party election leaflet which refers to numbers of miners and others killed or injured in industrial accidents.	Document	Archives	
MNA/PP/15/1	John Davies (Gwaun Cae Gurwen)	1915	Handwritten notebook – Coal Mines (Minimum Wage) Act 1912, copied from SWMF leaflets. Refers to 'infirm workman' and disability from illness or accident. Instructions relating to disability, or absence from work from accident or illness, and medical examinations.	Document	Archives	
MNA/PP/15/2 and 11	John Davies (Gwaun Cae Gurwen)	Inter-war period	John Davies's essay regarding East Pit, Gwaun-Cae-Gurwen Collieries. Paragraph including references to accidents.	Document	Archives	
MNA/PP/16/1	S. O. Davies	1951–2	NUM memo; Social Insurance, Workmen's Compensation Act, Beveridge Report, National Insurance Acts, balance sheet for Industrial Injuries Fund. NUM memo and Parliamentary motion regarding transfer of Workmen's Compensation to Industrial Injuries Act.	Document	Archives	
MNA/PP/16/11/1–34	S. O. Davies	1944–8	24 November 1948: Welsh Affairs reference to mining accidents.	Document	Archives	
MNA/PP/16/12	S. O. Davies	1930s–1940s	Review of Socialist Medical Association pamphlet, references to mining accidents and injuries. 1937: Parliamentary speech reference to mining accidents and dangers. May Day resolution relating to Compensation Bill. Notes; Industrial Injuries Bill.	Document	Archives	

Reference Code	Collection	Dates	Description	Media	Location	DP
MNA/PP/16/50/2, 6, 8, 9, 10	S. O. Davies	1940-4	Constituency correspondence. 1940: compensation for worker at ROF. 1942: compensation for Government contract workers. 1944: Workmen's Compensation – heart, lungs, dermatitis, ROF worker (lost fingers), copy Treasury memo Scheme of Compensation no. 133 (injury to workmen in government establishments). 1946: ROF compensation claim. 1947: compensation claim for accident at government hostel (death of worker). 1948: Workmen's Compensation and miner's accident.	Document	Archives	Y
MNA/PP/16/50/7/1 and 2	S. O. Davies	1945	Constituency correspondence. ROF worker compensation for lost finger; Workmen's Compensation for factory worker's hand injury; letters regarding RAF aircraftman with second-degree burns; specialist nerve operation for wounded soldier. ROF compensation claims (e.g. dermatitis).	Document	Archives	Y
MNA/PP/16/85	S. O. Davies	1940s	Correspondence regarding compensation for injuries e.g. eye.	Document	Archives	Y
MNA/PP/22/1	D. L. Evans (Abercrave)	1902	Western Division Special Rules: abstract Coal Mines Regulation Act 1887- including references to accidents and deaths.	Document	Archives	
MNA/PP/28/10	James Evans (Tumble)	1937	Letters: light employment of workers certified suffering from disease or after accident. Conciliation Board Agreement for the Coal Trade of Monmouth and South Wales, compensation.	Document	Archives	
MNA/PP/28/25	James Evans (Tumble)	1908-37	Notes re accidents 1925-34, injured, killed, and jobs, deaths in slant and drift 1908-35.	Document	Archives	Y
MNA/PP/28/26	James Evans (Tumble)	1937–1950s	Memo of MFGB evidence relating to shaft accidents. Accidents at Mines details in relation to Coal Mines Act. Notes: Industrial Injuries Act, Assessments of Disabilities by Medical Boards and Medical Appeal Tribunals.	Document	Archives	Y

Reference Code	Collection	Dates	Description	Media	Location	DP
MNA/PP/34/11	Harold Finch	1939	Royal Commission on Workmen's Compensation minutes, 27–28 April 1939. Paper No. 7 Memo of Evidence by the Board of Trade 18 May 1939 and 1 June 1939.	Document	Archives	
MNA/PP/35/51	David Francis	1947	*Socialist Appeal* newspaper, refers to mine accidents.	Document	Archives	
MNA/PP/40/2–3	Robert Harrington (Hirwaun)	1916–22	Aberdare District Miners' Federation (MFGB) membership cards: Special notice regarding accidents – instructions to report to Compensation Secretary immediately in event of any accident.	Document	Archives	
MNA/PP/41/1, 3, 4, 5 and 6	David Harris (Glais) (exercise books containing bilingual manuscript reminiscences)	1970s, ref C19th	Two accidents at Bryncoch Colliery, case at House of Lords – company denied liability. Reference to Compensation Act 1900. Experiences of carrying fatally injured miner on stretcher through streets to home. Own injuries and accidents including at colliery. Pit accidents, e.g. water, roof fall.	Document	Archives	Y
MNA/PP/46/54	Arthur Horner (*Colliery Workers' Magazine* (SWMF))	1924	*Colliery Workers' Magazine* Vol. II, 10: The Workers' Charter (including accidents). Reports of district meetings (compensation cases).	Document	Archives	
MNA/PP/46/67	Arthur Horner (proposed constitution for British Mineworkers' Union)	c.1935	British Mineworkers' Union Constitution: reference to accidents, compensation and legislation.	Document	Archives	
MNA/PP/47/5	Noel Hufton (Bedwas) (*The Colliery Guardian*)	1905	Article: 'Electrical Shock', electrical accidents in mines. Article: Workmen's Compensation in 1904, refers to statistics issued by Home Office.	Document	Archives	
MNA/PP/5/2	Jesse Clark	1919–1960s	Diaries. 1919: mining injuries, time off and compensation.	Document	Archives	Y
MNA/PP/50/3	W. R. James (Trelewis) (Taff Merthyr Lodge minute book)	1946–52	Reference to fatal accident.	Document	Archives	
MNA/PP/54/5 and 6	Hubert Jenkins (Office diary)	1919–24	Injury cases, fatalities. Compensation cases.	Document	Archives	

Reference Code	Collection	Dates	Description	Media	Location	DP
MNA/PP/63/6	I. G. Jones (Cwmtwrch)	1941	Desk diary, including fatal accident (crush) details, inquest and inspection.	Document	Archives	Y
MNA/PP/73/6	James Lewis (Maesteg) (papers re James Lewis's tenure of office as secretary of Llynfi Sundries Lodge)	1930–47	Reporting of accidents and compensation. MFGB blank forms for Compensation claims. Light work and incapacitated miners.	Document	Archives	
MNA/PP/73/7	James Lewis (Maesteg) (miscellaneous pamphlets and printed material)	1933–46	Pamphlet: SWMF Compensation Department, *Workmen's Compensation (Temporary Increases) Act 1943*. MFGB Minutes of Executive Committee Meeting, 24 January 1940, reference to Workmen's Compensation and SWMF. 1936: SWMF balance sheet, refers to Compensation Insurance Fund.	Document	Archives	
MNA/PP/86/1	W. J. Nind (photocopied pages from *The South Wales Miner* newspaper)	1933	*The South Wales Miner*, 22 June 1933: letter re 'Danger in the Pit' – pit accident and pay (SWMF securing pay for injured miner).	Document	Archives	
MNA/PP/86/3	W. J. Nind (analysis of underground accidents)	1936–7	Bedwas Navigation Colliery Co., analysis of accidents, January–March 1937, including rock falls and fatalities. Report including details of ages, shifts, occupations, areas of pit. Handwritten version including personal details. Pamphlet, *An Analysis of Underground Haulage Accidents in South Wales, 1936*, by South Wales and Monmouthshire Safety in Mines Research Committee.	Document	Archives	Y
MNA/PP/87/1 and 2	Charles Parker (transcripts of interviews with miners and their wives)	1961, ref interwar period	Husband's death, pit accident. Miners' accidents. Gas explosions, roof falls. Damp explosion.	Document	Archives	Y
MNA/PP/9/5 and 6	H. W. Currie	1927–1930s	(5) Newspaper cutting: pit fatality of boy (15), 1936. (6) Newspaper cuttings (1937): mine safety, accidents, compensation.	Document	Archives	

Reference Code	Collection	Dates	Description	Media	Location	DP
MNA/PP/92/2–4	A. L. Powell (court papers)	1913–24	Judgement in arbitration proceedings, and award paper, re Workmen's Compensation Act 1906 claim by dependants of collier.	Document	Archives	
MNA/PP/93/26	Leo Price	1936–41	SWMF Members Contribution Cards, with Compensation Act 1923 notes on reverse (reporting of accidents and entitlements), (cards for 1936, 1938 and 1941).	Document	Archives	
MNA/PP/93/28	Leo Price	1933	SWMF Rules 1933: Compensation for injuries and fatal accidents, enforcing rights of claimants.	Document	Archives	
MNA/PP/98/1 and 2	Gwilym Richards	1913–20	Newspaper cuttings: 1920: Compensation and disablement.	Document	Archives	
MNA/PP/118/12	John Thomas (Aberavon) (*The Dockers' Record* (24 monthly reports of the DWRGWU))	1901–16	June 1911: Factory Inspectorate; more needed and information to be given about numbers of accidents, disabilities, injuries, deaths, diseases to dock workers. Factory Acts in docks. February 1907: Sick Benefit Society meeting, letter relating to Compensation Act, need to include all dangerous trades and occupational disease. February 1907 (letter from Ben Tillett): Most dock workers not covered under Workmen's Compensation Act. Dock Regulations: structural defects in ships a danger. Safety relating to docks, wharves and quays, questionable whether registered for inspection, or subject to Factory Act. Reports of Legal Department: Compensation for injuries, case lists, amounts. Points made at 1904 conference regarding health and safety, decrease in work hours, legislation for injured workers, appointment of inspectors under Factory and Workshops' Act, laws regarding proper compensation, full wages during disablement. December 1909: reference to two serious accidents, Home Office involved, view of getting more efficient inspection of gear. June 1911: reference to accidents and claiming compensation, National Insurance, Invalidity and Unemployment Insurance.	Document	Archives	

Reference Code	Collection	Dates	Description	Media	Location	DP
MNA/PP/118/14	John Thomas (Aberavon)	1888–99	(Correspondence, circulars, agendas and other papers for South Wales, Monmouthshire and Gloucestershire Tinplate Workers' Union) Tinplate Workers' Union meeting agendas: 1891: reference to accidents, causes to be investigated, whether eligible for compensation or not. 1891: fund for relief of workmen who had had an accident.	Document	Archives	
MNA/PP/118/47	John Thomas (Aberavon) (annual report and balance sheet for Monmouthshire and South Wales Miners' Permanent Provident Society)	1895	Conference report 26 March 1895: coalfield accidents, Albion Colliery and others, lost 424 members; non-fatal accidents 12,917 (very heavy); Benefit for aged and infirm miners; miners' mortality rates; statistics for payments and benefits; Ferndale (1867) and Mardy Colliery's explosions funds.	Document	Archives	
MNA/PP/118/50	John Thomas (Aberavon) (*The Ironworkers' Journal*)	1900	*The Ironworkers' Journal*, June 1900: Workmen's Compensation Act and casual labour; fatal accident and Workmen's Compensation case.	Document	Archives	
MNA/PP/118/52	John Thomas (Aberavon) (Ness Edwards, *The Industrial Revolution in South Wales*)	1924	Working conditions: accidents, safety, illness, ventilation, injuries, lung disease.	Document	Archives	
MNA/PP/122/1	Wilfred Timbrell (Tumble) (memoirs of Tumble)	1896– c.1960s	Working conditions, fatal accident, compensation.	Document	Archives	
MNA/PP/127/1	D. J. Williams	1900–38	Compensation form book. Notices of Claim in cases of injury and death, to Manager of Gwaun-Cae-Gurwen collieries. Sum claimed, name, address, date of death and injury, cause, place. Causes including accidents, falls, crush.	Document	Archives	Y
MNA/PP/132/9	James Winstone	1902	Executive Committee meeting 1902: Vochriw Colliery Disaster (gas explosion), details, victims, evidence. Notification of accidents. Scottish compensation case and 2 appeals cases (relating to accidents).	Document	Archives	

141

Reference Code	Collection	Dates	Description	Media	Location	DP
MNA/PP/132/9	James Winstone (scrapbook of news-cuttings and handwritten notes)	1912	Fatality at Pontnewynydd Works (crushed). Labour statistics relating to deaths, lead poisoning. Medical and compensation cases including fatalities.	Document	Archives	
MNA/TUG/2/1	British Iron, Steel and Kindred Trades Association, British Steel Smelters Reports	1892–7	1892–4: Funeral levy, benefits, obituaries (including names and cause of death and family members' deaths). Employers' Liability Bill 1894 details. Compensation case for accident and death, details (knocked down by crane), at Briton Ferry. Accident at Flemington, lost hand.1895–7: Funeral levy, obituaries, causes of death (men and family members). Accident claims and grants. Workmen's Compensation Act 1897, details and schedules.	Document	Archives	
MNA/TUG/1/A2	Coaltrimmers' Union (Cardiff, Penarth and Barry Branch) (annual, general, committee, and Executive Committee minutes)	1890–5	Accident pay claims references, injury, Compensation. Pontypridd Colliery Disaster Appeal 1893. Applications for benefits. 1894: funds to Cilfynydd Explosion Fund. 1894: balance sheet including accident pay. Swansea docks explosion on steamer, newspaper cutting, two deaths and two injured. 1895: Union memo, Inspector sent from London to report. Newspaper cuttings; fire on ship, spontaneous combustion whilst taking in coal cargo, 1895: Cardiff, five men, serious injuries and burns, sent to Hamadryad Hospital.	Document	Archives	
MNA/TUG/3/0/1	National Association of Colliery Overmen, Deputies and Shotfirers (minute book of conference and committees of General Federation of Colliery Firemen of GB)	1910–25	1914: Senghenydd Disaster Enquiry, Firemen's Certificates (and other years), gas testing, ventilation, dust. 1921: Poisoning from explosive fumes. 1921: Woodhorn Colliery Disaster, Report of Inquest (gas explosion, fatalities). Compensation. 1923: Report of Haigh Pit Disaster (Cumberland), explosion. Accidents, falls of roof. 1925: Llay Mine Explosion Enquiry.	Document	Archives	

Reference Code	Collection	Dates	Description	Media	Location	DP
MNA/TUG/5/1	South Wales and Monmouthshire Enginemen, Stokers, and Craftsmen's Association (quarterly report of the Association)	1906	Section re compensation, fatal accident case and widow's claim, court case. Claim details for another fatal accident, fall. TUC delegate's report referring to Workmen's Compensation Amendment Bill.	Document	Archives	
MNA/TUG/6/1	Tin and Sheet Millmen's Association (monthly report books; minutes of Executive Council meetings, balance sheets, contributions etc.)	1905	Numbers of members on sick list, and deaths. Distress grants paid per branch, amounts and illness. Wattstown Disaster (explosion). Workmen's Compensation Act Amendment Bill. Accident levy for member. Compensation cases references.	Document	Archives	
MNA/TUG/7/1/C/1-2	Iron and Steel Trades Confederation (reports, circulars, minutes and papers)	1934-48	1934: Workmen's Compensation Act 1925, letter reporting accidents. 1943: Memo re Workmen's Compensation (Temporary Increases) Act. 1944: Workmen's Compensation (calculations). Memo: legal services, accidents at work and compensation. 1946: Letter, reporting of accidents. 1948: Letter, accidents caused by explosion of live shells.	Document	Archives	
MNA/TUG/9/1	Amalgamated Engineering Union (minute book)	1922-6	Accident case, dependents to claim sick benefit, visit to hospital by Sick Steward.	Document	Archives	
MNB/COL/9	Deep Navigation Colliery (account book: weekly advances and compensation payments)	1940	Details of compensation amount, name, occupation, accident details.	Document	Archives	Y
MNB/COL/11/E1-2	Fernhill Colliery (contract books)	1942-53	Conciliation Board Agreements for the Coal Trade of Monmouth and South Wales, Schedule II, principles for periodical ascertainments; including Workmen's Compensation.	Document	Archives	

Reference Code	Collection	Dates	Description	Media	Location	DP
MNB/COL/12/1–3	Garch No. 3 Colliery (register of workmen employed)	1923–54	Includes: doctor's name and if medical certificate issued; if 'Applicant a healthy workman'; details of any accidents to the workmen and if compensation paid.	Document	Archives	Y
MNB/COL/17/C12	Morlais Colliery (Home Office (Mines Dept) Circulars)	1916–42	1925: reference to series of accidents – inrushes of water into mine workings, Water Dangers Committee appointed, reference to plans of abandoned mines. Accident forms for Mine Department (blank). Refers to return of forms relating to non-fatal accidents. 1925: Working Committee of Safety in Mines Research Board investigation into effect of machine work on accidents at the coalface.	Document	Archives	
MNB/COL/17/C19	Morlais Colliery	1916–42	(General correspondence with Thomas Williams and Sons (Llangennech) Ltd); 1930 letter: Colliery tips and injuries to persons.	Document	Archives	
MNB/COL/17/C25D	Morlais Colliery (Secretarial Department circulars)	1939–42	Refers to Fire Prevention (Business Premises). (2) 1941: Compensation for injuries. Grant to workmen entitled to compensation.	Document	Archives	
MNB/COL/17/C25E	Morlais Colliery (Secretarial Department circulars)	1934–42	Cost sheets including Workmen's Compensation. 1940: letter re Ex Gratia Compensation Grant and pre-1924 cases. References to Workmen's Compensation.	Document	Archives	
MNB/COL/17/C25F	Morlais Colliery (Secretarial Department circulars)	1939–41	Termination of contracts relating to sickness and accidents. Compensation, light work, War Advance, ex-gratia payment.	Document	Archives	
MNB/COL/17/C25H	Morlais Colliery (Secretarial Department circulars)	1934–8	Cost sheet, 1934, including Workmen's Compensation. Levy and compensation suspension, 1938. Holidays with pay for compensation workmen.	Document	Archives	
MNB/COL/17/C28	Morlais Colliery (Transport Department circulars)	1923–32	1925: The Prevention of Accidents Rules 1911 and The Prevention of Accidents (Extension of Time) Rules 1920, relating to wither side brake levers.	Document	Archives	

Reference Code	Collection	Dates	Description	Media	Location	DP
MNB/COL/17/C32B	Morlais Colliery (miscellaneous memoranda, resolutions, agreements etc.)	1915–42	1927: Monmouthshire and South Wales Coal Owners' Association Reports 1927, including: Home Office copy of notice regarding Lead Paint (Protection against Poisoning Act 1926); fencing of machinery; accidents at colliery sidings. Memos of Agreement relating to accidents. 1928: Cost sheet including Workmen's Compensation.	Document	Archives	
MNB/COL/17/C6B	Morlais Colliery (Board of Conciliation circulars)	1925–42	Cases commuted (accidents). Details including name, age, address, nature of injury, amount of compensation, date recorded in court. Injuries including; fractures, burns, hernia, amputations, paralysis, wounds, crush Injuries, injuries to eye, head and spine.	Document	Archives	Y
MNB/COL/17/C6B and C	Morlais Colliery (Board of Conciliation circulars)	1928–38	Cases commuted 1928–31 (monthly): accident date, personal details, injury, commutation amount, date recorded in court. Amputations, electric shock, burns, hernia, fractures, spine, eye, head, ulcers, deafness.	Document	Archives	Y
MNB/COL/17/F1-4	Morlais Colliery (colliery workmen's contract book)	1926–42	Including Memo of Agreement, with references to accidents, Workmen's Compensation and Insurance, National Health Insurance, Miners' Welfare Levy.	Document	Archives	
MNB/COL/17/M6	Morlais Colliery (Talyclyn Colliery; notices of accidents)	1942–3	Completed accident forms; personal details, accident details, injuries, if taken to hospital, if due to 'quarrel or play', if 'violation of Mines Act or Specific Orders or Rules', witnesses, remarks (e.g. visit to doctor), Mutual Indemnity Society.	Document	Archives	Y
MNB/I/3/D19	Abergorki Workmen's Hall and Institute	1926–9	Newspaper cuttings relating to SWMF affairs; *South Wales Journal of Commerce*, 6 February 1929, relating to miners' compensation claims.	Document	Archives	
MNB/NUM/1/D/179	Dillwyn (correspondence with colliery managements)	1902–55	Compensation.	Document	Archives	Y

Reference Code	Collection	Dates	Description	Media	Location	DP
MNB/NUM/1/D/343	Seven Sisters (correspondence with colliery managements)	1942–56	Compensation.	Document	Archives	Y
MNB/NUM/1/D/460	International (correspondence with Lodge Secretaries)	1940–54	Injuries and compensation.	Document	Archives	Y
MNB/NUM/1/D/464	Maesmarchog (correspondence with Lodge Secretaries)	1942–55	Compensation.	Document	Archives	Y
MNB/NUM/1/D/483	Seven Sisters (Correspondence with Lodge Secretaries)	1943–56	Compensation.	Document	Archives	Y
MNB/NUM/1/D/49	Abercrave and International (correspondence with colliery managements)	1944–54	Compensation.	Document	Archives	Y
MNB/NUM/1/D/504	NUM circulars (correspondence with Lodge Secretaries)	1947–59	NUM rehabilitation and compensation circulars.	Document	Archives	
MNB/NUM/E/1–145	NUM Records (compensation case-papers and correspondence)	1941–81	Colliery and lodge compensation case-papers and correspondence.	Document	Archives	Y
MNB/NUM/E/146	NUM Records	1940–7	Miscellaneous court proceedings relating to compensation claims.	Document	Archives	Y
MNB/NUM/E/147–150	NUM Records	1930–52	Circulars, reports and general correspondence relating to compensation claims.	Document	Archives	Y
MNB/NUM/E/147–152	NUM Records	1924–67	Miscellaneous legal papers relating to compensation cases including court proceedings, solicitors' correspondence and opinions, report on Compensation Acts etc.	Document	Archives	Y
MNB/NUM/J/1/11	Abercynon Lodge (SWMF Conference resolutions on wages)	1939	Call upon MFGB to give attention to needs of men injured in mining industry to ensure receive equal treatment in compensation payments to correspond with increased payments to employed miners related to increased cost of living.	Document	Archives	

Reference Code	Collection	Dates	Description	Media	Location	DP
MNB/NUM/L/1/6	Abercynon Lodge (Lodge Secretary's carbon-copy letter book)	1938	Compensation cases including accidents. Light employment and compensation cases. Lump sum and compensation. Compensation conference in Cardiff.	Document	Archives	
MNB/NUM/L/15/E1	Mountain Lodge (minutes of Safety Committee Meeting)	1945	Accident (shot firing). Roof falls. Accident numbers (fatal and non-fatal).	Document	Archives	
MNB/NUM/L/16/1	Rhas Lodge (Onllwyn No. 2 Pit) (minute book)	1940–53	Accident – fracture and rheumatism.	Document	Archives	
MNB/NUM/L/2/10	Ammanford No. 2 Lodge (Lodge Secretary's general correspondence)	1929–35	1933: Letter: damage to artificial teeth. 1933: Circular: Workmen's Colliery Examiners and Section 16 of Coal Mines Act.	Document	Archives	
MNB/NUM/L/2/11	Ammanford No. 2 Lodge (medical reports on compensation claimants)	1926	Doctors' letters to solicitors re miners' compensation claims. Discuss wounds, hearing and eye problems, neurasthenia, hypertropic astigmatism, head injuries, bone fractures, septicaemia, leg injuries, lost fingers.	Document	Archives	Y
MNB/NUM/L/3/1	Blaenserchan Lodge (account book)	1918–63	Expenditure: deputation visiting scene of accident and inspecting scenes of accidents, attending Compensation School, medicals, Medical Tribunal.	Document	Archives	
MNB/NUM/L/4/1	Caerau Lodge (statement of accounts)	1929	Expenditure: Dependants of fatal accident victims.	Document	Archives	
MNB/NUM/L/9/1	Ffaldau Lodge (minute book)	1939–41	Fatal accident, widow's compensation appeal. Accidents. Compensation claim relating to 'shock' and fatal accident of another. Various compensation cases.	Document	Archives	
MNB/POL/6/A6	Newport Constituency Labour Party (Executive and General Committee minutes)	1930–3	Explosions at Ship Yard.	Document	Archives	

Reference Code	Collection	Dates	Description	Media	Location	DP
MNB/PP/10/H31	S. O. Davies	1937-47	Copies: Workmen's Compensation Bill 1937; Workmen's Compensation (Supplementary Allowances) Bill 1940; Disabled Persons (Employment) Act 1944. Summary of provisions of National Assistance Bill 1947. National Assistance Bill Financial Memorandum 1947 (terminating existing poor law, provision for disabled).	Document	Archives	
MNB/PP/11/B1	W. A. Davies (Ystalfera) (National Association of Colliery Managers Conference papers)	1936	NACM Conference address by J. E. Lambert (ICI Ltd.) – 'The Safe Use of Explosives'. Refers to accidents and roof falls.	Document	Archives	
MNB/PP/12/A19 and A20	William Henry Davies (Penclawdd)	1911-36	Workmen's Compensation certificate 1911, (under Workmen's Compensation Acts 1897, 1900 and 1906) for injuries caused by accident (includes dates and payment amounts).	Document	Archives	Y
MNB/PP/12/B2 and B3	William Henry Davies (Penclawdd)	1929-43	Penclawdd Distress Fund: 1929-30: newspaper cuttings for 24 dependents of 7 victims of Wernbwll Colliery Disaster (explosion), lists subscribers; 1929-43: correspondence and papers relating to compensation claims, names of deceased and payments to widows.	Document	Archives	Y
MNB/PP/22/1	Harold Finch (minute book, Miners' Group)	1942-6	Workmen's Compensation 1942 Bill, rates details. Benefit scheme, rejected cases. Supplementary benefit, disablement, part-compensation. Safety Stemming Plug Co. Law Reform (Contributory Negligence) Bill 1945.	Document	Archives	
MNB/PP/34/A1	Berwyn Howells	1934	Memo of Agreement (Injury by Accident). Workmen's Compensation case 1934 – lump sum payment. Details of accident (fall of coal) and injury. Full and partial compensation.	Document	Archives	Y
MNB/PP/34/A5	Berwyn Howells	1942	1942 Agreement, Personal Injury (Accident) of collier. Workmen's Compensation to be paid by company, lump sum settlement.	Document	Archives	Y

Reference Code	Collection	Dates	Description	Media	Location	DP
MNB/PP/34/A6	Berwyn Howells	1944	Lists of compensation cases. Name, date of birth, date of accident, nature of injury, compensation rate, outstanding liability. Injuries – fracture, amputated limb, wound, eye injury, crush, head injury.	Document	Archives	Y
MNB/PP/34/C6	Berwyn Howells	1941	1941: letter: payment of lump sum for Workmen's Compensation.	Document	Archives	Y
MNB/PP/55	Eiragwyn Rees (letters)	1941	Letter: Compensation claim at Trimsaran Colliery. Two letters: re-employment of colliers (one accident case).	Document	Archives	
MNB/PP/57/1 and 2	Thomas Richards	1901–5	(1) Senghenydd Explosion Relief Fund account book, listing payments to dependants (names and amounts). (2) Separate list of Relief Fund payments.	Document	Archives	
MNB/PP/63/4	Howell Davy Williams (printed material re coal-mining industry)	1943	SWMF Compensation Dept. pamphlet: *Workmen's Compensation (Temporary Increases) Act 1943.*	Document	Archives	
MNB/PP/72/26	Alistair Wilson (compensation case examination cards and notes)	1939–42	Handwritten notes relating to compensation cases.	Document	Archives	Y
MNC/COP/1/1	Aberdare Co-operative Society (minute book)	1929–32	Injured employee and compensation. Staff accidents at work (one fatal). Staff member on compensation, doctor's examination.	Document	Archives	
MNC/COP/3/1	Abersychan Co-op Society (minute book)	1908–12	Staff sickness and injury absences. Workmen's Compensation Insurance.	Document	Archives	
MNC/COP/6/5	Blaenavon Co-op Society (minute book)	1937–54	Staff accidents. HM Factory Inspector letter regarding fencing of machine.	Document	Archives	
MNC/COP/15/2	Penarth Co-op Society (minute book)	1937–9	Staff accidents, compensation, sick pay, medical fees. Dispute between Insurance Society and employee's doctor re fitness of person to return to work.	Document	Archives	
MNC/COP/16/1	Penygraig Co-op Society (minute book)	1912–16	Accidents, compensation claim.	Document	Archives	

Reference Code	Collection	Dates	Description	Media	Location	DP
MNC/COP/27/1, 14, 27	*People's Yearbooks* (Annual of the Co-operative Wholesale Society Ltd)	1920–48	1920: Industrial accidents and diseases, statistics of deaths and disability. 1933: UK Statistics, including from trade unions (work fatalities, industrial accidents). 1948: Reference to Industrial Injuries Acts.	Document	Archives	
MNC/ISTC/1/1	National Union of Blastfurnacemen, Ore Miners, Coke Workers and Kindred Trades. (Annual Conference Reports)	1919–25	Compensation and reporting of accidents and injuries. 1919: Workmen's Compensation (War Addition) Amendment Act 1919 details. 1920: *Fatigue in the Iron and Steel Industry*, report of Industrial Fatigue Research Board, issued by MRC and Department of Scientific and Industrial Research, initiated by Home Office 1918, 12-hr shift replaced by 8 hour, investigation ongoing. 1919: Refers to Workmen's Compensation.	Document	Archives	Y
MNC/ISTC/3/1	National Union of Blastfurnacemen, Ore Miners, Coke Workers and Kindred Trades. (Delegate Board Minutes)	1922–31	1923: Accident and compensation, three deaths from injuries. Gas poisoning case and compensation. Reference to gassing. Compensation cases relating to Ebbw Vale and Dowlais (4 fatal), 1930. 1931: Compensation cases (Dowlais and Cardiff). Notice of cases of Workmen's Compensation – National Executive Committee to submit amendments to Compensation Acts to General Council of TUC. Accidents and compensation cases.	Document	Archives	
MNC/ISTC/4/1	National Union of Blastfurnacemen, Ore Miners, Coke Workers and Kindred Trades. (Annual General Meeting reports)	1938–41	Details of Workmen's Compensation (Supplementary Allowances) Act 1940, applicable in cases where accident happened on or after 1 January 1924. 1941: report of Compensation Department, Personal Injuries (Civilians Act), Supplementary Allowances Act, Amendment of Compensation Acts (1938 Royal Commission).	Document	Archives	

Reference Code	Collection	Dates	Description	Media	Location	DP
MNC/NUM/2/5/1-3	NUM South Wales Area	1948	Minutes of Proceedings at Summer School for Compensation Secretaries, Barry, 14 June 1948. History of compensation, Industrial Injuries Act, Social Insurance, Beveridge Report and NHS, National Insurance Act, disability and disease in mining, Sickness Benefit, disablement, accidents, Medical Boards, doctors' certificates.	Document	Archives	
MNC/NUM/5/182	NUM South Wales Area (SWMF Eastern Valleys District Monthly Meeting minutes (D2/F53))	1915 and ud	Compensation cases. Fatal Accident agreement (ud); Benefits to widow and dependents, removal of body, ambulance men.	Document	Archives	
MNC/NUM/L/24/1-4	Newlands Lodge	1935-64	Compensation correspondence files including SWMF, and Midlands Employers Mutual Assurance Ltd. Relating to industrial injuries and accidents. Certificates; examinations under Workmen's Compensation Act 1925.	Document	Archives	Y
MNC/NUM/L/27/41	Penallta Lodge	1942-63	Accident reports file. Contains accident report forms and notices of accidents or dangerous occurrences.	Document	Archives	Y
MNC/NUM/L/27/43	Penallta Lodge	1910	Copies of Workmen's Compensation Acts. Contains complete copies of the Workmen's Compensation Acts of 1906 and 1909.	Document	Archives	
MNC/NUM/L/29/22	Arrael Griffin Lodge	1939-46	Compensation counterfoil books. Contains notices of injury and claims for compensation. Including name, address, occupation, cause of injury, date of accident of injured person, amount claimed.	Document	Archives	Y
MNC/NUM/L/8/49-50	Blaenavon Lodge	1934-8	Compensation counterfoil books. notices of injury and claims for comp. Including name, address, occupation, cause of injury, date of accident of injured person, amount claimed.	Document	Archives	Y
MNC/NUM/L/8/60	Blaenavon Lodge	1906	Workmen's Compensation Act pamphlet 1906. Explanatory notes relating to Workmen's Compensation Act.	Document	Archives	

Reference Code	Collection	Dates	Description	Media	Location	DP
MNC/PP/15/10	Dr Gwent Jones (newspaper cuttings)	c.1938–c.1948	'What Science is Doing for the Miner – Precautions Against Accidents and Silicosis', by Prof. Granville Poole. Refers to accidents, falls, gas, firedamp, explosions.	Document	Archives	
MNC/PP/15/7	Dr Gwent Jones (copies of SWMF Compensation Dept papers)	1940–3	Circular relating to Workmen's Compensation (Supplementary Allowances) Act 1940, and Workmen's Compensation (Temporary Increases) Act 1943. Copy of the Act issued by the SWMF (pamphlet).	Document	Archives	
MNC/PP/15/8	Dr Gwent Jones (copies of Industrial Injury Insurance Scheme proposals and statutory rules and orders)	1940–4	Proposals for Industrial Injury Insurance Scheme (HMSO 1944). Workmen's Compensation (Supplementary Allowances) Bill, 1940. Statutory Rules and Orders 1943 (s. 885, 886 (Pneumoconiosis)) Workmen's Compensation. Workmen's Compensation (Temporary Increases) Act 1943, Chapter 49.	Document	Archives	
MNC/PP/18/3	David Lewis	1942	SWMF membership cards. On back cover, reference to Compensation Act, reporting of accidents and injuries and claiming compensation.	Document	Archives	
MNC/PP/26/10	Lance Rogers	1939	House of Lords Judgement 1939. Caswell v Powell Duffryn Associated Collieries Ltd. Caswell killed underground. Mother sued under Fatal Accidents Act to recover damages on ground that death caused by breach of statutory duty. Safety of machine.	Document	Archives	Y
MNC/PP/3/1	Idris Cox		Pit accidents (father's and own). Comment regarding danger and accidents underground.	Document	Archives	
MNC/PP/35/1	Anon (Envelope XX)	1906	Photocopy of colliery accident statistics from book (by Henry Davies), relating to British statistics.	Document	Archives	
MNC/PP/35/1	Anon (Envelope II)	c.1930s	MFGB Report on Explosion at Garswood Colliery near Wigan 12 November 1932, references to ventilation, gas and rescue. 1934: MFGB minutes regarding compensation.	Document	Archives	Y

Reference Code	Collection	Dates	Description	Media	Location	DP
TN295 COL	*The Coal Miner: His Health, Diseases and General Welfare* (pamphlet)	c.1924	Occupational diseases and accidents; accidents (first aid, rescue).	Document	SWML	
TN63 HOM	Reports of Inspectors of Mines for Cardiff and Swansea Districts (Mines and Quarries)	1906–12	Details relating to accidents, fatalities and prosecutions.	Document	SWML	
	Scrapbooks of newspaper cuttings (unlabelled green scrapbook)	1946–8	Colliery Medical Treatment Centres. Spinal Injuries treatment. Deaths underground, e.g. firedamp, gas, falls. Fatal accidents statistics. Records kept by some medical centres, including working conditions and accidents.	Document	SWML	

153

Community Health

~ 5 ~
Infectious Diseases

The causes and treatment of infectious diseases in the nineteenth century were linked to sanitary reform and the public health movement. Although transmission had been previously associated with air and water, lack of hygiene and cleanliness were gradually accepted as contributory factors: a position exemplified in Edwin Chadwick's *Report on the Sanitary Condition of the Labouring Population*, which was published in 1842. The Public Health Act of 1875 legislated for local authorities to supply water and sanitation, and gave them powers to disinfect houses and bedding after the occurrence of infectious diseases.

The development of bacteriology in the late nineteenth century, pioneered by Louis Pasteur and Robert Koch, enabled the identification of cholera, diphtheria, tetanus, tuberculosis and typhoid bacteria. Laboratories were created to identify diseases and develop treatments, and patients were isolated in specialist institutions. In 1889 the Infectious Diseases Notification Act made notification of the more important infectious diseases to local authorities compulsory in all areas. Successive Annual Reports from medical officers of health – a compulsory appointment after the Public Health Act of 1872 (see Chapter 7, 'Housing and Sanitation') – printed statistics relating to every notifiable disease, for example, smallpox, scarlet fever, diphtheria, whooping cough, typhoid, acute poliomyelitis, tuberculosis, influenza, typhus fever, chicken pox, rabies, dysentery, bronchitis, cancer and pneumonia. New notifiable diseases continually joined the list, anthrax being added in 1921 and enteric fever, enteritis and puerperal pyrexia in 1939.

Edward Jenner's 1798 discovery that vaccination with cowpox was a successful deterrent for smallpox led ultimately to legislation in 1840 that made vaccinations – administered by the Poor Law Medical Service – voluntary for infants, on the decision of their parents. By 1853, however, parents were being compelled to have their children vaccinated. The 1896 Royal Commission on Vaccination proposed the continuation of smallpox vaccination due to its success in limiting the disease. A minimum age limit of three months was set, and the procedure was to take place at home in a clean environment. The isolation of smallpox cases and immediate notification were to be used in conjunction with the vaccination programme, and parents were to be fined for non-compliance, unless they had serious objections (SWCC: HV686 R3).

Between 1890 and 1895, Emhil Behring discovered and first used a vaccination for diphtheria, and in 1920 Béla Schick developed a test for the presence of the disease (subsequently called Schick testing). However, the Ministry of Health – which took over responsibility for the Poor Law from the Local Government Board in 1919 – was slow to introduce testing to the UK, partly for financial reasons but also because of public opposition to smallpox vaccination in the nineteenth century. During the 1920s, Schick testing and immunization did take place in several institutions and schools in cities across the country, including Cardiff, but general immunization was not introduced until the 1940s (SWCC: HV686 RV; MNA/PP/16/50/2).

In 1906 Albert Cammette developed the BCG vaccination for tuberculosis, and by 1924 a vaccine for the prevention of the disease had been developed in France. However, the Ministry of Health was satisfied that the United Kingdom already had a sufficient network of public health facilities for the prevention and treatment of TB. Again, therefore, no action was taken until the 1940s when a vaccination programme began for vulnerable groups of the population, including children.

Nevertheless, tuberculosis was an ongoing health concern in the early twentieth century, which provoked a number of community as well as institutional policies (see chapter 13, 'Medical Institutions: Sanatoria'). In Wales no sanatoria were developed under the Isolation Hospitals Act of 1893, but some local education authorities did establish sanatorium schools, the Poor Law authorities maintained cases in infirmaries and sanatoria, and sanitary authorities began to treat pulmonary tuberculosis in dispensaries. However, voluntary societies contributed much to the battle, and services were run by private charities. In Wales the King Edward

VII Welsh National Memorial Association was set up in 1910 to organize a national campaign for the prevention and treatment of tuberculosis (SWCC: RC773 POW). After the 1929 Local Government Act enhanced the power of local authorities to improve public health services, they financed the association through the block grants allocated by central government. Ten years later the agency agreement between the association and Welsh local government was the subject of a report by a Ministry of Health Committee of Inquiry, which investigated the anti-tuberculosis service and asked what steps should be taken to improve the arrangements for prevention, treatment and cure. In 1947 the response to TB was transformed by the discovery of an effective antibiotic, streptomycin.

Reference Code	Collection	Dates	Description	Media	Location	DP
	Scrapbooks of newspaper cuttings (unlabelled green scrapbook)	1946–8	Newspaper cutting referring to TB.	Document	SWML	
	The Welsh Housing and Development Year Book	1925	Housing and its bearing on tuberculosis.	Document	SWML	
AUD/172	Mrs J Evans (Maerdy Community Study)	1920–c.1960	TB in family, and Maerdy in general.	Transcript of audio	SWML	Y
AUD/481	Mrs Bessie Webb and Mrs Hannah Katie Evans	1920–75	TB of family members.	Audio tape	SWML	Y
HV686.R3	Reports of the MOH, and School MO, Rhondda UDC	1914–47	Schools; statistics of diseases and defects. Infectious/zymotic diseases. Disinfection. TB. Influenza. 1916: Venereal diseases (The Public Health (Venereal Diseases) Regulations 1916). German measles (The Measles and German Measles Order, 27 Nov 1915). 1917: Typhus fever. Contagious ophthalmia. VD clinics at King Edward VII Hospital, Cardiff. 1918: Influenza epidemic of 1918. 1919: Public health (acute encephalitis lethargica and acute polio-encephalitis) Regulations 1918. Rabies (hydrophobia). Lousiness and itch. Trench fever. Public Health (pneumonia, malaria, dysentry etc.) Regulations 1919 . 1920: Acute influenza and primary pneumonia. Malaria. Dysentry. Ystrad and Ynyshir Clinics (School MO report). 1922: Crippling defects (e.g. TB and rickets). Acute poliomyelitis. Bronchitis. Anthrax (compulsorily notifiable, 1 July 1921). Erysipelas. Cancer. 1923: Smallpox outbreak, Tylorstown, June 1923. Chicken pox. 1924: Death statistics: bronchitis, organic heart disease, congenital debility, phthisis, pneumonia, cancer, cerebral haemorrhage, violence (excluding suicide). 1927: School MO report: infectious diseases,	Document	SWML	

Reference Code	Collection	Dates	Description	Media	Location	DP
			exceptional prevalence of diphtheria (Clydach Vale, Treherbert, Pentre), and scarlet fever (Porth). 1930: School MO: prevalence of smallpox in area. 1932: School MO: diphtheria outbreaks at Treorchy and Maerdy; scarlet fever at Gelli. 1939: Notifiable diseases – additions including enteric fever, enteritis. Schools; diphtheria at Clydach Vale. 1940: Diseases, and immunization against diphtheria. 1942: School MO: government evacuation scheme; emergency sick bay at Penrhys Smallpox Hospital, for contagious skin diseases. 1943: Provision of Insulin Circular 2734 Ministry of Health (1943), consent to local authorities to supply insulin to poorer inhabitants with diabetes. TB Dispensary (Welsh Memorial Association) at Porth House, Porth. VD treatment facilities at Central Homes, Pontypridd.		Archives	Y
MNA/COL/2/56	Clydach Merthyr Colliery (compensation correspondence to Manager)	1938–45	Details of medical examinations of persons seeking employment, with their health history, e.g. scarlet fever, whooping cough, anaemia, diphtheria, measles, double pneumonia, deafness and hearing tests, sight test results, condition of teeth.	Document	Archives	
MNA/COP/7/1–13	Ton Co-op Society (general and committee minutes)	1884–1927	Employees: diphtheria case.	Document	Archives	
MNA/COP/7/14–15	Ton Co-op Society (Board Meetings minutes)	1928–48	Sanitary Inspections re Treherbert smallpox epidemic 1930, staff member vaccinated.	Document	Archives	
MNA/I/16/3	Forest of Dean District Welfare Association (committee minutes)	1929–35	Applications: heart disease, rheumatoid arthritis, bronchitis, injury, cancer, tumour, diabetes, pneumonia, TB. Grant for travel to Standish House to visit children confined with TB.	Document	Archives	Y
MNA/NUM/L/10/1	Bedwas Lodge (annual, general and committee meetings minutes)	1925–33	Smallpox epidemic, Newport 1928.	Document	Archives	

Reference Code	Collection	Dates	Description	Media	Location	DP
MNA/POL/2/1	Aberdare Trades and Labour Council (annual and monthly meetings minutes)	1925–35	Smallpox Hospital. TB patients and pensions.	Document	Archives	
MNA/POL/2/2	Aberdare Trades and Labour Council (annual and monthly meetings minutes)	1935–44	Mention of 1939 Report on TB. References to council addresses relating to public health, including VD, cancer and TB.	Document	Archives	
MNA/POL/3/1 and 3	Ammanford, Llandebie and District Trades and Labour Council (annual, general and Executive Council minutes)	1931–48	(1) Outbreak of diphtheria in area. Treatment of school children at Glanamman Cottage Hospital and charge relating to adenoids. (3) County scheme for aftercare of TB patients. 1947: County services enlarged for medical treatment of TB and cancer research.	Document	Archives	
MNA/POL/6/5	Caerphilly Labour Party (Caerphilly Area Labour Party minutes)	1940–50	TB: positive milk samples; care of patients by fever nurses; cost of care; numbers of cases in hospital; aftercare of curable cases; incurable cases; Welsh National Memorial Committee using part of Caerphilly and Gelligaer Isolation Hospitals; cases increase; nurse shortage. School children's health and TB. School medical report: Scabies. Smallpox Hospital, evacuees' sick bay for contagious diseases; isolation hospital, staff wages; Port Talbot Hospital, US Army request to use part for VD cases.	Document	Archives	
MNA/POL/6/7	Caerphilly Labour Party (Bargoed Ward Labour Party minutes)	1939–42	Isolation Hospital and blood transfusion case. 1940: Scabies in district; MOH report regarding abnormal epidemic period. Decontamination squad. 1940: TB report comments; King Edward Memorial doctor's research in Denmark, on his return put in charge of X-ray dept. X-rays at Rhymney Cottage Hospital. 1940: Chester Sanatorium taken over by military authorities for soldiers with bad chests and lung problems. Discharges from army with TB, every person to be examined before joining Forces or ammunition factories. TB: aftercare, housing; examination of children.	Document	Archives	

Reference Code	Collection	Dates	Description	Media	Location	DP
MNA/POL/6/8	Caerphilly Labour Party (Gelligaer Area Labour Party minutes)	1940–9	Early treatment of cancer and TB. TB: radiological van touring county; numbers examined; examination of workers and school children; cost.	Document	Archives	
MNA/POL/14/14/1	Newport Trades and Labour Council and Labour Party (annual report and balance sheet for County Borough of Newport)	1929	Port sanitation: prevention of infectious diseases and treatment in isolation hospitals; disinfection of crews' quarters and clothes; clearing ships and warehouses of rats. Smallpox epidemic in Monmouth. TB and King Edward VII Welsh National Memorial Association.	Document	Archives	
MNA/POL/14/14/2	Newport Trades and Labour Council and Labour Party (annual report and balance sheet for County Borough of Newport)	1938	TB and Welsh National Memorial Association; hospitals, sanatoria and centres. Public health including disease prevention, vaccination, general health administration, port health, public conveniences.	Document	Archives	
MNA/POL/14/3	Newport Trades and Labour Council and Labour Party (group and Executive Committee minutes)	1944–13	Request to Ministry of Health to coordinate cancer research and treatment. TB clinic premises.	Document	Archives	
MNA/POL/24/1	Ynyshir Ward Labour Party (Rhondda Borough Trades and Labour Council and Labour Party Executive Committee minutes)	1936–8	Isolation hospital; provision of car for patients; complaint about child who was sent home too early and another child infected as result; employment conditions. Porth TB clinic complaint regarding patients' long wait.	Document	Archives	
MNA/POL/24/2	Ynyshir Ward Committee minutes	1947–51	Mass radiography of 17,000 children (11 had TB). Reference to Welsh National Memorial Association report including TB incidence among teachers. Asthma specialist treatment in area, free in special cases.	Document	Archives	

Reference Code	Collection	Dates	Description	Media	Location	DP
MNA/PP/9/17/2	H. W. Currie	1937–48	Newspaper cuttings: J. B. S. Haldane articles regarding disease and new drugs; and disease and dirt.	Document	Archives	
MNA/PP/9/6 and 8	H. W. Currie	1937–43	(6) 1937: Newspaper cuttings; stemming flu epidemics. (8) 1943: Newspaper cuttings: moral self-control and VD.	Document	Archives	
MNA/PP/12/11	Mrs Beatrice Davies (née Phippen), Ystrad Rhondda	1924	Rhondda Urban District Council election poster for Dr W. E. Thomas. Refers to water supply and related outbreaks of infectious diseases (smallpox, diphtheria, typhoid, scarlet fever)	Document	Archives	
MNA/PP/16/8	S. O. Davies	1927	1927: page (*Manchester Guardian*) reference to smallpox.	Document	Archives	
MNA/PP/16/9/1	S. O. Davies	1939	Article in *Western Mail*, 1939 – 'Tackling Economic Aspect of TB', referring to anti-tuberculosis service report. Causes of bad health (poverty, housing, nutrition).	Document	Archives	
MNA/PP/16/11/1–34	S. O. Davies	1943–8	*Parliamentary Debates* (Hansard). 17 February 43 – Written answers regarding prisoners (medical examination and treatment for VD); lost medical forms (British Army); Tuberculosis Wales (milk supply). *Parliamentary Debates* (Hansard). 17 June 48: National Assistance Regulations, uniform scale but special provision for blind and TB sufferers.	Document	Archives	
MNA/PP/16/12	S. O. Davies	1930s–1940s	Notes regarding Welsh anti-TB services; National Assistance Bill (referring to TB).	Document	Archives	
MNA/PP/16/50/2, 5 and 8	S. O. Davies	1941–6	(2) Constituency correspondence; requests for discharge from forces on medical grounds, including TB. MOH letter relating to diphtheria immunization of children. (5) 1943: Constituency correspondence; scheme for treatment for TB in Wales. (8) 1946: Constituency correspondence; detailed pensions appeal tribunal relating to TB.	Document	Archives	Y

Reference Code	Collection	Dates	Description	Media	Location	DP
MNA/PP/16/50/7/1 and 7/2	S. O. Davies	1945	(7/1) Constituency correspondence; letter from medical superintendent of Glan Ely TB hospital describing patient's state, medical certificate from TB clinic. (7/2) Constituency correspondence; 1943: speech by Medical Officer of Health to Health Committee, regarding care and aftercare of TB patients and allowances for TB patients.	Document	Archives	Y
MNA/PP/16/50/67	S. O. Davies	1940s	Notes regarding MOH information relating to growth of children, TB, diets survey.	Document	Archives	
MNA/PP/67/17	W. Eddie Jones	1932	Medical report regarding TB, Cefn Mably Institute. Surgical intervention and lack of facilities, no surgeons for chest surgery. Cancer deaths on increase.	Document	Archives	
MNA/PP/67/29 and 80	W. Eddie Jones (newspaper cutting)	1930s	(29) 1935:TB and Welsh National Memorial Association. (80) 1933: Cardiff Corporation article: grants to Edward Nichol Home (Penylan), infectious diseases, TB treatment and prevention (and Welsh National Memorial Association).	Document	Archives	
MNA/PP/87/2	Charles Parker (transcripts of interviews with miners and their wives (Banwen))	1961	Reference to interwar period, illness and disease, including TB.	Document	Archives	Y
MNA/PP/91/12	William Picton (Maerdy) (committee agenda)	c.1939	TB report for Wales and adverse effects of reduction of child nourishment allowances.	Document	Archives	
MNA/PP/115/35-37	George Thomas (Treherbert)	1932-5	1932, 1933 and 1935 election pamphlets (UDC and CC), Evan George Thomas (Communist). Refers to TB, influenza and other diseases.	Document	Archives	

Reference Code	Collection	Dates	Description	Media	Location	DP
MNA/PP/118/81/1	John Thomas (Aberavon) (C1)	1893	Borough of Aberavon, Highway Committee Minutes: MO's Monthly Report (Dr J. Arnallt Jones) including smallpox case, placards for public regarding vaccination, scarlatina and erysipelas cases, need for infectious diseases hospital and accommodation sought, zymotic death rate (scarlatina, whooping cough, diarrhoea), infant mortality, cases of scarlatina, measles, whooping cough, typhoid fever (and poor living conditions), Smallpox handbills – distribution. Fees under Infectious Disease (Notification) Act 1889. Coffin bought for smallpox case.	Document	Archives	
MNA/PP/118/95	John Thomas (Aberavon) (C15) (annual reports of MOH Aberavon)	1893–5	Precautions against infectious diseases. Isolation and disinfection. Smallpox outbreak 1893–4. Vaccination officer, Howard Beynon, visit to houses in infected districts and others, over 700 vaccinations. Smallpox case details, treatment, reference to lack of hospital or disinfector. Details relating to cases of scarlatina, measles, typhoid fever, influenza, phthisis and cancer. Birth and death rates. Zymotic diseases including smallpox, measles, scarletina, diarrhoea. Infant mortality. Infectious Diseases Notifications including smallpox, scarlet fever, membranous croup, erysipelas, typhoid fever, puerperal fever, continued fever.	Document	Archives	
MNA/PP/118/96	John Thomas (Aberavon) (C16) reports of the Inspector of Nuisances to Aberavon Town Council	1893–4	Infectious diseases; smallpox (trained nurse cared for cases), typhoid fever, scarlatina, erisipelas, membranous croup and puerperal fever.	Document	Archives	
MNA/PP/122/1	Wilfred Timbrell (Tumble) (memoirs of Tumble)	1896–c.1960s	1917: typhoid epidemic, cesspits removed, night soil removed in special carts. Method used until 1926 when flushing toilets supplied.	Document	Archives	
MNA/PP/131/9	Dr Alistair Wilson	1938	Aberdare UDC election leaflet for Alistair Wilson (Communist). Re poverty and disease, Ministry of Health Inquiry into Welsh anti-tuberculosis services.	Document	Archives	

Reference Code	Collection	Dates	Description	Media	Location	DP
MNA/PP/132/9	James Winstone (scrapbook of news cuttings and handwritten notes)	1912	School clinics, Monmouthshire's scheme established by Dr Rocyn Jones (MOH), Welsh National Memorial Association, TB, hygiene, medical inspections.	Document	Archives	
MNA/TUG/9/5	Amalgamated Engineering Union (Superannuation Benefit and Benevolent Fund book)	1920–49	Benevolent Fund: names, dates, grant amounts, illness (including heart disease, cerebral haemorrhage, bronchitis, TB, cancer, gangrenous foot, gastric ulcers, senility and dementia, pneumonia).	Document	Archives	Y
MNB/POL/6/A8	Newport Constituency Labour Party	1938–44	Executive and General Committee minutes, and Health Committee report. TB aftercare, allowances and conference.	Document	Archives	Y
MNB/PP/10/H31	S. O. Davies	1937–47	Report of Inter-departmental Committee on Rehabilitation and Resettlement of Disabled Persons 1943, including TB.	Document	Archives	
MNB/PP/12/C2/1–15	William Henry Davies (Penclawdd) (annual reports: MOH, Gower Rural Sanitary Authority)	1895-7, 1899, 1900, 1902–11	General: Population statistics, birth and death rates (e.g. cancer, heart disease, suicide, TB), zymotic diseases. 1895: Notification of Infectious Diseases Act January 1896. 1896: Scarlet fever epidemic. Diphtheria, membrous croup, enteric or typhoid fever, including drinking polluted water. 1900: Enteric (typhoid fever) case of man who drank from stream passing through farm where polluted by excreta from enteric fever patient. Diphtheria cases, anti-toxin serum used, all 5 cases did well. 1902: Typhoid fever outbreak, Durwant, water and milk supplies analysed but cause not ascertained. Sanitary improvements. Penclawwd, smallpox case, patient at Swansea Fever Hospital, relative also caught it, row of houses visited and all contacts vaccinated. 1903: new MOH. Increased death rate from severe climatic changes affecting aged and young. Bodies recovered from shipwrecks on coast. Measles prevalent and led to school closures. Swansea Isolation Hospital to receive Gower cases if room. 1906: measles epidemic, schools closure. Outbreak of impetigo, spread through Gower from school.	Document	Archives	

Reference Code	Collection	Dates	Description	Media	Location	DP
MNB/PP/56/7	Miss E. Leyshon (Swansea) (East Side District Nursing Association annual reports and accounts)	1905–40	Water analysis. Causes of death including alcoholism. Infantile mortality including whooping cough, congenital defects, atrophy, debility, marasmus, convulsions. 1907: Deaths including influenza. 1909: Measles, whooping cough, school closures. Disinfection of schools. Death of 102-year-old. 1910: TB control, MOH recommendation that it should be notifiable as 14 deaths had occurred. 1911: Epidemics of scarlet fever and diphtheria. Schools prevention of disease spread, 'Memo on closure of and exclusion from school 1909'. Phthisis; no sanatorium or hospital accommodation. Supply of disinfectants during infectious disease and fumigation afterwards. Chemical and bacterial examinations. Council arrangements with Clinical Research Association Ltd. Swansea General Hospital admittance of TB cases if enough space. (1923 missing) Case statistics including TB.	Document	Archives	
MNB/PP/72/13–14	Alistair Wilson (2 'Wellcome' medical diaries and visiting lists)	1920–8	182 printed pages of therapeutic notes. Index of diseases and treatment. Infectious diseases and notification	Document	Archives	Y
MNB/PP/72/28	Alistair Wilson	1933	Enid M. Williams MD, *The Health of Old and Retired Coalminers in South Wales*, Cardiff: University of Wales Press Board.	Document	Archives	Y
MNC/COP/1/6	Aberdare Co-operative Society (minute book)	1945–8	Employee's wife, diphtheria. Another employee's typhoid contact.	Document	Archives	Y
MNC/COP/3/3	Abersychan Co-op Society (minute book)	1924–31	1927: reference to smallpox epidemic.	Document	Archives	

Reference Code	Collection	Dates	Description	Media	Location	DP
MNC/ISTC/1/1	National Union of Blastfurnacemen, Ore Miners, Coke Workers and Kindred Trades (Annual Conference reports)	1919–25	NHI Section Accounts: list of diseases and average cases per week (including bronchitis and throat, influenza and colds, catarrh, pneumonia, pleurisy, TB, rheumatism, hernia). 1919: East Midland Report regarding December 1918 and influenza epidemic, death grants increased by 300% (heavier than war casualty years).	Document	Archives	
MNC/PP/11/1	G. James (newspaper cuttings)	c.1910–1920s	Article; Welsh National Memorial Association, Grove House Cardiff for TB hospital not bought. Glamorgan Insurance Committee meeting, doctors' treatment of TB patients.	Document	Archives	
MNC/PP/17/9	Selwyn Jones	1930s	(Merthyr Royal Commission Special, July 1935) (Merthyr Borough Sub-District of Communist Party) Health of workers' children, poverty, malnutrition, tonsils, adenoids, scarlet fever, diphtheria, infantile death rate.	Document	Archives	
RA44.T7 CHA	Socialist Medical Association (pamphlet)	1953	'Challenge of the Rhondda Fach Survey'. Reprint from *Medicine Today and Tomorrow*, January–February 1953. TB situation in a typical Welsh mining valley' – reference to report by A. L. Cochrane, J. G. Cox, and T. F. Jarman, BMJ, 18 October 1952.	Document	SWML	
RA44.T7 COM	*Tuberculosis: The White Scourge, The War and Wales* (pamphlet)	1940	(Cardiff: South Wales District Committee of the Communist Party of Great Britain, 1940). Clement Davies Inquiry 1938. TB, war and social conditions. Housing, nutrition, wartime industrial conditions, blackout, air-raid shelters, evacuation. Anti-TB services of Wales, provision of beds, Welsh National Memorial Association, Conference 1938. Shortage of nursing staff. Chepstow hutted hospital. Rehabilitation and aftercare. Pasteurization of milk. Prevention and control of TB. 13-point programme.	Document	SWML	
RA44.T7 NEW	*New Weapons Against Tuberculosis. An explanation of Mass X-ray Examination and the New Financial Allowances* (pamphlet)	1943	Prepared by Labour Research Department in collaboration with Socialist Medical Association. Mass radiography. Financial allowances to patients. Home treatment, sanatorium, institute. Prevention and health of the people. Wartime TB increase. Details relating to TB including reference to infected milk.	Document	SWML	

Reference Code	Collection	Dates	Description	Media	Location	DP
RA644.T7 PRO	*Programme of the South Wales Tuberculosis Campaign* (pamphlet)	ud	Home treatment; home helps, home nursing service, laundry, library, occupational therapy, extra nourishment, allowances or meals service, lodging allowance or rehousing. BCG inoculation of all school-leavers, miners and other adults to be considered. Banish TB from Wales. Case finding, e.g. Rhondda Fach Survey, chest clinics. Treatment facilities, hospital beds, new units. Financial arrangements, prevent hardship of patients and families. Bone TB, drinking infected milk, pasteurized milk, TB testing of herds.	Document	SWML	
RA644.T7 WAR	Socialist Medical Association (pamphlet)	1942	'The War, Tuberculosis, and the Workers'. Reprint from *Medicine Today and Tomorrow*, June 1941. Financial position of patient (food shortage), present war (food, income, wages), earlier diagnosis, financial difficulties (NHI, sanatoriums, benefits), rehabilitation.	Document	SWML	
RC773 Gre	Ministry of Health Report	1939	Report of the Committee of Inquiry into the Anti-Tuberculosis Service in Wales and Monmouthshire.	Document	SWML	
RC773 Ind	Symposium Report	1945	*Industry Tuberculosis and Compensation, A Symposium* (National Tuberculosis Association), New York, 1945).	Document	SWML	
RC773 POW	The King Edward VII Welsh National Memorial Association (for the Prevention, Treatment, and Abolition of Tuberculosis in Wales and Monmouthshire) Report (Pamphlet)	1940	Report by D. A. Powell (Principal MO) and memo by T. W. Davies (TB Officer) on *Industrial Pulmonary Fibrosis (with Special Reference to Silicosis) in Wales*. Published April 1940, Cardiff. Treatment and cost. Nature of silicosis. Pathology. Relationship between silicosis and TB. Silicosis in south Wales coalfield. Diagnosis and prognosis. Complications and sequelae. Compensation. Medical examinations and certificates. Prevention. Non-compensateable industrial fibrosis (including anthracosis).	Document	SWML	

~ 6 ~

Illness and Disability

The population of the South Wales Coalfield experienced a broad spectrum of illnesses, which ranged from bronchitis and pneumonia to heart complaints and cancer, fractures and ulcers, diabetes, depression and dementia (SWCC: MNC/ISTC/1/1; HV686.R3; MNA/I/34/G20; MNA/1/16/3; MNA/PP/16/50/2). The management of several of these ailments advanced during the first half of the twentieth century. New techniques for treating wounds and fractures, for instance, were transported from the military medicine of the First World War to the civilian medicine of the interwar period; and there were also innovations in the use of radium as a treatment for cancer and insulin as a treatment for diabetes. However, the heavy industries of the coalfield and its high level of social deprivation ensured that physical disabilities – in particular, blindness, deafness and orthopaedic conditions (SWCC: MNA/POL/14/14/2; MNC/COP/3/4; MNA/PP/67/29) – were prominent morbidities.

Throughout the period to 1948, the charitable sector played a major role in promoting services for disabled people. In 1868, for example, the National Institute for the Blind was founded, to be followed in 1911 by the National Bureau for Promoting the General Welfare of the Deaf, the forerunner of the National Institute for the Deaf. Complementing these national bodies were local organizations, set up and financially supported by individuals and groups like the Co-operative societies (SWCC: MNA/COP/7/1–13; MNC/COP/3/3) and the workmen's mutual aid schemes (SWCC: MNA/I/3/2; MNA/NUM/L/35/1). Thus, in south Wales there were local institutes for people with sensory impairments, among them the Rhondda Institute for the Blind (SWCC: MNA/NUM/3/1/1) and the Glamorgan Mission to the Deaf and Dumb (SWCC: MNC/COP/1/6).

In 1889 the Report of the Royal Commission on the Blind, the Deaf and the Dumb was published, dealing with the incidence and the conditions of the 'blind, deaf and dumb, idiots and imbeciles'. A dominant theme was education and training for work to prevent disabled people from becoming idle paupers. From a trade union perspective, the National League of the Blind began a campaign for employment rights in the 1890s. And in 1920 the Blind Persons Act finally instructed local authorities to provide work for blind and partially sighted employees. The employment of deaf people was later addressed in the 1930 Poor Law Act, although it was not obligatory that local authorities assist them in finding work. In 1935, a Ministry of Health subcommittee recommended regulations for the assessment and assistance of the unemployable blind.

Work, and hence the achievement of self-sufficiency, was equally central in the treatment and rehabilitation of physical disabled people. The Central Council for the Care of Cripples – later the Royal Association for Disability and Rehabilitation – was set up in 1919. Its aim was to create a system of orthopaedic hospitals and clinics, initially for children but subsequently for adults as well. Though the new artificial-light treatments introduced in the interwar period were used for rickets and other bone defects, rehabilitation was also pursued through workshops and through employment arranged by local groups. Labour shortages during the Second World War drew previously jobless disabled people into work. Reflecting on this experience, the Inter-departmental Committee on the Rehabilitation and Resettlement of Disabled Persons recommended that the majority of disabled workers should be employed in equal competition with the able-bodied; only a minority needed employment in a sheltered workshop, or the protection of a quota scheme that required most larger employers to recruit 3 per cent of their workforce from those registered as disabled with the Ministry of Labour. These proposals were incorporated into the 1944 Disabled Persons (Employment) Act, which fixed the parameters of policy for over thirty years.

Reference Code	Collection	Dates	Description	Media	Location	DP
	Gomer Evans (Pamphlet Box 4)	c.1920	Pamphlet for the People No. 4, *A Peep Behind the Scenes on a Board of Guardians*, by Councillor Glyde. Refers to poverty, starvation, sickness, lunacy, imbecile wards, poor food and conditions in workhouse.	Document	SWML	
	Gomer Evans (Pamphlet Box 6)	1945	*Labour Party Bulletin* No 12, Vol. IV, 1945: Reference to Register of Disabled Persons.	Document	SWML	
AUD/165	Trevor Davies	1916–c.1960	Blindness. Member of Salvation Army band in 1930s with 2 other blind men (one astagma, other weak sight). Death of brother falling on exposed electrical transformer wires near pit, severe burns, treated by neighbours with olive oil on skin, no compensation.	Transcript of audio	SWML	Y
AUD/199	Will Lake	1900–c.1973	WWI injuries: leg abscess, and medical recovery hut in Liverpool; voice loss, treatment by doctors at Brecon barracks. Sister's death from TB.	Transcript of audio	SWML	Y
AUD/222	Dick Cook	c.1910–1974	Blindness of father. Disabled brother. Illness as child (TB). 1925: Anthracite Strike, injuries received from police.	Transcript of audio	SWML	Y
AUD/342	Mrs Nancy Davies (Seven Sisters)	1920s–1940s	Refers to girl who stayed at home to nurse sick mother.	Transcript of audio	SWML	Y
AUD/462	Mrs Thomas	c.1910–c.1950	Rheumatic fever.	Audio tape	SWML	
HD6661.TRA	TUC Annual Reports of Proceedings (incomplete set)	1904–15	1924: Pensions for blind and National League of Blind.	Document	SWML	
HD9552.3 MIN	*The Miner*, Vol. I, No. 2	Nov 1944	Articles: 'Social Insurance Plan (Part I)', sickness benefits, invalidity, medical and hospital treatment.	Document	SWML	

Reference Code	Collection	Dates	Description	Media	Location	DP
HD9552.3 MIN	*The Miner*, Vol. I, No. 9/10	June/July 1945	Article: 'Welfare Activities in Mining Communities, South Wales Coalfield', St John Ambulance, rehabilitation, Blind Institutes.	Document	SWML	
HD9552.3 MIN	*The Miner*, Vol. II, No. 12	Oct 1946	Articles: 'Factories in South Wales for Disabled Persons'; Disabled Persons' Employment Act, numbers of disabled people, training centres, workers and jobs at other establishments, sheltered employment. 'Training and Employment of Severely Disabled Persons under Special Conditions', re Section 15 of Disabled Persons (Employment) Act 1944.	Document	SWML	
HD9552.3 MIN	*The Miner*, Vol. III, No. 3	Jan 1947	Tables for Disabled Persons (Employment) Act (1946 figs), and Government Vocational and Disabled Training Schemes 1946.	Document	SWML	
HV686.R3	Reports of the MOH, and School MO, Rhondda UDC	1914–47	1922: Acute poliomyelitis. Bronchitis. Anthrax (compulsorily notifiable, 1 July 1921). Erysipelas. Cancer. 1924: Death statistics: bronchitis, organic heart disease, congenital debility, phthisis, pneumonia, cancer, cerebral haemorrhage, violence (excluding suicide), 1930: District Coroners' death statistics (including colliery accidents, suicide, heart disease, burns or scalds, run over or knocked down by motor vehicles). 1943: Provision of Insulin Circular 2734 Ministry of Health (1943), consent to local authorities to supply insulin to poorer inhabitants with diabetes. TB Dispensary (Welsh Memorial Association) Porth House, Porth. VD treatment facilities at Central Homes, Pontypridd. 1945: Rheumatism Clinic, Carnegie Welfare Centre. 1946: Paratyphoid fever. 1947: Rheumatism Clinic report by MO in charge. Anthrax, unconfirmed notification of patient at Isolation Hospital.	Document	SWML	

Reference Code	Collection	Dates	Description	Media	Location	DP
MNA/COL/2/56	Clydach Merthyr Colliery (compensation correspondence to Manager)	1938–45	Details of medical examinations of persons seeking employment with health history, e.g. scarlet fever, whooping cough, anaemia, diphtheria, measles, double pneumonia, deafness and hearing tests, sight test results, condition of teeth.	Document	Archives	Y
MNA/COP/2/1–11	Ammanford Co-op Society (general and committee Meetings minutes)	1900–38	Donations to health-related charities e.g. National Institute for the Blind.	Document	Archives	
MNA/COP/3/2	Briton Ferry and Neath Co-op Society (balance sheets and committee reports)	1919–24	Accounts including Health Insurance payments and claims, and health-related donations e.g. Deaf and Dumb Institute.	Document	Archives	
MNA/COP/7/1–13	Ton Co-op Society (general and committee minutes)	1884–1927	Employees: sickness; diphtheria case. Donations: National Institute of the Blind, Glamorgan Mission to the Deaf and Dumb, Rhondda Institute for the Blind.	Document	Archives	
MNA/COP/7/14–15	Ton Co-op Society (Board Meetings minutes)	1928–48	Health-related subscriptions; Glamorgan Mission to Deaf and Dumb, National League for Blind, Rhondda Institute for the Blind, Llanelly Medical Aid. Rheumatic case to Droitwich or Bath. National League of Blind request to Glamorgan County Council to provide welfare for the blind. 1920: Blind Persons Act, reference to local authorities having to erect and maintain workshops for the blind and provide for the unemployed blind. Petition placed in all Co-op branches, 1934.	Document	Archives	
MNA/COP/7/18	Ton Co-op Society (quarterly and half-yearly meetings minutes)	1918–47	Reference to Beveridge Report and lack of disability benefits.	Document	Archives	
MNA/COP/7/57	Ton Co-op Society (general administration book)	ud	Index book; convalescent applications; sickness records; subscription list (including charities).	Document	Archives	
MNA/COP/7/70	Ton Co-op Society (press cuttings book)	1928–36	Refers to employee's illness and wages. Photograph of personal weighing machine c.1929.	Document	Archives	

Reference Code	Collection	Dates	Description	Media	Location	DP
MNA/I/19/C3	Lily of the Valley Lodge of the Unity of Oddfellows, Ystrad Rhondda (health certificates)	1899–1950	1899: 2 doctors' certificates re unable to work (no illness details). 1930: 8 doctors' certificates including 3 from Mid-Rhondda Medical Aid Society, some have illness details.	Document	Archives	Y
MNA/I/2/1–7	Abertridwr Institute (minute books)	1927–39	Refers to Health and Unemployment Insurance contributions. Donation to Pontypridd Institute for the Blind.	Document	Archives	
MNA/I/3/2	Ammanford and District Miners' Welfare Association (Finance Committee minutes)	1945–7	Doctor's notes (two) for member unable to attend work, including asthma. Collection for Swansea Blind Institute. Compensation payment to staff member. Cinema use granted to Blind Committee.	Document	Archives	Y
MNA/I/16/3	Forest of Dean District Welfare Association (committee minutes)	1929–35	Applications: neurasthenia, sciatica, artificial eye, silicosis, gastric ulcer, spectacles. Cost of invalid chair. Assistance of hospitals re expenditure on cases attending for treatment. Home help whilst wife in mental hospital. Applications: heart disease, rheumatoid arthritis, bronchitis, injury, cancer, tumour, diabetes, pneumonia, hearing aid, artificial teeth, hernia, dental treatment, truss, artificial limbs, appendicitis, TB, nervous breakdown, septic poisoning.	Document	Archives	Y
MNA/I/34/G1	St David's Unity of Ivorites (Bud of Hope Lodge)	1892	Two 1892 sick notes for Treherbert resident suffering from rheumatism.	Document	Archives	
MNA/I/34/G18 and G23	St David's Unity of Ivorites (Bud of Hope Lodge)	c.1870s–1929	Lists of society members either died or sick, and payments 1870s/1880s. Annual returns re Sick and Funeral Fund (Friendly Societies Acts 1896 to 1929), in English and Welsh.	Document	Archives	

Reference Code	Collection	Dates	Description	Media	Location	DP
MNA/I/34/G20	St David's Unity of Ivorites (Bud of Hope Lodge)	1860–99	17 Doctors' certificates (1882–99), Treherbert, including name, date, address, illnesses (including rheumatism, abscess, fracture, catarrh). Letter from member relating to sickness and that in care of local doctor. Sick notes (including bronchitis and kidney problem), certificates, claims (1860–99). (English and Welsh)	Document	Archives	
MNA/I/34/R5	The Glais Friendly Society (correspondence re sick benefit claims)	1814–77	Handwritten notes from members – claims for sick relief and funeral benefits. Also several death certificates, and certificates from Bath Mineral Water Hospital confirming admittance of members as patients. Signatures on notes including local doctors and church ministers.	Document	Archives	
MNA/I/34/R6	The Glais Friendly Society (correspondence re sick benefit claims)	1814–77	Handwritten notes from members – claims for sick relief and funeral benefits. One example re 'asthmatic complaint'.	Document	Archives	
MNA/NUM/3/1/1	Minutes of the SWMF Exec Council, and annual and special conferences	1907–40	Blindness: National League for the Blind, National Institute of the Blind, Pontypridd Institute for the Blind, Swansea Institute for the Blind, Rhondda Institute for the Blind, blinded soldiers (1918).	Document	Archives and SWML	
MNA/NUM/3/3/2	Correspondence (bound volume of circulars)	1916–27	1918: letter regarding Blinded Soldiers' Children Fund, to assist blind men to get married.	Document	Archives	
MNA/NUM/3/3/24/6	Bargoed Housecoal Lodge (Correspondence with lodges)	1937–40	1940: correspondence relating to compensation claim for muscular rheumatism. 1937: correspondence relating to deaf boy, SWMF Secretary (area no. 6) recommended him to Cymric Press for work (print works).	Document	Archives	Y

Reference Code	Collection	Dates	Description	Media	Location	DP
MNA/NUM/3/5/14	SWMF: Compensation Records (Compensation Secretary's correspondence)	1938	Public Health Department Cardiff, booklet; Cardiff Municipal Accident Service (talk to Cardiff Medical Society); fracture clinic, rehabilitation of disabled workmen.	Document	Archives	Y
MNA/NUM/3/8/17 (H)	Area No. 2 correspondence re Pneumoconiosis, (district, area and combine records)	1930s	Three-page story of Cardiff medical student with rheumatoid arthritis, and treatment at mineral water baths at Royal National Hospital for Rheumatic Diseases, Bath.	Document	Archives	Y
MNA/NUM/L/10/1	Bedwas Lodge (annual, general and committee meetings minutes)	1925-33	Smallpox epidemic, Newport 1928. Institute of the Blind.	Document	Archives	
MNA/NUM/L/10/3	Bedwas Lodge (annual, general and committee meetings minutes)	1940-2	Donations: National League of the Blind.	Document	Archives	
MNA/NUM/L/3/16	Abergorki Lodge (Lodge Secretary's correspondence book)	1930-1	Mental illness case, Pontypridd Homes and Bridgend Institute.	Document	Archives	Y
MNA/NUM/L/3/7	Abergorki Lodge (Lodge Secretary's correspondence book)	1917-18	Complaint regarding treatment of men at medical examinations by military authorities, kept waiting long periods whilst undressed. Call-up of member and ill health. Exemption requests from military service on grounds of ill health of families, or being sole provider. Blind Institute contribution.	Document	Archives	
MNA/NUM/L/32/1	Emlyn Lodge (lodge account book)	1937-51	Payments to Blind Account (Blind Institute).	Document	Archives	
MNA/NUM/L/34/1 and 6	Fforchaman Lodge (annual, general and committee minutes)	1938-49	Blind Welfare Committee references.	Document	Archives	Y
MNA/NUM/L/35/1	Fochriw No. 1 and Nantwen lodges (minute books)	1917-34	Swansea Blind Institute donations and National Institute for Blind South Wales (Cardiff). £1,000 donation to blind soldiers fund by district. Nantwen Lodge 1925 on, Local Blind Institute, delegates and conference, and collections.	Document	Archives	

Cwmfelinfach Miners Rat-catching, 1916

RULES FOR NURSES.

1. The services of the Nurses are for cases of the sick poor and working classes in their own homes. Patients are not excluded who, though unable to incur the expense of a private Nurse, are able to make some contribution to the fund of the local Association.

2. All applications for the services of the Nurse should be made in writing, stating the nature of the case.

3. The Nurse should be responsible to the local Committee, keeping register of patients, etc., and reporting regularly upon her work.

4. The Nurse shall work under the medical men, and shall apply to them at once in cases of difficulty. When she has anything to communicate to them she shall do it in writing, and it is hoped that the medical men will also do this, so as to avoid leaving verbal messages with patients or their friends.

5. The Nurse shall not attend cases of scarlet fever, small pox, or typhus, unless in emergency, and then only with the sanction of the medical men, and if due provision can be made for the nursing of her other cases.

6. The Nurse shall not act as midwife, but may attend cases after child-birth, where skilled nursing is considered necessary by the medical man in attendance.

7. The Nurse shall be on duty eight hours daily—this time to be extended only under exceptional circumstances. On Sunday she shall only attend cases needing special or immediate attention.

8. The Nurse shall only be employed on night duty under exceptional circumstances, when due provision can be made for the efficient nursing of other cases under her charge.

9. The Nurse, when on duty, shall wear the uniform dress and no ornaments. She will be entitled to a month's holiday in the year, and a half-day off duty at least every three weeks.

10. The Nurse must be punctual in going to, and returning from, her district, entering the time at which she returns in the time-book provided.

11. The Nurse is strictly forbidden to interfere in any way with the religious opinions of the patients, or of the members of their families.

12. The Nurse shall be responsible for the personal cleanliness of patients. She shall endeavour to improve their general surroundings, and when the relations of the patient can be taught how to keep the room in nursing order, they shall be encouraged to do so.

13. The Nurses shall be responsible for all appliances, clothing, etc., lent by the local Association to her patients, and must see that they are returned in good condition.

14. The Nurse must not accept presents of any kind from patients, or friends of patients. She should encourage them, when able, to give a small donation to the funds of the Association.

15. The Nurse is not allowed, unless in cases of extreme necessity, to give nourishment or other relief. She shall report at the weekly meeting any case of urgent necessity.

16. The Nurse should arrange to be in her rooms from 3 to 4 o'clock p.m. on one or more fixed days weekly.

17. When private donations are received to assist a special case, the patient must be informed that this help comes from a private source, and not from the Association. All such donations will be acknowledged in the Annual Report.

18. In cases of necessity arising outside the district, the medical man attending shall (if the Nurse's other cases admit of it) have power to send the Nurse to such cases, the expense of conveyance being provided.

East Side District Nursing Association: Report, 1910

Hill's Plymouth Collieries: No. 2 Rescue Brigade, 1914

MAY DAY, 1939

All Workmen in the Amman Valley are invited to celebrate May-Day this year in a way entirely different from that of the past.

A PAGEANT is to be staged to depict the enormous struggle we are conducting against Unemployment, Inadequate Pensions, and the terrible disease which affects Miners and known as Silicosis.

All Collieries from the Emlyn, at the lower end, to Ynys, G.C.G. and Cwmgorse, in the upper end, are called upon to take part in this affair.

The Miners will present the struggle for (a) the inclusion of this disease for which Compensation is paid, and the provision of measures for the prevention of the disease.

The period which the Pageant will depict is from 1934 to the present 1939. In view of the huge number of cases which we have recorded during that period, it is necessary that a few thousands of our men shall play their part in the Pageant.

In order to make it successful, each Colliery Lodge is asked to find the complement of men required for that purpose. It is intended to show—

(a) The number of Applicants for Certificates for that period ... 1100
(b) The number of Certificates granted for Partial Disablement ... 240
(c) The number of Certificates granted for Total Disablement ... 350
(d) The number of Certificates granted in case of Death 130
(e) The number of Cases in which Certificates have been refused ... 370

Each Section will be shown in the Pageant by the men wearing berets or caps of a different colour, and the whole procession will be arranged in such a way as will give a complete picture of our fight against this malicious disease.

The Bands of the Valley will take part in the Pageant, and the Procession will carry many Banners to indicate the different phases of the struggle.

On this day it is hoped that the Workers of the Valley will give a "picture" of their struggles during the last few years.

The Organising Committee makes a most earnest appeal to all Workers to join in a mighty effort to make May-Day a Workers' Day in the real sense.

On behalf of the Committee,

Coun. D. R. OWEN (Chairman).
Coun. E. PHILLIPS (Secretary).

Silicosis Pageant: May Day, 1939

THE BOARD OF CONCILIATION FOR THE COAL TRADE OF MONMOUTHSHIRE AND SOUTH WALES.

INSTITUTE OF ENGINEERS,
PARK PLACE,
CARDIFF.

Reference   *6th May*, 1941.
Secretarial
No. 13,819.

INCREASED FOOD SUPPLIES FOR COLLIERY WORKPEOPLE.

JOINT MEMORANDUM

TO

COLLIERY COMPANIES AND
COLLIERY WORKMEN'S REPRESENTATIVES.

DEAR SIRS,

The Owners' and Workmen's Representatives on the Conciliation Board have given serious consideration to the question of the means of distribution of certain increased food supplies to be made available for colliery workmen at the Collieries, and have decided that the Joint Pit Committees should be instructed to view this matter as part of their duties.

It is understood that the Ministry of Food have decided to increase the cheese ration through the normal suppliers in respect of workmen employed underground and application has been made to have this concession extended to workmen employed on the surface.

The Ministry of Food have decided that a special additional supply of meat shall be provided for colliery workmen on condition that it is consumed at the colliery by the workmen. The quantity of meat to be so supplied is to the value of 1½d. per person per day.

The Joint Pit Committee is recommended by the Owners' and Workmen's Representatives to consider ways and means of ensuring the proper distribution of these supplies.

It is suggested that the distribution should be in the form of meat pies, meat and vegetable pies, rissoles, or sausage rolls, or

Morlais Colliery: Memorandum regarding 'Increased food supplies for Colliery Workpeople', 1941

SAFETY IN MINES RESEARCH BOARD

AN

EXHIBITION

OF

PROGRESS AND RESEARCH

IN

MINE SAFETY

WILL BE HELD AT

THE UNIVERSITY COLLEGE

SINGLETON PARK

SWANSEA

by the consent of the College Authorities
on
AUGUST 12th, 13th, 15th, and 16th.

The Exhibition will be open on each afternoon and evening.

SPECIAL LECTURES each evening at 7 p.m.

Friday 12th. "The Physical Properties of Coal Measure Strata,"
by. D. W. Phillips,B.Sc.
Saturday 13th. "Roof Control on Advancing Longwalls,"
by L. J. Barraclough,B.Sc.
Monday 15th. "Firedamp Explosions," by C. S. W. Grice.

Tuesday 16th "Explosives' by C. S. W. Grice.

The exhibition will deal with Coal and Coal Dust Explosions, Firedamp,
Flameproof Electrical Apparatus, Support of Workings, Haulage,
Explosives, and Mine Lighting.
Admission Free.

Morlais Colliery: Safety in Mines Exhibition, 1936

Mountain Ash and Penrhiwceiber General Hospital.

Mountain Ash and Penrhiwceiber Hospital: *Annual Report*, 1924

Mountain Ash and Penrhiwceiber General Hospital

S E R V I C E

1 9 2 4 - 1 9 3 8

Building Fund Debt:

£2,191   2s.   2d.

WILL YOU HELP

To Clear this Debt on the New Out-Patient Dept. and Nurses' Home?

Notable Facts

SERVICE DURING FOURTEEN YEARS:

In-Patients	...	...	...	9,176
Out-Patients	...	...	...	21,063
School Children Patients for 1 day		...		2,871
Total		...		33,110

Will you pause and reflect for one moment what these figures mean? The Hospital deserves your help, and we implore you to give it.

Mountain Ash and Penrhiwceiber Hospital: *Annual Report*, 1938

Neath Soup Kitchen Committee during the General Strike, 1926

PROGRAMME

OF THE

SOUTH WALES
TUBERCULOSIS
CAMPAIGN

BANISH TUBERCULOSIS FROM WALES.

About 3,500 fresh cases of Lung Tuberculosis are discovered each year in Wales, and are notified as needing medical care. While death rates have been falling, they still remain higher than in England. We have the opportunity now to realise a dream of earlier generations—to rid Wales of Tuberculosis. Cholera, Typhoid, Smallpox have all now been banished. It is the turn of Tuberculosis.

What must be done?

CASE FINDING.

Tuberculosis is an infectious disease. If we are to eradicate it, all existing cases must be sought out and treated. This is necessary in the interests alike of the sufferer and the community he may infect.

To judge by the Rhondda Fach Survey, there may be as many as 25,000 cases of Lung Tuberculosis needing treatment in Wales at this moment. That is one in every 100 of the population. Half of these are probably able to infect others, and the other half may become so at any moment, unless they are discovered and treated in time.

For every two cases of infectious Tuberculosis already known, there is probably an additional one whose presence in our midst is unknown. That was the conclusion of the Rhondda Fach Survey, and even this covered only 90 per cent. of the populations of the valley.

South Wales Tuberculosis Campaign: Front Cover, undated

A67616997

Ton Co-operative Society: Weighing Scales, 1929

Reference Code	Collection	Dates	Description	Media	Location	DP
MNA/NUM/L/39/1 and 2	Gellyceidrim Lodge (lodge account book)	1923-44	Donations to Swansea and South Wales Institute for the Blind.	Document	Archives	
MNA/NUM/L/39/5	Gellyceidrim Lodge (Lodge Sick Fund account book with ambulance accounts)	1938-44	Rules of Colliery Workmen's Fund including sickness and benefits, and contributions to Swansea General and Eye Hospital. Personal details, complaint (e.g. flu, gastritis, rheumatism, bronchitis, lumbago, abscess), dates away, and amount paid.	Document	Archives	Y
MNA/NUM/L/43/A8	Graig Merthyr Lodge (general and committee minutes)	1948	Factories for disabled, pressure to have factories built, Tumble and Ponthenry factories to take 50% men and women. Under new scheme, Insurance certified men to continue work unless have TB. Blind Institute references, anxious that contributions continue until government takes over, otherwise a number of blind workers to be laid off.	Document	Archives	Y
MNA/NUM/L/50/33	Maerdy Lodge (Lodge Secretary's correspondence and papers)	c.1920	Lodge ballot paper for vote on contributions to Rhondda Institute for the Blind.	Document	Archives	
MNA/NUM/L/62/A3	Park and Dare Lodge (minute book for annual, general and committee meetings; also special and colliery workers meetings and subscribers to Pentwyn Cottage Hospital, 1943)	1941-3	Institute for Blind delegates. Donation for disabled man's wheelchair.	Document	Archives	
MNA/NUM/L/89	Abercynon Lodge (explanatory leaflet on the work of the Cardiff and District Hospital Society)	1942	Cases where responsibility not accepted, e.g. TB, mental cases, Infectious Diseases, Incurable.	Document	Archives	
MNA/NUM/L/9/2	Bargoed Housecoal Lodge (account book)	1941-50	Expenditure relating to Blind Institute.	Document	Archives	

Reference Code	Collection	Dates	Description	Media	Location	DP
MNA/POL/1/2	Aberdare Town Ward Labour Party (committee minutes)	1943–52	District Psychologist and Child Guidance clinic. Health Committee. Visit to Bridgend Blind School. Factory for blind – move from Pontypridd to Treforrest.	Document	Archives	
MNA/POL/13/1	Neath Rural District Labour Party (minute book)	1935–40	Glamorgan Federation of Labour Parties Conference 1936, reference to blind appeal and march to London. Refers to Anti-TB Service in Wales report.	Document	Archives	
MNA/POL/13/5	Neath Rural District Labour Party (area conference reports)	1935–40	1936: Treatments; orthopaedic, dental, eye, ENT. Hospital cases.	Document	Archives	
MNA/POL/14/2 and 3	Newport Trades and Labour Council and Labour Party (group and Executive Committee minutes)	1914–18	(2) 1914–18: References to pensions for disabled soldiers. (3) 1944–53: Request to Ministry of Health to coordinate cancer research and treatment. TB clinic premises. National Blood Transfusion Service speaker.	Document	Archives	
MNA/POL/14/14/1	Newport Trades and Labour Council and Labour Party (annual report and balance sheet for County Borough of Newport)	1929	Smallpox epidemic in Monmouthshire. TB and King Edward VII Welsh National Memorial Association. Blind welfare and workshops.	Document	Archives	
MNA/POL/14/14/2	Newport Trades and Labour Council and Labour Party (annual report and balance sheet for County Borough of Newport)	1938	Welfare of blind: registration; education and training; workshops; home employment and teaching; social welfare; grant. Woolaston House Institute and Infirmary. Cost of Poor Relief for people in hospital. Outdoor relief costs including medical services. Mental deficiency and Crindau Occupation Centre.	Document	Archives	
MNA/POL/15/1	New Tredegar Trades and Labour Council (Trades and Labour Council minutes)	1938–51	1947: County council report references to work done for the blind.	Document	Archives	

Reference Code	Collection	Dates	Description	Media	Location	DP
MNA/POL/2/1	Aberdare Trades and Labour Council (annual and monthly meetings minutes)	1925–35	ASLEF lecture: teeth and health. Industrial Health Society. Local Blind Aid Committee. National League of the Blind. Blind Persons Act 1920. Blind workshops.	Document	Archives	
MNA/POL/2/10	Aberdare Trades and Labour Council (balance sheets with annual reports)	1907–62	1942: references to affiliation fees including Aberdare National League of the Blind, and expenditure including 'Starving children fund'.	Document	Archives	
MNA/POL/2/2	Aberdare Trades and Labour Council (annual and monthly meetings minutes)	1935–44	PAC medical attention. Soldiers' dependants' free medical service. Council addresses relating to public health, including VD, cancer and TB. Blind pensions, medical examinations. Pontypridd; District Blind Inst, and workshops for the blind. National League of the Blind. Blind League. South Wales League of the Blind. Aberdare Blind Welfare Association.	Document	Archives	
MNA/POL/2/3	Aberdare Trades and Labour Council (annual and monthly meetings minutes)	1944–52	Soldiers' pay if in hospital. Pontypridd Institute for Blind. National Institute of Blind and Aberdare Blind Institute.	Document	Archives	
MNA/POL/2/7	Aberdare Trades and Labour Council (Executive Committee minutes)	1941–51	Disabled miners' Committee relating to light industries. Disabled Persons Employment Act.	Document	Archives	
MNA/POL/24/2	Ynyshir Ward Labour Party (committee minutes)	1947–51	Public institutions: rent payments (Social Welfare Committee); pension books taken from inmates; cases of women in Institute including starvation and death of husband, and request for payment whilst a patient. Transport for Rheumatic clinic. Increased allowances to blind.	Document	Archives	

181

Reference Code	Collection	Dates	Description	Media	Location	DP
MNA/POL/3/3	Ammanford, Llandebie and District Trades and Labour Council (annual, general and Executive Council minutes)	1941–8	1944: Carmarthen MOH, Dr Lloyd, lecture on VD. Reference to Blind Persons Act. County scheme for aftercare of TB patients. 1947: County services enlarged for medical treatment of TB, and cancer research. Disabled Persons Act and registration of disabled workers.	Document	Archives	
MNA/POL/3/3/1	Ammanford, Llandebie and District Trades and Labour Council (annual, general and Executive Council minutes)	1938–41	1941: campaign for establishment of light industries in area for injured workers. 1940: TUC resolutions regarding blind allowance and cost of living. Refers to National League of the Blind, and Blind Committee of Trades Council.	Document	Archives	
MNA/POL/6/1	Caerphilly Labour Party (Executive Committee minutes)	1938–41	Blind Institute and administration of blind welfare.	Document	Archives	
MNA/POL/6/7	Caerphilly Labour Party (Bargoed Ward Labour Party minutes)	1939–42	PAC, work relating to artificial limbs and dental treatment. League of Blind; 1920 Act regarding workshops, work and training. Ambulances. Isolation Hospital – blood transfusion case. 1940: Scabies in district; MOH report regarding abnormal epidemic period. Decontamination squad.	Document	Archives	
MNA/POL/6/8	Caerphilly Labour Party (Gelligaer Area Labour Party minutes)	1940–9	Mental health: patient numbers; clinics; voluntary treatment. Cancer and TB early treatment. TB: radiological van touring county; numbers examined; examination of workers and school children; cost.	Document	Archives	
MNA/PP/9/6	H. W. Currie	1937	Newspaper cuttings; control of patent medicines; stemming flu epidemics; clinics for mental and nervous diseases; psychology.	Document	Archives	
MNA/PP/9/17/2	H. W. Currie	1937–48	Newspaper cuttings; J. B. S. Haldane articles re disease and new drugs; disease and dirt; diagnosing deafness.	Document	Archives	
MNA/PP/16/2	S. O. Davies	1948–1951	Letter to Prime Minister relating to disabled workers, Remploy factories, numbers of Unemployed Registered Disabled Persons.	Document	Archives	

Reference Code	Collection	Dates	Description	Media	Location	DP
MNA/PP/16/11/1–34	S. O. Davies	1944–8	*Parliamentary Debates* (Hansard). 17 October 44 – Written answers relating to the British Army; vaccinations, sickness (hospital cases). *Parliamentary Debates* (Hansard). 17 June 48 – National Assistance Regulations, uniform scale but special provision for blind and TB sufferers. Written answers relating to NHS; hearing aids, medical services (NI contributions).	Document	Archives	
MNA/PP/16/12	S. O. Davies	c.1930s–1940	Notes on Welsh anti-TB services; National Assistance Bill (reference to blind, TB, handicapped, elderly, infirm, disabled); Disablement Employment Act; refers to 1943 report Committee on the Rehabilitation and Resettlement of Disabled Persons.	Document	Archives	
MNA/PP/16/50/10	S. O. Davies	1948	Constituency correspondence; war pensions, disablement and discharge; TB pension; Ministry of Supply Depot closure, impact on disabled workforce.	Document	Archives	Y
MNA/PP/16/50/10	S. O. Davies	1948	Constituency correspondence; clothing allowance re false limb; working party for services for blind; hearing aids; Sandbrook House Rheumatic School (Merthyr).	Document	Archives	Y
MNA/PP/16/50/2	S. O. Davies	1941–2	1941: requests for discharge from forces for illness, e.g. TB, skin disease, rheumatoid arthritis, neurasthenia, blindness. 1942: requests for discharge from forces on medical grounds (e.g. TB, arthritis, weak heart, nervous breakdown) or for dependants' need.	Document	Archives	Y
MNA/PP/16/50/5	S. O. Davies	1943	Constituency correspondence; neurasthenia of workers; nervous breakdown of soldier; psychiatric examination of gunner; seaman's will, father in mental hospital. Discharges from forces with hyper-pituitarism and epilepsy; serviceman unable to afford clothing for son going to TB sanatorium; scheme for	Document	Archives	Y

183

Reference Code	Collection	Dates	Description	Media	Location	DP
			treatment of TB in Wales; disability pensions. Constituency correspondence; requests for discharge from forces on medical grounds or families sick (many detailed).			
MNA/PP/16/50/6	S. O. Davies	1944	Constituency correspondence; request to leave ROF due to illness (family died of TB and meningitis). Disability and war service pensions – bronchitis, eczema, psychoneurosis; recall and discharge from forces – sick families; soldier's death from meningitis; mental and physical state of soldier on service in India.	Document	Archives	Y
MNA/PP/16/50/7/1 and 2	S. O.Davies	1945	File 1: Constituency correspondence; requests for discharge and leave from forces due to illness or family sickness (detailed); doctors' certificates; pension claims for dependants of servicemen, disabled and sick war veterans (both world wars); medical certificate from TB clinic. File 2: Constituency correspondence; requests for discharge and leave from forces re illness or family sickness (detailed); doctors' certificates; pension claims; servicemen at Pentsam TB Sanatorium; notice of soldier's death.	Document	Archives	Y
MNA/PP/16/50/8	S. O. Davies	1946	Constituency correspondence; detailed pensions appeal tribunal relating to TB; Ministry of Pensions notes on war pensions and disablement, hospitals and clinics, allowances. Requests for discharge and leave from forces due to illness or family sickness (detailed). Request for Merthyr welfare and workshop centre for blind.	Document	Archives	Y

Reference Code	Collection	Dates	Description	Media	Location	DP
MNA/PP/16/50/9	S. O. Davies	1947	Constituency correspondence; Sandbrook Rheumatic Hospital School (minutes extracts); removal of patient from Glamorgan County Mental Hospital; clothing allowance for person with artificial limb. Requests for discharge and leave from forces due to illness or family sickness (detailed); pensions claims (both world wars).	Document	Archives	Y
MNA/PP/16/59	S. O. Davies	1962-3	Correspondence relating to closure of Remploy factory at Merthyr (orthopaedic footwear). Letters from local hospitals and people. Majority of employees disabled – concerns about redundancies.	Document	Archives	
MNA/PP/16/86	S. O. Davies	c.1948-58	NHS supply, prescriptions, fitting for surgical appliances and artificial limbs. Also mentions invalid chairs and clothing coupons.	Document	Archives	
MNA/PP/21/6	D. Evans	1919-43	1919: National League for the Blind affiliated to Trade Council. 1920: braille literature in Free Library.	Document	Archives	
MNA/PP/28/51	James Evans (Tumble)	1952	NUM (SW) Executive Committee minutes – National League of the Blind,	Document	Archives	
MNA/PP/30/3	Sonia Evans (Porth)	1925	Unionist Labour Party election leaflet for Pontypridd Board of Guardians; refers to aged and disabled.	Document	Archives	
MNA/PP/5/6	Jesse Clark	1940s–1960s	Undated letter about cold remedies, addressed to newspaper. Undated copied notes relating to genetic inheritance.	Document	Archives	
MNA/PP/50/3	W. R. James (Trelewis) (Taff Merthyr Lodge minute book)	1946-52	Collection for National League for Blind. Training of disabled persons.	Document	Archives	
MNA/PP/54/5 and 6	Hubert Jenkins (office diary)	1919-24	Vaccination exemptions. Meetings attended regarding 'mental defectives' at Bridgend Asylum and Caerphilly Hospital.	Document	Archives	

Reference Code	Collection	Dates	Description	Media	Location	DP
MNA/PP/67/17	W. Eddie Jones	1932	Speech transcript: Means Test and two suicides 1932. Medical report re TB, Cefn Mably Institute. Surgical intervention and lack of facilities, no surgeons for chest surgery. Cancer deaths on the increase.	Document	Archives	
MNA/PP/67/18	W. Eddie Jones	1932	Monmouthshire County Marchers Council speaker's notes, 'The effect of our Demands upon Rates'. Public Assistance; relief, mental patients, drugs, appliances. Cost of Poor Relief including Institutional Relief, persons in mental hospitals, domiciliary relief. Public Assistance Institutions cost per inmate; Cambrian House (Caerleon), Coed y Gric (Pontypool), Hatherleigh Place (Abergavenny), Hill House (Monmouth), Ty-Bryn (Tredegar).	Document	Archives	
MNA/PP/67/25	W. Eddie Jones	1935	1935: statement by man sent by Pontypool Labour Exchange to Shobden Hardening Centre. Harsh conditions, contracted muscular rheumatism and under doctor's treatment for five weeks. Trainees unable to afford medical services there.	Document	Archives	
MNA/PP/67/29	W. Eddie Jones (newspaper cutting)	1935	Reference to eye clinic examinations and eye problems. Nose and throat conditions. Ear diseases. Deformities. Heart conditions. Rheumatism. TB and Welsh National Memorial Association. Royal National Orthopaedic Hospital, Dr Arthur Rocyn Jones, Consultant orthopaedic surgeon saw cases at Newport clinic.	Document	Archives	

Reference Code	Collection	Dates	Description	Media	Location	DP
MNA/PP/67/80	W. Eddie Jones (newspaper cuttings)	c.1930s	1933: *Cardiff Corporation* article: vaccination, orthopaedic treatment, nose and throat treatment, spectacles, grants to voluntary institutions. 1933: *Cardiff Corporation* article: grants to Edward Nichol Home (Penylan), Salvation Army Home, Blind Institute, infectious diseases, TB treatment and prevention (and Welsh National Memorial Association), Diseases of Animals Acts. Articles relating to suicide of man forced to apply for Public Assistance Relief, Pontrewynydd – undernourished, depressed and suffering from neuritis and bronchitis.	Document	Archives	
MNA/PP/98/18	Gwilym Richards	ud	*The Disabled Person's Charter* pamphlet by G. Richards. Refers to disablement benefit.	Document	Archives	
MNA/PP/113/9	Emlyn Thomas (Maerdy) (SWMF Mardy Lodge, statement of accounts)	1920	Charity and Distress Funds including Deaf and Dumb Institute (Swansea), National League of Blind and Rhondda Blind Institution.	Document	Archives	
MNA/PP/118/95	John Thomas (Aberavon) (C15) (annual reports of MOH Aberavon)	1893–5	Smallpox case details, treatment, reference to lack of hospital or disinfector. Details: scarlatina, measles, typhoid fever, influenza, phthisis, cancer.	Document	Archives	
MNA/TUG/10/1	Amalgamated Society of Engineers (minute book)	1917–22	Government Training Scheme for disabled sailors and soldiers.	Document	Archives	
MNA/TUG/5/1	South Wales and Monmouthshire Enginemen, Stokers, and Craftsmen's Association (quarterly report of the Association)	1906	TUC delegate's report refers to Helping the Blind (League of Blind).	Document	Archives	

Reference Code	Collection	Dates	Description	Media	Location	DP
MNA/TUG/7/1/B/70	Iron and Steel Trades Confederation (general office correspondence files and papers)	1945	DAC Memo No. 5, 'Quota and Designated Employment Schemes 1944'. 'Disabled Persons (Employment) Act 1944, Registration' (1945 pamphlet from Ministry of Labour and National Service).	Document	Archives	
MNA/TUG/7/1/B/70	Iron and Steel Trades Confederation (general office correspondence files and papers)	1945	Disablement Advisory Committees – required under Disabled Persons (Employment) Act 1944. Copy of Act, Memo (No. 23) for Disablement Advisory Committees, DAC Memo No. 2, 'Applications for Entry of Name in (or Removal of Names from) Register of Disabled Persons 1944'.	Document	Archives	
MNA/TUG/9/5	Amalgamated Engineering Union (Superannuation Benefit and Benevolent Fund Book)	1920–49	Benevolent Fund: names, dates, grant amounts, illness (including heart disease, cerebral haemorrhage, bronchitis, TB, cancer, gangrenous foot, gastric ulcers, senility and dementia, pneumonia, and lost in action during wartime).	Document	Archives	Y
MNB/NUM/L/1/1	Abercynon Lodge (minute book)	1939–41	Pontypridd Institute for the Blind donations, and nominations to Board. Support re municipalization of blind workshops, payment of trade union wages to blind workers, increased allowances to dependants, and abolition of Means Test (via delegate to Pontypridd Institute for the Blind). Pontypridd Institute for Deaf, collection. Red Cross Fund donations.	Document	Archives	
MNB/NUM/L/1/21	Abercynon Lodge (wage sheets)	1940	Deductions for Institute for Blind.	Document	Archives	
MNB/NUM/L/1/24	Abercynon Lodge (news sheet issued by Joint Committee of Action for South Wales)	1936	The New Starvation Rates. UAB and National Government Law – New Regulations and Scales. Refers to blind people, those in receipt of sick pay from Friendly Societies, NHI Benefit and Disability Pension.	Document	Archives	

Reference Code	Collection	Dates	Description	Media	Location	DP
MNB/POL/1/12	Ammanford Trades and Labour Council (balance sheet and annual report)	1948	Radiologists' visit with mobile X-ray unit (Welsh National Memorial Hospital). Part-disabled workers and road schemes.	Document	Archives	
MNB/POL/2/2	Bridgend Trades Council (minute book)	1945–52	National League of Blind donation. Blood donors scheme.	Document	Archives	
MNB/POL/6/A1	Newport Constituency Labour Party (minutes of Labour Representational Committee and annual executive and general committees of Newport Labour Party)	1918–21	Election leaflets references to Health, Blind Welfare and Act, open air schools for children with Phthisis. League of Blind and Parliamentary Bill re financial provisions, also conference relating to Welfare of Blind Act 1920.	Document	Archives	
MNB/POL/6/A6	Newport Constituency Labour Party (Executive and General Committee minutes)	1930–3	National League of Blind appeal. Blind Persons Committee, pensions for blind and unemployment.	Document	Archives	
MNB/POL/6/A8	Newport Constituency Labour Party (Executive and General Committee minutes, and Health Committee report)	1938–44	TB aftercare, allowances, conference. Appeal for pillows for military hospitals. Disablement Allowances conference. First aid posts and ambulances. Blind subcommittee and donations to blind. Reference to post-war reconstruction of Wales's medical services and Beveridge Report.	Document	Archives	Y
MNB/POL/6/A30	Newport Constituency Labour Party (miscellaneous letters and papers)	1918–76	1948: copy Parliamentary Questions 137/3/48, Question to Minister of Labour regarding disabled ex-servicemen in Newport and work in new factory. Reply about disabled unemployed in area.	Document	Archives	
MNB/POL/7/5	South Wales District, Communist Party of Great Britain (miscellaneous political handbills)	1942–8	Part of handbill 'Vote for Communist Candidates' (Maerdy Lodge) – reference to Rheumatic Clinic (had been proposed by Communist), Glyncorrel.	Document	Archives	

189

Reference Code	Collection	Dates	Description	Media	Location	DP
MNB/PP/10/H31	S. O. Davies	1937–47	Copies: Disabled Persons (Employment) Act 1944. Summary of Provisions of National Assistance Bill 1947. National Assistance Bill Financial Memorandum 1947 (termination of existing Poor Law, provision for disabled). Report of Inter-departmental Committee on Rehabilitation and Resettlement of Disabled Persons 1943 (references to TB, orthopaedics, medical rehabilitation, Emergency Hospital Scheme, cardiac cases, blind, deaf, neuroses/psychoses, industrial diseases, artificial limbs, and disabled).	Document	Archives	
MNB/PP/12/C2/1–15	William Henry Davies (Penclawdd) (annual reports: MOH, Gower Rural Sanitary Authority)	1895–7, 1899, 1900, 1902–11	General: Population statistics, birth and death rates (e.g. cancer, heart disease, suicide, TB), zymotic diseases. 1908: Damp weather cause of sheep 'fluke', farmers lost many sheep. Reference to no losses from glanders, anthrax, hydrophobia. Deaths including meningitis, diabetes, senile decay.	Document	Archives	
MNB/PP/20/M2	Glyn Evans (Garnant)	1937	Circular from National League of the Blind 1937, to London and Home Counties District Council. Reference to conditions of the blind, workers and workshop employees, home workers and unemployable. Refers to Labour Party publication, *The Blind Persons Charter* relating to blind welfare policy.	Document	Archives	
MNB/PP/72/28	Alistair Wilson (book)	1933	Contents: physical condition, cardiac condition, blood picture, X-ray examination, TB and pneumoconiosis. Appendix with case details.	Document	Archives	Y
MNC/COP/1/1	Aberdare Co-operative Society (minute book)	1929–32	Donations: St Dunstan's Institute for the Blind.	Document	Archives	
MNC/COP/1/3	Aberdare Co-operative Society (minute book)	1937–40	Donations: Aberdare Blind Welfare.	Document	Archives	

Reference Code	Collection	Dates	Description	Media	Location	DP
MNC/COP/1/6	Aberdare Co-operative Society (minute book)	1945–8	Employee's wife, diphtheria. Employee's typhoid contact. Employment of disabled. Donations: Aberdare Blind Institute, Abercwmboi Nursing Association, Glamorgan Mission to Deaf and Dumb.	Document	Archives	Y
MNC/COP/13/1	Mid-Rhondda Co-op Society (minute book)	1920–6	Donations: St Dunstan's Home for the Blind, Deaf and Dumb Institute, and National League of the Blind (refused).	Document	Archives	
MNC/COP/13/3	Mid-Rhondda Co-op Society (minute book)	1946–54	Donations to Blind Institution, and room granted for their use.	Document	Archives	
MNC/COP/15/2	Penarth Co-op Society (minute book)	1937–9	Donations: Swansea Blind, Cardiff Royal Infirmary, Western Section Convalescent Fund, Deaf and Dumb Missions Appeal.	Document	Archives	
MNC/COP/27/1	*People's Yearbooks* (Annual of the Co-operative Wholesale Society Ltd)	1920	Labour legislation 1919, including employment and training of disabled men. National Scheme for Employment of Disabled Ex-Service Men, CWS statistics.	Document	Archives	
MNC/COP/27/14	*People's Yearbooks* (Annual of the Co-operative Wholesale Society Ltd)	1933	Advertisements: Co-operative Health Insurance Section benefits (including dental, convalescence, ophthalmic and glasses, maternity); Royal Albert Institute, Lancaster; 'A Training Home for the Feeble-Minded'. Photograph of 'Women's League of Health and Beauty'.	Document	Archives	
MNC/COP/3/1	Abersychan Co-op Society (minute book)	1908–12	Donations: Royal Institute for the Deaf and Dumb (Derby), Cardiff Institute for the Blind. Reference to Cardiff Poor Cripples Aid Society.	Document	Archives	
MNC/COP/3/3	Abersychan Co-op Society (minute book)	1924–31	Donations: Cardiff and National Institute for the Blind, Royal Institute for the Deaf and Dumb, Glamorgan and Monmouthshire Mission for the Adult Deaf and Dumb. Newport and Monmouthshire Blind Aid Society subscription.	Document	Archives	

191

Reference Code	Collection	Dates	Description	Media	Location	DP
MNC/COP/3/4	Abersychan Co-op Society (minute book)	1945-9	Donations: Glamorgan and Monmouthshire Mission for Adult Deaf and Dumb, Royal Institute for Deaf and Dumb. Disablement Advisory Committee of Co-op (re Disabled Persons (Employment) Act 1945). Spectacles complaint.	Document	Archives	
MNC/COP/9/1	Cardiff Co-op Retail Society (minute book)	1933-4	Donations: National League of the Blind, Cardiff Institute for the Blind.	Document	Archives	
MNC/ISTC/1/1 and 4/1	National Union of Blastfurnacemen, Ore Miners, Coke Workers and Kindred Trades (Annual Conference reports)	1919-25	(1/1) 1919–25: NHI Section Accounts (sick, disabled), list diseases and average cases per week (including accidents, bronchitis and throat, influenza, colds, catarrh, pneumonia, pleurisy, TB, rheumatism, hernia). (4/1) 1938–41: 1941 grants to League of the Blind.	Document	Archives	
PHO/DIS/33	Coal mining dispute photographs (disputes of 1921)	c.1921	Photograph of painting by Andrew Turner depicting 1921 Miners' Dispute. Images of miners and railwaymen. Three banners, including '1921 Cripple Alliance – Loganea Branch'.	Photographs	Archives	

~ 7 ~
Housing and Sanitation

In south Wales, many communities were established or expanded around existing sites to service the coal industry. While some were close to collieries and other industrial bases, others were in more remote rural areas. General sanitation was poor where these developments were away from mains drainage, sewerage and water supplies, and, even if rural properties had their own natural water source, this was easily contaminated (SWCC: MNA/PP/118/95–6; MNB/PP/12/C/2/1–15). The style of housing varied according to the local geography. In the eastern and central areas of the coalfield, terraced housing predominated due to the steep valley sides and hence the limited space for building. In the western area, semi-detached housing was more common due to the flatter terrain. Much accommodation was rented, which encouraged potential landlords to construct and buy more housing. However, overcrowding became a problem as the local workforce increased, and as families rented rooms to lodgers to supplement their income.

The nineteenth century saw the introduction of significant legislation to tackle the public health problems associated with industrialization. Following largely permissive legislation in 1848, the Public Health Act of 1872 created local sanitary authorities and made the appointment of a medical officer of health (MOH) obligatory. In 1875 a basic sanitary code was established under the direction of the medical officer of health, which included the control of building design and standards through by-laws, and the supply and quality of domestic water supplies. Three years later an amendment enabled local sanitary authorities to purchase water rights and charge consumers, while the Local Government Act of 1888 made local authorities responsible for the health services managed by the MOH. The 1936 Public Health Act consolidated the law in relation to sanitation, drainage, water supply and infectious diseases.

Early twentieth-century Wales was the subject of several public health investigations. Between 1901 and 1916, for example, a series of reports were produced by the Royal Commission on Sewage Disposal, which looked at the processes for the disposal and purification of waste, the protection of waterways from pollution and the effects of discharge into the sea. In 1921, a Ministry of Health committee undertook a *South Wales Regional Survey* '[t]o enquire and report upon the special circumstances affecting the distribution and location of the houses to be erected with State aid in the Region of the coalfields of South Wales . . .' One of the five headings was 'economy in the provision of water supply, sewerage and other services'. The committee reported that '[s]anitation provision was poor and sometimes altogether absent', and recommended that a Regional Water Supply Board should be set up, 'trunk sewers from the valleys with sea outfalls . . . encouraged', and '[a]menities such as baths . . . the control and levelling of dumps and the cessation of river pollution . . . provided for'.

Throughout the late nineteenth and early twentieth centuries, housing projects in south Wales were undertaken by private investors, colliery companies, coal owners, local authorities, and philanthropic organizations such as the Welsh Garden Cities Company. Building clubs also allowed potential owner-occupiers to become collective shareholders in building developments (SWCC: MNA/PP/81/48). The 1909 Housing and Town Planning Act further promoted the construction of local authority housing, which subsequently benefited from government financial assistance. Under the Housing and Town Planning Act of 1919, housing requirements were assessed by local authorities and plans drawn up for subsequent provision, with the Ministry of Health overseeing any work that was undertaken. The Housing (Additional Powers) Act of the same year involved Ministry of Health plans for five house types, called 'Addison Houses'. These 'Addison' Acts, and the associated cash incentives, came to an end in 1921. The 1923 'Chamberlain' Act inaugurated subsidies for housing that was certified by local authorities as meeting set criteria. It also allowed for local authorities to receive financial help from the government to build their own housing, if this was a preferable alternative to private initiatives. The 1924 'Wheatley' Act likewise granted subsidies to approved local authority and private housing schemes. These provisions were discontinued by an Act of 1933, which ended subsidies for all schemes except those agreed by the Ministry of Health before the end of the year.

Between 1919 and 1930, slum clearance and rehousing schemes got underway, although their impact was limited and problems with accommodation remained (SWCC: AUD/221; MNA/PP/12/2; MNC/COP/27). The 1930 'Greenwood' Act subsidized local authorities to demolish and clear away properties that were considered unfit for human habitation or a major health risk. Anyone whose home had been demolished was entitled to rehousing, which facilitated the provision of council housing. Over-crowding was tackled under the 1935 Housing Act, when local authorities were required to survey their districts and acknowledge where areas needed redevelopment (SWCC: MNA/POL/2/1–2). Councils were also given broader capacities to combine their previous housing subsidies and vary property rents accordingly. The 1936 Housing Act consolidated previous legislation, while in 1938 subsidy scales for all new schemes were standardized and an Overcrowding Act established more financial support for local authority slum clearance. During the Second World War, extensive bomb damage was sustained in Cardiff and Swansea. This offered post-war opportunities for building and redevelopment in both cities.

Reference Code	Collection	Dates	Description	Media	Location	DP
	Gomer Evans (Pamphlet Box 4)	c.1920	Pamphlet for the People No. 4, *A Peep Behind the Scenes on a Board of Guardians*, by Councillor Glyde. References to poverty, starvation, sickness, lunacy, imbecile wards, poor food and conditions in workhouse.	Document	SWML	
	Gomer Evans (Pamphlet Box 6)	1945	*Labour Party Bulletin*, No 12, Vol. IV, 1945: Emergency housing, spare rooms, cooking facilities; housing.	Document	SWML	
	The Welsh Housing and Development Year Book	1916–17	The housing problem in Wales. Municipalities and housing reform. Cottage-building after the War. Town planning in the Welsh Valleys. The cost of slums. The regeneration of rural Wales. Bad housing and disease. The improvement of colliery districts.	Document	SWML	
	The Welsh Housing and Development Year Book	1918–19	1918: A Ministry of Health. Housing problems from the standpoint of a woman. 1919: The regional treatment of housing and development problems in Wales. House planning from a woman's point of view.	Document	SWML	
	The Welsh Housing and Development Year Book	1920–2	1920: The housing problem in Wales. A Water Board for Wales. 1921: Pithead baths. Smoke abatement. 1922: Fuel economy and smoke abatement. The prevention of smoke pollution. The recommendations of the Smoke Abatement Committee.	Document	SWML	
	The Welsh Housing and Development Year Book	1925	Housing in its bearing on tuberculosis. Smoke abatement. A congested Welsh Valley (re the housing shortage in Rhondda UDC).	Document	SWML	
	The Welsh Housing and Development Year Book	1926	The Public Health Act, 1925, as it affects Public Health administration. Dietary studies: their importance and significance. Miners' Welfare Work in the South Wales Coalfield. Housing in colliery districts.	Document	SWML	

Reference Code	Collection	Dates	Description	Media	Location	DP
AUD/173	David John Davies	1900–c.1973	Describes a large family living in a small house.	Transcript of audio	SWML	Y
AUD/193 and 194	Will Picton	1910–c.1973	Description of home life, lodgers, housing interiors, sand on stone floors.	Transcript of audio	SWML	Y
AUD/192	Mr and Mrs Fred Morris (Maerdy)	1900–c.1973	Miners bathing at home, details of preparation and washing.	Transcript of Audio	SWML	Y
AUD/221	Jim Evans	1910–c.1972	Rhymney valley; river black (coal dust/sewerage), no fish or trees. Houses in Tirphil infested with beetles, unable to destroy with traps or powder. Welsh slum houses, and women's housework.	Transcript of audio	SWML	Y
AUD/301	Jim Minton	1882–c.1973	Rat infestation in house.	Transcript of audio	SWML	Y
AUD/316	Mr Oliver Powell (Tredegar)	1900–c.1973	Poor state of council houses (cockroaches).	Transcript of Audio	SWML	Y
AUD/481	Mrs Bessie Webb and Mrs Hannah Katie Evans	1920–75	Miners bathing at home.	Audio tape	SWML	Y
AUD/488	Mrs. Exon	1910–75	Bathing and cleaning the house.	Audio tape	SWML	Y
HD9550 EBB	The Ebbw Vale Works Magazine, Vol. 10, No. 40	Oct 1931	Article: 'Ebbw Vale'; water supply; houses; Local Board of Health drainage scheme; reservoir (C19th).	Document	SWML	
HV686.R3	Reports of the MOH, and School MO, Rhondda UDC	1914–47	Housing. Water supply, sewerage, drainage, river pollution. 1920: Statistics relating to housing conditions.	Document	SWML	
MNA/COP/7/19	Ton Co-op Society (General Purposes Committee minutes)	1921–33	House repairs for Co-op rental properties.	Document	Archives	
MNA/I/7/A1-2	Bodwigiad Club Records (minute book and club accounts)	1875–1925	Tenants' housing repairs.	Document	Archives	

Reference Code	Collection	Dates	Description	Media	Location	DP
MNA/NUM/1/1	Records of the Miners' Federation of Great Britain (minute books of Executive Committee, and annual and special conferences)	1921–24	Housing conditions and needs.	Document	Archives and SWML	
MNA/NUM/1/1–2	Records of the Miners' Federation of Great Britain/NUM (minute books of MFGB/NUM Executive Committee, and annual and special conferences)	1902–48	General themes: Housing, miners' houses, evictions.	Document	Archives and SWML	
MNA/NUM/3/1/1	Minutes of the SWMF Executive Council, and annual and special conferences	1907–40	Reference to housing.	Document	Archives and SWML	
MNA/NUM/3/3/1	Correspondence (bound volume of circulars)	1899–1915	Conference Agenda 1911, including reference to housing.	Document	Archives	
MNA/NUM/3/3/2	Correspondence (bound volume of circulars)	1916–27	1918: conference references including housing, 1920: Labour Party Resolutions Annual Conference: housing. Women's Labour Section meet re cost of living, price comparisons, 1920. Report of Coal Industry Commission including pithead baths and housing.	Document	Archives	
MNA/NUM/L/35/1	Fochriw No. 1 and Nantwen Lodges (minute books)	1917–34	Reference to 1920 Housing Scheme.	Document	Archives	
MNA/NUM/L/43/A8	Graig Merthyr Lodge (general and committee minutes)	1948	Housing and pithead baths, pressing for both projects.	Document	Archives	Y
MNA/NUM/L/43/C44	Graig Merthyr Lodge (Lodge Secretary's correspondence and papers)	1946–77	1948: letter from House of Commons – David Grenfell, relating to housing and facilities to bath and dry clothes (for miners).	Document	Archives	

Reference Code	Collection	Dates	Description	Media	Location	DP
MNA/NUM/L/59/109	Oakdale Navigation Lodge (Lodge Secretary's correspondence and papers)	1923–47	Miscellaneous printed material, including Welsh Housing and Development Association pamphlet and circulars.	Document	Archives	
MNA/POL/2/1 and 2	Aberdare Trades and Labour Council (annual and monthly meeting minutes)	1925–35	1925–1935: Rent Acts; property conditions, facilities, Sanitary Inspector's certificate. Slum Clearance Act. 1935–1944: Council addresses regarding public health. Council's housing campaign and Overcrowding Act.	Document	Archives	
MNA/POL/2/3 and 7	Aberdare Trades and Labour Council (annual, monthly, and Executive Committee minutes)	1941–52	Ministry of Health and house prices.	Document	Archives	
MNA/POL/3/3 and 3/3/1	Ammanford, Llandebie and District Trades and Labour Council (annual, general and Executive Council minutes)	1941–48	(3/3) References to post-war housing standards, and reconstruction of sewerage and water schemes. Council house size increases, Ammanford. Points system relating to council houses; condemned houses, overcrowding, medical grounds (TB). Refuse collection. (3/3/1) House overcrowding and applications for council houses. Complaints re lack of water supply.	Document	Archives	
MNA/POL/5	Bedling Independent Labour Party, press cuttings (in account book)	1934–36	*The Western Mail* ; 1935 article 'Spending £100,000 for Health and Work in the Rhondda', references to drainage, sewerage, water supplies, 1933 typhoid outbreak.	Document	Archives	
MNA/POL/6/5	Caerphilly Labour Party (minutes)	1940–50	Sanitary Inspector. Rat infestation. Refuse collections. Public and individual baths for residents. Poor living conditions in old houses, Nantgarw. Water supplies and sewers. Housing. Public conveniences.	Document	Archives	
MNA/POL/6/6	Caerphilly Labour Party (Women's Section minutes)	1934–53	Women's Housing Advisory Group (and other references to housing).	Document	Archives	

Reference Code	Collection	Dates	Description	Media	Location	DP
MNA/POL/6/7	Caerphilly Labour Party (Bargoed Ward Labour Party minutes)	1939–42	TB and housing.	Document	Archives	
MNA/POL/6/8	Caerphilly Labour Party (Gelligaer Area Labour Party minutes)	1940–9	Housing allocations.	Document	Archives	
MNA/POL/13/5	Neath Rural District Labour Party (Area Conference reports)	1935–40	1935: Housing. Housing Committee's work from 1919. Deputation to Ministry of Health re 'terrible' housing conditions in area, and subsequent sanction to erect more houses.	Document	Archives	
MNA/POL/14/1 and 2	Newport Trades and Labour Council and Labour Party (annual report and balance sheet for County Borough of Newport)	1929–38	1929: Housing. Refuse collection and disposal. Sewers. Port sanitation: disinfection of crews' quarters and clothes; clearing ships and warehouses of rats. 1938: Housing, replacement, relief of overcrowding. Refuse collection and disposal. Sewers. Public health including public conveniences.	Document	Archives	
MNA/POL/15/1	New Tredegar Trades and Labour Council (Trades and Labour Council minutes)	1938–51	References to water supply and shortages in area. Street refuse collection. House repairs and grants from Welsh Board of Health.	Document	Archives	
MNA/POL/24/1	Ynyshir Ward Labour Party (Rhondda Borough Trades and Labour Council and Labour Party Executive Committee minutes)	1936–8	Provision of public conveniences. Housing; infestation with rats and cockroaches; repairs and improvements; ash collections.	Document	Archives	
MNA/POL/24/2	Ynyshir Ward Labour Party (Ynyshir Ward Committee minutes)	1947–51	Sanitary conditions in area. 'Bad' housing. Tips opened. Refuse and salvage collection.	Document	Archives	
MNA/PP/12/2, 5 and 11	Mrs Beatrice Davies (née Phippen), Ystrad Rhondda	1908–12	Rhondda UDC election leaflets for W. M. Phippen. Refers to slums and housing problems in Rhondda, Housing of Working Classes Act. (11) 1924: Rhondda UDC election poster for	Document	Archives	

Reference Code	Collection	Dates	Description	Media	Location	DP
MNA/PP/15/8	John Davies (Gwaun Cae Gurwen)	1952	Dr W. E. Thomas, referring to Public Health and Housing Acts, water supply and related outbreaks of infectious diseases (smallpox, diphtheria, typhoid, scarlet fever).	Document	Archives	
MNA/PP/16/2	S. O. Davies	1948–51	Letter to Prime Minister regarding unemployment, disabled workers, Remploy factories, housing, removal of industrial debris and tips, reafforestation of valleys, numbers of Unemployed Registered Disabled Persons.	Document	Archives	
MNA/PP/16/3/1	S. O.Davies	1934	Merthyr Tydfil by-election leaflet. Reference to housing conditions and poverty.	Document	Archives	
MNA/PP/16/5	S. O. Davies	1934	Election newspaper. References to poverty, Poor Law, housing and social amenities.	Document	Archives	
MNA/PP/16/9/1	S. O. Davies	1922–39	1922: Poster 'Labour's Call to the People', references to housing, slums, and health. Article in *Western Mail*, 1939: 'Tackling Economic Aspect of TB', reference to anti-tuberculosis service report and causes of bad health including poverty and housing.	Document	Archives	
MNA/PP/16/11/1–34	S. O. Davies	1944–8	*Parliamentary Debates* (Hansard). 24 November 48: Welsh Affairs reference to disabled, housing, mining accidents.	Document	Archives	
MNA/PP/16/40	S. O. Davies	1943	Labour Party preliminary document, South Wales Regional Council of Labour. Reference to housing and public health.	Document	Archives	
MNA/PP/16/50/2	S. O. Davies	1941	Constituency correspondence: complaints relating to workers' lodging conditions.	Document	Archives	Y
MNA/PP/16/50/10	S. O. Davies	1948	Constituency correspondence: house overcrowding.	Document	Archives	Y

Reference Code	Collection	Dates	Description	Media	Location	DP
MNA/PP/21/6	D. Evans	1943	Pontypridd Trades Council and Labour Party pamphlet, referring to housing, open spaces, water supply, sanitation and public lavatories.	Document	Archives	
MNA/PP/24/13	Edgar Evans (Bedlinog)	1948	Election leaflet, Bedwas and Machen UDC, Communist; referring to housing and improving welfare facilities for people including swimming baths.	Document	Archives	
MNA/PP/30/3, 4 and 5	Sonia Evans (Porth)	1925	(3) Unionist Labour Party election leaflet for Pontypridd Board of Guardians, refers to housing, the aged, and disabled. (4) Labour Party election leaflet for Pontypridd Board of Guardians, refers to housing. (5) Independent candidate (Jack Davies – chemist) election leaflet for Rhondda UDC, refers to health and housing.	Document	Archives	
MNA/PP/46/33/2	Arthur Horner (election handbill)	1933	'Mainwaring's Election Special' election handbill for W. H. Mainwaring (Labour). Refers to Labour Party and housing.	Document	Archives	
MNA/PP/46/54	Arthur Horner (*Colliery Workers' Magazine* (SWMF))	1924	*Colliery Workers' Magazine*, Vol. II, No. 10; The Workers' Charter (including housing). Labour Councillor's Diary (health of miners' families).	Document	Archives	
MNA/PP/46/66	Arthur Horner (report of Annual Convention of American Federation of Labour)	1945	Report of 64th Annual Convention 1944: refers to health and housing.	Document	Archives	
MNA/PP/50/3	W. R. James (Trelewis) (Taff Merthyr Lodge minute book)	1946–52	Refers to bad condition of housing.	Document	Archives	
MNA/PP/54/1	Hubert Jenkins (election address of Hubert Jenkins, Labour candidate in Caerphilly UDC election)	1911	References: water, gas and electric supplies; street improvements; refuse bins; enforcement of new Housing and Town Planning Act and improvement in public health.	Document	Archives	
MNA/PP/54/5 and 6	Hubert Jenkins (office diary)	1919–24	County Public Health and Housing Committee.	Document	Archives	

Reference Code	Collection	Dates	Description	Media	Location	DP
MNA/PP/67/15, 16 and 20	W. Eddie Jones	c.1930s	(15) Speech transcript referring to bad housing conditions of workers, primitive sanitary and sewerage conditions (open sewers, no flushing tanks), road schemes, hospitals, schools, drainage, delays by local authorities. (16) MOH Abercarn: house repairs declined, overcrowding. (20) Speakers' notes on work schemes. The new government's Housing Bill: slum clearance, housing shortage. Public health. Sanitary Inspector's report for Abersychan, 1933.	Document	Archives	
MNA/PP/67/34, 37 and 80	W. Eddie Jones	1938	(34) 1938: *Cardiff Vanguard* newsletter (Cardiff Communist Party). Reference to housing in Cardiff; poor conditions, overcrowding, Sanitary Inspector, insufficient number of houses, and high rents. (37) 1934: Abersychan UDC Election leaflet, Communist (Reg Jones and W. Eddie Jones). Refers to housing – unsanitary, unfit, and effect on health. (80) 1933: Cardiff Corporation newspaper article: Sanitary services, mortuary and disinfection station. Housing.	Document	Archives	
MNA/PP/81/1	Abel Morgan (minute book)	1946–8	Committee members, reference to public health. Shortage of materials for house repairs. Non-continuance of payment to Sanitary Inspectors under Rat Infestation Order 1943. 1947: refers to building of aluminium houses, and inspection of sites. Allotments Committee. 1948: Housing, and need for more traditional family houses.	Document	Archives	
MNA/PP/81/48	Abel Morgan	ud	The Housing Reform Building Co. (Cardiff), *Proposals for Building at Ynysybwl* (pamphlet). Formation of Ynysybwl Co-operative Garden Village Ltd, registered under the Industrial and Provident Societies Act. Society the legal owner of the houses, but members could purchase permanent occupation. Include bathrooms and hot and cold water.	Document	Archives	

203

Reference Code	Collection	Dates	Description	Media	Location	DP
MNA/PP/91/30/2 and 3	William Picton (Maerdy)	1946	Election leaflet and address for William Picton, referring to housing supply and repairs.	Document	Archives	
MNA/PP/98/1 and 2	Gwilym Richards	1913–20	Newspaper cuttings: Re 1913 Annual report of Chief Medical Officer of Government Board, Dr Newsholme, and extension of public health services which led to decline in infant mortality; refers to housing conditions, and fresh air (*Labour Leader*, 31 July 1913).	Document	Archives	
MNA/PP/111/1	Bryn Thomas ('Llandybie Over the Ages')	Early 1900s	Water collected from well. Extreme poverty. Few homes with baths or water-flushed toilets.	Document	Archives	
MNA/PP/115/35–37	George Thomas (Treherbert)	1932–5	1932, 1933 and 1935: election pamphlets (UDC and CC), Evan George Thomas (Communist). References to living conditions, poor housing.	Document	Archives	
MNA/PP/118/50	John Thomas (Aberavon) (*The Ironworkers' Journal*)	1900	*The Ironworkers' Journal*, June 1900: reference to 'Housing of the Working Classes'.	Document	Archives	
MNA/PP/118/52	John Thomas (Aberavon), Ness Edwards, *The Industrial Revolution in South Wales*	1924	Social conditions, women and children, housing (poor housing), drainage and cleansing, water supplies, health effects.	Document	Archives	
MNA/PP/118/81/1	John Thomas (Aberavon) (C1)	1893	Borough of Aberavon, Highway Committee Minutes: MOH's Annual Report including sanitary work relating to sewers, housing, privies built and repaired, general nuisances. Appointment of same Medical Officer for Aberavon Urban Sanitary District. County Medical Officer's report regarding drainage, sewers, poor housing, disinfection and isolation, cleaning of streets, inspection of district for sanitary purposes, adoption of Clauses I and II of Housing of the Working Classes Act 1890.	Document	Archives	

Reference Code	Collection	Dates	Description	Media	Location	DP
MNA/PP/118/95	John Thomas (Aberavon), (C15) annual reports of MOH Aberavon	1893-5	Inspection of houses and schools, ashpits and privies, refuse and manure deposits, drainage of houses, pigsties, precautions against infectious diseases. MOH – J. Arnallt Jones. Details of overcrowding and poor housing. Water supply, sewerage, drainage, river pollution. Lodging houses. Housing of working classes.	Document	Archives	
MNA/PP/118/96	John Thomas (Aberavon) (C16) (reports of the Inspector of Nuisances to Aberavon Town Council)	1893-4	Dwelling houses and schools; defects, unsanitary, poor ventilation, water closets, overcrowding, unfit for human habitation. Ashpits and privies. Lodging houses; drains. Pigsties. Deposit of refuse and manure. Drainage, sewers, river pollution. House drainage, defective water closets and drains. Water supply. General nuisances.	Document	Archives	
MNA/PP/118/104 and 105	John Thomas (Aberavon) (D2) and (D3)	c.1900-5	(D2) Election handbill, Mr J Littlejohn (Labour) Swansea District. Refers to poor housing, conditions. (D3) ILP Annual Conference Report 1905, reference to minimum space for dwelling houses.	Document	Archives	
MNA/PP/122/1	Wilfred Timbrell (Tumble), memoirs of Tumble	1896–c.1960s	Pigsties in gardens. Building Society formed to help buy houses for colliery workers, subsidized by colliery.	Document	Archives	
MNA/PP/131/9	Dr Alistair Wilson	1938	Aberdare UDC Election leaflet for Alistair Wilson (Communist). References to poverty, disease, poor living conditions and housing.	Document	Archives	
MNA/PP/132/8	James Winstone	1916	'Miners and the Housing Question', regarding The Welsh Housing Yearbook 1916 and article. Reference to overcrowding, discomfort, unsanitary conditions and lack of amenities.	Document	Archives	
MNA/PP/132/9	James Winstone (scrapbook of news cuttings and handwritten notes)	1912	South Wales and Monmouthshire News, reference to children, and health and mortality. Eastern Valleys Sewerage, Joint Sewage Disposal Board. The Cottage Famine, shortage of housing for workers, disease and bad housing, slum clearance. Miners and	Document	Archives	

205

Reference Code	Collection	Dates	Description	Media	Location	DP
			Housing Reform, poor housing and health, child deaths. Miners' International Congress, reference to poor housing in south Wales.			
MNB/COL/17/C7D	Morlais Colliery (South Wales District Control Board circulars)	1930-46	Letter to 'Owners of Collieries producing Anthracite or Dry-Steam Coals', details of 'Good Heating for Every Home Exhibition', London, March 1946 – held by Solid Smokeless Fuels Federation.	Document	Archives	
MNB/POL/6/A1	Newport Constituency Labour Party	1918-21	Minutes of Labour Representational Committee and annual executive and general committees of Newport Labour Party. Election leaflets referring to health, housing, water. Housing problem and health.	Document	Archives	
MNB/POL/6/A8	Newport Constituency Labour Party (Executive and General Committee minutes, and Health Committee report)	1938-44	Council conference including housing. Sanitary and health requirements. 1938: Conference report including housing.	Document	Archives	Y
MNB/PP/12/C/2/1-15	William Henry Davies (Penclawdd), (annual reports: MOH, Gower Rural Sanitary Authority (incomplete))	1895-1948	1895: Workhouse at Penmaen deaths. Drains, emptying of slops. Drinking water. Poor water supplies in districts. Water from open wells, new pipes, summer shortage, polluted stream at Blackpill. Notification of Infectious Diseases Act with effect from January 1896. Recommended code of by-laws regarding new buildings. 1903: water supplies and sewage disposal. Disinfection, fumigation, washing walls. Reports to council regarding housing and water. 1911: Housing, Rivers and streams. 1948: notes, longstanding need for Sewerage Inquiry, Gower MOH complained of sanitary arrangements at schools 50 years earlier, but no changes. Few houses with flushing privies. 1932 scheme delayed by the War.	Document	Archives	
MNB/PP/22/1	Harold Finch (minute book, Miners' Group)	1942-6	Housing in mining areas.	Document	Archives	

Reference Code	Collection	Dates	Description	Media	Location	DP
MNC/COP/1/1	Aberdare Co-operative Society (Minute book)	1929–32	Sanitary Inspector notice to repair 3 Co-operative Society houses.	Document	Archives	
MNC/COP/3/1	Abersychan Co-op Society (minute book)	1908–12	References to Sanitary Inspector certificates; houses and water closets.	Document	Archives	
MNC/COP/13/1	Mid-Rhondda Co-op Society (minute book)	1920–6	MOH correspondence relating to Co-operative house conversion into shop. Rhondda UDC Notice re works to living accommodation at shop (Housing Acts).	Document	Archives	
MNC/COP/27/1, 14 and 27	People's Yearbooks, Annual of the Co-operative Wholesale Society Ltd.	1920–48	1920: Housing Progress, 1919 Act. Domestic legislation 1919 and Ministry of Health Act. 1933: Housing and slum clearance. 1948: Interwar period, slums, Addison Housing Scheme.	Document	Archives	
MNC/NUM/L/26/6	Pantyffynon Lodge	1945–7	Lodge correspondence referring to housing.	Document	Archives	Y
MNC/PP/14/1	Arthur Lewis Jones (notebook)	1938	Housing, and building with Sanitary Authority's Certificate for Repairs sent to owners, regarding 'disgusting conditions'. Public meeting flyer relating to high rents for 'rat holes and bug infested hovels'.	Document	Archives	
MNC/PP/17/9 and 10	Selwyn Jones, Merthyr Royal Commission Special, July 1935 (Merthyr Borough Sub-District of Communist Party)	1930s	(9) Health of workers' children, poverty, poor housing. Unemployment camps (Glangwili), poor conditions and sanitary arrangements. (10) 1935 Election pamphlet for Harry Pollit (Communist) referring to the unemployed and work on houses, piped water supply, baths at home.	Document	Archives	
	Scrapbooks of newspaper cuttings (labelled scrapbook (green); 'Cuttings Book, 1945–1947')	1945–7	Housing requirements in South Wales.	Document	SWML	

~ 8 ~
Food and Nutrition

The home production of food was not uncommon on the South Wales Coalfield, as the childhood memories of ex-miners testify (SWCC: AUD/461; AUD/481; MNA/PP/41/1–2, 4–6). Families often grew vegetables and fruit in their gardens or allotments, and some kept chickens and other livestock. Potatoes were especially popular because they were easy to grow and rich in carbohydrate (SWCC: MNA/I/10/4; MNA/PP/104/2). The Second World War 'Dig for Victory' campaign encouraged people to produce their own fruit and vegetables to supplement their diet. Despite this cultivation of home produce, there were many concerns about the diet of coalfield families. Therefore, during periods of depression and strike – as in 1921 and 1926 – soup kitchens were formed and staffed by local people, with provisions donated, paid for with donated money, or bought cheaply from local outlets. Their purpose was to feed the men who were out of work or on strike – and sometimes their family members too, where they were at risk of undernourishment due to lack of income. Young children were included, while those past the school-leaving age of fourteen were often excluded; school-age children were only fed if they were not in receipt of school meals (see chapter 10, 'Children's Health'). There was a strict ticket system, and food was eaten at canteens set up in local community venues such as church halls and welfare institutes. Hot meals were provided at least once a day, with other cold meals additionally offered where possible. These usually consisted of the staples like bread, cheese and tea (SWCC: AUD/249; MNA/PP/130; PHO/DIS/45).

Most industrial areas received their fresh milk via companies that had contracts with local dairy farmers. The milk and the farms were subject to quality and hygiene inspections and in 1901 the Sale of Milk Regulations legally defined and enforced a minimum level of fat in milk, to control adulteration by 'watering down' (SWCC: MNA/POL/3/3). In south Wales, the Co-operative Society provided a milk delivery service, and purchased its own dairy production unit at Llanharan. Milk from local farms was regularly tested at the society's own laboratories, and any sub-standard produce triggered a visit to the offending supplier's farm by co-operative representatives (SWCC: MNC/COP/1/1, 3, 6).

Milk was also tested by local authority laboratories for bovine tuberculosis. The link between milk and the transmission of bovine TB to humans was the cause of much debate from the early 1900s until the Second World War. Robert Koch – a pioneer of bacteriology – was one of many who questioned whether such a link existed in a 1901 speech at the International Congress on Tuberculosis in London. Pasteurization, or heat-sterilization, was thought to remove the threat of tuberculosis; and only milk that had undergone this process was put in bottles, which had begun to appear by 1900 (SWCC: HD2951 A5; MNC/COP/9/1). Support-ers saw it as a way to increase the longevity of their product, suiting the larger companies that supplied wider geographical and often urban areas. Opponents saw it as interfering with a natural product, which was clean if organic farming traditions were followed. Pasteurization was also expensive, and often added another link to the chain between producer and customer because milk had to be transported to processing depots.

In both World Wars, food control and rationing took place due to shortages in supply as normal trade was suspended, and key workers – such as miners and those in other heavy industries – received additional rations (SWCC: MNA/NUM/1/1–2; MNA/NUM/L/13/1; MNB/COL/17/C6A). During the First World War (1914–18), the government post of Food Controller was created in 1916 and two years later the rationing of sugar, meat, butter and margarine for civilians was introduced. The Ministry of Food continued in existence until 1920. During the Second World War (1939–45), a rationing scheme – in which consumers were given 'points' for certain foods – was launched at the end of 1941 (SWCC: MNA/POL/3/3/1; MNA/POL/6/7). British Restaurants were also set up. Originally emergency feeding centres, they subsequently became more widespread and by 1943 there were 2,115 restaurants across the country. Open to the general public, they tended to be concentrated in industrial areas without can-teens. Such restaurants opened in the South Wales Coalfield, for example at Ammanford (SWCC: MNA/POL/3/3).

Reference Code	Collection	Dates	Description	Media	Location	DP
	Gomer Evans (Pamphlet Box 4)	c.1920	Pamphlet for the People No. 4: *A Peep Behind the Scenes on a Board of Guardians*, by Councillor Glyde. References to starvation and poor food and conditions in workhouse.	Document	SWML	
	The Welsh Housing and Development Year Book	1926	'The Public Health Act, 1925, as it affects Public Health Administration'. 'Dietary Studies: Their Importance and Significance'.	Document	SWML	
AUD/81	Bryn Thomas	c.1900s–c1920s	Living conditions WWI in Ffairfach village, near starvation, food scarce and bad quality, little meat, family poor.	Transcript of audio	SWML	Y
AUD/193 and 194	Will Picton	1910–c.1973	Description of home life, lodgers. Unemployment, diet, allotments, malnutrition.	Transcript of audio	SWML	Y
AUD/168	Ben Davies	1919–c.1960	1921: lockout; soup kitchens, meals, fruit and nut picking in summer.	Transcript of audio	SWML	Y
AUD/170	Lee Hutchinson	1875–c.1960	1921: strike, food, soup kitchens, co-op dividends.	Transcript of audio	SWML	Y
AUD/173	David John Davies	1900–c.1973	Describes living in a large family in a small house. Food sharing, e.g. one egg between two people. 1910 strike and soup kitchens.	Transcript of audio	SWML	Y
AUD/222	Dick Cook	c.1910–1974	1926: soup kitchens, food restricted to workers.	Transcript of audio	SWML	Y
AUD/247	Mr Dai Coity Davies	1926–c.1975	1926: lockout – soup kitchen. One of 6 children, little or no food, lived in abject poverty. Mother died of pernicious anaemia (caused by starvation) 1930: she sacrificed herself so that family could have food.	Transcript of audio	SWML	Y
AUD/249	David Brown	1895–c.1973	1926: soup kitchens. Food: took bread, cheese and cake to work; did not eat cooked dinner often; ate cheese and eggs (1 between 2 in family).	Transcript of audio	SWML	Y

211

Reference Code	Collection	Dates	Description	Media	Location	DP
AUD/300	Percy James Matthews	1898–c.1973	Poverty and lack of food/starvation, soup kitchen (1926).	Transcript of audio	SWML	Y
AUD/374	Dr Thomas	1900–1960s	Silicosis and pneumoconiosis, and nutritional factors in resistance to dust diseases.	Audio tape	SWML	Y
AUD/461	Mrs Alexander	c.1910–c.1950	One of 12 children. Describes self-sufficiency of family life, own livestock, vegetable garden, types of food eaten.	Audio tape	SWML	Y
AUD/462	Mrs Thomas	c.1910–c.1950	Details of work in grocery shop (inter-war) and food shopping habits of the poor (food types and shops used). 1926 Strike, food and soup kitchens.	Audio tape	SWML	Y
AUD/481	Mrs Bessie Webb and Mrs. Hannah Katie Evans	1920–75	Large family (15 children). Food; vouchers, soup kitchen, own produce, black market (WWII).	Audio tape	SWML	Y
AUD/488	Mrs Exon	1910–75	Food; 1926 soup kitchens, producing own food, buying food.	Audio tape	SWML	Y
HD2951.A5	Annual Co-operative Congress Reports (missing: 1914, 1917–24, 1932, 1943, 1949, 1951, 1965)	1913–76	1930: Advertisement for CWS Pure Foods (guaranteed pure food). Sale of bottled milk, extension of Co-op Milk Service. Medicine Stamp Duty. 1940: Meat Trade Association. Application of Poisons Act, and Drug Trade Association's Report. Food Control Committees. Milk Trade Association.	Document	SWML	
HD6661.TRA	TUC Annual Reports of Proceedings (incomplete)	1904–85	1924: Establishment of public abattoirs and humane slaughtering of animals. Prevention of meat contamination.	Document	SWML	
HD7269 M62 Oce	After Ten Years: A Report of Miners' Welfare Work in the South Wales Coalfield 1921–1931 (pamphlet)	1931	(Ocean Collieries, Treorchy: The Ocean Area Recreation Union.) Reference to canteens.	Document	SWML	

Reference Code	Collection	Dates	Description	Media	Location	DP
HD7269.M62.OTH	*The Other Side of the Miner's Life: A Sketch of Welfare Work in the Mining Industry* (pamphlet)	1936	Issued by Philip Gee (Lincoln's Inn) with authority of The Mining Association of Great Britain. Contents include colliery canteens.	Document	SWML	
HD9552.3 MIN	*The Miner*, Vol. II, No. 9	July 1946	Report, NUM Annual Conference, references to food and soap supplies. Article: 'Bread and Soap Rationing', re miners, and canteens.	Document	SWML	
HD9552.3 MIN	*The Miner*, Vol. II, No. 1/2	Oct/Nov 1945	Articles: 'Pit Welfare', including canteens.	Document	SWML	
HD9552.3 MIN	*The Miner*, Vol. III, No. 3	Jan 1947	Article: 'Miners' Welfare', including canteens.	Document	SWML	
HD9552.3 MIN	*The Miner*, Vol. I, No. 11/12	Aug/Sept 1945	Articles: 'Outdoor Welfare in the South Wales Coalfield'; 'Colliery Canteens, Food Supplies and Permits'; 'Mining Enters a New Era', including canteens.	Document	SWML	
HD9552.3 MIN	*The Miner*, Vol. I, No. 9/10	June/July 1945	Article: 'Welfare Activities in Mining Communities, South Wales Coalfield', refers to canteens.	Document	SWML	
HD9552.3 MIN	*The Miner*, Vol. II, No. 11	Sept 1946	Articles: Food – world food shortage, including mortality statistics; and 'Miners' Meat Rations'.	Document	SWML	
HV686.R3	Reports of the MOH, and School MO, Rhondda UDC	1914–47	Nutrition, milk and food supplies. 1917: Food Control (Local Authorities (Food Control) Order No. 1, 1917). 1920: Food, and supplies. Milk, and (Mothers and Children) Order 1919. Meat and slaughterhouses. 1922: Milk and Dairies (Amendment) Act. Provision of Meals Acts, 1906–1914. 1924: Milk supplied for Maternity and Child Welfare Scheme. 1925: Public Health (Meat Regulations) 1924. 1927: Milk Assistance Scheme. 1928: School MO report on Provision of Meals. 1939: Maternity and Child Welfare Centres. Supervision of expectant mothers. Provision of milk and medicinal foods. Reference to Food and Drugs Act	Document	SWML	

Reference Code	Collection	Dates	Description	Media	Location	DP
			1938. 1940: Maternity and child welfare: provision of milk and medicinal foods – sale of dried milk, and cod liver oil. Food and Drugs Act, summary of samples submitted to public analysts (including milk). 1943: Health visiting (children). Inspection and supervision of food (milk). 1945: Care of debilitated children under school age. 1945: Milk (Special Designations) Regulations and National Milk Testing – Advisory Scheme; licences re graded milks issued by council ('Tuberculin Tested', 'Accredited' and 'Pasteurised' Milk). 1946: Vitamin supplements (children and expectant mothers – cod liver oil and fruit juices).			Y
MNA/1/16/3	Forest of Dean District Welfare Association (committee minutes)	1929-35	Grants for extra nourishment.	Document	Archives	
MNA/COL/2/1	Clydach Merthyr Colliery	1942-7	Rough minutes of arbitration meetings held to resolve disputes: reference to canteens.	Document	Archives	Y
MNA/COL/2/4-38	Clydach Merthyr Colliery (Manager's carbon-copy correspondence books)	1937-48	Food rations and canteens.	Document	Archives	Y
MNA/COP/1/17	Aberdare and District Co-op Society Ltd (general and Board Meeting minutes)	1932-5	Milk analysis and school supplies.	Document	Archives	Y
MNA/COP/1/19	Aberdare and District Co-op Society Ltd (resolution book)	1897-9	Soup kitchens.	Document	Archives	
MNA/COP/7/1-13	Ton Co-op Society (general and committee Minutes)	1884-1927	Soup kitchens and Distress Committees, 1926. Bottled milk regulations, 1926. Public Health Regulations relating to food preservatives 1927. Sale of Food (Drugs) Act 1927.	Document	Archives	

214

Reference Code	Collection	Dates	Description	Media	Location	DP
MNA/COP/7/14–15	Ton Co-op Society (Board Meetings minutes)	1928–48	Foot-and-mouth outbreak and slaughter of pigs, 1925. Bread, flour and food quality. Request for staff meal facilities and sanitary conveniences, Co-op butchery. Purchase of bronchial mixture for resale. 1929: Avery personal weighing machine at Treherbert shop. 1931: butchery department; slaughter of livestock due to foot-and-mouth outbreak. 1932: butchery department – slaughter of pigs because of suspected swine fever. Technical Committee butchery report 1936 on handling of home-killed meat. Food and Drugs Act samples 1935. Milk quality, testing, contamination, complaints, prosecution. 1934: Milk Licence (pasteurized milk). School milk supplies. RUDC Maternity and Child Welfare Scheme milk supplies. Committee against Malnutrition and War, Cardiff.	Document	Archives	
MNA/J/10/4	Cwmaman Institute (annual, general and committee minutes)	1932–6	Regular donations of potatoes to the hospital from allotment holders.	Document	Archives	
MNA/J/21/1–6	Maesteg Distress Fund (minutes, accounts and correspondence)	1926–9	Refers to food, meals, canteens, feeding and relief. Lists of people receiving food.	Document	Archives	
MNA/J/22/1–2	Maesteg Medical Fund (balance sheets)	1925–47	1925 including list of members attending canteens.	Document	Archives	
MNA/NUM/I/1 and 2	Records of the Miners' Federation of Great Britain and NUM (minute books of Executive Committee, and annual and special conferences)	1937–47	(1) 1937–44: Food: rationing, shortages, supplementary allowances including cheese, milk rations including for large families, pithead canteens, underground food in event of air raid; allowances. (2) 1947: Food rationing. Supply of hot food underground.	Document	Archives and SWML	

Reference Code	Collection	Dates	Description	Media	Location	DP
MNA/NUM/3/1/1/	Minutes of the SWMF Executive Council, and annual and special conferences	1907–40	Food – prices, supplies, for children. Communal kitchens (1926). Co-op Societies and Relief Fund. National Kitchens and Restaurants in industrial areas (1919). Sugar and soap rations (1940).	Document	Archives and SWML	
MNA/NUM/3/3/1	Correspondence (bound volume of circulars)	1899–1915	1915: conference re 'High Prices for Food and Fuel', proposals for reduction in prices.	Document	Archives	
MNA/NUM/3/3/14	Correspondence with SWMF No. 1 Area, (File 17)	1931–42	File 17: 1942; Ammanford, Llandebie and District Trades Council and Local Labour Party Statement of Accounts and Reports 1941–42, food rationing and British Restaurants.	Document	Archives	Y
MNA/NUM/3/3/14	Correspondence with SWMF No. 1 Area (File 15)	1931–42	File 15: 1940: Correspondence regarding extra rations for silicosis and TB cases.	Document	Archives	Y
MNA/NUM/3/3/2	Correspondence (bound volume of circulars)	1916–27	1917 Conference: reference to food supplies and prices. 1920 Labour Party Resolutions Annual Conference: including food supplies, milk supply. Women's Labour Section meeting regarding cost of living and price comparisons for 1920.	Document	Archives	
MNA/NUM/3/3/3	Correspondence (bound volume of circulars)	1927–35	Poor Law Administration report c.1928, complaints about Bedwellty Union, investigated by Medical Officer of Ministry of Health – refers to malnutrition, lack of food and clothing.	Document	Archives	
MNA/NUM/3/4/45	SWMF/NUM Misc. office papers and reports	1938–54	Daily Worker newspaper cutting, May 1939: Cardiff, food for schoolchildren – 'dirty, ill-ventilated and insanitary' as argued by Labour councillors, and private caterers should be replaced by council administration or money given to parents. TB partly blamed on malnutrition. Milk refused when no medical certificate.	Document	Archives	

Reference Code	Collection	Dates	Description	Media	Location	DP
MNA/NUM/3/4/45	SWMF/NUM office papers and reports (May Day Pageants 1938–9; Inter-colliery Sports 1939; wartime film scenarios)	1938–54	Script 'Full Employment' (film/documentary); family living in poverty – scene re doctor's visit, giving them extra rations as wife is starved, recommends they eat milk, butter, eggs. Family eating only potatoes and bread.	Document	Archives	Y
MNA/NUM/3/5/14 and 15	SWMF: Compensation Records (Compensation Secretary's correspondence)	1934–41	Food rations for silicotics.	Document	Archives	Y
MNA/NUM/3/8/17 (A)	Area No. 2 Council Minutes (register of ordinary accident cases)	1934–52	Clothing, boot, food and soap coupons for miners. Colliery canteens.	Document	Archives	
MNA/NUM/3/8/20	Forest of Dean Miners' Association/ Area (district, area and combine records)	1919–61	Cash book 1920–32; including Feeding Centre tradesmen's accounts, 1921.	Document	Archives	
MNA/NUM/L/1	Abercrave Lodge (annual and general meetings minutes)	1935–57	Canteen.	Document	Archives	
MNA/NUM/L/10/3 and 5	Bedwas Lodge (annual, general and committee meetings minutes)	1940–6	(3) 1940–42: 1942 reference to coupons for cheese, clothing, towels. (5) 1944–46: Canteen – insects, fumigation, food supplies.	Document	Archives	
MNA/NUM/L/11/41	Blaenavon Lodge (Lodge Secretary's correspondence and papers)	1940	Notice regarding extra rations, 1 February 1940.	Document	Archives	
MNA/NUM/L/13/1	Blaengwrach Lodge (annual and committee meetings minute book)	1946–8	Decision to allow industrial workers to use Lodge Bread Coupons for domestic purposes instead of canteens. Extra meat rations for underground workers.	Document	Archives	
MNA/NUM/L/20/134	Cambrian Lodge	1926	Register of men fed at relief canteens and of members entitled to food vouchers.	Document	Archives	

217

Reference Code	Collection	Dates	Description	Media	Location	DP
MNA/NUM/L/23/126	Coegnant Lodge (Lodge Secretary's correspondence and papers)	1912	Book containing records for minimum wage claims, 1918. (At front, attendance register for Siloh Feeding Centre, 1912)	Document	Archives	
MNA/NUM/L/28/30	Deep Duffryn Lodge (Lodge Secretary's correspondence and papers)	1943–5	Ration coupon allocation register.	Document	Archives	
MNA/NUM/L/3/7	Abergorki Lodge (Lodge Secretary's correspondence book)	1917–8	1918: Food Control Office and scarcity of food in locality, and retention of food by shopkeepers especially cheese and jam, cheese a chief food in mining community.	Document	Archives	
MNA/NUM/L/41/46	Glyncorrwg Lodge (South Pit)	1930–49	Account book containing canteen accounts, 1941–2.	Document	Archives	
MNA/NUM/L/47/34	Lady Windsor Lodge	1921	Account book including Ynysbwl Distress Fund Account 1921, and Ynysybwl Relief Kitchen lists of articles loaned and gifts in kind, 1921.	Document	Archives	
MNA/NUM/L/50/ E1	Maerdy Distress Committee Records (minute book)	1926	Feeding of school children and adults. Canteen and meal details. Types of food. Tenders for food supplies. Decisions relating to feeding unemployed and people on Sick Benefit.	Document	Archives	
MNA/NUM/L/50/ E2	Maerdy Distress Committee Records (minute book)	1926–31	Soup kitchens, food details, supplies during strikes. Food and clothing donations.	Document	Archives	
MNA/NUM/L/50/64 and 72	Maerdy Lodge (Maerdy Distress Committee records)	1929	Letter from Medical Officer of Health, Rhondda UDC to Samuel Davies, regarding food vouchers. Lodge notice giving information as to food supplies.	Document	Archives	
MNA/NUM/L/58/1	Norchard and Princess Royal Lodges (minute book of Norchard Lodge Pit Head Committee meetings)	1942–9	Bread rations, supplementary allowances for unemployed and compensation cases	Document	Archives	

Reference Code	Collection	Dates	Description	Media	Location	DP
MNA/NUM/62/A3	Park and Dare Lodge (minute book for annual, general and committee meetings; also special and colliery workers meetings and subscribers to Pentwyn Cottage Hospital 1943)	1941–3	Donation to Cwmparc Allotment Society. Food distribution, feeding centres for Rhondda. Rations for cheese, clothes, soap.	Document	Archives	
MNA/NUM/L9/1	Bargoed Housecoal Lodge (committee minutes)	1947–50	Rationing and shortages at hospital. Nominations for Boards (including canteen). General references to canteen.	Document	Archives	
MNA/POL/13/5	Neath Rural District Labour Party (Area Conference reports)	1935–40	1936: Assisted milk scheme, provision and costs. Cod liver oil supplies.	Document	Archives	
MNA/POL/14/24/4	Newport Trades and Labour Council and Labour Party (Labour Party leaflet)	c.1948–50	Labour party leaflet for women: refers to food and rationing; school meals and milk.	Document	Archives	
MNA/POL/14/3	Newport Trades and Labour Council and Labour Party (Group and Executive Committee minutes)	1944–53	Food distribution and rationing.	Document	Archives	
MNA/POL/15/1	New Tredegar Trades and Labour Council (Trades and Labour Council minutes)	1938–51	1939: Food Control Committee set up. 1939: reference to diet of school children. 1947: British Restaurant in Aberbargoed. 1941: Sickness scheme for school cooks and assistants. 1947: reference to county council report on school food.	Document	Archives	
MNA/POL/2/1–3	Aberdare Trades and Labour Council (annual and monthly meetings minutes)	1925–35	(1) 1925–35: Reference to councillor's talk on medical examination of school children; reference to malnutrition. (2) 1935–44: Reference to conference on 'War and Malnutrition'. (3) 1944–52: Trecynon Dairies, working conditions. Food rationing cuts.	Document	Archives	

Reference Code	Collection	Dates	Description	Media	Location	DP
MNA/POL/24/1	Ynyshir Ward Labour Party (Rhondda Borough Trades and Labour Council and Labour Party Executive Committee minutes)	1936–8	School meals. School milk: provision over weekends and holidays; 1937 Ministry of Health standards. Complaint about milk supplied by council's scheme.	Document	Archives	
MNA/POL/3/3	Ammanford, Llandebie and District Trades and Labour Council (annual, general and Executive Council minutes)	1941–8	Food Controller. Food supplies, costs, communal feeding centres, school meals (elementary and high schools). British Restaurants (Ammanford). Extra food for mining areas. 1943: Clean milk campaign: refers to MOH (Dr. Lloyd) and press report; investigation into town's milk supply; pasteurization; testing; Llandilo RDC Sanitary Inspector's farm visits and milk grading; TB cases in children decreased. Dr Lloyd talk relating to clean milk and bovine TB.	Document	Archives	
MNA/POL/3/3/1	Ammanford, Llandebie and District Trades and Labour Council (annual, general and Executive Council minutes)	1938–41	1939–40 complaints to Ministry of Food regarding rationing, workers' needs, prices, meat shortage. 1940 reference to Llandilo Food Control Committee.	Document	Archives	
MNA/POL/5	Bedlinog Independent Labour Party	1934–6	*Western Mail* newspaper cutting; 1934 article relating to school milk supplies and licences to supply pasteurized milk.	Document	Archives	
MNA/POL/6/1 and 2	Caerphilly Labour Party (Executive Committee minutes)	1938–41	(1) 1938–41: County Council work: diet in county institutions. Food rationing. (2) 1940–6: Setting up of British Restaurants. School meals.	Document	Archives	
MNA/POL/6/5	Caerphilly Labour Party (minutes)	1940–50	PAC, food and communal feeding. TB: milk samples positive.	Document	Archives	
MNA/POL/6/6	Caerphilly Labour Party (Women's Section minutes)	1934–53	Food prices campaign. Food for elementary school children.	Document	Archives	

Reference Code	Collection	Dates	Description	Media	Location	DP
MNA/POL/6/7	Caerphilly Labour Party (Bargoed Ward Labour Party minutes)	1939–42	Food Control Committee, subcommittee to deal with food contamination, 1941. Refers to wasted milk. Malt and milk for children with doctor's certificate. Milk in schools – summer holidays. Food controller, Food Committee, rationing. British Restaurant. Malnutrition. Evacuees: food rations. Schools used for feeding evacuated mothers and children.	Document	Archives	
MNA/POL/6/8	Caerphilly Labour Party (Gelligaer Area Labour Party minutes)	1940–9	Food Control Committee. British Restaurants. School meals, malnourished children.	Document	Archives	
MNA/POL/6/9	Caerphilly Labour Party (Secretary's correspondence)	1948–55	1948: letter from Ministry of Food relating to distribution of food to needy, sent from overseas.	Document	Archives	
MNA/PP/104/2	Mrs Margaret Roberts (Tonypandy)	1914	Group photograph of GNR (Glamorgan National Reserves) Tonypandy, September 1914, 'Potato Cleaning'.	Photograph	Archives	
MNA/PP/111/1	Bryn Thomas ('Llandybie Over the Ages')	Early 1900s	Food: no school meals, ate lunch on roadway or went home; WWI food shortages, collected horse chestnuts to be sent away and ground for flour, ate black bread, black treacle instead of sugar, no sweets, butter and meat at premium; WWII rationing fairer.	Document	Archives	
MNA/PP/115/35-37	George Thomas (Treherbert)	1932–5	1932, 1933 and 1935 election pamphlets (UDC and CC), Evan George Thomas (Communist). Refers to malnutrition and school feeding.	Document	Archives	
MNA/PP/118/104	John Thomas (Aberavon) (D2)	c.1900	Election handbill, Mr J Littlejohn (Labour) Swansea District. Reference to food and school food.	Document	Archives	
MNA/PP/118/81/1	John Thomas (Aberavon) (C1)	1893	Borough of Aberavon, Highway Committee Minutes: MO's Annual Report including sanitary work relating to meat and dairy and slaughterhouses.	Document	Archives	

Reference Code	Collection	Dates	Description	Media	Location	DP
MNA/PP/118/81/6	John Thomas (Aberavon) (C1)	1893	Borough of Aberavon, Markets Committee Minutes 1893. References to slaughterhouses, scarcity of water for cleansing them, slaughterhouse rules and facilities for animals. Market drains and pipes, trough, water leak.	Document	Archives	
MNA/PP/118/95	John Thomas (Aberavon) (C15) (annual reports of MOH Aberavon)	1893–5	Inspection of dairies, milk sheds and milk shops, bakehouses and slaughterhouses.	Document	Archives	
MNA/PP/118/96	John Thomas (Aberavon) (C16) (reports of the Inspector of Nuisances to Aberavon Town Council)	1893–4	Dairies, milk shops and cowsheds. Bakehouses. Slaughterhouses. Offensive Trades (tripe boilers and tallow melter). Seizure of unwholesome food.	Document	Archives	
MNA/PP/118/98	John Thomas (Aberavon) (C18)	1895	Aberavon Borough Bye-laws: Water Street Slaughter-House (1895). For inspection of slaughterhouse and keeping same in cleanly and proper state, removing filth and refuse at least once every 24 hrs, provided with sufficient supply of water and preventing cruelty.	Document	Archives	
MNA/PP/122/1	Wilfred Timbrell (Tumble)	1896–c.1960s	Pigsties in gardens, meat stored for winter. 1921: Strike and meals.	Document	Archives	
MNA/PP/130	R. Williams (Tylorstown), (order book for Tylorstown Relief Committee)	1926	Daily food list e.g. bags of potatoes, meals (stew, roast beef), numbers of meals – for Tylorstown, Pontrygwaeth and Stanleytown.	Document	Archives	
MNA/PP/131/9	Dr Alistair Wilson	1936	The New Starvation Rates 1936, Unemployment Assistance Board and National Government new regulations. Poster, Joint Council of Action for South Wales, school meals provision.	Document	Archives	
MNA/PP/131/9	Dr Alistair Wilson	1928	The Spectator, 22 December 1928, photocopied pages, Aberdare Fund (for distress) – refers to lack of food, unemployment, poverty.	Document	Archives	

Reference Code	Collection	Dates	Description	Media	Location	DP
MNA/PP/131/9	Dr Alistair Wilson	1938	Aberdare UDC Election leaflet for Alistair Wilson (Communist). Refers to school food and milk schemes (tested and pasteurized milk).	Document	Archives	
MNA/PP/16/11/1-34	S. O. Davies	1944-8	Parliamentary Debates (Hansard). 17 October 44 – Welsh Affairs reference to nutrition (livestock, milk), poverty.	Document	Archives	
MNA/PP/16/11/1-34	S. O. Davies	1943	Parliamentary Debates (Hansard). 17 February 43 – Written answers re Tuberculosis Wales (Milk Supply).	Document	Archives	
MNA/PP/16/50/2	S. O. Davies	1940	Constituency correspondence; concerns about food rationing for ill (diabetics, rheumatics); food shortage in Merthyr due to influx of evacuees.	Document	Archives	Y
MNA/PP/16/50/67	S. O. Davies	1940s	Papers regarding Merthyr school meals service. Details of food, cost of service. 1947: report on meal provision. 1948: report re staffing, conditions of school restaurants, and Ministry's observations. Notes about MOH information regarding growth of children, TB, diets survey.	Document	Archives	
MNA/PP/16/9/1	S. O. Davies	1939	Article in Western Mail 1939: 'Tackling Economic Aspect of TB', anti-tuberculosis service report. Causes of bad health (poverty, housing, nutrition).	Document	Archives	
MNA/PP/21/6	D. Evans	1943	1918: Food Committee and rationing. 1922: free milk for pregnant. 1926 General Strike and school feeding. Economic depression in 1930s, poverty and hunger.	Document	Archives	
MNA/PP/24/1	Edgar Evans (Bedlinog)	1926-7	Bedlinog Council of Action minute book: feeding children during strike. Merthyr Board of Guardians and Poor Law Institute, meals for aged.	Document	Archives	

Reference Code	Collection	Dates	Description	Media	Location	DP
MNA/PP/28/24	James Evans (Tumble)	1937-42	1942: SWMF proposals for annual conference agenda – including food rations.	Document	Archives	
MNA/PP/35/21	David Francis	1942	1942 correspondence regarding works colliery canteen.	Document	Archives	
MNA/PP/41/1–2 and 4-6	David Harris (Glais), (exercise books containing bilingual manuscript reminiscences)	1970s, ref C19th	1921 and 1926: soup kitchen details. 1914: Garden Society, Dig for Victory and allotment. Food, storage for winter, home-produced potatoes and pork, food prices, milk, bread, baking. WWII Poultry Club, taught how to kill and prepare chicken, and egg production. Butter making on farms. Skimmed milk cheap – given to children and fed to pigs. Details of food taken for lunch underground, effects of heat, mice problem. Food and way of living; soup kitchens 1921-6, preparing for winter, home-produced potatoes and pig, fruit storage, butter, beer and ale, eggs, milk, women making wine for winter, bread. Food and lunch boxes. Cray Water Works and healing properties of water. Allotment Society and Dig for Victory 1914. Food and meals when a child, family's own produce, e.g. potatoes, bread and baking, sweets, pig.	Document	Archives	Y
MNA/PP/46/54	Arthur Horner, *Colliery Workers' Magazine* (SWMF)	1924	*Colliery Workers' Magazine* Vol. II, No 10; Labour Councillor's Diary, health and miners' families including food and nutrition.	Document	Archives	
MNA/PP/46/60	Arthur Horner	1943	Newspaper cutting from *Sunday Express*: reference to food shortages and vegetables.	Document	Archives	
MNA/PP/5/6	Jesse Clark	1948	Printed letter (pink paper) from Mid-Rhondda Co-op Society regarding milk re-registration. States dangers of untreated milk, and why Co-op milk healthy. Pencilled notes on remedy for kidney and bladder problems and recipe for drink, copied from *Virtue's Twentieth-century Medica*.	Document	Archives	

Reference Code	Collection	Dates	Description	Media	Location	DP
MNA/PP/50/3	W. R. James (Trelewis) (Taff Merthyr Lodge minute book)	1946-52	Reference to canteen.	Document	Archives	
MNA/PP/54/5 and 6	Hubert Jenkins (office diary)	1919-24	1919: Food Control Committee and ration books.	Document	Archives	
MNA/PP/59/1	E. M. Jones	1921	Pontardulais Canteen Committee minute book. Soup kitchens, list of school children, foodstuffs, provision of 2 meals, ticket system. School meals – County Education Authorities decided not to provide.	Document	Archives	
MNA/PP/59/4	E. M. Jones	1926	Newspaper cuttings; canteen fund (Pontardulais), lists committee and contributions, goods received. Number of meals, cost.	Document	Archives	
MNA/PP/67/18	W. Eddie Jones	1932	Monmouth County Marchers Council speaker's notes, 'The effect of our Demands upon Rates'. Public Assistance; including drugs.	Document	Archives	
MNA/PP/67/26	W. Eddie Jones	1935	1935: letter; centre for unemployed and poor food.	Document	Archives	
MNA/PP/70/1	William Henry Knipe	c.1960	Newspaper cuttings of articles on the Tonypandy riots (photocopy); Article: poverty and starvation.	Document	Archives	
MNA/PP/73/1	James Lewis (Maesteg) (Maesteg Medical Fund Committee minute book)	1929-39	Chemists' application to sell medicated wines. UAB Nourishment allowances.	Document	Archives	
MNA/PP/73/6	James Lewis (Maesteg)	1930-47	Papers regarding James Lewis's tenure of office as secretary of Llynfi Sundries Lodge, refers to meat rations.	Document	Archives	
MNA/PP/8/8-9	W. H. Crews	1926-1950s	Essay re 1926 lockout (written later), mentions soup kitchens and parish relief.	Document	Archives	
MNA/PP/81/1	Abel Morgan (minute book)	1946-8	Food control committee members. Distribution of food gifts for those in receipt of Public Assistance. Allotments and Committee.	Document	Archives	

Reference Code	Collection	Dates	Description	Media	Location	DP
MNA/PP/81/8	Abel Morgan	1935	The Wheatsheaf, September 1935 (Ynysybwl Industrial Co-op Society Ltd). Article: Allotments.	Document	Archives	
MNA/PP/87/1 and 2	Charles Parker (transcripts of interviews with miners and their wives)	1961 (refers to interwar period)	Starvation. Food during Depression years, horsemeat, tinned rabbit and margarine (were told it was better for them than butter).	Document	Archives	Y
MNA/PP/9/16	H. W. Currie	1939–47	Newspaper cutting re typhoid danger in ice cream.	Document	Archives	
MNA/PP/9/17/2	H. W. Currie	1937–48	Newspaper cuttings of J. B. S. Haldane articles: disease and new drugs; food production.	Document	Archives	
MNA/PP/9/17/3	H. W. Currie	1939–48	Newspaper cuttings of J. B. S. Haldane articles: food and nutrition.	Document	Archives	
MNA/PP/9/31, 34, 35	H. W. Currie	1937–47	Postal course notes 1937–8 (National Council of Labour Colleges) Local Government including Ministry of Health details and legislation. Two notebooks containing handwritten notes: psychology, physiology and nutrition.	Document	Archives	
MNA/PP/9/5	H. W. Currie	1927–1930s	Newspaper cutting: International Co-operative Women's Guild pure food campaign 1927.	Document	Archives	
MNA/PP/90/4	J. M. Phillips (newspapers and newspaper cuttings)	1921–6	The Communist newspaper, 27 August 1921. Russian famine week, large cartoon 'Blockade – Famine – Cholera' re stoppage of medicine imports to Russia by Allies. Communist Party of GB 'Famine Fund' to send food and medicines to Russian workers.	Document	Archives	
MNA/PP/91/31	William Picton (Maerdy) (newspaper cuttings)	1936–65	1938: walkout at Training Camp for Unemployed, Cynarth (Carmarthenshire); poor food and housing conditions. Article (1930s–1940s) regarding families on UAB, not enough food, woman suffering starvation, children fed on bread and butter and never eaten eggs.	Document	Archives	

226

Reference Code	Collection	Dates	Description	Media	Location	DP
MNA/PP/91/6	William Picton (Maerdy) (letter)	1938	Claims for extra nourishment allowances, and invalids travelling to be examined by Regional Medical Officer. SWMF complaint about poor food and conditions at Treglog Instructional Centre for Unemployed, Brechfa (Carms).	Document	Archives	
MNA/TUG/10/1	Amalgamated Society of Engineers (minute book)	1917–22	References: Food Control Committee and food prices and distribution. Refers to member's report of Labour Association concerning food situation.	Document	Archives	
MNA/TUG/7/1/C1–2	Iron and Steel Trades Confederation (reports, circulars, minutes and papers)	1934–48	1944: Minutes of local conferences including food rationing, canteens.	Document	Archives	
MNB/COL/17/C17A and B	Morlais Colliery (Miners' Assoc of GB Circulars)	1921–44	1941: letter re food supplies for miners, canteens and increased food rations.	Document	Archives	
MNB/COL/17/C25D	Morlais Colliery (Secretarial Dept circulars)	1939–42	Colliery canteens. Food in wartime.	Document	Archives	
MNB/COL/17/C25E	Morlais Colliery (Secretarial Dept circulars)	1934–42	Increased food supplies for colliery workers. Canteens.	Document	Archives	
MNB/COL/17/C32C	Morlais Colliery (misc. memoranda, resolutions, agreements etc.)	1915–42	1927 report, ref to National Food Canning Council posters and increased consumption of home-grown fruit and vegetables, thus promoting increased employment in steel, tin and coal Industries.	Document	Archives	
MNB/COL/17/C6A	Morlais Colliery (Board of Conciliation circulars)	1925–42	Arrangements for increased food supplies (e.g. cheese and meat) for colliery workmen. 1941 pamphlet: 'Increased Food Supplies for Colliery Work People'.	Document	Archives	
MNB/NUM/L/1/1	Abercynon Lodge (minute book)	1939–41	Additional meat ration for miners, distributed at pithead.	Document	Archives	

Reference Code	Collection	Dates	Description	Media	Location	DP
MNB/NUM/L/1/17	Abercynon Lodge (circular re colliers' food supplies)	1941	Increased Food Supplies for Colliery Workpeople. Joint memo to Colliery Companies and Workmen's Representatives. Additional cheese and meat to be distributed in a form suitable to be taken to workplace in food box.	Document	Archives	
MNB/NUM/L/1/24	Abercynon Lodge (news sheet issued by Joint Committee of Action for South Wales)	1936	'The New Starvation Rates'. UAB and National Govt Law – New Regulations and Scales. Reference to School Meals.	Document	Archives	
MNB/NUM/L/2/1-4	Ammanford No. 2 Lodge (minute books)	1924-34	Soup kitchen 1925. Milk supply to workmen.	Document	Archives	
MNB/POL/1/12	Ammanford Trades and Labour Council (balance sheet and annual report)	1948	Food distribution.	Document	Archives	
MNB/POL/1/6	Ammanford Trades and Labour Council (balance sheet and minutes)	1942	Food: rationed commodities; interview with Food Controller; support of British Restaurant movement including one at Ammanford.	Document	Archives	
MNB/POL/6/A26	Newport Constituency Labour Party (Crindau Ward Committee minutes)	1932-9	1934: Refers to Health Department activities and destruction of meat (fresh and tinned).	Document	Archives	
MNB/POL/6/A6	Newport Constituency Labour Party (Executive and General Committee minutes)	1930-3	Food for inmates of casual Ward and Woolaston House. Meals for children where parents on PAC Benefit. Meals for school children and food type. Bread supply.	Document	Archives	
MNB/POL/6/A8	Newport Constituency Labour Party (Executive and General Committee minutes and Health Committee report)	1938-44	Woolaston House Infirmary: 1943 report by Social Welfare Committee, including reference to diet, and treatment of patients. Supplementary rations for manual workers.	Document	Archives	Y

Reference Code	Collection	Dates	Description	Media	Location	DP
MNB/PP/12/C/2/1–15	William Henry Davies (Penclawdd), (annual reports: MOH, Gower Rural Sanitary Authority)	1895–7, 1899, 1900, 1902–11	1910: Milk supply sampled. Other foods, inspection of slaughterhouses. Pollution of stream by carcase. 1911: Reference to report MOH sent to Council regarding washing cockles at Penclawdd. 6 Bakehouses and 26 slaughterhouses registered and inspected. Milk supply, no action relating to TB milk, supplied direct from farms.	Document	Archives	
MNB/PP/22/1	Harold Finch (minute book, Miners' Group)	1942–6	Mining areas and food allocations.	Document	Archives	
MNB/PP/31/3	Cornelius Gronow (correspondence)	1917–21	1919 letters: Rhondda Food Control Committee; Divisional Food Commissioner and prosecutions per committee and fines.	Document	Archives	
MNB/PP/38/1–2	Willie James (Newport)	1926	New Tredegar, Tirphil and District Central Relief Committee Food Kitchens; list of centres, number of meals and cost, number of children's meals.	Document	Archives	
MNB/PP/56/1	Miss E. Leyshon (Swansea)	1914	(Report of Executive Committee for Swansea of Prince of Wales' National Relief Fund) Vegetable Products Committee: to collect fruit, vegetables, jam and assist in organization and development of fruit and vegetable industries; cultivation of beer as source of sugar supply. Canadian cheese and flour.	Document	Archives	
MNB/PP/56/2	Miss E. Leyshon (Swansea)	1915	(Report of Executive Committee for Swansea of Prince of Wales' National Relief Fund) Canadian cheese and flour for distribution.	Document	Archives	
MNB/PP/56/4	Miss E. Leyshon (Swansea)	1929	(Coalfields Distress Fund circulars regarding family eligibility for assistance from Lord Mayor's Fund) Circular: Limits of Family Income for Grant of Assistance from Lord Mayor's Fund in form of Food Vouchers.	Document	Archives	

Reference Code	Collection	Dates	Description	Media	Location	DP
MNB/PP/56/6	Miss E. Leyshon (Swansea)	1929	(Summary of instructions to Swansea Committee of Coalfield Distress Fund) Instructions from Divisional Committees; food vouchers and school food, and family food.	Document	Archives	
MNB/PP/64/K1	J. S. Williams (Dowlais) (miscellaneous printed material, press cuttings and circulars)	c.1924–37	1934 Parliamentary papers: Questions for Oral Answer, and not for Oral Answer, reference to food supplies in UK.	Document	Archives	
MNB/PP/72/13–14	Alistair Wilson (2 'Wellcome' medical diaries and visiting lists)	1920–8	182 printed pages of Therapeutic Notes. Index of Diseases and Treatment. Poisoning; Symptoms and Treatment. Diet Tables. Feeding of Infants and Children (including milk). Average weights and heights.	Document	Archives	Y
MNC/COP/1/1, 3 and 6	Aberdare Co-operative Society (minute book)	1929–48	(1) 1929-32: Milk: summons – sample taken by police, analytical reports of routine sampling, list of farms, CWS Ltd Research Department statistics, complaints, farmer and unclean premises, milk fat % legal limits, pasteurization, school supply. Analysis of butter, lard, margarine. Aberdare General Hospital: tender for meat and bread supplies, waste bread used at piggery. (3) 1937–40: Milk under-pasteurized – Aberdare MOH reference to milk sample, UDC involved. Distribution of BMA leaflets regarding pasteurized milk. Milk tests and analysis results. Complaint about contaminated milk bottle. Tender for supply of milk to schools, also bread and biscuits. (6) 1945–8: Aberdare Food Control Committee. Bread rationing. Milk analysis test results. Complaint about bread from shop.	Document	Archives	Y
MNC/COP/12/1	Lower Cwmtwrch Co-op Society (minute book)	1908–10	1909: Patent Medicine Licence procured. 1909: Loose page from order book with advert header for 'Milkmaid Full Cream Milk' – refers to 'Children thrive on "Milkmaid" Milk'.	Document	Archives	

Reference Code	Collection	Dates	Description	Media	Location	DP
MNC/COP/13/1	Mid-Rhondda Co-op Society (minute book)	1920–6	MOH correspondence: slaughterhouse alterations; shop. Rat problems at shop (2 terriers bought), and at bakery (stock destroyed). Complaint of cigarette in bread. Reference to meat supply for Porth Cottage Hospital.	Document	Archives	
MNC/COP/15/1	Penarth Co-op Society (minute book)	1922–39	1926: reference to pasteurized milk project and milk depot.	Document	Archives	
MNC/COP/15/2	Penarth Co-op Society (minute book)	1937–9	Bread: complaints about quality (string found in loaf), and handling of bread by delivery person. School milk provision regulations 1937 referring to pasteurized. Planarian Dairy advised by Penarth MOH, visits by MOH and Sanitary Inspector 1938 regarding technical problems. Milk bottle tops, change from card to tin foil. Delivery of milk by coal lorry stopped. 1938 Milk Bill and Conference.	Document	Archives	
MNC/COP/27/1	*People's Yearbooks* (Annual of the Co-operative Wholesale Society Ltd)	1920	Articles: food supply, production, prices, consumption, rations, distribution, control, legislation (e.g. milk, meat, flour, vegetables). Family grocery bill comparisons over 37 years. Photograph of CWS laboratory where analysis of milk and food, and soil and fertilizer tests taking place.	Document	Archives	
MNC/COP/27/14	*People's Yearbooks* (Annual of the Co-operative Wholesale Society Ltd)	1933	Milk publicity week. Co-operative Drug Trade Association.	Document	Archives	
MNC/COP/27/27	*People's Yearbooks* (Annual of the Co-operative Wholesale Society Ltd)	1948	Food distribution, rationing, production (including milk). National Co-operative Chemists Ltd, pharmacy and drug trade. Interwar period starvation, milk consumption.	Document	Archives	
MNC/COP/3/4	Abersychan Co-op Society (minute book)	1945–9	Reference to supply contract for school canteens, and milk. Bread rationing.	Document	Archives	

Reference Code	Collection	Dates	Description	Media	Location	DP
MNC/COP/6/1	Blaenavon Co-op Society (minute book)	1915–18	Food control and supplies (e.g. sugar). Sugar Registration Cards. Ration cards. Meat shortage.	Document	Archives	
MNC/COP/6/5	Blaenavon Co-op Society (minute book)	1937–54	Complaint about milk. Blaenavon Food Control Committee. Supplies to baths canteen.	Document	Archives	
MNC/COP/9/1	Cardiff Co-op Retail Society (minute book)	1933–4	1934: Hunger Marchers appeal for assistance to feed the people. 1934: reference to supply of patent medicines, Walfox Ltd and Co-operative Wholesale Society. Reference to hospital tenders. CWS Dairy Llanharan. All branches licensed to sell milk – MOH advised. Complaints about milk. Pasteurized milk. Milk tenders. School supplies. Advertisement for pasteurized milk; 'The Only Safe Milk', in 'Hygienic Cartons'. Milk Sub Committee Conference.	Document	Archives	
MNC/ISTC/4/1	National Union of Blastfurnacemen, Ore Miners, Coke Workers and Kindred Trades	1938–41	(Annual General Meeting Reports) 1941 Cost of Living Index Figure details, reference to food prices.	Document	Archives	
MNC/ISTC/D6/3/1	South Wales Siemens Steel Trade, Joint Board Meeting (minutes)	1941	Canteen services (where not provided), reference to exhaustion of workers and heat (especially regulations of blackout) – refreshments needed. Not accepted by management as too much capital expenditure. Canteen Committee to be set up.	Document	Archives	
MNC/NUM/5/182	NUM S Wales Area, SWMF Eastern Valleys District monthly meetings minutes (D2/F53)	1915	Food and drug prices under National Insurance Act.	Document	Archives	

Reference Code	Collection	Dates	Description	Media	Location	DP
MNC/NUM/5/228	Cambrian Lodge (correspondence and papers)	1938–41	Rhondda Communist Party meeting notice (ud) regarding nutrition and malnutrition. 1938: SWMF Committee Memo relating to Unemployed Assistance, and diet necessary 'to support health and working capacity' (BMA) and details of food and costs. SWMF Conference agendas 1940 and 1941 including food rationing.	Document	Archives	
MNC/PP/11/1	G. James (newspaper cuttings)	c.1910–1920s	1912: miners' living conditions, reference to makeshift meals (e.g. potted meat and fish instead of fresh fish, and chips).	Document	Archives	
MNC/PP/15/2	Dr Gwent Jones	c.1940s	Advertisement: 'Benerva' Vitamin B, Deficiency of Antineuritic Vitamin. Report: 'Benecol' (Benger), preparation for the treatment of arthritis and allied conditions. Report: 'New Data on Saline Therapy in relation to Inefficient Defaecation', by Manufacturing Chemist.	Document	Archives	
MNC/PP/15/3	Dr Gwent Jones (correspondence)	1942-4	Letters: South Wales and Monmouthshire Council of Social Service re Dr Jones' silicosis pamphlet, relating to diet – survey of expenditure on food during Depression years.	Document	Archives	
MNC/PP/15/5	Dr Gwent Jones	1944	MFGB Minutes of Executive Committee Meeting, 07 January 1944. Reference to mineworkers' food rations.	Document	Archives	
MNC/PP/17/10	Selwyn Jones (election pamphlet, Harry Pollitt, Communist)	1935	Reference to the unemployed (provision for free milk, clothes and boots for children), and workers (abolish taxes on food).	Document	Archives	
MNC/PP/17/13	Selwyn Jones (minute book, Social Service Guild)	c.1928	Committee to relieve local distress, soup kitchen for unemployed, food and clothes 'tickets', food parcels.	Document	Archives	
MNC/PP/17/38	Selwyn Jones	c.1940s	Leaflet: Ministry of Information film, details. 'Food is Man's Security Number One', 'World of Plenty', re post-war plans (made during WWII).	Document	Archives	

Reference Code	Collection	Dates	Description	Media	Location	DP
MNC/PP/17/9	Selwyn Jones, Merthyr Royal Commission Special, July 1935 (Merthyr Borough Sub-District of Communist Party)	1935	Health of workers' children, including malnutrition, and free school meals.	Document	Archives	
MNC/PP/18/6	David Lewis	c.1940s	Newspaper cuttings: food and drink, and herbal remedies. 2 'Dig for Victory' leaflets nos. 10 (Jam and Jelly Making) and 11 (Bottling and Canning Fruit and Vegetables) issued by Ministry of Agriculture and Fisheries.	Document	Archives	
MNC/PP/27/10	Claude Stanfield (copy of Merthyr Tydfil Corporation Act)	1948	Registration of hawkers of food and premises. Power to prohibit persons in advanced state of TB from selling food. Precautions against contamination of food (not milk or meat).	Document	Archives	
MNC/PP/3/1	Idris Cox		1921: Strike, Maesteg Relief Committee, 2 meals per day for children under 14, Cwmfelin canteen. 1926: strike canteens.	Document	Archives	
PHO/DIS/31	Coal Mining Dispute Photographs (disputes of 1921)	1921	Formal photograph of Penyrenglyn Canteen District Committee, men and women. A stove can be seen in the photograph.	Photographs	Archives	
PHO/DIS/32	Coal Mining Dispute Photographs (disputes of 1921)	1921	Formal photograph of Tonypandy Mission Hall Canteen officials and staff during 1921 lockout. Group outside Mission Hall, board in front reads 'Out but appy'.	Photographs	Archives	
PHO/DIS/43	Coal Mining Dispute Photographs disputes of 1926	1926	Formal photograph of Banwen Canteen staff, men and women, outside the independent vestry they used for the soup kitchen during the 1926 strike.	Photographs	Archives	
PHO/DIS/44	Coal Mining Dispute Photographs (disputes of 1926)	1926	Formal photograph of the staff of Duffryn Canteen during the 1926 strike, including men, women and children.	Photographs	Archives	
PHO/DIS/45	Coal Mining Dispute Photographs (disputes of 1926)	1926	Formal photograph of the staff of Salem Canteen at Nantyffyllon during the 1926 strike, including men, women and children.	Photographs	Archives	

Reference Code	Collection	Dates	Description	Media	Location	DP
PHO/DIS/47–49	Coal Mining Dispute Photographs (disputes of 1926)	1926	3 formal photographs of Neath Soup Kitchen Committee during the 1926 strike. In one, Tom Nicholas is holding a bag of flour. Groups include men, women and children.	Photographs	Archives	
PHO/DIS/55	Coal Mining Dispute Photographs (disputes of 1927)	1927	Images of 1927 Hunger March including cooking staff waiting on the road to serve hot soup.	Photographs	Archives	
PHO/DIS/76	Coal Mining Dispute Photographs (disputes of 1936)	1936	4 photographs of demonstration by children about the imprisonment of their fathers after the Taff Merthyr Riots. Banners include 'Our Daddies must fight or we will starve', and 'Mammies worry how to feed us UAB scales won't allow'.	Photographs	Archives	
PHO/DIS/79	Coal Mining Dispute Photographs (disputes of 1937)	1937	Photograph of Communist Party march in Cardiff. Banners include 'Houses for the people, more food for heavy workers'.	Photographs	Archives	
R489 W1	Thomas Wakley (pamphlet)	1962	*Thomas Wakley*, by Charles Brook (SMA Publication). Founder – *The Lancet* 1823. Paved way for first food and drug legislation and appointment of public analysts, MP, introduced first Medical Registration Bill leading to Medical Act 1858.	Document	SWML	
TN295 COL	'The Coal Miner: His Health, Diseases and General Welfare' (pamphlet)	c.1924	Reprint from *Journal of Industrial Hygiene*, by E. L. Collis (Welsh National School of Medicine). Physiological needs; food, drink, salt.	Document	SWML	
	Scrapbooks of newspaper cuttings, unlabelled scrapbook (green)	1946–8	Food, extra fats for miners, more meat and fruit, Ministry of Food urged to make bigger allocation of fats to fish-fryers in mining areas.	Document	SWML	
	Scrapbooks of newspaper cuttings, labelled (green): 'Cuttings Book, 1945–1947'.	1945–7	Poor food rations for miners, colliery canteens.	Document	SWML	

~ 9 ~

Women's Health

Though women were pivotal to family life on the South Wales Coalfield, their health – and hence their capacity to support male workers and dependent children – was undermined by poor housing (see Chapter 7, 'Housing and Sanitation') and an inadequate diet (see Chapter 8, 'Food and Nutrition'), which were the outcome of poverty and unemployment. Indeed, women sometimes went without food so that they could provide enough for their families, thus damaging their own health and in extreme cases dying of pernicious anaemia or starvation (SWCC: AUD/247; MNA/PP/91/31). Their well-being was further undermined by the exhaustion and overwork caused by housekeeping and childcare, and preparing baths and doing the daily laundry. Therefore, the gradual introduction of pithead baths from the early twentieth century was an important asset for women as well as miners (see Chapter 3, 'Safety and Welfare').

Pregnant and nursing mothers faced additional risks to their health, which the regulation of midwifery attempted to tackle. The 1902 Midwives Act required that births be attended either by a licensed midwife or by a doctor. In the same year, the Central Midwives Board was established to maintain a register of midwives; and from April 1905 only registered midwives were allowed to practise. The 1911 National Insurance Act allowed midwives to claim the same payment as doctors for being present at births, and the 1936 Midwives Act 'nationalized' the profession through the salaried employment of practitioners by local authorities. Under the National Health Service (NHS), however, many services offered by midwives were taken over by general practitioners or hospitals.

The health of mothers (and their children) was addressed in other ways besides the reform of midwifery, catalysed by the poor condition of military recruits and concern about the efficiency of future generations. In 1918 the Maternity and Child Welfare Act enabled local authorities to open clinics and employ health visitors; and, during the interwar years, the Annual Reports of Medical Officers of Health catalogued a number of such schemes like the allocation of milk to malnourished mothers by Rhondda Urban District Council; statistics for births and deaths, puerperal fever, maternal nutrition, and midwifery services were also published (SWCC: HV686 R3).

In 1928 the charitable National Birthday Trust Fund was set up to provide maternity services for disadvantaged 'Special Areas', and food for pregnant women who were poor. Five years later, Lady Williams initiated a scheme in the Rhondda Valley, whereby two district sister-superintendents from London worked as assistant inspectors of midwives in the area. Additional antenatal care was made available as well as courses for local midwives, and an obstetric consultant was employed at Llwynypia Hospital, where emergency care was provided (SWCC: MNA/POL/2/1).

Throughout the economic Depression, additional food was distributed to combat malnutrition, and maternity and child welfare centres provided milk and dietary supplements as well as supervising expectant mothers. These services continued into the 1940s with district councils supplying dried milk, cod liver oil, vitamin supplements and fruit juice for expectant mothers – and for children (SWCC: HV686 R3; MNA/POL/13/5). Home helps were added to the list of maternity and child welfare services during the Second World War.

Reference Code	Collection	Dates	Description	Media	Location	DP
AUD/310, 311	Abel Morgan	1878	Women's use of maternity home in Mountain Ash, and doctor's undertaking of payment responsibilities.	Transcript of audio	SWML	Y
AUD/461	Mrs Alexander	c.1910–c.1950	One of 12 children. Describes mother's and own pregnancies and midwife attending births.	Audio tape	SWML	Y
AUD/481	Mrs Bessie Webb and Mrs Hannah Katie Evans	1920–75	Large family (15 children), living conditions, pregnancy and births.	Audio tape	SWML	Y
MNA/PP/12/11 and 14	Mrs Beatrice Davies (née Phippen), Ystrad Rhondda	1924	(11) 1924: Rhondda UDC election poster for Dr W. E. Thomas; refers to maternity and childwelfare centres. (14) 1935: Rhondda UDC election leaflet for Eliza Williams (collier's wife). Includes issues of social legislation relating to mothers and children and death during childbirth.	Document	Archives	
MNA/PP/16/3/2	S. O. Davies	1935	Merthyr Tydfil Parliamentary election leaflet; references to health and maternity services.	Document	Archives	
MNA/PP/9/6 and 7	H. W. Currie (newspaper cuttings)	1937–8	1937: Midwives Act. 1938: birth rates, maternity provision and Midwives Act; sex education and relationships; abortion.	Document	Archives	
MNA/PP/9/17/1 and 2	H. W. Currie (newspaper cuttings)	1937–48	Newspaper cuttings relating to pain in childbirth, and maternity and child welfare.	Document	Archives	
MNA/POL/1/1	Aberdare Town Ward Labour Party (committee minutes)	1933–42	Aberdare Maternity Hospital to take abnormal cases if home surroundings unsuitable. Home nursing scheme at Abernant and Cwmbach.	Document	Archives	
MNA/PP/24/1	Edgar Evans (Bedlinog)	1926–7	Bedlinog Council of Action minutebook: scheme by Women's Committee to assist mothers (reference to midwives).	Document	Archives	
MNA/PP/21/6	D. Evans	1943	1922: reference to free milk for pregnant women.	Document	Archives	

238

Reference Code	Collection	Dates	Description	Media	Location	DP
MNA/COP/7/1–13	Ton Co-op Society (general and committee minutes)	1884–1927	Maternity Committee appeal and Treorchy Maternity Scheme.	Document	Archives	
MNA/POL/2/1	Aberdare Trades and Labour Council (annual and monthly meetings minutes)	1925–35	District Council Health and Medical Committee; Maternity Home. Maternity Home (Mountain Ash). Maternity Benefit. Llwynypia Hospital (General and Maternity).	Document	Archives	
MNA/POL/2/2	Aberdare Trades and Labour Council (annual and monthly meetings minutes)	1935–44	Aberdare General Hospital, election of vice-president. General Hospital appointments of staff. Provision of Maternity Hospital for Aberdare. Midwifery Act.	Document	Archives	
MNA/COP/7/14–15	Ton Co-op Society (Board Meetings minutes)	1928–48	RUDC Maternity and Child Welfare Scheme milk supplies.	Document	Archives	
MNA/POL/5	Bedling Independent Labour Party (press cuttings (in account book))	1934–6	*Western Mail* newspaper cuttings, including reference to maternity homes.	Document	Archives	
MNA/POL/13/5	Neath Rural District Labour Party (Area Conference reports)	1935–40	1936: Maternity and child welfare. Doctor (MOH), Sanitary Inspectors, health visitors. Welfare centres. Clinics. Neath Antenatal clinic. Assisted milk scheme, provision and costs. Cod liver oil supplies. Treatments; orthopaedic, dental, eye, ENT. Hospital cases.	Document	Archives	
MNA/POL/14/2	Newport Trades and Labour Council and Labour Party (group and Executive Committee minutes)	1914–18	1917: reference to Co-operative Women's Guild resolutions relating to maternity Welfare.	Document	Archives	
MNA/POL/14/14/1 and 2	Newport Trades and Labour Council and Labour Party (annual report and balance sheet for County Borough of Newport)	1929–38	(1) 1929: Maternity and child Welfare. (2) 1938: Maternity and child welfare: centres and clinic; hospital provision; convalescent homes; midwives; milk; dental; orthopaedics; Municipal Midwifery Service.	Document	Archives	

Reference Code	Collection	Dates	Description	Media	Location	DP
MNA/POL/6/5	Caerphilly Labour Party (Caerphilly Area Labour Party minutes)	1940–50	Maternity and child welfare. Caerphilly and Gelligaer possible joint Maternity Home (part of Miners' Hospital). Home for Mothers and Children. Poor care of evacuees at Senghenydd House, Senghenydd and appointment of new matron. Treatment of child with appendicitis. Clinic for children. Midwives shortage.	Document	Archives	
MNA/POL/6/8	Caerphilly Labour Party (Gelligaer Area Labour Party minutes)	1940–9	Birth rates. Maternity welfare. Midwifery service. Appeal for Maternity Home. Ambulance services and costs. Home equipment; gas and air for women in labour. Maternity Hospital. Maternity and child welfare clinics.	Document	Archives	
MNA/POL/24/1	Ynyshir Ward Labour Party (Rhondda Borough Trades and Labour Council and Labour Party Executive Committee minutes)	1936–8	Complaint about milk supplied by council's scheme. Maternity services; midwives (numbers, appointments, complaint regarding councillor's interference in their work).	Document	Archives	
MNA/POL/14/24/4	Newport Trades and Labour Council and Labour Party (Labour Party leaflet)	ud	Labour party leaflet for women: refers to Health Service (including free medical care for women in the home); National Insurance (including when husband ill, and maternity benefits).	Document	Archives	
MNC/COP/27/14	People's Yearbooks (Annual of the Co-operative Wholesale Society Ltd)	1933	Advertisements: Co-operative Health Insurance Section benefits (including maternity provision).	Document	Archives	
MNC/COP/27/27	People's Yearbooks (Annual of the Co-operative Wholesale Society Ltd)	1948	Interwar period infant and maternal mortality.	Document	Archives	
HV686.R3	Reports of the MOH, and School MO, Rhondda UDC	1914–47	Birth and death statistics. Maternity and child welfare. Puerperal fever. Infantile mortality. Illegitimacy. Ophthalmia neonatorium. 1920: Maternity and Child Welfare Committee. Milk, and (Mothers and Children) Order 1919.	Document	SWML	

Reference Code	Collection	Dates	Description	Media	Location	DP
			1924: Milk supplied for Maternity and Child Welfare Scheme. 1939: Maternity and child welfare centres. Supervision of expectant mothers. Provision of milk and medicinal foods. Travel expenses of mothers attending welfare centres (vouchers). Midwives Act 1936: compensation on ceasing practice; Municipal Midwifery Service. 1940: Maternity and child welfare: provision of milk and medicinal foods, sale of dried milk and cod liver oil. 1944: Home helps, maternity and child welfare. 1946: Glyncornel Maternity Home. Vitamin supplements (children and expectant mothers, cod liver oil and fruit juices). 1947: Maternity and child welfare.	Document	Archives	
MNB/POL/7/5	South Wales District, Communist Party of Great Britain (miscellaneous political handbills)	1942–8	Part of handbill, 'Vote for Communist Candidates' (Maerdy Lodge) – reference to Rheumatic Clinic (proposed by Communist), Glyncornel, and only 18 maternity beds reserved for Rhondda instead of the 28 pledged.	Document	Archives	
MNB/NUM/L/1/24	Abercynon Lodge (news sheet issued by Joint Committee of Action for South Wales)	1936	The New Starvation Rates. UAB and National Government Law – New Regulations and Scales. Reference to Maternity Benefit (NHI).	Document	Archives	
MNB/POL/6/A8	Newport Constituency Labour Party	1938–44	(Executive and General Committee minutes, and Health Committee report) Health Committee work relating to maternity and child welfare.	Document	Archives	Y
MNB/J/3/D19	Abergorki Workmen's Hall and Institute (newspaper cuttings relating to SWMF affairs)	1926–9	*Western Mail* 21 October 29; Victoria Cottage Hospital, Abergavenny – Laying of foundation stone for new maternity wards (extensions cost £5,000).	Document	Archives	
MNB/POL/6/A26	Newport Constituency Labour Party (Crindau Ward Committee minutes)	1932–9	1934: Reference to maternity and child welfare and new machine for treatment of deafness.	Document	Archives	

Reference Code	Collection	Dates	Description	Media	Location	DP
MNB/PP/56/8	Miss E. Leyshon (Swansea)	1905–35	(Summary of work done by district nurses, Swansea's East Side) Lists number of visits 1905–35. Maternity nurse appointed 1916.	Document	Archives	
MNB/PP/56/7	Miss E. Leyshon (Swansea) [East Side District Nursing Association annual reports and accounts)	1905–40	(1923 missing) Case numbers and visits. Balance sheets. Case statistics including TB. Rules. New appointments and resignations. Maternity nurse (from 1916), midwifery statistics, 1937 Maternity Act. Penny-a-month scheme, 1907. Surgical nurse appointment. Queens' nurses.	Document	Archives	
MNB/PP/56/6	Miss E. Leyshon (Swansea)	1929	(Summary of instructions to Swansea committee of Coalfield Distress Fund) Instructions from Divisional Committees regarding food vouchers and school food, family food, maternity outfits, boots and clothing, coal.	Document	Archives	
MNA/PP/91/30/2 and 3	William Picton (Maerdy) (election leaflet and address)	1946	Maternity Hospital at Glyncornel. Clinics for ante- and post-natal, and mothers and children. Home helps.	Document	Archives	
MNC/PP/17/9	Selwyn Jones, *Rhondda Vanguard* newspaper, Feb 1936 (Rhondda Communist Party)	1930s	Council clinics at Treherbert and Ferndale, not yet built, bus fares of women attending not paid. Statistics of MOH Report, December 1935, deaths of children under 1 year old.	Document	Archives	
MNB/PP/20/E11	Glyn Evans (Garnant) (Borough Council circular re Midwives Act)	1936	Metropolitan Borough of St Pancras Public Health Department circular; Midwives Act 1936. Administration of Act, MOH Public Notice. Midwifery and maternity nursing in home, midwives' details, hospitals and associations (e.g. Maternity Nursing Association), medical consultants.	Document	Archives	
MNB/PP/64/K1	J. S. Williams (Dowlais) (miscellaneous printed material, press-cuttings and circulars)	c.1924–37	Notice of meetings (Amalgamated Union of Building Trade Workers, Altogether Builders' Labourers and Constructional Workers' Soc, National Health Section) Approved Society Section and National Health Benefits, including maternity.	Document	Archives	

Reference Code	Collection	Dates	Description	Media	Location	DP
MNA/NUM/L/34/1	Fforchaman Lodge (annual, general and committee minutes)	1938–40	Hospital committee report regarding maternity cases, and if going to charge for them.	Document	Archives	Y
MNA/PP/81/1	Abel Morgan (minute book)	1946–8	Maternal and Child Welfare Committee Members and public health.	Document	Archives	
MNA/PP/131/9	Dr Alistair Wilson	1938	Aberdare UDC Election leaflet for Alistair Wilson (Communist). Refers to Maternity Hospital.	Document	Archives	
MNA/PP/115/35–37	George Thomas (Treherbert)	1932–5	1932, 1933 and 1935 election pamphlets (UDC and CC), Evan George Thomas (Communist). Refers to infant and maternal mortality, clinics, maternity home.	Document	Archives	
MNA/I/34/A21	St David's Unity of Ivorites	ud	(Central Records) National Health Insurance Maternity Benefit Form (ud), blank.	Document	Archives	
MNA/PP/67/37	W. Eddie Jones	1934	Abersychan UDC Election leaflet, Communist (Reg Jones and W. Eddie Jones). References to free medical and maternity services for unemployed and increased child allowances.	Document	Archives	
MNA/PP/67/16 and 18	W. Eddie Jones	1930s	(16) Reference to 1931 report about undernourished condition of Monmouthshire schoolchildren, Dr Mary Scott, Assistant MO Pengam; rickets, maternal problems, poor feeding, overcrowding. (18) 1932: Monmouthshire County Marchers Council speaker's notes, 'The Effect of our Demands upon Rates', and the latest reports on the children's health. Maternity and child welfare statistics and provision of food and milk.	Document	Archives	
MNA/PP/67/80	W. Eddie Jones (newspaper cuttings)	c.1930s	1933 Cardiff Corporation article: maternity and child welfare (including food, milk and doctor's fees).	Document	Archives	

Reference Code	Collection	Dates	Description	Media	Location	DP
MNA/PP/46/33/2	Arthur Horner (election handbill)	1933	'Mainwaring's Election Special', election handbill for W. H. Mainwaring (Labour). Reference to maternity services, health and social services.	Document	Archives	
MNC/ISTC/1/1	National Union of Blastfurnacemen, Ore Miners, Coke Workers and Kindred Trades	1919–25	(Annual Conference Reports) NHI Section Accounts (including maternity).	Document	Archives	
MNC/ISTC/4/1	National Union of Blastfurnacemen, Ore Miners, Coke Workers and Kindred Trades	1938–41	(Annual General Meeting Reports) 1940, National Insurance section, why members should join Approved Society, details, NHI benefits, e.g. maternity.	Document	Archives	

~ 10 ~
Children's Health

Since the health of school-age children was closely intertwined with their education, the 1870 Education Act was a significant milestone. But, although school boards were required to fill the gaps in charitable education by opening elementary schools for five- to ten-year-olds, attendance – for those under the age of ten only – did not become compulsory until 1880. Furthermore, there was no provision for disabled children. Legislation in 1893 made elementary education for blind and deaf children the duty of local authorities, which were required to develop their own special schools or subsidize schools in the charitable sector. The identification of children judged as 'mentally defective' (or as having a learning difficulty) was obligatory under the Mental Deficiency Act of 1913 (SWCC: HV686 R3; MNA/POL/2/1–2). However, it was not until 1914 that the permissive power to organize elementary education for 'defective' and epileptic children – in existence since 1899 – was made compulsory. The 1918 Education Act made schooling obligatory for physically as well as mentally 'defective' children; while, with the famous 1944 Act, all pupils who were considered capable of benefiting from education became the responsibility of local authorities.

From the early twentieth century, schools became the loci for the distribution of food and milk to children whose health was threatened by malnourishment that lowered their resistance to disease and exposed them to conditions like rickets. Impoverished families were not always able to afford regular hot meals and so school meals were invaluable. So too was fresh milk, substituted at home with tinned, condensed milk that was less nutritious. The 1906 Education (Provision of Meals) Act established the supply of school meals by local authorities, which were free if parents were unable to pay towards them. Building on this service, the 1914 Education (Provision of Meals) Act allowed for school meals to be provided on non-school days, with previous spending restrictions removed. Milk was also offered to school children under these Acts. Furthermore, the National Milk Publicity Council set up the 'Penny-a-Bottle' scheme in 1923, which meant that by the early 1930s approximately 90,000 elementary school children were receiving free milk and around 80,000 were paying a penny a bottle. This scheme was joined by a government 'Milk in Schools' project, which was started in 1934 by the Milk Marketing Board with the aim of supplying one third of a pint of milk daily to 50 per cent of elementary school children, either free or at half cost. This proportion was achieved by 1939. Subsequently, the 1944 Education Act provided free milk for all school children.

Children were also caught up in the growing regulation of health after 1900. Under an Act of 1907, local authorities were enabled to make the notification of births compulsory in their district and to collect statistics in relation to the birth rate; later legislation in 1915 made notification compulsory across the UK as a whole. More importantly, the 1908 Children's Act consolidated the law with regard to the protection of infant life and the prevention of cruelty. In addition, however, parents and guardians were deemed guilty of neglect if they treated a child 'in a way likely to cause injury to his health' and if they failed 'to provide adequate food, clothing, medical aid or lodging.'

A year earlier, the Education (Administrative Provisions) Act had established a national system of school medical inspection and school clinics run by local authorities. On the basis of regular inspections, school medical officers compiled statistics relating to children for the Annual Reports of Medical Officers of Health. These reports included information about diseases and defects, hygiene, ringworm, teeth, tonsils and adenoids, ears and hearing, eyes and vision, tuberculosis, height and weight, 'crippling defects' and so-called 'defective' children (SWCC: HV686 R3; MNA/PP/ 67/29). Emphasis was placed on hygiene, physical exercise, sanitation and nutrition. Statistics relating to outbreaks of communicable diseases, such as diphtheria and scarlet fever, were also recorded. Vaccinations for some diseases were available to children (see chapter 5, 'Infectious Diseases'); in the Rhondda, for example, immunization against diphtheria was under way in 1940 (SWCC: HV686 R3).

The Second World War also witnessed the state's intervening more generally in the field of childcare. In particular, nurseries were set up for younger children whose mothers were working, and an evacuation scheme to remove school children from areas at risk of enemy bombing was implemented (SWCC: MNA/POL/6/5–7).

Reference Code	Collection	Dates	Description	Media	Location	DP
AUD/212	Edgar Evans	c.1910–73	Edgar Evan's childhood illnesses, leg problems and hospital treatment.	Transcript of audio	SWML	Y
AUD/222	Dick Cook	c.1910–74	Illness as child (doctor diagnosed TB).	Transcript of audio	SWML	Y
AUD/342	Mrs Nancy Davies (Seven Sisters)	1920s–1940s	Food and milk for schoolchildren, 1926. Girl who stayed at home to nurse sick mother (diabetic, heart problems and partially blind).	Transcript of audio	SWML	Y
HD9550 EBB	The Ebbw Vale Works Magazine, Vol. 9, No. 34	April 1930	Article: 'Massage and Manipulations'. Hospital treatment and 'The Guinea Subscriber's Scheme' at King's College Hospital, London – facilities also available for wives and children.	Document	SWML	
HV686.R3	Reports of the MOH and School MO, Rhondda UDC	1914–47	Infantile mortality. Schools; medical inspections, hygiene, clinics, nurses, physical exercise, openair. Sanitation. Nutrition. Diseases and defects statistics. Uncleanliness. Ringworm. Teeth. Tonsils and adenoids. Ears and hearing. Eyes/vision. TB. Height/weight. 'Defective' children. 1917: Typhus fever. Contagious ophthalmia. School children – Dental treatment. 1919: School MO report on the Ystrad Clinic. 1920: Ystrad and Ynyshir Clinics (School MO report). 1922: Crippling defects and orthopaedics; open-air education; physical training; Provision of Meals Acts, 1906–1914; School baths; 'Blind, Deaf, Defective and Epileptic Children'; eye disease; defective vision/squint; crippling defects (e.g. TB and rickets). 1923: Chicken pox. Schools: dental defects; Ynyshir Dental Clinic. 1924: Schools: Assistant School MO – Dr Ellen Mackenzie; incidence of heart	Document	SWML	

Reference Code	Collection	Dates	Description	Media	Location	DP
			disease in relation to rheumatism; Goitre (enlargement of thyroid gland). 1926: School MO report: Crippling defects and orthopaedics – Carnegie Welfare Centre, Trealaw, and Prince of Wales Hospital, Cardiff. 1927: Milk Assistance Scheme. School MO report: Infectious diseases, exceptional prevalence of diphtheria (Clydach Vale, Treherbert, Pentre) and scarlet fever (Porth). Provision of glasses. Anthropometric measurements. Training of stammering children.1928: School MO report on provision of meals. 1930: School MO: prevalence of smallpox in area. 1931: Infant Life Protection – reference to Children Act, 1908. 1932: School MO: Diphtheria outbreaks – Treorchy and Maerdy; scarlet fever – Gelli. 1939: Schools – diphtheria (Clydach Vale). School MO report: influx of evacuees into district; orthopaedic treatment for secondary and higher schools; school camps (Pendine, Gileston, Ogmore, Rhoose). 1940: Maternity and child welfare: provision of milk and medicinal foods – sale of dried milk and cod liver oil. Diseases – immunization against diphtheria. School MO: Scabies and other contagious skin affections; Crippling defects and orthopaedics – appointment of Mr N. Rocyn Jones FRCS as Orthopaedic Consultant, and appointment of Orthopaedic Nurse – clinics at Carnegie Welfare Centre (including ultraviolet light treatment). 1942: Wartime nurseries. School MO: Government Evacuation Scheme – emergency sick bay (Penrhys Smallpox Hospital) for contagious skin diseases, hostel for persistent bed-wetters (Maindy Hall, Pentre), hostel (Glyncornel House, Llwynypia) for behavioural problems. 1943:			

Reference Code	Collection	Dates	Description	Media	Location	DP
			Health visiting (children). Inspection and supervision of food (milk). Care of debilitated children under school age. 1946: Handicapped children. Statistics of children notified by LEA to Local Mental Deficiency Authority, 1947: Infestation, e.g. nits. School MO: 'Return of all Handicapped Children in the Area', including blind, partially sighted, deaf, partially deaf, delicate, diabetic, educationally subnormal, epileptic, maladjusted, physically handicapped, speech defects, multiple disabilities.			
MNA/COP/7/14-15	Ton Co-op Society (Board meetings minutes)	1928-48	Subscription to North Devon Convalescent Children's Home. School milk supplies. RUDC Maternity and Child Welfare Scheme milk supplies.	Document	Archives	
MNA/1/16/3	Forest of Dean District Welfare Association (minutes)	1929-35	Grant for travel to Standish House to visit children confined with TB.	Document	Archives	Y
MNA/NUM/1/1-2	Records of the Miners' Federation of Great Britain/NUM (minute books of Executive Committee and annual and special conferences)	1902-48	General themes include employment of women and children.	Document	Archives and SWML	
MNA/NUM/3/3/2	Correspondence (bound volume of circulars)	1916-27	1917: Conference on food, including for children. 1918: letter relating to Blinded Soldiers' Children Fund to assist soldiers to get married.	Document	Archives	
MNA/NUM/3/4/45	SWMF/NUM Miscellaneous office papers and reports	1938-54	*Daily Worker* newspaper cutting, May 1939: Cardiff food for schoolchildren; 'dirty, ill-ventilated and insanitary' argued Labour councillors, and private caterers should be replaced by council administration or money to parents. TB partly blamed on malnutrition. Milk refused when no medical certificate.	Document	Archives	

Reference Code	Collection	Dates	Description	Media	Location	DP
MNA/NUM/3/5/14	SWMF: Compensation Records (Compensation Secretary's correspondence)	1938	Public Health Department Cardiff booklet regarding Cardiff Municipal Accident Service (talk to Cardiff Medical Society); including handicraft classes for disabled children.	Document	Archives	Y
MNA/NUM/3/7/6	Pit Disaster Records	1914–38	Senghenydd Relief Fund Minute Book, reference to grants for children in ill health.	Document	Archives	Y
MNA/NUM/L/10/1	Bedwas Lodge (annual, general and committee meetings minutes)	1925–33	1926: Relief, Ministry of Health and Guardians, feeding of schoolchildren.	Document	Archives	
MNA/NUM/L/50/E1 and E2	Maerdy Distress Committee Records (minute book)	1926–31	(E1) Feeding of school children and adults. (E2) Children 'adopted' and 'sent away' during disputes.	Document	Archives	
MNA/NUM/L/62/A3	Park and Dare Lodge (minute-book for annual, general and committee meetings; also special and colliery workers' meetings and subscribers to Pentwyn Cottage Hospital 1943)	1941–3	1942: 2 children in need of operations, could not be done by Dr Armstrong, Pentwyn Hospital not prepared to bear expense, appeal to hospital committee.	Document	Archives	
MNA/POL/1/1 and 2	Aberdare Town Ward Labour Party (committee minutes)	1933–52	(1) Free milk for children with malnutrition and at Domestic Training Centres. Child Welfare Committee nominations. (2) District Psychologist and Child Guidance clinic. Visit to Bridgend Blind School.	Document	Archives	
MNA/POL/2/1 and 2	Aberdare Trades and Labour Council (annual and monthly meetings minutes)	1925–44	(1) District Council Health and Medical Committee; child mortality, school children (eye and dental examinations), school meals. School meals and milk. Extraction of children's teeth. Child Welfare Act. Reference to councillor's talk about medical examination of school	Document	Archives	

Reference Code	Collection	Dates	Description	Media	Location	DP
			children; malnutrition, orthopaedic work, eye and dental clinics, treatment of adenoids, autorhoea (ear discharge), infectious diseases (Mardy Hospital), deaf, dumb and blind, nursery schools, school baths. Pendine School Camp, Greenhill Occupational Centre for Mentally Defective Children (Aberaman), mental and physical defectives (the Open Air School). (2) Mardy and Merthyr Child Welfare Committee.			
MNA/POL/3/1, 3 and 4	Ammanford, Llandebie and District Trades and Labour Council (annual, general and Executive Council minutes)	1931–57	(1) Outbreak of diphtheria in area. Treatment of school children at Glanamman Cottage Hospital and charge relating to adenoids. School medical services including 'crippled' children, appointment of orthopaedic surgeon. (3) Food supplies, costs, communal feeding centres, school meals (elementary and high schools), 1943: Clean milk campaign: reference to MOH (Dr Lloyd) and press report; TB cases in children decreased. X-raying of all children on leaving school. TB scheme 1945, X-ray of schoolchildren aged 14–18. (4) 1949: complaint to Welsh Regional Hospital Board that schoolchildren with ear, nose and throat defects not receiving adequate attention under new Act.	Document	Archives	
MNA/POL/6/1 and 2	Caerphilly Labour Party (Executive Committee minutes)	1938–46	(1) County Council work: diet in county institutions; nurse shortage; child welfare. (2) School meals.	Document	Archives	

Reference Code	Collection	Dates	Description	Media	Location	DP
MNA/POL/6/5	Caerphilly Labour Party (Caerphilly Area Labour Party minutes)	1940–50	Milk and children's nurseries. Cod liver oil for under-5s. School children's health: ENT, teeth, TB. School meals. School medical report: numbers of dental surgeons; scabies; orthopaedic clinics and operations; Bridgend Blind School. Poor care of evacuees at Senghenydd House, Senghenydd and appointment of new matron. Treatment of child with appendicitis. Clinic for children.	Document	Archives	
MNA/POL/6/6	Caerphilly Labour Party (Women's Section minutes)	1934–53	Food for elementary school children.	Document	Archives	
MNA/POL/6/8	Caerphilly Labour Party (Gelligaer Area Labour Party minutes)	1940–9	School meals, malnourished children. Immunization against fever. Bedlinog Children's Hospital. TB: radiological van touring county; numbers examined; examination of school children; cost.	Document	Archives	
MNA/POL/6/7	Caerphilly Labour Party (Bargoed Ward Labour Party minutes)	1939–42	Evacuees: medical attention, dentures, food rations. Schools used for feeding evacuated mothers and children. Huts to be built by hospital for evacuees. Malt and milk for children with doctor's certificate. Milk in schools and provision for summer holidays. TB: examination of children.	Document	Archives	
MNA/POL/14/2	Newport Trades and Labour Council and Labour Party (group and Executive Committee minutes)	1914–18	1914: reference to Feeding of School Children Bill.	Document	Archives	

253

Reference Code	Collection	Dates	Description	Media	Location	DP
MNA/POL/15/1	New Tredegar Trades and Labour Council (minutes)	1938–51	1939: Food Control Committee set up. 1939: diet of school children. 1947: reference to County Council report on work done on school food. 1944: ambulance use for child tonsil operation cases. 1948: New Tredegar Modern Secondary School temporary classrooms for 'backward children', and house bought at Chepstow for care of 'maladjusted' children.	Document	Archives	
MNA/POL/24/1	Ynyshir Ward Labour Party (Rhondda Borough Trades and Labour Council and Labour Party Executive Committee minutes)	1936–8	School meals. School milk: provision over weekends and holidays. Isolation Hospital: complaint about child sent home too early and another child infected as result.	Document	Archives	
MNA/POL/24/2	Ynyshir Ward Labour Party (committee minutes)	1947–51	School meals. Reference to high number of children born with 'hare lips' in area, no local treatment – sent to Great Ormond Street Hospital, London. New residential schools for handicapped children. Child health and immunization. Dentists: shortage; provision at secondary schools. Mass radiography of 17,000 children (11 had TB).	Document	Archives	
MNA/PP/9/6	H. W. Currie	1937	Newspaper cuttings including child health.	Document	Archives	
MNA/PP/9/16	H. W. Currie	1939–47	Newspaper cuttings including infantile paralysis.	Document	Archives	
MNA/PP/12/2 and 5	Mrs. Beatrice Davies (née Phippen), Ystrad Rhondda	1908–12	Rhondda UDC election leaflets for W. M. Phippen. Refers to Medical Inspection Act (Schools) and Feeding of School Children Act.	Document	Archives	
MNA/PP/13/1	J. Davies (Neath)	1933	Communist Party poster, Neath Borough elections (for Roper). Refers to lack of school food and cost of milk for school children.	Document	Archives	

Reference Code	Collection	Dates	Description	Media	Location	DP
MNA/PP/16/3/3	S. O. Davies	1951	Merthyr Tydfil – Parliamentary election leaflet. Refers to infantile mortality.	Document	Archives	
MNA/PP/16/5	S. O. Davies	1934	Election newspaper: feeding school children.	Document	Archives	
MNA/PP/16/50/2	S. O. Davies	1942	Constituency correspondence; MOH letter – diphtheria immunization of children.	Document	Archives	Y
MNA/PP/16/50/8, 9, 10	S. O. Davies	1946–8	(8) Constituency correspondence; letters relating to termination by employers of supplementary allowances under Workmen's Compensation Acts for children and family allowances. (9) Sandbrook Rheumatic Hospital School (minutes extracts). (10) School meals; hearing aids; Sandbrook House Rheumatic School (Merthyr).	Document	Archives	Y
MNA/PP/16/50/67	S. O. Davies	1940s	Papers relating to Merthyr school meals service. Details of food, cost of service. 1947: report on meal provision. 1948: report re staffing, conditions of school restaurants and Ministry's observations. Notes on MOH information relating to growth of children, TB, diets survey.	Document	Archives	
MNA/PP/21/5	D. Evans	1922	*Government Offensive against Unemployment* (Lloyd George, Liberal pamphlet). Refers to weekly payments for dependent wives and children in winter and school meals for children.	Document	Archives	
MNA/PP/21/6	D. Evans	1943	1915 medical inspection of school children. 1926 General Strike, reference to school feeding.	Document	Archives	
MNA/PP/24/1	Edgar Evans (Bedlinog)	1926–7	Bedlinog Council of Action minute book: feeding children during strike.	Document	Archives	

255

Reference Code	Collection	Dates	Description	Media	Location	DP
MNA/PP/28/24	James Evans (Tumble)	1937–42	1942: SWMF proposals for annual conference agenda – clinics and school food for children.	Document	Archives	
MNA/PP/30/4	Sonia Evans (Porth)	1925	Labour Party election leaflet for Pontypridd Board of Guardians; reference to children under care of Guardians.	Document	Archives	
MNA/PP/55/4	J. D. Jenkins (MOH, Rhondda UDC) (correspondence and papers re miners' nystagmus)	1921	Request for information from Health Department by doctor, for research purposes. Details supplied including defective vision in school children.	Document	Archives	
MNA/PP/59/1	E. M. Jones	1921	Pontardulais Canteen Committee minute book. Soup kitchens' list of school children, foodstuffs, provision of 2 meals, ticket system. School meals – County Education Authorities decided not to provide.	Document	Archives	
MNA/PP/59/4, 5, 6	E. M. Jones	1926	Boots needed for some children, health endangered of some by bad boots and shoes. Handwritten request for boots for child, sent to Pontardulais Distress Committee. Notebook (bank book) of same.	Document	Archives	
MNA/PP/67/1	W. Eddie Jones	1936	1936: letter from headmaster, references to parents' having gone without food to make sacrifices for children. Suggests health of children deteriorated and pupils 'half-fed'. Special MO from London visit, stated no evidence of malnutrition.	Document	Archives	Y
MNA/PP/67/12/1	W. Eddie Jones (leaflet)	1936	Leaflet by Abertillery Marchers' Committee, Programme of Demands to County PAC, Education Committee to give 2 substantial meals per day to school children.	Document	Archives	
MNA/PP/67/16	W. Eddie Jones	c.1930s	Talk. Demand that Monmouth Education Authority provide 2 meals per day (7 days per week) to all children in need. Abertillery Education Committee already doing so	Document	Archives	

Reference Code	Collection	Dates	Description	Media	Location	DP
			6 days per week. 1931: report re undernourished condition of Monmouth school children, Dr Mary Scott, Assistant MO Pengam; rickets, maternal problems, poor feeding, overcrowding. Abertillery MO report; no boots for small children, poor clothing. 1931: Monmouthshire Health Authority investigation, state of nutrition of school children. Poor food, clothing, rest. School children refused meals if parents' income over £2. Starvation rate reflected in death returns (including flu). Deteriorating physical standards. Diets.			
MNA/PP/6/7/17	W. Eddie Jones	1932	Blaenavon clinic, children attending for teeth extractions, no transport. Abertillery Feeding Centre. Malnutrition, subnormality, school food, insufficient clothing and footwear.	Document	Archives	
MNA/PP/6/7/18	W. Eddie Jones	1932	Monmouth County Marchers' Council speaker's notes, The effect of our Demands upon Rates and the latest reports on the children's health. Maternity and child welfare, provision of food and milk.	Document	Archives	
MNA/PP/6/7/20	W. Eddie Jones	c.1930s	Speakers' notes on Work Schemes. Public health, starvation of workers by refusal to operate School Feeding Act to full (Means Tested).	Document	Archives	
MNA/PP/6/7/21	W. Eddie Jones	c.1930s	Abertillery UDC Education Committee. Brief description of scheme for feeding necessitous school children. Centres established, meals provided, dietary details, supplies, numbers fed and cost. School MO and Sanitary Inspectors – attention to food quality. Cleanliness of centres.	Document	Archives	

Reference Code	Collection	Dates	Description	Media	Location	DP
MNA/PP/67/22	W. Eddie Jones	1933	Letter from Monmouth County Council to National Unemployment Workers Movement. PAC and school meals.	Document	Archives	
MNA/PP/67/29	W. Eddie Jones (newspaper cuttings)	1935	'Health of the School Children of the County', 1935 Medical Report by Medical Inspection Department – Dr D Rocyn Jones, School MO for Monmouthshire. Reference to medical and dental examinations of pupils, dental treatments and needs, malnutrition, school dinners and milk, cleanliness, clothing and footwear. Reference to open-air education, Barry School Camp, Ogmore School Camp and other classes. Physical instruction, training. Children at institutions for the blind, deaf and dumb, epileptics. Multiple defects. Mental defectives.	Document	Archives	
MNA/PP/67/37	W. Eddie Jones (leaflet)	1934	Abersychan UDC Election leaflet, Communist (Reg Jones and W. Eddie Jones). Refers to 2 meals per day for school children and increased child allowances.	Document	Archives	
MNA/PP/67/80	W. Eddie Jones (newspaper cuttings)	c.1930s	1932 article: Monmouthshire children's health, medical inspection findings including nutrition, vision, dentists, teeth, TB, open-air classes, physical education, school meals, milk. Article: Malnutrition in Schools, statistics for inspections. 1933 article: Cardiff Corporation accounts: Lord Pontypridd Hospital at Dulwich House for children with rheumatic cardiac disease.	Document	Archives	
MNA/PP/82/1 and 2	D. Morgan (general correspondence, miscellaneous letters and circulars re Rhymney Workingmen's Medical Aid Fund)	1942–9	Form for payment for hospital treatment of school child. Monmouthshire County Scheme of Payment for Hospital Treatment of School Children, e.g. orthopaedics, ophthalmic, ENT, skin disease.	Document	Archives	Y

Reference Code	Collection	Dates	Description	Media	Location	DP
MNA/PP/85/1	T. Nicholas (minute book of Neath Branch of the Independent Labour Party)	1930–3	Reference to School Children's Feeding Act in operation at school, and need at Crynant.	Document	Archives	
MNA/PP/91/12	William Picton (Maerdy) (committee agenda)	c.1939	Milk for necessitous school children. UAB assessment of milk granted to school children, and reduction of nourishment allowances. TB report for Wales and adverse effects of reduction of child nourishment allowances. Medical examinations at Pontypridd.	Document	Archives	
MNA/PP/91/30/2	William Picton (Maerdy)	ud	Election leaflet; William Picton. Refers to School Feeding Scheme (1 hot meal per day in canteens). Milk for school children.	Document	Archives	
MNA/PP/98/1 and 2	Gwilym Richards	1913–20	Newspaper cuttings: Re 1913 annual report of Chief Medical Officer of Government Board, Dr. Newsholme - extension of public health services led to decline in infant mortality (in *Labour Leader*, 31 July 1913).	Document	Archives	
MNA/PP/111/1	Bryn Thomas ('Llandybie Over the Ages')	Early 1900s	Schools: Sanitation; earth and bucket toilets, yard used as urinal. Nowhere to dry clothes or wash. No drinking water. Medical examinations; weighed and head searched. Ringworm, impetigo, lice, fleas common in children. Long walks to school. Overcrowding.	Document	Archives	
MNA/PP/115/35–37	George Thomas (Treherbert)	1932–5	1932, 1933 and 1935 election pamphlets (UDC and CC), Evan George Thomas (Communist). Refers to child health, clinics, school feeding.	Document	Archives	
MNA/PP/118/11	John Thomas (Aberavon) (circulars and other papers re DWRGWU)	1899–1916	1906 poster – Adequate inspection to prevent infringement of clauses regarding child, youth and women workers.	Document	Archives	

Reference Code	Collection	Dates	Description	Media	Location	DP
MNA/PP/118/105	John Thomas (Aberavon) (D3)	1905	ILP Annual Conference Report 1905. References: hungry children and the unemployed. State maintenance of school children (including meals).	Document	Archives	
MNA/PP/118/107	John Thomas (Aberavon) ((D5) (South Wales Labour Annual)	1902	Adverts: 'Fennings' family medicines including 'Children's' powders ('Do not contain Antimony, Calomel, Opium, Morphia'), 'Steedman's Powders' (for children cutting teeth).	Document	Archives	
MNA/PP/118/81/1	John Thomas (Aberavon) (C1)	1893	Borough of Aberavon, Highway Committee Minutes: Water for school supply. MO's annual report including infant mortality.	Document	Archives	
MNA/PP/118/95	John Thomas (Aberavon) ((C15) (annual reports of MOH Aberavon)	1893–5	Birth and death rates and infant mortality.	Document	Archives	
MNA/PP/118/52	John Thomas (Aberavon) (Ness Edwards, *The Industrial Revolution in South Wales*)	1924	Social conditions, women and children.	Document	Archives	
MNA/PP/131/9	Dr Alistair Wilson	1938	1936: The New Starvation Rates 1936, reference to Unemployment Assistance Board and National Government new regulations. Poster, Joint Council of Action for South Wales, school meals provision. 1938: Aberdare UDC Election leaflet for Alistair Wilson (Communist). Refers to school food and milk schemes.	Document	Archives	
MNA/PP/132/9	James Winstone (scrapbook of news cuttings and handwritten notes)	1912	*South Wales and Monmouthshire News*, regarding children's health and mortality. Housing Reform, refers to child deaths. Details annual report School Clinic and Health Centre Deptford, medical treatments, dental,	Document	Archives	

Reference Code	Collection	Dates	Description	Media	Location	DP
			operations, infants, open-air schools, night camp, breathing exercises. School clinics, Monmouth's scheme established by Dr Rocyn Jones (MOH), Welsh National Memorial Association, tuberculosis, hygiene, medical inspections.			
MNB/I/3/C12	Abergorki Workmen's Hall and Institute (Secretary's carbon-copy letter book)	1948-9	Hensol Castle admission request for 'mental case' boy, ref to other children in family 'abnormal'.	Document	Archives	Y
MNB/I/6/9	Merthyr Miners' Hall ('The Crusade', National Committee for the Prevention of Destitution), 1911	1911	Reference to medical inspection of school children, and parental responsibility (including case of child with defective eyesight).	Document	Archives	
MNB/I/7/2, 4, 8	Mountain Ash and Penrhiwceiber Hospital (annual reports and financial statements)	1933-47	1933 (2): References to: possible new Children's Ward. 1938 (4): Reference to Temporary Children's Ward of 8 beds in hospital 'Flat', and need for funding of project. 1947 (8): Children's Ward – never achieved.	Document	Archives	
MNB/NUM/L/1/24	Abercynon Lodge (news sheet issued by Joint Committee of Action for S Wales)	1936	The New Starvation Rates. UAB and National Government Law – New Regulations and Scales. Reference to school meals.	Document	Archives	
MNB/POL/1/13	Ammanford Trades and Labour Council (balance sheet and annual report)	1949	Representations to Welsh Regional Health Board relating to inadequate facilities for treatment of children with ENT defects.	Document	Archives	
MNB/POL/6/A1	Newport Constituency Labour Party	1918-21	(Minutes of Labour Representational Committee and annual executive and general committees of Newport Labour Party) Election leaflets referring to open-air schools for children with phthisis.	Document	Archives	

Reference Code	Collection	Dates	Description	Media	Location	DP
MNB/POL/6/A4	Newport Constituency Labour Party (Executive and General Committee minutes)	1921–5	Woolaston House [Poor Law Institute], appointment of Master and Matron. Labour Guardians' support of Matron for Children's' Homes. Collection for 'Margaret Macdonald Baby Clinic'.	Document	Archives	
MNB/POL/6/A6	Newport Constituency Labour Party (Executive and General Committee minutes)	1930–3	Meals for children where parents on PAC Benefit. Meals for school children and food type.	Document	Archives	
MNB/POL/6/A8	Newport Constituency Labour Party (Executive and General Committee minutes and Health Committee report)	1938–44	Transport of children to clinics. Milk supply to children. First-aiders in schools. Mental Deficiency Committee nomination.	Document	Archives	Y
MNB/PP/12/C2/1–15	William Henry Davies (Penclawdd) (annual reports: MOH, Gower Rural Sanitary Authority)	1895–7, 1899, 1900, 1902–11 and 1948	1896: New privies for schools, dry earth system instead of cesspits. 1903: Measles prevalent – school closures. 1906: measles epidemic, schools closure. Outbreak of impetigo spread through Gower from school. Infantile mortality including whooping cough, congenital defects, atrophy, debility, marasmus, convulsions. 1908: Detailed infant mortality statistics and numbers of illegitimate. 1909: Measles, whooping cough – school closures. Disinfection of schools. 1910: Medical Inspector of Schoolchildren to be appointed. TB control, MOH recommended that should be notifiable, as 14 deaths. 1911: Schools prevention of disease spread, 'Memo on closure of and exclusion from school 1909'. MOH appointed as School Medical Inspector. Infant mortality, illegitimate births. 1948 notes; Sewerage Inquiry– long-standing need, GowerMOH complained of sanitary arrangements at schools over 50 years before, no changes.	Document	Archives	

Reference Code	Collection	Dates	Description	Media	Location	DP
MNB/PP/38/1–2	Willie James (Newport)	1926	New Tredegar, Tirphil and District Central Relief Committee Food kitchens – list of centres, number of meals and cost, number of children's meals.	Document	Archives	
MNB/PP/56/6	Miss E. Leyshon (Swansea) (Summary of instructions to Swansea committee of Coalfield Distress Fund)	1929	Instructions from Divisional Committees regarding food vouchers and school food, family food, maternity outfits, boots and clothing.	Document	Archives	
MNB/PP/72/13–14	Alistair Wilson (2 'Wellcome' Medical diaries and visiting lists)	1920–8	182 printed pages of Therapeutic Notes. Index of diseases and treatment. Feeding of infants and children (and milk).	Document	Archives	Y
MNC/COP/27/1	People's Yearbooks (Annual of the Co-operative Wholesale Society Ltd)	1920	UK birth and death rates statistics and infant mortality.	Document	Archives	
MNC/COP/27/14	People's Yearbook (Annual of the Co-operative Wholesale Society Ltd)	1933	Women's Co-operative Guild: 'To Help the Deficient', request government grants – schools for physically and mentally deficient children.	Document	Archives	
MNC/PP/11/1	G. James (newspaper cuttings)	c.1910–1920s	Coroner's letter relating to children scalded or killed falling into baths prepared for miners. Reference to Mr M Roberts-Jones (Coroner South Monmouthshire), inquests re scalded children and baths for miners.	Document	Archives	
MNC/PP/17/9	Selwyn Jones (Rhondda Vanguard! newspaper, Feb 1936 (Rhondda Communist Party))	1930s	Article re Llwynypia Hospital; treatment of children of unemployed parents refused admission even after certified by local doctors as needing operations. Dispute re responsibility for maintenance of children in hospital (Councils, MOH, Relieving Officers). Statistics of MOH Report December 1935, deaths of children under 1 year old.	Document	Archives	

Reference Code	Collection	Dates	Description	Media	Location	DP
MNC/PP/17/9	Selwyn Jones (Merthyr Royal Commission Special, July 1935 (Merthyr Borough Sub-District of Communist Party))	1930s	Health of workers' children, poverty, malnutrition, tonsils, adenoids, scarlet fever, diphtheria, infantile death rate, spectacles, poor housing, free school meals.	Document	Archives	
MNC/PP/17/10	Selwyn Jones (Eelection pamphlet, Harry Pollitt (Communist))	1935	Reference to unemployed and schools, provision for free milk, clothes and boots for children.	Document	Archives	
MNC/PP/27/10	Claude Stanfield (Merthyr Tydfil Corporation Act)	1948	Notifiable diseases: information to be furnished, parents to notify, restrictions on attendance at schools, power to close schools and exclude children.	Document	Archives	
PHO/DIS/76	Coal Mining Dispute Photographs (disputes of 1936)	1936	Four photographs of demonstration by children about the imprisonment of their fathers after the Taff Merthyr Riots. Banners include 'Our Daddies must fight or we will starve', and 'Mammies worry how to feed us UAB scales won't allow'.	Photographs	Archives	

~ 11 ~
Health Care Personnel

Doctors

The Medical Act of 1858, which created the General Medical Council, was a significant reorganization of the medical profession. It established a medical register of persons qualified in medicine or surgery, and prevented unregistered practitioners from holding public appointments, such as medical officer of health or posts with mutual aid societies. The Medical Act of 1886 established a common set of qualifications (in general medicine, surgery and midwifery). Voluntary hospitals provided a major source of medical training (see Chapter 13, 'Medical Institutions: Hospitals'), and the increase in the number of mutual aid and friendly societies provided increased opportunities for medical attendance (see chapter 12, 'Health Insurance and Medical Aid'). Thus the second half of the nineteenth century saw a substantial increase in the number of qualified medical practitioners.

The 1911 National Insurance Act improved access to free medical care by forming 'panels' of doctors to treat the working population, though not their wives and children (see chapter 12, 'Health Insurance and Medical Aid'). In 1937, this service was extended to workers aged fourteen to sixteen years. By the end of 1938, between two-thirds and three-quarters of general practitioners had joined the scheme, and more than 21 million workers and pensioners derived some kind of benefit.

In some areas of the South Wales Coalfield, doctors were employed by local medical aid societies, or by communities like Bedlinog. The 'Doctor's Poundage' system was extremely unusual. Collieries employed local doctors to examine workmen before employment, to treat cases of accident or illness, and to follow up claims for workmen's compensation. Disputes sometimes arose about the individual's choice of medical practitioner because some companies insisted that only their 'official' doctor be used. The payslips of colliery workmen list the deductions made for payments to the doctor or to the medical scheme (SWCC: MNA/PP/ 78/1–2; MNB/COL/14).

Reference Code	Collection	Dates	Description	Media	Location	DP
AUD/45	Dr Anne Cockroft	1970–82	Work at Pneumoconiosis Unit (MRC). References to scientists, doctors and training.	Audio tape	SWML	Y
AUD/56	Haydn Mainwaring	1910–80	Visits to compensation doctor at colliery office.	Audio tape	SWML	Y
AUD/199	Will Lake	1900–c.1973	First World War: leg abscess and medical recovery hut in Liverpool; treatment by doctors.	Transcript of audio	SWML	Y
AUD/212	Edgar Evans	c.1910–73	Doctor's practice owned by workmen, who employed the doctor (with preference given to a Labour Party supporter).	Transcript of audio	SWML	Y
AUD/217	Mr O. Edwards	1903–c.1973	Retirement of two local doctors and introduction of new appointment system.	Transcript of audio	SWML	Y
AUD/303	Mr. B. Edwards (Tonypandy)	c.1890s	Pay deductions for doctor. Treatment of men at surgery. Sick fund run by lodge and company. Details regarding use of doctor. Accident cases used their own doctor.	Transcript of audio	SWML	Y
AUD/336	Harold Finch (SWMF Compensation Secretary) (permission needed for use)	1920–c.1973	Reference to Dr Harper and pneumoconiosis. Llandough Hospital research unit. Health Service cuts, A. Bevan, BMA.	Transcript of audio	SWML	Y
AUD/344	Mr W. Knipe	1905–c.1973	Tonypandy Riots 1910, casualties of fighting, Dr Llewellyn at Llwynypia attended over 500 casualties.	Transcript of audio	SWML	Y
AUD/391	Mrs Gwen Netherway	1914–50	Brother made wooden leg supports for father's use, and later became doctor specializing in miners' spinal injuries (invented metal spinal support).	Audio tape	SWML	Y
AUD/394	Mr and Mrs D. J. Davies	1910–c.1974	Mrs Davies's experiences of nursing work with Dr Pritchard (Aberdare MOH) in orthopaedics.	Transcript of audio	SWML	Y

Reference Code	Collection	Dates	Description	Media	Location	DP
HD9550 EBB	*The Ebbw Vale Works Magazine*, Vol. 7, No. 25	Dec 1927	Article: William Garland and his campaign for separate consulting rooms for local doctors. Doctor's Fund Committee and improvements in service.	Document	SWML	
HD9550 EBB	*The Ebbw Vale Works Magazine*, Vol 7, No. 26	Mar 1928	Reference to colliery worker's son qualifying as doctor at Cardiff School of Medicine – appointed Senior House Surgeon at Cardiff Infirmary	Document	SWML	
HD9552.3 MIN	*The Miner*, Vol. II, No. 10	Aug 1946	Whole issue – Talygarn Miners' Rehabilitation Centre. References to staff including doctors.	Document	SWML	
HD9552.3 MIN	*The Miner*, Vol. III, No. 3	Jan 1947	Article: 'Organisation of Pneumokoniosis Research in South Wales under the Medical Research Council', re Llandough Hospital, Drs D'Arcy Hart and Aslett, Cardiff Royal Infirmary Pathologists.	Document	SWML	
HV686.R3	Reports of the MOH, and School MO, Rhondda UDC	1939-40	Appointments, including Dr Ruth Penlon Jones (Assistant Medical Officer). School MO: appointment of Mr N Rocyn Jones FRCS as Orthopaedic Consultant.	Document	SWML	
MNA/COP/7/1-15	Ton Co-op Society (general and committee minutes)	1884-1927	References to doctors' rental of Co-op properties as surgeries.	Document	Archives	
MNA/1/16/3	Forest of Dean District Welfare Association (committee minutes)	1929-35	1929: grant to assist injured miners. Copy letter from doctors dealing with cases regarding fees and retaining fees. Limitation on number of cases due to cost. Details of discussions.	Document	Archives	Y
MNA/POL/2/3	Aberdare Trades and Labour Council (annual and monthly meetings minutes)	1944-52	Reference to disagreement between doctors and Board.	Document	Archives	

Reference Code	Collection	Dates	Description	Media	Location	DP
MNA/POL/2/7	Aberdare Trades and Labour Council (Executive Committee minutes)	1941–51	Patients' complaints regarding preferential treatment and moving hospitals. Hospital Boards; doctors' complaints (5+1 woman) regarding only 3 surgeons to do operations at hospital, improvements needed.	Document	Archives	
MNA/POL/6/7	Caerphilly Labour Party (Bargoed Ward Labour Party minutes)	1939–42	Hospital: staff salary increases; recruitment problems. Reference to MOH, Medical Superintendent of hospital. Ministry of Health fees to doctor who examined the Fire Service. Welsh Board of Health requesting release of MOH for war service. Pay for doctors in charge of: Isolation Hospital; clinics (female doctor); Bargoed Hostel; ARP. Gelligau Hospital – resignation of doctor. Problems for medical services as many doctors in army.	Document	Archives	
MNA/POL/6/8	Caerphilly Labour Party (Gelligaer Area Labour Party minutes)	1940–9	Reference to shortage of doctors.	Document	Archives	
MNA/POL/13/5	Neath Rural District Labour Party (Area Conference reports)	1935–40	1936: Reference to doctor (MOH).	Document	Archives	
MNA/POL/15/1	New Tredegar Trades and Labour Council	1938–51	(Trades and Labour Council minutes) 1948: reference to appointment of Medical Officer of Health applicants.	Document	Archives	
MNA/POL/24/1	Ynyshir Ward Labour Party	1936–8	(Rhondda Borough Trades and Labour Council and Labour Party Executive Committee minutes) Reference to Public Assistance doctor's resignation, and patients' free choice of doctor.	Document	Archives	
MNA/POL/24/2	Ynyshir Ward Labour Party	1947–51	(Committee minutes) Reference to shortage of doctors. Payments to doctors, and reporting of exploitation by practitioners.	Document	Archives	

269

Reference Code	Collection	Dates	Description	Media	Location	DP
MNA/PP/3/1–4	H. H. Chick (Clydach Vale)	1915	3 Colliery price list booklets including a list of doctors.	Document	Archives	
MNA/PP/9/4/2	H. W. Currie	1937–9	Card with doctor's name and address stamped on front. List of payments inside.	Document	Archives	
MNA/PP/9/7	H. W. Currie	1938	Newspaper cuttings with references to doctors' pay and regulation.	Document	Archives	
MNA/PP/9/29	H. W. Currie	1943–4	Newspaper cutting: Government white paper for NHS, doctors. Booklet, 'Forward – By the Right!', 1943 statement by Tory Reform Committee – section on doctors and patients (freedom of choice).	Document	Archives	
MNA/PP/16/7/1	S. O. Davies	1917–49	Newspaper cuttings re death of Llanelly doctor (Insurance Act panel doctor, works' medical attendant, school inspector); and specialists for Merthyr and Aberdare Hospital.	Document	Archives	
MNA/PP/16/12	S. O. Davies	1930s–1940s	Review of Socialist Medical Association pamphlet, including reference to doctors.	Document	Archives	
MNA/PP/16/50/2	S. O. Davies	1942	Constituency correspondence: Indian conscript medical student and racial prejudice.	Document	Archives	Y
MNA/PP/16/50/5	S. O. Davies	1943	Constituency correspondence: Czech doctor (acting as army medical orderly) request for Commission; medical student requesting release or move to RAMC.	Document	Archives	Y
MNA/PP/16/50/9 and 10	S. O. Davies	1947–8	Constituency correspondence: 1947: Car manufacturers' priority for doctors. 1948: Doctor's petrol use.	Document	Archives	Y
MNA/PP/30/4	Sonia Evans (Porth)	1925	Labour party election leaflet for Pontypridd Board of Guardians, including reference to doctors.	Document	Archives	

270

Reference Code	Collection	Dates	Description	Media	Location	DP
MNA/PP/41/1, 2, 5 and 6	David Harris (Glais) (exercise books containing bilingual manuscript reminiscences)	1970s, ref C19th	(1) References to local doctors, including mix-up of pills by one non-Welsh-speaking doctor. (2) Including list of Clydach doctors. (5) Clydach Hosp 1918, brief history including names of doctors. Photograph of Dr Varley at his son's birthday party (pre WWII). Reference to doctors' extracting teeth from patients. (6) Reference to pit accidents, including the ambulance room and doctor.	Document	Archives	Y
MNA/PP/73/1	James Lewis (Maesteg) (Maesteg Medical Fund committee minute book)	1929–39	Various references to medical fees and doctors. Disputes regarding payments and fee quotas. Complaints about waiting time for doctor and availability on Sundays.	Document	Archives	
MNA/PP/73/3	James Lewis (Maesteg) (Secretary of the Maesteg Medical Fund; papers relating to Maesteg Medical Fund)	1932–47	Contribution cards for 2 doctors. Payments to doctors. Correspondence with doctors. Handwritten notes from various doctors on receipt of fees.	Document	Archives	Y
MNB/PP/72/15–18	Alistair Wilson	1937–55	Doctor's house-call books, with brief personal details and notes re treatment and medicines.	Document	Archives	Y
MNB/PP/72/25	Alistair Wilson	1915–37	Day book with details of professional medical charges. Details of professional medical charges, bills, correspondence.	Document	Archives	Y
MNA/PP/73/2	James Lewis (Maesteg)	1940–1	Account book with lists of contributions to doctors.	Document	Archives	
MNA/PP/78/1 and 2	Glyn Mathias (Gorseinon)	1933	Bryngwyn Sheet Works payslips, including deductions for doctor.	Document	Archives	

Reference Code	Collection	Dates	Description	Media	Location	DP
MNA/PP/82/1	D. Morgan (general correspondence; Rhymney Workingmen's Medical Aid Fund)	1946–9	Memorial money for Dr Redwood. Redwood Memorial Hospital, Rhymney (Cardiff and District Hospital Society). Rhymney Cottage Hospital (transferred to Minister of Health 1947), tax and employment status of Dr E Thomas. Payments to doctors.	Document	Archives	Y
MNA/PP/82/2	D. Morgan (misc. papers; Rhymney Workingmen's Medical Aid Fund)	1942–8	1948: Income and Expenditure sheet, including doctors. House purchase for Medical Officer of Fund, Dr Redwood.	Document	Archives	Y
MNA/PP/111/1	Bryn Thomas ('Llandybie Over the Ages')	Early 1900s	Reference to having to pay to see a doctor.	Document	Archives	
MNA/PP/119/1 and 2	John B. Thomas (Bedlinog Medical Committee meetings minute book)	1912–13 1920–32	(1) 1912–13: References to doctor's employment. (2) 1920–32: Copy of doctor's appointment agreement (Dr T. H. Evans), including liberty to engage in private practice and public appointments. Complaints re doctor. Dispensing done by doctor as no qualified dispenser available.	Document	Archives	Y
MNA/PP/119/3	John B. Thomas (copy agreement appointing Dr E. L. M. Hopkins, Medical Attendant)	1908	Lists 8 conditions of employment including employee contributions, provision of Medical Attendance (free for poor and elderly), payment of arrears by unemployed, complaints, workmen pledging to be faithful to the doctor, and terms of notice.	Document	Archives	Y
MNA/NUM/1/1	Records of the Miners' Federation of Great Britain (minute books of Executive Committee, and annual and special conferences)	1944	Reference to Mines Medical Service and functions of the doctors.	Document	Archives and SWML	

Reference Code	Collection	Dates	Description	Media	Location	DP
MNA/NUM/3/1/1	Minutes of the SWMF Exec Council, and annual and special conferences	1907–40	Doctors – employment, complaints against, refusal to examine, drafted into army. BMA (boycott of medical funds) 1914.	Document	Archives and SWML	
MNA/NUM/3/3/21	Correspondence with SWMF No. 8 Area	1934–42	Appointment of Certifying Surgeon for district.	Document	Archives	
MNA/NUM/3/5/14	SWMF: Compensation Records (Compensation Secretary's correspondence)	1938	Public Health Department Cardiff, booklet re Cardiff Municipal Accident Service (talk to Cardiff Medical Society); including reference to doctors and medical students learning about industrial medicine.	Document	Archives	Y
MNA/NUM/3/8/17 (A)	Area No. 2 Council Minutes (register of ordinary accident cases)	1934–52	X-ray levy for doctors' fees and prices.	Document	Archives	Y
MNA/NUM/J/3/1	Abergorki Lodge (annual, general and committee meetings minute book)	1913–15	Dispute regarding a doctor forcing men to return to work, and Compensation Committee. References to Doctors' Committee and to doctors' poundage.	Document	Archives	
MNA/NUM/J/3/6	Abergorki Lodge (receipts for minor payments to SWMF Central funds)	1936–42	Payments for medical referee, and deputations to doctor and colliery office.	Document	Archives	
MNA/NUM/J/10/1	Bedwas Lodge (annual, general and committee meetings minutes.)	1925–33	Complaints about compensation doctor. Doctors' fees and unemployed contributions.	Document	Archives	
MNA/NUM/J/10/5	Bedwas Lodge (annual, general and committee meetings minutes)	1944–6	Hospital scheme and additional doctors.	Document	Archives	

Reference Code	Collection	Dates	Description	Media	Location	DP
MNA/NUM/L/32/1	Emlyn Lodge (Lodge account book)	1937–51	Payments to Dr Harper's scheme.	Document	Archives	
MNA/NUM/L/39/12 and 13	Gellyceidrim Lodge (Lodge Secretary's carbon-copy letter book)	1927–31	References to doctors.	Document	Archives	Y
MNA/NUM/L/39/15–21	Gellyceidrim Lodge (letters and circulars)	1898–1942	1917: letter requesting additional doctor for area (Carmarthenshire).	Document	Archives	
MNB/COL/14	Glanamman Colliery (Medical Fund account book)	1939–40	Weekly payments to doctors (including names and amounts paid). Lists deductions from pay for Dr Harper.	Document	Archives	
MNB/COL/17/D2–11	Morlais Colliery (weekly wage sheets)	1940–4	Lists deductions from wages, including doctor.	Document	Archives	Y
MNB/COL/17/H6	Morlais Colliery (Brynlliw Colliery; wages Book)	1909–11	Deductions from wages including doctor. Payments to doctors.	Document	Archives	
MNB/I/3/A6	Abergorki Workmen's Hall and Institute (abstracts of general committee minutes re colliery medical services)	1923–5	References to Drs Armstrong and Cohen. Request to transfer from colliery doctor to a local doctor. Colliery doctors to record visits to accident victims. New boys advised to report to colliery doctors. References to increased money to doctors, and their equal status.	Document	Archives	
MNB/I/7/1	Mountain Ash and Penrhiwceiber Hospital	1925	(Statement of accounts for year ending 31 December 1924). Lists staff, and reference to surgeons from Cardiff Infirmary.	Document	Archives	
MNB/I/7/5	Mountain Ash and Penrhiwceiber Hospital (annual report and financial statement)	1939	Appointment of Orthopaedic Surgeon, Dr Nathan Rocyn Jones (of Cardiff). Honorary medical staff including a female doctor, Dr Nora Thomas.	Document	Archives	

Reference Code	Collection	Dates	Description	Media	Location	DP
MNB/NUM/1/1/6	Abercynon Lodge (Lodge Secretary's carbon-copy letter book)	1938	Reference to Certifying Surgeon's fees.	Document	Archives	
MNB/NUM/1/1/21	Abercynon Lodge (wage sheets)	1940	Deductions including for Surgeon.	Document	Archives	
MNB/POL/2/1 and 2	Bridgend Trades Council (minute book)	1944–52	(1) Reference to shortage of doctors. (2) Reference to shortage of doctors at Aberkenfig.	Document	Archives	
MNB/PP/12/C/2/1–15	William Henry Davies (Penclawdd) (annual reports: MOH, Gower Rural Sanitary Authority)	1903	1903: reference to new MOH. 1911: MOH appointed as School Medical Inspector.	Document	Archives	
MNB/PP/72/13–14	Alistair Wilson (2 'Wellcome' medical diaries and visiting lists)	1920–8	182 printed pages of 'Therapeutic Notes and Index of Diseases and Treatment'. Includes 'Income Tax for Medical Men'. Handwritten entries regarding patients and visits.	Document	Archives	Y
MNC/COP/1/6	Aberdare Co-operative Society (minute book)	1945–8	Specialists at hospitals, references to enquiry into decision of Aberdare General Hospital regarding service.	Document	Archives	Y

Nurses

The voluntary and poor law hospitals of south Wales trained general nurses, with courses of typically three years leading to a certificate. The foundation of the General Nursing Council in 1919, and the commencement of nurse registration in 1921, attempted to standardize nurse training and registration, but hospitals retained a high degree of autonomy over the courses they delivered. The asylums and mental hospitals of the region provided training for mental nurses under the scheme run by the Medico-Psychological Association.

Outside the medical institution, midwives and district nurses played a significant role in the everyday lives of the coalfield population. District nurses were often provided by local voluntary district nursing associations, funded by private subscriptions (SWCC: AUD/212; [Local Area Collection] LAC/64). In addition, they were employed by the medical aid societies and workplace schemes that arranged doctors (SWCC: MNA/POL/8/1; MNB/NUM/L/9/1). Welfare organizations, trade unions and co-operative societies also made regular payments to local nursing associations (SWCC: MNA/I/16/1; MNC/COP/3/3–4; MNB/NUM/L/2/1–4).

Local authorities had no powers to employ district nurses or support district nursing associations until the Public Health Act of 1936, when this responsibility was allocated to the Medical Officer of Health. However, local authorities could provide midwifery (see Chapter 9, 'Women's Health'), school nursing and rural health visiting, and make arrangements to attend patients with infectious diseases. Furthermore, the poor law authorities were able to fund the home attendance of patients on poor relief. The statutory provision of district nursing did not come into being until the National Health Service of 1948.

The Queen's Nursing Institute, and its famous 'Queen's Nurses', made an important contribution to the development of community nursing. The institute was founded in 1887 to organize home nursing for the sick poor and to promote district nursing. Nurses were not employed directly, but they were affiliated, trained and inspected by the institute. In 1897 County Nursing Associations were introduced, which coordinated smaller rural associations and employed qualified midwives with an elementary training in home nursing. The Glamorgan County Nursing Association included the Abercynon and Ynysboeth District, and Mid-Rhondda (SWCC: HV686 R3; MNA/PP/9/4/1). However, the institute did not represent all district nurses because independent associations also existed, which in the South Wales Coalfield included Aberdare and District, Abersychan and District, Ammanford District, Bedlinog, Cinderford District (Forest of Dean), Monmouth, Pontnewydd, Pontycymmer and District, and Porth (SWCC: AUD/212; MNB/NUM/L/9/1).

Reference Code	Collection	Dates	Description	Media	Location	DP
	Gomer Evans (Pamphlet Box 6)	1945	*Labour Party Bulletin* No. 12, Vol. IV, 1945: Increased salaries for nurses; nursing and midwifery services, general training, mental, TB and industrial nursing, midwifery.	Document	SWML	
	Scrapbooks of newspaper cuttings (unlabelled green scrapbook)	1946–8	Colliery Medical Treatment Centres and colliery nurse.	Document	SWML	
AUD/212	Edgar Evans	c.1910–73	Bedlinog Hospital Committee and Nursing Association – politics.	Transcript of audio	SWML	Y
AUD/249	David Brown	1895–c.1973	Sister was a nurse: trained at Newport, worked at Rotherhyde Hospital (London), Whitchurch Military Hospital (WWII), and became a 'Queen's' nurse.	Transcript of audio	SWML	Y
AUD/310, 311	Abel Morgan	1878–c.1972	Hospital and Nursing Fund. Full-time Queen Alexandra's nurse paid for by subscription.	Transcript of audio	SWML	Y
AUD/394	Mr and Mrs D. J. Davies	1910–c.1974	Experiences of nurse training of Mrs Davies: SRN (London); midwifery certificate (Plymouth); private nursing work; district nursing; continuation of career whilst married; work with Dr Pritchard (Aberdare MOH) in orthopaedics.	Transcript of audio	SWML	Y
HD9550 EBB	*The Ebbw Vale Works Magazine*, Vol. 4, No. 16	Sept 1925	Note regarding Ebbw Vale branch of Monmouthshire Nursing Association annual fete.	Document	SWML	
HD9550 EBB	*The Ebbw Vale Works Magazine*, Vol. 6, No. 21	Dec 1926	Article: 'Ebbw Vale Nurses' Home' – Ebbw Vale branch, Monmouth Nursing Association; staff and nurses' work with doctors in district.	Document	SWML	
HD9550 EBB	*The Ebbw Vale Works Magazine*, Vol. 6, Nos 23–4	Jun–Sept 1927	June and September; Newbridge Nursing Association and Ebbw Vale Nurses' Association fetes.	Document	SWML	

Reference Code	Collection	Dates	Description	Media	Location	DP
HD9550 EBB	The Ebbw Vale Works Magazine, Vol. 7, No. 28	Sept 1928	Reference to Nursing Association annual fete.	Document	SWML	
HD9550 EBB	The Ebbw Vale Works Magazine, Vol. 8, Nos 30–2	Mar–Sept 1929	Abertillery Nursing Division winning prize. Ebbw Vale Nurses' Association fete.	Document	SWML	
HD9550 EBB	The Ebbw Vale Works Magazine, Vol. 10, No. 39	Jul 1931	Cwm Ambulance and Nursing Divisions awards evening.	Document	SWML	
HD9550 EBB	The Ebbw Vale Works Magazine, Vol. 10, No. 40	Oct 1931	Ebbw Vale Nursing Association fete.	Document	SWML	
HD9552.3 MIN	The Miner, Vol. III, No. 3	Jan 1947	Article: 'Miners' Welfare', including reference to nurse.	Document	SWML	
HV686.R3	Reports of the MOH, and School MO, Rhondda UDC	1914–47	Schools; medical inspections, hygiene, clinics and nurses. 1918: List of health visitors and school nurses, indicating if they have nursing experience. 1925: Llwynypia Hospital (converted from Poor Law Institute 1925) and approved training school for nurses. Nursing facilities, provision of nurses by voluntary and other agencies, lectures on home nursing. 1928: Ambulance and nursing facilities: scarcity of nurses in district (3; 1 from Association in Porth; 1 employed by Medical Aid Society in Mid-Rhondda; 1 engaged by GP). 1930: Ambulance and nursing facilities: Nursing Association affiliated with Queen's Institute of District Nursing and Glamorgan County Nursing Association, organised in Mid-Rhondda 1930 – 2 nurses. 1940: School MO: Appointment of orthopaedic nurse – clinics at Carnegie Welfare Centre. 1947: School nurses, certificate details including 'Obstetric Analgesia'.	Document	SWML	

Reference Code	Collection	Dates	Description	Media	Location	DP
LAC/64	Miss E. Leyshon (Swansea) (summary of work done by district nurses in Swansea's East Side)	1905–35	List of no. of visits 1905–35. Maternity nurse appointed 1916.	Document	Archives	
LAC/64	Miss E. Leyshon (Swansea) (East Side District Nursing Association annual reports and accounts)	1905–40	(1923 missing) Case numbers and visits. Balance sheets. Case statistics including TB. Rules. New appointments and resignations. Maternity nurse (from 1916), midwifery statistics, 1937 Maternity Act. Penny-a-month scheme 1907. Surgical nurse appointment. Queens' nurses.	Document	Archives	
MNA/COP/1/17	Aberdare and District Co-op Society Ltd (general and Board Meeting minutes)	1932–5	Aberdare and District, District Nursing Associations.	Document	Archives	Y
MNA/COP/5/1/1–14	Pembroke Dock Co-op Society (general and committee meetings minutes)	1888–1951	Reference to Victoria Nurses Home Committee.	Document	Archives	
MNA/I/10/4	Cwmaman Institute (annual, general and committee minutes)	1932–6	Reference to Glamorgan Nursing Association to discuss forming a District Nursing Association at Cwmaman (1935).	Document	Archives	
MNA/I/16/1	Forest of Dean District Welfare Association (committee minutes)	1921–4	Cinderford District Nursing Association (new), grant given for 2 bicycles for nurses.	Document	Archives	
MNA/NUM/L/43/A1	Graig Merthyr Lodge (general and committee minutes)	1937–40	Appointment of representatives for Nursing Association.	Document	Archives	Y
MNA/POL/1/2	Aberdare Town Ward Labour Party (committee minutes)	1943–52	Reference to Nursing Committee.	Document	Archives	

Reference Code	Collection	Dates	Description	Media	Location	DP
MNA/POL/3/3	Ammanford, Llandebie and District Trades and Labour Council (annual, general and Executive Council minutes)	1941–8	Reference to dismissed nurse at Mental Hospital, and withheld superannuation. St John's Nursing Association collection.	Document	Archives	
MNA/POL/5	Bedlinog Independent Labour Party (press cuttings)	1934–6	*Western Mail* newspaper cuttings; 1934: Lady Windsor Colliery Nursing Fund receipts and disbursements .	Document	Archives	
MNA/POL/6/1 and 2	Caerphilly Labour Party (Executive Committee minutes)	1938–46	(1) County council work including with regard to nurse shortage. UDC and nurses' housing. Extension of Isolation Hospital, staff working conditions and houses. (2) Reference to letter by nurses from Llwyncelyn Hospital regarding poor condition of building and employment problems	Document	Archives	
MNA/POL/6/5	Caerphilly Labour Party (Caerphilly Area Labour Party minutes)	1940–50	TB: care of patients by fever nurses; nurse shortage. Llwynypia Hospital, nurses' lecture rooms heating. Nurses' pay. Housing for midwives. Training centre for nurses, Pontypridd. Nurses' grants for cars and bicycles. Nursing services overseen by Divisional Health Committee 1948.	Document	Archives	
MNA/POL/6/7	Caerphilly Labour Party (Bargoed Ward Labour Party minutes)	1939–42	Nurse shortage – use of male nurses to be tried, 1941. Midwives and work during air raids. New Midwifery Act. Hospital nurses and 48-hour week. Reference to matron and duties. Nurse at Gelligau Hospital case (no details).	Document	Archives	
MNA/POL/6/8	Caerphilly Labour Party (Gelligaer Area Labour Party minutes)	1940–9	Nurses: Training Centre Pontypridd; shortage; leaving rate high; poor working conditions at Church Village Hospital; number of full-time nurses. Refers to training hospitals (e.g. Cardiff Infirmary).	Document	Archives	

Reference Code	Collection	Dates	Description	Media	Location	DP
MNA/POL/8/1	Ebbw Vale Branch Iron and Steel Trades and Labour Council (cash book)	1899–1919	Receipts and expenditure including Nursing Association.	Document	Archives	
MNA/POL/13/1	Neath Rural District Labour Party (minute book)	1935–40	1937: reference to nursing profession and trade union organization.	Document	Archives	
MNA/POL/15/1	New Tredegar Trades and Labour Council (minutes)	1938–51	1938: references to circulars, TUC – Health Insurance and compensation for work absence re contact with infectious diseases, and Health Services Federation, appropriate union for nurses. Maternity nurse shortage in area.	Document	Archives	
MNA/POL/24/2	Ynyshir Ward Labour Party (Ynyshir Ward Committee minutes)	1947–51	Doctors and nurses shortage. Clinic staff shortage and long waiting list. Married nurse given temporary job. Probationer nurse advertisements and certificates. Regional Hospital Boards taking over midwifery. District nurses, replacement of voluntary organizations with central service.	Document	Archives	
MNA/PP/9/4/1	H. W. Currie	1936	Abercynon and Ynysboeth District Nursing Association subscribers' contribution card. Affiliated to Queen's Institute of District Nurses and Glamorgan County Nursing Association. Lists officials' names and addresses, and 6 rules re services.	Document	Archives	
MNA/PP/9/17/1–2	H. W. Currie	1937–48	Newspaper cuttings: training and recruitment of nurses, and ban on 'coloured' nurses.	Document	Archives	
MNA/PP/12/14	Mrs Beatrice Davies (née Phippen), Ystrad Rhondda	1935	Rhondda UDC election leaflet for Eliza Williams (collier's wife). Includes unsatisfactory condition of nurses at isolation hospitals.	Document	Archives	
MNA/PP/16/50/5	S. O. Davies	1943	Constituency correspondence; nurse at mental hospital, dislike of work.	Document	Archives	Y

Reference Code	Collection	Dates	Description	Media	Location	DP
MNA/PP/24/4	Edgar Evans (Bedlinog)	1936	References to District Nursing Assoc (Bedlinog) and to individual nurse (Secretary of Association – Edgar Evan's wife).	Document	Archives	Y
MNA/PP/30/4	Sonia Evans (Porth)	1925	Labour party election leaflet for Pontypridd Board of Guardians; references to nurses.	Document	Archives	
MNA/PP/41/1	David Harris (Glais) (exercise books containing bilingual manuscript reminiscences)	1970s, ref C19th	List of local nurses c.1900.	Document	Archives	Y
MNA/PP/67/34	W. Eddie Jones (newsletter)	1938	*Cardiff Vanguard* newsletter (Cardiff Communist Party). Reference to Cardiff Royal Infirmary lack of funds, affecting patients, nurses, doctors.	Document	Archives	
MNA/PP/78/1 and 2	Glyn Mathias (Gorseinon)	1933	Bryngwyn Sheet Works payslips, including deductions for nursing.	Document	Archives	
MNA/PP/82/1 and 2	D. Morgan (general correspondence, letters and circulars re Rhymney Workingmen's Medical Aid Fund)	1942–9	(1) Ministry of Health Circular 63/47 'Nurses' Salaries'. (2) Nurses' Record of Hospital or Institutional Service, G. Haskell, SRN, RFM Midwifery Part I (Sister). British Hospitals Association (S Wales and Monmouth) meeting re Beveridge Report, nurses' salaries (Rushcliffe Committee), Medical Planning Commission.	Document	Archives	Y
MNA/PP/104/4	Mrs. Margaret Roberts (Tonypandy) (Christmas card)	1914	Christmas card depicting nurse and injured soldier, entitled 'A Woman's Part'.	Document	Archives	
MNA/PP/119/2	John B. Thomas	1920–32	Bedlinog Medical Committee Meetings minute book, accounts, agreement re Dr T. H. Evans. Copy of doctor's appointment agreement, including provision of district nurse. Nursing classes.	Document	Archives	Y
MNA/PP/122/1	Wilfred Timbrell (Tumble) (memoirs of Tumble)	1896–c.1960s	Nursing Association in village.	Document	Archives	

Reference Code	Collection	Dates	Description	Media	Location	DP
MNB/COL/14	Glanamman Colliery (Medical Fund account book)	1939–40	Lists deductions from pay including for nurse.	Document	Archives	
MNB/NUM/L2/1–4	Ammanford No.2 Lodge (minute books)	1924–34	Ammanford District Nursing Association Scheme, and midwifery services.	Document	Archives	
MNB/NUM/L2/8	Ammanford No. 2 Lodge (Lodge balance sheet for 1938)	1939	Nursing Association.	Document	Archives	
MNB/NUM/L9/1	Ffaldau Lodge (minute book)	1939–41	Ballot for Local Nurses Association (and copy ballot paper), Pontycymmer and District Nursing Association, re penny-a-week scheme.	Document	Archives	
MNB/POL/6/A6	Newport Constituency Labour Party (Executive and General Committee minutes)	1930–3	Woolaston House; work hours of nurses, and position of OAP inmates including cost.	Document	Archives	
MNB/POL/6/A8	Newport Constituency Labour Party (Executive and General Committee minutes, and Health Committee report)	1938–44	National Advisory Council for Training and Allocation of Nurses. Woolaston House Infirmary: 1942: prosecution of 2 wartime nurses; 1943: report by Social Welfare Committee concerning diet, and treatment of patients; poor treatment of probationer nurses; PAC Relieving Officer and admittance note.	Document	Archives	Y
MNB/PP/12/C2/1–15	William Henry Davies (Penclawdd)	1895–1911	(Annual reports: MOH, Gower Rural Sanitary Authority) 1911: Two district nurses both certified midwives, not to attend cases without medical supervision.	Document	Archives	
MNB/PP/20/E11	Glyn Evans (Garnant) (Borough Council circular re Midwives Act)	1936	Metropolitan Borough of St Pancras Public Health Department circular; Midwives Act 1936. Administration of Act, MOH Public Notice. Midwifery and maternity nursing in home, midwives' details, hospitals and associations (e.g. Maternity Nursing Association), medical consultants.	Document	Archives	

Reference Code	Collection	Dates	Description	Media	Location	DP
MNC/COP/1/3	Aberdare Co-operative Society (minute book)	1937–40	Donations: Nursing Associations at Aberaman, Penrhiwceiber and Mountain Ash.	Document	Archives	
MNC/COP/1/6	Aberdare Co-operative Society (minute book)	1945–8	Donations: Abercwmboi Nursing Association.	Document	Archives	Y
MNC/COP/3/3 and 4	Abersychan Co-op Society (minute Book)	1924–31	(3) Donations: Monmouthshire Nursing Association, Abersychan and District Nursing Association. Pontnewydd Nursing Association subscription. (4) Donations: District Nursing Associations.	Document	Archives	
MNC/COP/5/1	Allwen and Pontardawe Co-op (minute book (Welsh))	1914–17	Subscriptions to Pontardawe and District Nursing Association.	Document	Archives	
MNC/NUM/5/182	NUM S Wales Area, SWMF Eastern Valleys District monthly meetings minutes (D2/F53)	1915	Dr Rocyn Jones, presentation ceremony and speech details, relating to Monmouthshire Nursing Association.	Document	Archives	
MNC/PP/17/13	Selwyn Jones (minute book, Social Service Guild)	c.1928	Committee to relieve local distress, baby clothes to be made, soup kitchen for unemployed, distributing clothing, food and clothes 'tickets', involvement of district nurse, aid in sickness (and medical certificates), food parcels.	Document	Archives	
PHO/COL/49	Colliery Photographs (collieries)	1916	Formal photograph of people who attended Glamorgan Colliery ambulance and home nursing classes.	Photographs	Archives	

Dentists

The first register of qualified dentists was opened in 1921. Although no new unqualified dentists were permitted to work, many already practising were allowed to register. Dentists, based in private practices, charged their own fees. In middle-class districts, they were able to achieve the social standing of a professional and generate an income that was consistent with that lifestyle. In working-class areas, on the other hand, both social status and earnings were low because merely a few approved societies included dentistry in their benefits, and even they usually paid just part of the cost.

The only fully salaried dentists paid in the state sector were those who worked in the school and infant welfare clinics, which were run by local authorities. These clinics ensured free dental treatment for expectant mothers until their children were five years old, and for infants and children until they left school at the age of fourteen. A shortage of dentists often prevented adequate treatment, encouraging extractions in preference to fillings, even for children. In 1948 the Spens Report concluded that large parts of the country were either without or short of dentists. Therefore, when the National Health Service offered free dental treatment, there was an enormous demand (SWCC: R1.5513). However, the dentists who met this demand remained independent. Unlike general practitioners, they did not 'sell' their practices to the state; nor did they receive a capitation fee for every registered patient. Instead, they were paid an agreed sum for every treatment undertaken, regardless of whether the patient was on their list.

Between 1914 and 1947, the Rhondda medical officer of health – acting as school medical officer – reported on the dental defects found in school children in the district, and on the treatments that they received (SWCC: HV686 R3). Children underwent dental examinations from a school dentist, who was assisted by a dental nurse. Adults could obtain treatment if they paid for it themselves, or were covered by a welfare, workplace, or Co-operative Society scheme (SWCC: MNB/PP/64/K1; MNC/COP/3/1). Claims by miners for dental treatment and dentures were often associated with minor accidents that had taken place while working (SWCC: MNA/COL/2/4–38; MNA/NUM/3/5/5).

Reference Code	Collection	Dates	Description	Media	Location	DP
HV686.R3	Reports of the MOH, and School MO, Rhondda UDC	1923	1923: Schools: Dental defects; School Dentist Miss Poole, Ynyshir Dental Clinic; Dental Nurses. 1939: Appointments: Miss Rhoda Kelso (Assistant Dental Surgeon).	Document	SWML	
MNA/COP/3/2	Briton Ferry and Neath Co-op Society	1919–24	Balance sheets and committee reports: Co-op dental scheme for treatment by registered dental surgeon.	Document	Archives	
MNA/I/25/13	Markham and District Welfare Association (Secretary's correspondence)	1928	Leaflet of Industrial Health Education Society advertising health talks. Speakers included doctors and dentists, free of charge, to talk to meetings of workers re health matters.	Document	Archives	
MNA/POL/24/2	Ynyshir Ward Labour Party (committee minutes)	1947–51	Dentists: shortage and provision at secondary schools.	Document	Archives	
MNA/POL/6/5	Caerphilly Labour Party (minutes)	1940–50	School medical report, including numbers of dental surgeons.	Document	Archives	
MNA/POL/6/7	Caerphilly Labour Party (Bargoed Ward Labour Party minutes)	1939–42	Dentists and medical services – problems with shortages as many in army.	Document	Archives	
MNA/PP/16/11/1-34	S. O. Davies	1948	Written answers re NHS – hearing aids, medical services (NI contributions), dentists; mental hospitals.	Document	Archives	
MNA/PP/24/5	Edgar Evans (Bedlinog)	1936	Personal correspondence; political letter of support from Aberystwyth dentist (re Edgar Evan's arrest and time in prison).	Document	Archives	Y
MNC/COP/3/1	Abersychan Co-op Society (minute book)	1908–12	Dentist's request to be on Society's list, reference to his County Court fine for Damages. Wholesale Co-op Artificial Teeth Supply Association.	Document	Archives	
RI.5513	Socialism and Health. The Future for Dentistry – a policy document (pamphlet)	ud	Published by Socialist Medical Association, Vol. 8, No 2. History of dentistry pre- and post-1948. Health centres. Solutions for the future.	Document	SWML	

Pharmacists

The Pharmaceutical Society of Great Britain was founded in 1841. The aims of the Society were to unite the profession into a single body, protect members' interests and advance scientific knowledge. Under legislation passed in 1815, the Society of Apothecaries acted as a licensing body for medical practitioners who held neither an MD nor a diploma from the Royal College of Surgeons. However, the qualifications of pharmaceutical chemists were first regulated by the 1852 Pharmacy Act. In 1865, the Chemists and Druggists (No. 2) Act prohibited trading under these titles without examination and registration, while three years later the Pharmacy Act recognized the chemist and druggist as custodian of named poisons (such as arsenic and opium) which had previously been unregulated and freely available (SWCC: [Local Area Collection] LAC/6).

The discretion of pharmacists was the only safeguard against the abuse of medicaments; and even if customers were turned away, they could go elsewhere to a less reputable pharmacy. Therefore, the 1908 Poisons and Pharmacy Act restricted the sale of poisonous material to registered chemists, on condition that the customer be known to the seller and that an entry be made in a Poisons Register. The 1920 Dangerous Drugs Act made the sale of drugs dependent on a doctor's prescription, replacing the old system of the chemist selling drugs to known customers. The Report of the Departmental Committee on the Poisons and Pharmacy Acts, published in 1930, distinguished the practice of pharmacy from the control of poisons, recommending that all chemists and druggists should be registered members of the Pharmaceutical Society, and that the Home Office should become the Central Authority for poisons.

Reference Code	Collection	Dates	Description	Media	Location	DP
LAC/6	Edward Bevan (Swansea), account books & balance Sheet	1859–1901	Cash books with references to pills, tablets, drugs, dried milk, Bristol Medicine Co., equipment (bottles, syphons), Potash Water, Pharmaceutical Society, powders, chemists, medical guide. 1896: Balance sheet, lists companies and people.	Document	Archives	
LAC/6	Edward Bevan (Swansea), pharmaceutical notebook and address book	c.1875	Handwritten notebook relating to opium. Notes on varieties, collection, composition. Opium test. Adulterations. Administration and dosage. Preparations with ingredients and amounts. Lists of pills, powders, syrups, tinctures. Student list. Address book.	Document	Archives	
LAC/6	Edward Bevan (Swansea), Lloyd's Bank passbooks	1896–1931	Payments to Bristol Drug Houses, National Drug, doctor, Beechams Pills, Distillery and Pharmaceutical Society.	Document	Archives	
MNC/COP/1/6	Aberdare Co-operative Society (minute book)	1945–8	Chemist shop (Aberdare): Licence applied for 1945, recruitment of manager, preparations for new shop, staff interviews, pay rates, additional shop in Hirwaun (1947), 1948 panel of chemists re new National Health Scheme. Mountain Ash Hospital prescriptions.	Document	Archives	Y
MNC/COP/3/3	Abersychan Co-op Society (minute book)	1924–31	1930: reference to the opening of a new chemist shop.	Document	Archives	
MNC/COP/3/4	Abersychan Co-op Society (minute book)	1945–9	Pontypool Drug Department staff problems. Abersychan Drug Department spoiled goods, and new chemist shop. Employment of qualified Pharmacist and compliance with Pharmaceutical Acts. Abersychan Drug Department, staff problems. Wage rates. Dispensing under new Insurance Act 1948. Reference to the investigation of prices in Drug Departments for gelatine and aspirins. Pharmaceutical Committee and Monmouth Insurance Committee. Trade union proposed wage increase for pharmacy and optical workers.	Document	Archives	

Reference Code	Collection	Dates	Description	Media	Location	DP
MNC/COP/16/11	Penygraig Co-op Society (minute book, Finance Committee)	1936–42	Copy of minutes 15 September 37: reference to Drug Department and appointment of apprentice. Pharmaceutical Society to inform regarding examination subjects which qualify applicant for registration as apprentice.	Document	Archives	
MNC/COP/16/22	Penygraig Co-op Society (minute book, Management Committee)	1948–9	Pharmacy Department: references to staffing, salaries, Pharmacy Agreement under negotiation, Indentured Apprentices (Chemist and Dispenser), Pharmacy opening hours, and Rules of the Pharmaceutical Society.	Document	Archives	
MNC/COP/27/27	People's Yearbooks (annual of the Co-operative Wholesale Society Ltd)	1948	References to the National Co-operative Chemists Ltd, pharmacy and drug trade.	Document	Archives	
MNC/PP/33/1	Peggy Williams	1885	Certificate of Apprentice's Indenture (4 years) for Chemist and Druggist in Cardigan, Carmarthenshire. Apprentice; George Hughes. Master; Joseph Rees.	Document	Archives	

Health Insurance and Medical Aid

Although medical care was available through the nineteenth-century poor law, the emphasis on economy and deterrence, and the promotion of self-help on the part of the lower classes, led to an extremely rudimentary service. Therefore, the introduction of a compulsory initiative by the state in the shape of the 1911 National Insurance Act was a path-breaking development. The new scheme was administered by government-approved friendly societies, trade unions and commercial insurance companies, and the cost was borne by workers, employers and the state; employers deducted contributions from workers' wages, and purchased stamps for each contributor's insurance card, which showed how much had been paid (SWCC: MNA/PP/118/11, 115; MNB/COL/17/C33B). Any insured worker was entitled to free medical treatment by a doctor who was a member of the 'panel'. Workers received sick pay, maternity and disablements benefits, and free treatment in a sanatorium or similar establishment if suffering from tuberculosis or another listed disease (SWCC: MNB/PP/64/K1; MNC/COP/27/1). However, the scheme had limitations. In particular, it provided for the workers but not their dependants and excluded those with a previous history of ill health.

The 1911 Act was subject to a number of amendments during the interwar years, the 1937 extension of medical benefit to young workers aged fourteen to sixteen years being especially notable. Furthermore, there was widespread discussion about future services. The Royal Commission on National Health Insurance (the Lawrence Commission), which sat between 1924 and 1926, recommended that inequalities in benefits offered by approved societies should be addressed, and that additional health services should be available to all members, financed by the societies. The commission suggested that 'expert out-patient services' should be provided, plus allowances for dependants on sick benefit and an extension of maternity benefit. Other suggestions included transferring the administration of the scheme to the local authorities. None of these changes took effect and in 1926 the government reduced its contributions to the fund. During the 1930s, some general practitioners did establish medical services for the dependants of their panel patients, and the British Medical Association argued for the expansion of the health insurance scheme, to incorporate specialist and dental services, nursing and pharmaceutical provisions. The Socialist Medical Association and the Labour Party went still further, suggesting that health services should be financed completely by local and central government, and available to the entire population free of charge. However, it was not until the creation of the National Health Service in 1948 that these ideas came to fruition.

In the absence of comprehensive state provision, working people turned to alternative sources of medical care, showing in the process that 'self-help' could emerge from collective as well as individual action in the bid to escape the stigma of the poor law and the workhouse. Friendly societies were one such option. Increasingly popular from the early nineteenth century – notably in industrial, urban areas – they were formed by small local groups and on a larger national scale, where greater funds and a wider range of benefits were available. In return for modest weekly payments, members benefited when they were sick or needed to pay for a funeral (SWCC: MNA/I/7; MNA/I/34). Nevertheless, these societies were beyond the reach of the most poorly paid workers, and those with irregular employment patterns, who were not uncommonly penalized by a system of fines for non-payment of subscriptions. Consequently, burial societies were a more affordable choice for many who were determined to avoid the indignity of a pauper's funeral (SWCC: MNA/PP/118/73; MNB/NUM/L/2/19; MNB/TUG/2/1). Following a Royal Commission, the 1875 Friendly Societies Act sought to regulate the societies more rigorously and protect their members from financial volatility.

Complementing the activities of friendly societies were workplace or occupational schemes run by trade unions and financed by membership subscriptions. These trade union welfare schemes supplied benefits during sickness and convalescence, as well as cover for dependants like maternity support (SWCC: MNA/PP/

118/12; MNA/PP/118/61). Similarly, co-operative societies offered provision for funerals – though, because dividends were based on the amount of money spent in their stores, poorer customers were at times excluded. The co-operative societies also introduced their own health insurance schemes, with additional benefits from dentists and opticians becoming available (SWCC: HD2951 A5; MNC/COP/27). Some of the larger employers also managed their own sickness benefit societies for employees (SWCC: MNA/TUG/ 1/1; MNA/TUG/9/5; MNB/I/1/1).

This variety of insurance schemes was represented among industrial workers in the South Wales Coalfield, their payslips listing deductions for doctors, nurses, hospitals, organizations (such as the Red Cross), and other health-related benefits (SWCC: MNA/COL/2/55; MNA/PP/78/1–2). In addition, however, medical aid schemes were popular. The schemes operated on a 'poundage' system, in which mutually agreed deductions were taken from the pay of workmen, who were also involved in the administration of the funds and election of officials. In return for their contributions, they received treatment from doctors and nurses, surgical appliances, access to local hospital and convalescent facilities, and benefits for their dependants (SWCC: AUD/215; MNA/I/19/C3; MNC/NUM/5/182). It is alleged that Aneurin Bevan derived his model for the National Health Service from Tredegar Medical Aid Society.

Reference Code	Collection	Dates	Description	Media	Location	DP
AUD/215	Walter Powell	c.1900–74	Medical Aid Societies; payments, membership, surgeries, doctors, sick scheme.	Transcript of audio	SWML	Y
AUD/219	Del Davies	1930–c.1973	Ynyscedwyn Sick Fund. Mutual Aid.	Transcript of audio	SWML	Y
AUD/336	Harold Finch (permission needed for use)	1920–c.1973	SWMF Compensation Secretary. South Wales and Monmouthshire Indemnity Society. History of legislation, silicosis and pneumoconiosis. Industrial Injuries Scheme.	Transcript of audio	SWML	Y
AUD/382	D. C. Davies	1930–c.1976	Social Insurance. Work as Lodge Compensation Secretary. Indemnity Societies employed by coal owners.	Transcript of audio	SWML	Y
HD2951.A5	Annual Co-operative Congress reports (incomplete set)	1913–76	1930: NHI prescriptions. Employees' sick pay. Medicine Stamp Duty. Distress Fund. Insurance.	Document	SWML	
HD9552.3 MIN	The Miner, Vol. I, No. 2	Nov 1944	Articles: 'Social Insurance Plan (Part I)', re sickness benefits, invalidity, medical and hospital treatment, NHS; 'Social Insurance Plan (Part II) Workmen's Compensation'; 'The Detector Order', re gas and firedamp regulations.	Document	SWML	
HD9552.3 MIN	The Miner, Vol. II, No. 5/6	Feb/Mar 1946	Article: 'Principles underlying the New Industrial Injuries Bill'.	Document	SWML	
HD9552.3 MIN	The Miner, Vol. II, No. 7	May 1946	Articles: 'Social Insurance – with Special Reference to the Industrial Injuries Bill'; 'Removing a Pestilence' re silicosis and pneumoconiosis, dust suppression. Pneumoconiosis 1946 Regulation details from General and Compensation Secretaries. Advertisement re compensation and inadequate lump sum settlements.	Document	SWML	
HD9552.3 MIN	The Miner, Vol. III, No. 4/5	Feb/Mar 1947	Article re The National Insurance Act 1946.	Document	SWML	
MNA/COL/2/55	Clydach Merthyr Colliery (Manager's correspondence)	1940–1	Insurance. Ambulances. Red Cross fund.	Document	Archives	Y

Reference Code	Collection	Dates	Description	Media	Location	DP
MNA/COP/1/17	Aberdare and District Co-op Society Ltd (general and Board Meeting minutes)	1932-5	Western Co-op Convalescent Fund. District Nursing Association. CWS Health Insurance.	Document	Archives	Y
MNA/COP/2/1-11	Ammanford Co-op Society (general and committee meetings minutes)	1900-38	Health Insurance allowances.	Document	Archives	
MNA/COP/3/2	Briton Ferry and Neath Co-op Society (balance sheets and committee reports)	1919-24	Accounts including health insurance payments and claims.	Document	Archives	
MNA/COP/7/43	Ton Co-op Society (reports and balance sheets)	1890-1956	Payments to Convalescent Fund, Health Insurance claims, National Health Insurance Sick Pay.	Document	Archives	
MNA/I/11/C13	Cwmllynfell Miners' Welfare Association (minute and daily account book of Old Cwmllynfell Colliery)	1875-6	Rules for workmen employed at Cwmllynfell Colliery, including deductions from wages for Medical and Surgical Attendance. Also refers to need for certificate from surgeon if ill.	Document	Archives	
MNA/I/16/1	Forest of Dean District Welfare Association (committee minutes)	1921-4	Meetings with Industrial Welfare Society. St Johns Ambulance Association, Forest of Dean Centre, grants, visit re establishing a sick room, stores.	Document	Archives	
MNA/I/16/3	Forest of Dean District Welfare Association (committee minutes)	1929-35	1929: grant to assist injured miners. Copy letter from doctors dealing with cases, fees and retaining fees. Limitation on no. of cases due to cost. Details of discussions.	Document	Archives	Y
MNA/I/19/A1	Lily of the Valley Lodge of the Unity of Oddfellows, Ystrad Rhondda (register of members)	1833-1905	Lists members' contributions and payments re relief for sickness, accidents, old age, funeral donations (including personal details).	Document	Archives	

Reference Code	Collection	Dates	Description	Media	Location	DP
MNA/I/19/A3–5	Lily of the Valley Lodge of the Unity of Oddfellows, Ystrad Rhondda (office books, secret book, and general rule book (bilingual))	c.1840–1900	References to visiting the sick and afflicted. Questions re health on initiation into Order. Ref to assisting members in ill health and old age, and dependants on death of member. Refers to relief payment and need for medical certificate.	Document	Archives	
MNA/I/19/B1	Lily of the Valley Lodge of the Unity of Oddfellows, Ystrad Rhondda (general account book)	1849–82	Monthly contributions paid by members including Funeral Fund. Payments for relief for sickness, accidents, old age (including personal details).	Document	Archives	
MNA/I/19/B26	Lily of the Valley Lodge of the Unity of Oddfellows	1888–98	2 Relief Books, 1888–93 and 1893–8. Names and amounts of relief paid to members.	Document	Archives	
MNA/I/19/B7	Lily of the Valley Lodge of the Unity of Oddfellows, Ystrad Rhondda (fines book with draft accounts)	1838–9	Refers to relief payments for sickness.	Document	Archives	
MNA/I/19/C1	Lily of the Valley Lodge of the Unity of Oddfellows, Ystrad Rhondda (Lodge Secretary's records)	1926–32	Subscriptions and privileges for Porth Cottage Hospital. Subscriptions and tickets for Cardiff Royal Infirmary, Bristol Royal Infirmary, Porthcawl Rest, Southerdown Rests. Subscription to St Mark's Cancer Research Hospital, London.	Document	Archives	
MNA/I/19/C2	Lily of the Valley Lodge of the Unity of Oddfellows, Ystrad Rhondda (general correspondence)	1881–1950	Requests for assistance and relief, and notes advising of illness and inability to work. Subscriptions for St Mark's Hospital London, Porth Cottage Hospital, Bristol Royal Infirmary, Porthcawl Rest. Sick allowance claim.	Document	Archives	Y
MNA/I/19/C3	Lily of the Valley Lodge of the Unity of Oddfellows, Ystrad Rhondda (health certificates)	1899–1950	1899: 2 doctors' certificates re unable to work (no illness details). 1930: 8 doctors' certificates including 3 from Mid-Rhondda Medical Aid Society, some have illness details.	Document	Archives	Y

Reference Code	Collection	Dates	Description	Media	Location	DP
MNA/I/19/C4	Lily of the Valley Lodge of the Unity of Oddfellows, Ystrad Rhondda (death certificates)	1892–1929	Certificates for purposes of a Registered Friendly Society. Including personal details, cause of death and when/where.	Document	Archives	Y
MNA/I/2/1–7	Abertridwr Institute (minute books)	1927–39	Refers to Health and Unemployment Insurance contributions. Donations to Caerphilly Miners' Hospital, and Pontypridd Institute for the Blind.	Document	Archives	
MNA/I/20/A1	Maerdy Workmen's Hall and Institute	1920s	Use of building as temporary hospital, use as surgery for New Medical Scheme. Loan to New Medical Scheme Committee. 1923: payment for insurance for servants under Workmen's Compensation Act.	Document	Archives	
MNA/I/22/1–2	Maesteg Medical Fund (balance sheets)	1925–47	Including money received from collieries and distribution of payments to named doctors. 1925: including list of members attending canteens.	Document	Archives	
MNA/I/23/6	Maesteg Miners' Welfare Fund (wages book)	1929–36	Including payments for hospital, health and employer's contributions to health insurance.	Document	Archives	Y
MNA/I/30/5	Onllwyn and District Miners' Welfare Association (account book)	1924–37	Compensation payments. Hospital attendance. Subscriptions to Industrial Welfare Society. Health insurance stamps.	Document	Archives	
MNA/I/32/1	Powell Duffryn Workmen's Hospital (balance sheet)	1938	Expenditure: staff, provisions, surgical, medical, cleaning, fuel, water. Income: donations. Statistics: patient numbers, x-rays, casualties, outpatients, massage, electric treatments, ultra violet ray, infra red therapy, operations, costs.	Document	Archives	
MNA/I/34/A2	St. David's Unity of Ivorites (rule books (in Welsh and English))	1848–1920	References: relief during sickness and infirmity; members in distress; Accident Fund; health questions re new members; contributions; benefit claims; benefit details; sick visitors; National Insurance Acts 1911 and 1922; hospitalization; provisions for women.	Document	Archives	

Reference Code	Collection	Dates	Description	Media	Location	DP
MNA/I/34/A4	St David's Unity of Ivorites (lecture books)	1865–1903	Reference to notices of distress, sickness or recovery of any members. New members asked if they, or wives, suffered from various medical conditions including rheumatism, scrofula ('King's Evil'), asthma, rupture, shortness of breath. (In Welsh and English)	Document	Archives	
MNA/I/34/A8	St. David's Unity of Ivorites (minutes and resolutions of Board Meetings)	1862–1916	Refers to sick payments, sick and funeral funds, Compensation, caring for the sick, rules, sickness allowances, National Health Insurance (1916). (In Welsh and English)	Document	Archives	
MNA/I/34/A9	St David's Unity of Ivorites (central records)	1916	1916: Ivorites Unity minutes and resolutions of Management Committee referring to compensation and sick claim, and certificate of disablement.	Document	Archives	
MNA/I/34/A16	St David's Unity of Ivorites (central records)	ud	Sick visitor's report form (blank, ud).	Document	Archives	
MNA/I/34/A21	St David's Unity of Ivorites (central records)	1883–ud	National Health Insurance Maternity Benefit form (ud), blank. 1883: doctor's notes (2) confirming good health of 2 men.	Document	Archives	
MNA/I/34/B2–B7	St David's Unity of Ivorites (Ystrad Rhondda District)		Application forms, rules, account statements. Rules refer to benefits, Distress Fund, Funeral Fund.	Document	Archives	
MNA/I/34/D5	St David's Unity of Ivorites (Gwenynen Lodge, Blaengarw)	1903–56	Sick pay account book, names and amounts.	Document	Archives	Y
MNA/I/34/F3	St David's Unity of Ivorites (Sibrwd Rhondda Lodge)	1929–c.1939	Sick visitor's book. Names and contributions.	Document	Archives	Y
MNA/I/34/G1	St David's Unity of Ivorites (Bud of Hope Lodge)	1892	Payments for funerals. Appointment of sick visitors. Two 1892 sick notes for Treherbert resident, suffering from rheumatism.	Document	Archives	
MNA/I/34/G18 and G23	St David's Unity of Ivorites (Bud of Hope Lodge)	c.1870s–1929	Lists of society members either died or sick, and payments made during the 1870s and 1880s. Annual returns re Sick and Funeral Fund (Friendly Societies Acts 1896 to 1929). (In Welsh and English)	Document	Archives	

Reference Code	Collection	Dates	Description	Media	Location	DP
MNA/I/34/G20	St David's Unity of Ivorites (Bud of Hope Lodge)	1860–99	17 doctors' certificates, (1882–99) Treherbert, including name, date, address, illnesses (including rheumatism, abscess, fracture, catarrh). Letter re sickness and in care of local doctor. Sick notes (including bronchitis and kidney problem), certificates, claims (1860–99). (In Welsh and English)	Document	Archives	
MNA/I/34/R1-4	The Glais Friendly Society (account books)	1809–71	Receipts from each member (names and occupations), and payment per month. Sick lists, funeral monies, and 'Ale Account'.	Document	Archives	
MNA/I/34/R5	The Glais Friendly Society (correspondence re sick benefit claims)	1814–77	Handwritten notes from members – claims for sick relief and funeral benefits. Also several death certificates and certificates from Bath Mineral Water Hospital confirming admittance of members as patients. Signatures on notes including local doctors and church ministers.	Document	Archives	
MNA/I/34/R6	The Glais Friendly Society (correspondence re sick benefit claims)	1814–77	Handwritten notes from members – claims for sick relief and funeral benefits. One example re 'asthmatic complaint'.	Document	Archives	
MNA/I/34/R7	The Glais Friendly Society (rules of the Society (approved by Quarter Sessions, 1816))	1809	Rules and articles of the Society.	Document	Archives	
MNA/I/34/R9	The Glais Friendly Society (contribution book)	1851	Lists contributions of members.	Document	Archives	
MNA/I/34/R11	The Glais Friendly Society (rule book of the 'Glaish Benefit Society')	1871	Reference to duty of sick visitor; sick pay; funeral money, table of contributions and benefits. (In Welsh and English)	Document	Archives	
MNA/I/7/A1-2	Bodwigiad Club Records (minute book and club accounts)	1875–1925	Contributions and payments including death, Board of Health, relief, ale and beer. Relief rules. Sick pay and certification. Sick visitors.	Document	Archives	

299

Reference Code	Collection	Dates	Description	Media	Location	DP
MNA/I/7/B1	Bodwigiad Club Records (account book)	1883–1910	Payouts for burials and sick pay (including names and length of time sick). Refers to asylum inmate payments.	Document	Archives	
MNA/I/7/C4	Bodwigiad Club Records (Secretary's correspondence and papers)	1927–72	1937: Rule book of Cambrian Lodge of the Old Unity of Oddfellows held at Bodwigiad Arms, Hirwaun, reference to assistance to sick members, funeral expenses, contributions and sick pay rules.	Document	Archives	
MNA/NUM/I/1	Records of the Miners' Federation of Great Britain (minute books of Executive Committee, and Annual and Special Conferences)	1921–40	1921–2 and 1931–3: National Health Insurance. 1934: Compulsory insurance against comp risks. 1937–40: National Health Insurance Act.	Document	Archives and SWML	
MNA/NUM/I/1–2	Records of the Miners' Federation of Great Britain/NUM (minute books of Executive Committee and Annual and Special Conferences)	1902–48	General themes include insurance and compensation laws.	Document	Archives and SWML	
MNA/NUM/1/2	Records of the Miners' Federation of Great Britain/NUM (minute books of National Executive Committee and Annual and Special Conferences)	1945–6	Medical service at mines. Miners' Medical Scheme. National Insurance (Industrial Injuries) Act.	Document	Archives and SWML	
MNA/NUM/2/3	Somersetshire Miners' Association (rules)	1928	Workmen's Compensation Act 1925, and Industrial Diseases –Instructions to Members. Sickness benefit under NHI. Objects of Miners' Association including legislation to protect health and lives of miners, and assisting members to improve moral, mental, industrial and social welfare.	Document	Archives	

Reference Code	Collection	Dates	Description	Media	Location	DP
MNA/NUM/2/4	Bristol Miners' Association (Agents' annual report)	1934	Pamphlet (4 pages). Including references to Workmen's Compensation (Coal Mines) Act 1934; Colliery owners' insurance or Special Trust; fund to cover liabilities to injured workmen; numbers of accidents and fatalities; insurance company medical examinations of injured workmen.	Document	Archives	
MNA/NUM/2/7	Somerset Area NUM (Guide to National Insurance [Industrial Injuries] Act, 1946)	1948	Pamphlet (31 pages) re the NI Act, contributions, benefits, medical boards, allowances, dependants, medical examinations, Workmen's Compensation, retirement pensions, supplementary schemes, common law, accidents, lump sums.	Document	Archives	
MNA/NUM/3/1/1	Minutes of the SWMF Executive Council, and Annual and Special Conferences (records of the SWMF/NUM (South Wales Area))	1907–40	Workmen's Compensation (and 1924 Amendments). Compensation Appeals. Insurance. National Insurance Act 1911. National Health Act 1919. Industrial Welfare Society. Workmen's Medical Societies (including Rhondda and Llanelly). Distress Fund. Red Cross Society.	Document	Archives and SWML	
MNA/NUM/3/3/1	Correspondence (bound volume of circulars)	1899–1915	Indemnity Scheme Insurance. Instructions re 1911 National Insurance Act. 1913 conference ref Medical Service and BMA meeting to set up Medical Scheme for Collieries in South Wales.	Document	Archives	
MNA/NUM/3/3/2	Correspondence (bound volume of circulars)	1916–27	1920: conference, Amendments to Coal Mines Act including National Insurance system of compensation for injuries.	Document	Archives	
MNA/NUM/3/3/3	Correspondence (bound volume of circulars)	1927–35	1935: May Day demonstrations, and references to National Health Insurance Act 1928.	Document	Archives	
MNA/NUM/3/3/14	Correspondence with SWMF No. 1 Area (File 2)	1931–42	(File 2) Compensation calculations. Notes for Amendment of Silicosis Scheme re Coal Mines (suggestions of Judge Rowlands). Insurance. (File 11) Correspondence with Indemnity Society (on behalf of Amalgamated Anthracite Collieries Ltd).	Document	Archives	Y
MNA/NUM/3/3/24/8	Bedlinog Lodge (correspondence with Lodges)	1934–40	1936: Health Insurance Act, correspondence relating to medical benefit and the unemployed.	Document	Archives	Y

301

Reference Code	Collection	Dates	Description	Media	Location	DP
MNA/NUM/3/3/33/2	Great Western Lodge (correspondence)	1934-42	Association of Approved Societies, Royal Commission on Workmen's Compensation, Statement of Evidence to be submitted on Behalf of the Association of Approved Societies (copy).	Document	Archives	
MNA/NUM/3/5/8	SWMF: Compensation Records (certified silicosis case papers)	1941-5	Correspondence from collieries, insurance companies, solicitors.	Document	Archives	Y
MNA/NUM/3/5/12	SWMF: Compensation Records (Returns of members contributing to the Fatal Accidents Scheme)	1951-3	Register of members (other than those through the Colliery Office) contributing to union and Special Fatal Accidents and Industrial Diseases Schemes. Lists for each lodge; name, address, rate per week, amount paid to schemes, amount paid to union.	Document	Archives	Y
MNA/NUM/3/5/14	SWMF: Compensation Records (Compensation Secretary's correspondence)	1938-41	1938: Mine owners' liability insurance. 1941: Sickness benefits paid under National Health Insurance Acts.	Document	Archives	Y
MNA/NUM/3/5/16	SWMF: Compensation Records (Compensation Secretary's correspondence: Area No. 5)	1934-41	National Health Insurance. Conference of Compensation Secretaries, Abercynon 1940. Registration card Workmen's Compensation, Deep Duffryn Colliery.	Document	Archives	Y
MNA/NUM/3/5/25	SWMF: Compensation Records (Compensation Department circulars)	1920-35	1920: SWMF Summary of Report re Home Office Inquiry into System of Compensation for Injuries to Workmen. 1923: Workmen's Compensation Act, weekly compensation tables. 1934: leaflet re Accidents to Federation Employees and Checkweighers, Compensation Insurance Fund.	Document	Archives	
MNA/NUM/3/5/25	SWMF: Compensation Records (Compensation Dept circulars)	1920-35	Typescript – National Health Insurance Bill 1935. Copy Central Compensation Department First report.	Document	Archives	Y
MNA/NUM/3/5/26	SWMF: Compensation Records (first report of SWMF Central Compensation Department and related material)	1934	Report re 1st year of SWMF Central Compensation Department. Notes re Workmen's Compensation, National Health Insurance Bill.	Document	Archives	Y

Reference Code	Collection	Dates	Description	Media	Location	DP
MNA/NUM/3/5/27	SWMF: Compensation Records (reports of Area Compensation Secretaries)	1938–40	Statistical tables from SWMF Areas re disputed compensation cases. Include personal details, colliery, insurance co., dispute details, costs, remarks.	Document	Archives	Y
MNA/NUM/3/8/7b	Maesteg District/Area (balance sheets)	1915–29	Insurance.	Document	Archives	
MNA/NUM/3/8/7c and d	Maesteg District/Area (Rules of Artifical Limb Fund and Benefit Fund)	1928–34	Five rules of Artificial Limb Fund, 1928. Benefit Fund rules for dependants in case of death of member, 1934.	Document	Archives	
MNA/NUM/3/8/17 (J)	Area No. 2 correspondence re pneumoconiosis (district, area and combine records)	1943–52	Memo re principles governing selection of diseases for insurance under National Insurance (Industrial Injuries) Act 1946. Notes of meeting of Pneumoconiosis Sub Committee at Coal Owners' Association.	Document	Archives	
MNA/NUM/3/10/22	Records of the NUM (South Wales Area) (printed material (pamphlet))	1927	SWMF, 'Outline of Work accomplished on behalf of the South Wales Colliery Workers'. Refers to contributions and death benefits.	Document	Archives	
MNA/NUM/L/1	Abercrave Lodge (annual and general meetings minutes)	1935–57	Health Insurance and Sick Fund. Fatal accidents and collections for dependants.	Document	Archives	
MNA/NUM/L/3/6	Abergorki Lodge (receipts for minor payments to SWMF central funds)	1936–42	Federation Compensation Insurance Fund. Deductions for Red Cross Penny-a-week Fund. Medical referee. Deputations to doctor and colliery office. Attendances, e.g. at courts, re compensation cases.	Document	Archives	
MNA/NUM/L/10/1	Bedwas Lodge (annual, general and committee meetings minutes)	1925–33	Sick workmen and pay. Doctors' fees and unemployed contributions.	Document	Archives	
MNA/NUM/L/20/124	Cambrian Lodge (Lodge Secretary's correspondence)	c.1915	Lists of weekly deductions for insurance, medical schemes, welfare, charities.	Document	Archives	

Reference Code	Collection	Dates	Description	Media	Location	DP
MNA/NUM/L 24/31	Cross Hands Lodge (Lodge Secretary's correspondence and papers)	1945–52	Cross Hands Collieries Benefit Scheme, Lodge contribution rates.	Document	Archives	
MNA/NUM/L34/6	Fforchaman Lodge (annual, general and committee minutes)	1947–9	Reference to 1948 Health Conference Cardiff. 1946 National Injuries Act, old and new cases of compensation.	Document	Archives	Y
MNA/NUM/L 43/A8	Graig Merthyr Lodge (general and committee minutes)	1948	Reference to conference at Barry, address by Harold Finch re NI, compensation, GP certificates to be accepted, no need for certifying surgeon's certificate, X-rays to be included in National Insurance.	Document	Archives	Y
MNA/NUM/L58/1	Norchard and Princess Royal Lodges (minute book of Norchard Lodge Pit Head Committee meetings)	1942–9	Federation Compensation Insurance Fund.	Document	Archives	
MNA/NUM/L 60/B15	Onllwyn Central Washery Lodge (lodge account book)	1945–53	Federation Compensation Insurance Fund.	Document	Archives	
MNA/NUM/L70/27	Trelewis Drift Lodge (Dowlais District correspondence)	1932–43	Miscellaneous papers including Dowlais District contributions to the Federation Compensation Insurance Fund, 1937.	Document	Archives	Y
MNA/NUM/L 70/8–14	Trelewis Drift Lodge (Lodge Secretary's correspondence and papers)	1921–33	Papers re insurance claims, awards, hearings, appeals.	Document	Archives	Y
MNA/NUM/L74/6	Windsor Lodge (correspondence)	1929–66	Correspondence of Lodge Secretary: File A including compensation and sickness, 1937–66. File C including insurance and Public Assistance, 1929–66.	Document	Archives	Y
MNA/NUM/L8/45 and 46	Ammanford Lodge (SWMF circulars and printed material)	1931–4	Information leaflets. Item 45: Industrial Diseases (March 1931). Item 46: Compensation Insurance Fund (December 1934).	Document	Archives	

Reference Code	Collection	Dates	Description	Media	Location	DP
MNA/NUM/L/89	Abercynon Lodge (explanatory leaflet on the work of the Cardiff and District Hospital Society)	1942	Benefits. Contributions. Dependants. Privileges. Surgical appliances. Reciprocity between contributory schemes. Municipal hospitals. Hospital vouchers. Non-contributors. Cases where responsibility not accepted, e.g. TB, mental illness cases, infectious diseases and the incurable.	Document	Archives	
MNA/POL/14/24/4	Newport Trades and Labour Council and Labour Party (Labour Party leaflet)	c.1948–50	Labour party leaflet for women: Health Service (including free medical care for women in the home); National Insurance (including when husband ill, and maternity benefits).	Document	Archives	
MNA/POL/3/1 and 3	Ammanford, Llandebie and District Trades and Labour Council (annual, general and Executive Council minutes)	1931–48	(1) National Health Insurance issues. (3) 1947: ref new Government Medical Health Scheme. Refers to Beveridge Report. NI Act, workers' panel Local Appeal Tribunal. NHS nominations for Hospital Management Committees.	Document	Archives	
MNA/PP/118/107	John Thomas (Aberavon) ((D5) South Wales Labour Annual)	1902	Lists of Friendly Societies. Borough Districts details including health committees and poor rates. Details of The Workers' Union, sick and funeral benefits.	Document	Archives	
MNA/PP/118/11	John Thomas (Aberavon) (Circulars and other papers re DWRGWU)	1899–1916	1912: DWRGWU Tinplate Section poster re National Insurance Act and Insurance Cards. Notification of Insurance Scheme Proposals (DWRGWU).	Document	Archives	
MNA/PP/118/115	John Thomas (Aberavon) (F38)	1921–32	National Health Insurance cards of J. Thomas, 1921–32. Medical card (1921) issued by Insurance Committee for County of Glamorgan.	Document	Archives	Y

Reference Code	Collection	Dates	Description	Media	Location	DP
MNA/PP/118/12	John Thomas (Aberavon) (*The Dockers' Record*, 24 monthly reports of the DWRGWU)	1901–16	1906: details re own insurance scheme. Various items re insurance scheme and benefits. December 1909: reference to 2 serious accidents, Home Office involved, view of getting more efficient inspection of gear. June 1911: refers to accidents and claiming compensation, National Insurance, Invalidity and Unemployment Insurance.	Document	Archives	
MNA/PP/118/12	John Thomas (Aberavon) (*The Dockers' Record*, 24 monthly reports of the DWRGWU)	1901–16	Feb 1907: Sick Benefit Society meeting, letter re Workmen's Compensation Act and need to including all dangerous trades and occupational disease.	Document	Archives	
MNA/PP/118/140	John Thomas (Aberavon) (F23)	1887	Booklet of instructions issued to agents of Prudential Assurance Co (Life Assurance, Medical Examinations, Certificate of Health for all Assurances).	Document	Archives	
MNA/PP/118/33	John Thomas (Aberavon) (correspondence and papers re tinplate union affairs)	1893–1928	Card: 'Welsh Artizans' United Association' (ud) re benefits including Workmen's Compensation Act and permanent disability.	Document	Archives	
MNA/PP/118/61	John Thomas (Aberavon) (B6)	1880	General rules of Independent Association of Tinplate Makers 1880 (in Welsh and English). Accidents, loss of limb, disabled by accident, or blinded, and unable to work – receive £20 on production of medical testimony. If resumed work, had to refund money.	Document	Archives	
MNA/PP/118/67 and 68	John Thomas (Aberavon) (B12 and B13)	1927–30	Rules of Tinplate and Kindred Workers' Special Fund (T and GWU Area No 4, Tinplate Section) 1927 and 1930. Sickness benefits, Workmen's Compensation, funeral benefit, Permanent Partial Disablement (Reduced Contributions), Permanent Disablement Grant (re accidents).	Document	Archives	

Reference Code	Collection	Dates	Description	Media	Location	DP
MNA/PP/118/69	John Thomas (Aberavon) (B14)	1890	Rules of Amalgamated Society of Engineers 1890. Sick stewards, keeping of sick records, visiting sick and medical attendants. Rules for sick benefit. Rules for members falling sick while on travel. Form of declaration on sick benefit. Rules relating to accidents.	Document	Archives	
MNA/PP/118/70	John Thomas (Aberavon) (B15)	1894	Rules of the trade union: Navvies', Bricklayers' Labourers', and General Labourers' Union. Benefit Section, rules of Sick, Accident and Funeral Fund. Branch sick visitors' duties, visiting members (or medical attendants in infectious cases), record keeping.	Document	Archives	
MNA/PP/118/73	John Thomas (Aberavon) (B18)	1898	Rules of National Amalgamated Labourers' Union 1898. Sick and Burial Fund, sick benefits, payments, conditions of allowance.	Document	Archives	
MNA/PP/118/75	John Thomas (Aberavon) (B20)	1899	Rules of National Amalgamated Union of Shop Assistants, Warehousemen and Clerks. Benefit claims, sick rules, benefits and contributions table. Payment at death. Benevolent grants (sick or distress). Marriage portion of female members (50% of contributions refunded on marriage).	Document	Archives	
MNA/PP/118/78	John Thomas (Aberavon) (B23)	1902	Rules of British Steel Smelters, Mill, Iron, and Tinplate Workers. Funeral and Accident Benefit rules.	Document	Archives	
MNA/PP/118/79	John Thomas (Aberavon) (B24)	1922	Rules of TGWU, 1922. NHI Officer. Contributions and benefits. Part II – NHI business including benefits, compensation, disablement and sickness benefits, medical certificates, married women.	Document	Archives	
MNA/PP/118/80/1	John Thomas (Aberavon) (B25)	1877	Rules of the Llanelly District Branch of the Merthyr Unity Philanthropic Institute (in Welsh and English). Benefits, including for accidents. Funeral fund.	Document	Archives	

Reference Code	Collection	Dates	Description	Media	Location	DP
MNA/PP/118/80/1	John Thomas (Aberavon) (B25)	1881	Rules and Orders of Friendly Society called Prince of Wales Society (Eng/Welsh). Reference to 'immoral life', 'disorders of disgraceful nature' (e.g. VD) – no assistance. Fighting, disability and sick benefit/relief. Sick pay rules. Death benefits. Sick Visitor. General health.	Document	Archives	
MNA/PP/118/80/1	John Thomas (Aberavon)	1880	Rules of the Gem of the Village Lodge, No. 355 of Llanelly District Branch, Merthyr Unity, Philanthropic Institution. Members who committed suicide, payment of funeral allowance. Funeral benefits. Accidents. Sick stewards. Appointment and duty of surgeon. Benefits.	Document	Archives	
MNA/PP/118/80/2	John Thomas (Aberavon) (B25)	1875–9	The Friendly Societies' Act 1875, and The Friendly Societies Amendment Act 1876, 6th edition 1879.	Document	Archives	
MNA/PP/119/1	John B. Thomas (Bedlinog Medical Committee meetings minute book)	1912–13	Refers to doctor's employment. Subscriptions for wives, families, uninsured boys, and for medical attendance in sickness or accidents. Withdrawal of confinement fees.	Document	Archives	Y
MNA/PP/124/1	W. S. Watkins (Neath)	1920s	Brief notes on interview. 1921: Provident fund for staff.	Document	Archives	
MNA/PP/132/9	James Winstone (scrapbook of news cuttings and handwritten notes)	1912	Labour statistics including Swiss Sickness and Accident Insurance. Review of New Insurance Act.	Document	Archives	
MNA/PP/16/1	S. O. Davies	1951–2	NUM memo: Social Insurance, Workmen's Compensation Act, Beveridge Report, National Insurance Acts, balance sheet for Industrial Injuries Fund. NUM memo and Parliamentary motion regarding transfer of Workmen's Compensation to Industrial Injuries Act.	Document	Archives	

Reference Code	Collection	Dates	Description	Media	Location	DP
MNA/PP/16/5	S. O. Davies	1934	Election newspaper. Refers to poverty, Poor Law, Unemployment and Health Insurance Acts. 1932 Health Insurance Act – removal of state medical benefit from unemployed as unable to pay insurance contributions.	Document	Archives	
MNA/PP/16/8	S. O. Davies	1927 and ud	1927 page (*Manchester Guardian*): reference to contributions to National Health Insurance Act. Cuttings relating to Workmen's Compensation transfer to Industrial Injuries scheme; south Wales poverty, Poor Law Scales.	Document	Archives	
MNA/PP/16/9/1	S. O. Davies	1940s–1950s	Questions and Answers: 'Compensation and Social Insurance' by Head of Compensation Department, reference to Industrial Injuries Act.	Document	Archives	
MNA/PP/16/11/1–34	S. O. Davies	1943	*Parliamentary Debates* (Hansard). Orders of Day – Social Insurance and Allied Services.	Document	Archives	
MNA/PP/16/50/7/2	S. O. Davies	1945	Constituency correspondence; Ministry of NI letter re case of Indemnity Society and workman (pneumoconiosis).	Document	Archives	Y
MNA/PP/28/20	James Evans (Tumble)	1931–43	1931 and 1937: SWMF Conciliation Board Agreement for Coal Trade of Monmouthshire and South Wales, refers to Welfare Levy, National Health contributions, compensation and insurance. 1943: SWMF Executive Council minutes reference to Cardiff Royal Infirmary, Pneumoconiosis Benefit Scheme.	Document	Archives	
MNA/PP/28/24	James Evans (Tumble)	1937–42	Insurance details for SWMF employees and Monmouthshire and South Wales Coal Mining Industry.	Document	Archives	
MNA/PP/28/26	James Evans (Tumble)	1937–1950s	1934: SWMF insurance fund for employees (accidents). 1938: SWMF Compensation Department letter regarding evidence for Royal Commission on Workmen's Compensation.	Document	Archives	

309

Reference Code	Collection	Dates	Description	Media	Location	DP
MNA/PP/28/37 and 39	James Evans (Tumble)	1938-49	1938: South Wales Miners' Pensions, summary of Draft Scheme. 1949: pamphlet Pwllbach Colliery Lodge NUM (SW) – refers to Sick Fund Benefit Scheme No. 2, and Sick and Accident Fund.	Document	Archives	
MNA/PP/28/47-49	James Evans (Tumble)	1942-6	NUM Conference Resolution re National Insurance and Industrial Injuries Acts. 1942: MFGB Executive Committee meeting minutes, Workmen's Compensation, pneumoconiosis schemes, part-disabled unemployed, dependants' allowances, disability payments. 1946: NUM National Executive meeting minutes, Workmen's Compensation Sub-Committee minutes.	Document	Archives	
MNA/PP/28/51	James Evans (Tumble)	1952	NUM (SW) Executive Committee minutes, Mineworkers' Special Fatal Accident Scheme.	Document	Archives	
MNA/PP/41/1	David Harris (Glais) (exercise books containing bilingual manuscript reminiscences)	1970s, ref C19th	Rulebook of Glanllwch Lodge (Ivorites): reference to sickness benefits and sick visitors.	Document	Archives	Y
MNA/PP/46/33/2	Arthur Horner (election handbill)	1933	'Mainwaring's Election Special', election handbill for W. H. Mainwaring (Labour): NHI Act, and Labour Party and housing, maternity services, health and social services.	Document	Archives	
MNA/PP/46/41	Arthur Horner (payslips: Arthur Horner at Standard Colliery)	1915-16	Payslips including payments for Health Insurance, Medical Fund, and Sick Fund.	Document	Archives	
MNA/PP/46/59	Arthur Horner, The Miners' Monthly (SWMF)	1936	The Miners' Monthly, Vol. III, No 10. Compensation men, Employers' Indemnity Society, insurance companies, warning against lump sum settlements.	Document	Archives	
MNA/PP/50/1	W. R. James (Trelewis)	1933	Life insurance policy of employee of Taff Merthyr Steam Coal Co.) Details of disability benefits.	Document	Archives	

Reference Code	Collection	Dates	Description	Media	Location	DP
MNA/PP/6/1/1–2	E. M. Collins	c.1930–33	Taff Vale Railway Co. book of regulations (undated); includes item relating to Accident Fund.	Document	Archives	
MNA/PP/73/1	James Lewis (Maesteg) (Maesteg Medical Fund committee minute book)	1929–39	Various references to medical fees and doctors. Disputes concerning payments and fee quotas. General reference to Medical Aid Schemes. Maesteg Fund committee details. Services for isolated districts. 1934: County scheme for men struck off Medical Benefit by NHI Act.	Document	Archives	
MNA/PP/73/3	James Lewis (Maesteg) (papers relating to Maesteg Medical Fund)	1932–47	Correspondence with and payments to doctors. Donations to Cardiff Royal Infirmary. Handwritten notes from various doctors on receipt of fees. (NB James Lewis was Secretary of the Maesteg Medical Fund).	Document	Archives	Y
MNA/PP/73/7	James Lewis (Maesteg) (miscellaneous pamphlets and printed material)	1933–46	Pamphlet: SWMF Compensation Department 'Workmen's Compensation (Temporary Increases) Act 1943'. MFGB minutes of Executive Committee Meeting 24/ January 40 – refers to Workmen's Compensation and SWMF. 1936: SWMF balance sheet, reference to grants for Compensation Insurance Fund.	Document	Archives	
MNA/PP/74/1	Elved Lewis (Tumble) (South Wales and Monmouthshire Colliery Examiners' Association contribution book)	1919–56	Members' contribution book, including 'Sick Members' Contributions'.	Document	Archives	
MNA/PP/78/4	Glyn Mathias (Gorseinon) (contribution card for British Steel Smelters, Mill, Iron, Tinplate and Kindred Trades Association)	1915–18	Distress Fund, Idle and Discharge Benefit (including Sickness), Accident Benefit, Workmen's Compensation Act.	Document	Archives	

Reference Code	Collection	Dates	Description	Media	Location	DP
MNA/PP/82/1	D. Morgan (general correspondence, miscellaneous letters and circulars re Rhymney Workingmen's Medical Aid Fund)	1946–9	Payment to Caerphilly Area Social Welfare Committee. Friendly Society's Medical Alliance re Ministry of Health grants for members. Rhymney Valley Hospital Management Committee and payments for inpatient treatment at Cardiff Royal Infirmary. Payments to doctors. Rhymney Cottage Hospital; Transfer of hospital to Minister of Health 1947, Glaxo Laboratories invoice, order of uniform for matron, money bequeathed. Welsh Board of Health re 'iron lungs' and polio, and testing. Tax Inspector and employment status of doctor. Donations from NCB Powell Dyffryn, Bernhard Baron Charitable Trust. British Hospitals Association; claim forms, clothing rationing. Memorial money for Dr Redwood. Redwood Memorial Hospital, Rhymney (Cardiff and District Hospital Society), and matron and sisters' annuities. Silicosis and Asbestosis (Medical Arrangements) Scheme 1931/1946 re X-ray of man. Supply of surgical belt via Aid Fund. Insurance re accident of child and bus. Monmouth County Public Health Dept scheme, payment for hospital treatment for school children. Ministry of Health Circular 63/47 'Nurses' Salaries'. Welsh Board of Health 'Hospital Services for Poles' re Polish Resettlement Act 1947.	Document	Archives	Y
MNA/PP/82/2	D. Morgan (miscellaneous papers re Rhymney Workingmen's Medical Aid Fund)	1942–8	British Hospitals' Association (South Wales and Monmouthshire) meeting re Beveridge Report, nurses' salaries (Rushcliffe Committee), Medical Planning Commission. Agenda; contributions from Royal Ordnance factories, Surveys of Hospital Accommodation in south Wales, Salaries, Emergency Medical Services and fracture cases. Rhymney Cottage Hospital building Insurance receipt. Invoice to Monmouth County Council for maintenance of patients at Monmouthshire County Hospital, Panteg. Specification of work to be done and materials for	Document	Archives	

Reference Code	Collection	Dates	Description	Media	Location	DP
			decorating Rhymney Cottage Hospital. Form re payment for hospital treatment of school child. Monmouth County Scheme of Payment for Hospital Treatment of School Children, e.g. orthopaedics, ophthalmic, ENT, skin disease. Ministry of Health Emergency Medical Services, Casualty Reporting Procedure – Polish personnel commissioned, enlisted or enrolled into the Polish Resettlement Corps. Vouchers; Rhymney Cottage Hospital, Cardiff and District Hospital Society, British Hospitals Association. Ministry of Supply, British Hospitals Association, Hospital Contributions in the Royal Ordnance Factories. Notes on Report of National Joint Council for Staff in Hospitals and Allied Institutions in England and Wales re pay, sick pay, disabled workers. Motor ambulance in use in area, details. 1948: Income and Expenditure sheet including doctors, drugs, wages, Insurance			
MNA/PP/98/18	Gwilym Richards	ud	*The Disabled Person's Charter*, pamphlet by G. Richards, re disablement benefit. South Wales Miners' Resolution re merger of all Friendly Societies, Insurance Schemes, Poor Relief Schemes into one national scheme to pay benefit re illness, accidents, unemployment, old age.	Document	Archives	
MNA/TUG/1/1	Amalgamated Society of Railway Servants (Merthyr) (minute book)	1888–95	Benevolent fund, claim for rheumatic fever. 1894: Employer's Liability Bill protest re contract out clause.	Document	Archives	
MNA/TUG/3/0/1	National Association of Colliery Overmen, Deputies and Shotfirers (minute book of conference and committees of General Federation of Colliery Firemen of GB)	1910–25	1921: Mine Owners' Benefit Schemes and Rules of Colliery Staffs Mutual Benefit Society (no trade union members), and fight against these.	Document	Archives	

313

Reference Code	Collection	Dates	Description	Media	Location	DP
MNA/TUG/7/1/C1–2	Iron and Steel Trades Confederation (reports, circulars, minutes and papers)	1934–48	1943: Memo re Workmen's Compensation (Temporary Increases) Act 1943. Minutes ref NHI (Approved Society) legal services. Letter re NHI Act 1946, sickness benefit.	Document	Archives	Y
MNA/TUG/9/5	Amalgamated Engineering Union (Superannuation Benefit and Benevolent Fund Book)	1920–49	Benevolent Fund: names, dates, grant amounts, illness (including heart disease, cerebral haemorrhage, bronchitis, TB, cancer, gangrenous foot, gastric ulcers, senility/dementia, pneumonia, and lost in action during wartime).	Document	Archives	
MNA/TUG/10/1	Amalgamated Society of Engineers (minute book)	1917–22	References: Sick Steward's reports. Sick Benefit cases. Sick member needing specialist doctor.	Document	Archives	
MNA/TUG/11/1	National Union of Vehicle Builders (Swansea Branch) (minute book)	1938–48	References to Mutual Aid Scheme, 1938.	Document	Archives	
MNB/COL/11/E1–2	Fernhill Colliery (contract books)	1942–53	Conciliation Board Agreements for the Coal Trade of Monmouthshire and South Wales, Schedule II re principles for periodical ascertainments; including Workmen's Compensation, National Health Insurance and Miners' Welfare levy.	Document	Archives	
MNB/COL/17/A14	Morlais Colliery, Commercial Committee (South Wales Coal Owners' Association)	1926–37	1926: letter from Ministry of Health re National Health Insurance and stamped Health Insurance cards to be returned.	Document	Archives	
MNB/COL/17/C25A	Morlais Colliery (Secretarial Department circulars)	1928–30	Re Coal Mines General Regulations (First-Aid) 1930. Cost sheets – 1930, including Workmen's Compensation, Health Insurance, Welfare Levy. Re Workmen's Compensation Act 1925 and Various Industries (Silicosis) Scheme 1928.	Document	Archives	
MNB/COL/17/C25E	Morlais Colliery (Secretarial Department circulars)	1934–42	Cost sheets including Health Insurance, Welfare Levy, Women's Compensation. 1940: letter, ex gratia compensation grant and pre-1924 cases. 1942: Essential Work (Coal Mining Industry) (No 3) Order, reference to sickness and pay.	Document	Archives	

Reference Code	Collection	Dates	Description	Media	Location	DP
MNB/COL/17/C25H	Morlais Colliery (Secretarial Department circulars)	1934–8	Cost sheet 1934, including health insurance, Workmen's Compensation, welfare levy. Levy and compensation suspension, 1938. Holidays with pay and compensation workmen.	Document	Archives	
MNB/COL/17/C32B	Morlais Colliery (miscellaneous memoranda, resolutions, agreements etc)	1915–42	1927: Monmouthshire and South Wales Coal Owners' Association Reports including: National Health Insurance Act 1924. 1928: Cost sheet including welfare levy, Workmen's Compensation and insurance.	Document	Archives	
MNB/COL/17/C32C	Morlais Colliery (miscellaneous memoranda, resolutions, agreements etc)	1915–42	1934: Cost sheet including welfare levy, Workmen's Compensation and health insurance.	Document	Archives	
MNB/COL/17/C33B	Morlais Colliery (welfare and safety circulars).	1922–79	National Health Insurance form re stamping of cards, 1922. Industrial Welfare Society 1923 booklet listing donations and subscriptions.	Document	Archives	
MNB/COL/17/C8A	Morlais Colliery (Monmouthshire and South Wales Employers' Mutual Indemnity Society circulars)	1916–38	Ordinary and Extraordinary Accident Funds Balance Sheets. List of collieries and members registered with Society. 1917: Certificate of Protection. 1917: refers to compensation awards, nystagmus, beat knee, beat elbow. AGM agenda and report to directors, 1917.	Document	Archives	
MNB/COL/17/C8B	Morlais Colliery (Monmouthshire and South Wales Employers' Mutual Indemnity Society circulars)	1916–38	Employers' Liability Policy Notice to Members re Provisions of Workmen's Compensation (Coal Mines) Act 1934. 1924: Compensation statistics; New Act cases (1906 and 1923), and Old Act Cases (1897). AGM agendas. Solicitor's/directors' reports to AGM re Workmen's Compensation. 1925: Partially Incapacitated Workmen, general stoppage. List of collieries and members registered. Extraordinary Accident Class, 1930. Insurance policy document, 1932.	Document	Archives	

Reference Code	Collection	Dates	Description	Media	Location	DP
MNB/COL/17/C8C	Morlais Colliery (Monmouthshire and South Wales Employers' Mutual Indemnity Society circulars)	1916–38	Ordinary and Extraordinary Account Funds. Compensation Costs, Old and New Acts. Statistics sent to Home Secretary re Accidents and Disability, and Compensation. Reports to AGMs, Solicitor and Directors, including Workmen's Compensation, Silicosis and Nystagmus. Insurance schedules. Statistics including accidents and injuries. Compensation cost statement. Summary of assets and liabilities. 1925: circular, Workmen's Compensation Acts 1906–23, fatal cases. Register for Protection of Members.	Document	Archives	Y
MNB/COL/17/F1–4	Morlais Colliery (colliery workmen's contract book)	1926–42	Including Memo of Agreement, with references to Workmen's Compensation and insurance, National Health Insurance and miners' welfare levy.	Document	Archives	
MNB/COL/17/M6	Morlais Colliery (Talyclyn Colliery; notices of accidents)	1942–3	Completed accident forms, including Employers' Mutual Indemnity Society details.	Document	Archives	Y
MNB/COP/2/1	Ynysybwl Co-op Society (report and balance sheet)	1947	1947: Report and Balance Sheet. Cash account lists with references to NHI Claims, Ambulance Car Fund, compensation and Staff Hospital Fund.	Document	Archives	
MNB/I/1/1	Abercrave Colliery Sick Fund (Welsh)	1909–52	Minute book of 'Y Ffund Fach': annual, general and committee meetings; also sick fund and lodge joint meetings.	Document	Archives	
MNB/I/1/1	Abercrave Colliery Sick Fund (minute book)	1909–52	Administration and rules. Sick and funeral benefits and accounts. Reference to Swansea Hospital. 'Sick Visitors'. Refers to individual applicants for benefits. Porthcawl, Talygarn, Southerndown Rest Homes and tickets. Refers to purchase of artificial foot. Insurance and Industrial Injuries Act 1948 reference.	Document	Archives	Y

Reference Code	Collection	Dates	Description	Media	Location	DP
MNB/I/1/2	Abercrave Colliery Sick Fund, rule book (Welsh)	1920	Sanctions and penalties if guilty of hindering recovery or refusal to see doctor. Have to leave note at home if go out whilst ill – or fined. Madhouses – no sick payments. Workhouse – no sick payments unless have dependants (no pay to them if in madhouse or workhouse). Association aims, constitution, committee. Trustees' duties. Payments. Rights of members to sick payments. Sick members not allowed out after 7 p.m. October to March, or after 9 p.m. April to September – fined if caught. Terms of acceptance for men over 55. Not accepted if in poor health. Provision of doctor's medical certificates. Need doctor's certificate if wish to go away due to ill health, no longer than 2 weeks away. No help if injured through fighting (except self-defence), sports or games, immoral living. Death benefits. Fund administration. Copy sick claim form.	Document	Archives	
MNB/I/12/1–3	Pontygwaith Division, St John Ambulance Brigade (minute books, correspondence and bills/receipts)	1939–60	1939-49: minute book including administration details, references to Medical Home Comfort Fund and Scheme. 1944: letter re examination arrangements. Bills and receipts for first aid classes.	Document	Archives	
MNB/I/13/1	Yniscedwyn Sick Fund (general and committee minute book)	1930–58	Sick benefit payments and rules. Membership conditions. Admin details. Reference to individual claimants. Burial benefit. Porthcawl Rest donation. Refers to Talygarn and Bournemouth Convalescent Homes. Silicosis claims. Refers to 'Sick Visitors'.	Document	Archives	Y
MNB/I/3/A6	Abergorki Workmen's Hall and Institute (abstracts of general committee minutes re colliery medical services)	1923–5	Refers to Drs Armstrong and Cohen. Request to transfer from colliery doctor to local doctor. Colliery doctors to record visits to accident victims. New boys advised to report to colliery doctors. Refers to increased money to doctors. Provision of nurse. Reference to equal status of doctors.	Document	Archives	

Reference Code	Collection	Dates	Description	Media	Location	DP
MNB/I/3/C12	Abergorki Workmen's Hall and Institute (Secretary's carbon-copy letter book)	1948–9	National Injuries Act – insurance payment for worker.	Document	Archives	Y
MNB/I/3/C28-32	Abergorki Workmen's Hall and Institute (Secretary's carbon-copy letter book)	1945–8	Treherbert Hospital request for donation. South-Western Divisional Welfare Convalescent Home facilities for women – applications for Hafod Boverton or Arosfa Porthcawl, and Scheme for Miners' Wives and Dependants.	Document	Archives	
MNB/I/3/D19	Abergorki Workmen's Hall and Institute (newspaper cuttings relating to SWMF affairs)	1926–9	*South Wales Journal of Commerce*, 6 February 29 re Miners' Compensation Claims.	Document	Archives	
MNB/I/8/17	North's Workmen's Institute (Maesteg) (statements of account and balance sheets)	1929–57	NHI (Health Insurance). Welfare scheme.	Document	Archives	
MNB/NUM/I/1/24	Abercynon Lodge (news sheet issued by Joint Committee of Action for South Wales)	1936	UAB and National Government Law – New Regulations and Scales. Refers to those in receipt of sick pay from Friendly Societies, NHI Benefit, Workmen's Compensation and Disability Pension.	Document	Archives	
MNB/NUM/I/2/10	Ammanford No. 2 Lodge (Lodge secretary's general correspondence)	1929–35	1935: Letter re Federation Compensation Insurance Fund.	Document	Archives	
MNB/NUM/I/2/19	Ammanford No. 2 Lodge (Colliery Sick and Burial Fund rules)	c.1930	Sick and Burial Fund cards. Sick Fund Rules (20).	Document	Archives	
MNB/NUM/I/2/8	Ammanford No. 2 Lodge (Lodge balance sheet for 1938)	1939	Payments for compensation, Sick Fund account, Health Insurance.	Document	Archives	
MNB/PP/22/1	Harold Finch (minute book, Miners' Group)	1942–6	National Insurance Industrial Injuries Bill 1946.	Document	Archives	

Reference Code	Collection	Dates	Description	Media	Location	DP
MNB/PP/23	B. A. Francis	C19th–C20th	History of co-operative movement, growth in south Wales, relief of distress.	Document	Archives	
MNB/PP/64/K1	J. S. Williams (Dowlais) (miscellaneous printed material, press cuttings and circulars)	c.1924–1937	(Kiii) Notice of meetings (Amalgamated Union of Building Trade Workers, Altogether Builders' Labourers and Constructional Workers' Society, National Health Section) re Approved Society Section and National Health Benefits; disablement, maternity, dental, optical, convalescence.	Document	Archives	
MNB/TUG/2/1	British Iron, Steel and Kindred Trades Association, British Steel Smelters Reports	1892–4	Funeral levy, benefits, obituaries (including names and cause of death, and family members' deaths). Employers' Liability Bill 1894 details. Compensation case re accident and death, details (knocked down by crane), at Briton Ferry. Accident at Flemington, lost hand.	Document	Archives	
MNB/TUG/2/1	British Iron, Steel and Kindred Trades Association, British Steel Smelters Reports	1895–7	Funeral levy, obituaries, causes of death (men and family members). Accident claims and grants. Workmen's Compensation Act 1897, details and schedules.	Document	Archives	
MNC/COP/1/1	Aberdare Co-operative Society (minute book)	1929–32	Reference to National Health Insurance.	Document	Archives	
MNC/COP/11/1	Garndiffaith Co-op Society (minute Book)	1928–30	References to Health Insurance, Convalescent Benefit and sick visiting.	Document	Archives	
MNC/COP/16/6	Penygraig Co-op Society (minute book (Finance Committee))	1924–30	1925: collection of Health Insurance cards.	Document	Archives	
MNC/COP/27/1	People's Yearbooks (Annual of the Co-operative Wholesale Society Ltd)	1920	Sidney Webb article: National Health Insurance, Poor Law, Ministry of Health. Domestic legislation 1919 and Ministry of Health Act. Co-op NHI advert including dental benefits.	Document	Archives	

Reference Code	Collection	Dates	Description	Media	Location	DP
MNC/COP/27/14	*People's Yearbooks* (Annual of the Co-operative Wholesale Society Ltd)	1933	Health Insurance Section details. Statistics for NHI, Trade unions (work fatalities, industrial accidents), Poor Law Relief including lunatics. Advertisements for Co-op Health Insurance Section benefits (including dental, convalescence, ophthalmic/glasses, maternity).	Document	Archives	
MNC/COP/27/27	*People's Yearbooks* (Annual of the Co-operative Wholesale Society Ltd)	1948	NHI and Industrial Injuries Acts. Health Insurance benefits.	Document	Archives	
MNC/COP/3/1	Abersychan Co-op Society (minute book)	1908–12	Insurance for ptomaine poisoning risks and Workmen's Compensation.	Document	Archives	
MNC/COP/3/4	Abersychan Co-op Society (minute book)	1945–9	1948: Sickness benefits, National Health Scheme. Co-op Insurance Society – Workmen's Compensation under Common Law, and National Insurance Scheme reference. Stanley Davies's appointment to Ministry of Health.	Document	Archives	
MNC/COP/9/1	Cardiff Co-op Retail Society (minute book)	1933–4	National Health Insurance applicants – numbers accepted.	Document	Archives	
MNC/ISTC/1/1	National Union of Blastfurnacemen, Ore Miners, Coke Workers and Kindred Trades (Annual Conference reports)	1919–25	NHI Section Accounts (sick, disabled, maternity), list diseases and average cases per week (including accidents, bronchitis/throat, influenza/colds, catarrh, pneumonia, pleurisy, TB, rheumatism, hernia). 1920: new rates of contributions and benefits. Leaflet re Union Approved Society. Approved Society Business (Benefits), including Dental treatment and dentures wef 1925 (details), and optical treatment and appliances (details). Convalescent Home Benefit. Compensation and reporting of accidents and injuries. Transfer from other approved societies details. Disablement and funeral grants (name, place, amt). Sickness and death rate benefits for stove cleaners. Various National Insurance references.	Document	Archives	

Reference Code	Collection	Dates	Description	Media	Location	DP
MNC/ISTC/4/1	National Union of Blastfurnacemen, Ore Miners, Coke Workers and Kindred Trades (Annual General Meeting reports)	1938–41	1941: Cost of Living Index Figure details, food prices. 1941: Additional Benefit No 14, Optical Treatment – renewal of glasses. 1941: increase in NHI benefits and extra contribution. 1942: Question of Social Security in post-war period. Accounts for union including benefits, convalescent homes, medical specialists, doctors' fees. 1941: report of Compensation Department – Personal Injuries (Civilians Act), Supplementary Allowances Act, Amendment of Compensation Acts (1938 Royal Commission), NHI. 1941: grants to League of Blind and Eye Infirmary. Personal Injuries (Emergency Provisions) Act 1939 details (civilian members who receive war injury, claim Injury Allowance). 1940: National Insurance section, why members should join approved society, details, NHI benefits, e.g. sickness, disabled, maternity, ophthalmic.	Document	Archives	
MNC/ISTC/4/1	National Union of Blastfurnacemen, Ore Miners, Coke Workers and Kindred Trades (Annual General Meeting reports)	1938–41	Cleveland District Convalescent Home Fund details (for members, wives, children). Accident and funeral benefits paid re members, wives, children (name, lodge, amount). Details Workmen's Compensation (Supplementary Allowances) Act 1940, application in cases where accident happened on or after 1 January 24.	Document	Archives	
MNC/NUM/ 2/5/1–3	NUM South Wales Area	1948	Notes of Proceedings at Summer School for Compensation Secretaries, Barry 14 June1948. History of compensation, Industrial Injuries Act, Social Insurance, Beveridge Report and NHS, National Insurance Act, disability and disease in mining, Sickness Benefit, disablement, accidents, Medical Boards, doctors' certificates.	Document	Archives	
MNC/NUM/5/182	NUM South Wales Area (SWMF Eastern Valleys District monthly meetings minutes (D2/F53))	1915	Compensation cases. Food and drug prices under National Insurance Act. NHI. Doctors' poundage system and agreement for collieries.	Document	Archives	

Reference Code	Collection	Dates	Description	Media	Location	DP
MNC/NUM/L/ 24/1–4	Newlands Lodge	1935–64	Compensation correspondence files including SWMF, and Midlands Employers' Mutual Assurance Ltd re industrial injuries and accidents. Certificates re examinations under Workmen's Compensation Act 1925.	Document	Archives	Y
MNC/NUM/L/27/43	Penallta Lodge	1911	Copy of National Insurance Act 1911, a handbook for employers.	Document	Archives	
MNC/PP/15/8	Dr Gwent Jones (copies of Industrial Injury Insurance Scheme proposals and statutory rules and orders)	1940–4	Proposals for Industrial Injury Insurance Scheme (HMSO 1944). Workmen's Compensation (Supplementary Allowances) Bill ,1940. Statutory Rules and Orders 1943 (Nos 885, 886 (Pneumoconiosis)) Workmen's Compensation. Workmen's Compensation (Temporary Increases) Act 1943, Chapter 49.	Document	Archives	
MNC/PP/15/8	Dr Gwent Jones (copies of Industrial Injury Insurance Scheme proposals and statutory rules and orders)	1940–4	The Coal Mines (South Wales) (Pneumoconiosis) Order 1943. Emergency Powers (Defence), Coal Mines (South Wales), Statutory Rules and Order 1943, No. 1696.	Document	Archives	
MNC/PP/35/1	Anon (Envelope II)	c.1930s	1934: MFGB minutes re compensation, insurance.	Document	Archives	Y

~ 13 ~
Medical Institutions

Hospitals

Hospital care on the South Wales Coalfield was delivered by the voluntary and the public sectors. Voluntary general hospitals – a concept which dated back to the eighteenth century – were funded by contributions from individuals and organizations such as trade unions, friendly societies, co-operative societies and workplace schemes (SWCC: MNA/COP/7/1–18; MNA/I/19/C1; MNA/NUM/ 3/3/2). Their services were free, but access was via the recommendation of a subscriber, except in emergencies, and certain categories of patient (for example, the mentally ill and pregnant women) were excluded. From the turn of the century, voluntary general hospitals were increasingly augmented by specialist institutions offering treatment for specific conditions or particular patient groups. Voluntary cottage hospitals, offering a basic level of medical services, also multiplied. Especially popular in rural areas, suburbs and small towns, these modest hospitals were staffed by general practitioners who referred more complex cases to the general and the specialist institutions where consultants were located. In south Wales, for example, the Cardiff Royal Infirmary, which opened in 1837 as the Glamorgan and Monmouthshire Infirmary and Dispensary, was joined by institutions like the Prince of Wales Orthopaedic Hospital (1918) and the Caerphilly and District Miners' Hospital (1924) (SWCC: MNA/ NUM/L/6/1; MNA/NUM/L/10/1; MNB/PP/53/1).

Public hospitals owed their origins to the Poor Law, which treated sick inmates in workhouse and infirmary wards until legislation in the 1860s permitted the construction of dedicated hospitals. The Royal Commission on the Poor Law, sitting between 1905 and 1909, recommended that local authorities take over the provision of Poor Law medical services to help unify the system and reduce the stigma for patients. Hospital care was not included under the 1911 National Insurance Act, which meant that the seriously ill or injured had no guaranteed cover. In 1929, however, the Local Government Act did transfer the Poor Law hospitals to local authorities, though few outside London seized the opportunity to remove them from the Public Assistance Committee and develop a municipal medical service under Public Health Committee.

Throughout the interwar period, there were attempts to improve the integration of health care. In 1919 the new Ministry of Health established a Consultative Council to look at the provision of medical services. A provisional report was published in 1920, which included recommendations for more specialist treatment at hospitals with consultants and sophisticated equipment, and the provision of health centres with better access to GPs and basic facilities. However, these recommendations were not implemented. In 1921 voluntary hospitals were the focus of the Cave Committee, which proposed a Voluntary Hospitals Commission with local committees to construct regional strategies. But the tangible outcomes were minimal and so regional collaboration and the amalgamation of resources with the public sector were still the message when the Sankey Committee reported in 1937. Hospital care thus showed little coordination until the advent of the National Health Service.

Reference Code	Collection	Dates	Description	Media	Location	DP
AUD/56	Haydn Mainwaring	1910–80	Membership of Porth Hospital Management Board.	Audio tape	SWML	Y
AUD/310, 311	Abel Morgan	1878–c.1972	Committee responsible for hospital treatment in Cardiff. Comparison of Mountain Ash and Ynysybwl medical facilities; X-rays only available from Ynysybwl (doctor authorized hospital visit). Hospital and Nursing Fund.	Transcript of audio	SWML	Y
HD6661.TRA	TUC Annual Reports of Proceedings (incomplete)	1904–85	1924: Manor House Hospital ('Labour Hospital'), Industrial Orthopaedic Society.	Document	SWML	
HD9550 EBB	The Ebbw Vale Works Magazine, Vol. 5, No. 20	Sept 1926	Notes and photograph; opening of Hospital 'Danybryn' – Ebbw Vale and District Hospital Fund (opened by Dr Rocyn Jones, MOH for Monmouthshire, and Sir Ewen Maclean, Cardiff).	Document	SWML	
HD9550 EBB	The Ebbw Vale Works Magazine, Vol. 10, No. 40	Oct 1931	Article: 'Abertillery Ambulance Division'; history, staff, Aberbeeg Hospital.	Document	SWML	
HD9552.3 MIN	The Miner, Vol. II, No. 3/4	Dec 1945 Jan 1946	Article: 'New Way with Medical Service', by Dr D. Stark Murray, Vice-President Socialist Medical Association, NHS, new health centres, hospitals.	Document	SWML	
HD9552.3 MIN	The Miner, Vol. II, No. 12	Oct 1946	Editorial: Miners' Medical Service, refers to Llandough Hospital.	Document	SWML	
HV686.R3	Reports of the MOH, and School MO, Rhondda UDC	1914–47	Tyntyla and Penrhys Isolation Hospitals. 1926: School MO report: crippling defects and orthopaedics – Carnegie Welfare Centre, Trealaw, and Prince of Wales Hospital, Cardiff. 1925: Hospitals: Pentwyn (for Ocean Colliery workmen), Porth and District, Llwynypia (converted from Poor Law Institute, 1925) and approved training school for nurses. Ambulance facilities; infectious patients (isolation hospitals); non-infectious – no ambulances; Porth and District Hospital – own ambulances;	Document	SWML	

Reference Code	Collection	Dates	Description	Media	Location	DP
MNA/COL/2/4–38	Clydach Merthyr Colliery (Manager's carbon-copy correspondence books)	1937–48	accident cases – St John Ambulance and British Red Cross ambulances can be used. 1939: Treatment centres and clinics: Ynyswen (Treorchy), Dyffryn Ffrwd (Ystrad), Carnegie Welfare Centre (Trealaw), Ynys Villa (Ynyshir), Oakland Terrace (Ferndale), Penrhys Smallpox Hospital. References to Clydach Cottage Hospital.	Document	Archives	Y
MNA/COP/1/17	Aberdare and District Co-op Society Ltd (general and Board Meeting minutes)	1932–5	General Hospitals; Mountain Ash, Aberdare and District.	Document	Archives	Y
MNA/COP/2/1–11	Ammanford Co-op Society (general and committee meetings minutes)	1900–38	Donations to hospitals (Swansea, Cwmamman, Amman Valley). Royal Mineral Hospital, Bath – treatment of Co-operative Society member.	Document	Archives	
MNA/COP/3/2	Briton Ferry and Neath Co-op Society (balance sheets and committee reports)	1919–24	Accounts including donations to Swansea General and Eye Hospital.	Document	Archives	
MNA/COP/5/1/1–14	Pembroke Dock Co-op Society (general and committee meetings minutes)	1888–1951	Donations to health-related charities, e.g. Swansea Hospital, Pembroke Infirmary.	Document	Archives	
MNA/COP/7/1–13	Ton Co-op Society (general and committee minutes)	1884–1927	Donations and tickets: Cardiff and Bristol Infirmaries, Seamen's Hospital, Manor House Hospital. Prince of Wales Hospital.	Document	Archives	

Reference Code	Collection	Dates	Description	Media	Location	DP
MNA/COP/7/14–15, and 18	Ton Co-op Society (Board meetings, and quarterly and half-yearly meetings minutes)	1918–48	(14–15) Subscriptions to Cardiff and Bristol Infirmaries, Treherbert Hospital and Pentwyn Hospital. Cardiff Infirmary elections. Rheumatic case to be sent to Droitwich or Bath Hospitals. (18) Donations: Cardiff and Bristol Infirmaries, Seamen's Hospital.	Document	Archives	
MNA/I/2/1–7	Abertridwr Institute (minute books)	1927–39	Donations to Caerphilly Miners' Hospital.	Document	Archives	
MNA/I/16/1	Forest of Dean District Welfare Association (committee minutes)	1921–4	Dilke Memorial Hospital: grants, e.g. for drainage, water and sewer mains; visit and tour with Matron. Lydney Cottage Hospital grant.	Document	Archives	
MNA/I/16/3	Forest of Dean District Welfare Association (committee minutes)	1929–35	Assistance of hospitals; expenditure on cases attending for treatment. Cases sent for treatment at Droitwich Baths, Bath Mineral Water Hospital, Bristol Infirmary, Cheltenham, Gloucester Infirmary, Dilke Hospital. Allowances and travel expenses.	Document	Archives	Y
MNA/I/19/C1	Lily of the Valley Lodge of the Unity of Oddfellows, Ystrad Rhondda (Lodge Secretary's records)	1926–32	Subscriptions and privileges for Porth Cottage Hospital. Subscriptions and tickets for Cardiff Royal Infirmary, Bristol Royal Infirmary. Subscriptions to St Mark's Cancer Research Hospital, London.	Document	Archives	
MNA/I/20/A1	Maerdy Workmen's Hall and Institute	1920s	Use of building as temporary hospital, use as surgery for New Medical Scheme. Loan to New Medical Scheme Committee.	Document	Archives	
MNA/I/34/R5	The Glais Friendly Society (correspondence re sick benefit claims)	1814–77	Includes certificates from Bath Mineral Water Hospital confirming admittance of members as patients.	Document	Archives	

Reference Code	Collection	Dates	Description	Media	Location	DP
MNA/NUM/1/1	Records of the Miners' Federation of Great Britain (minute books of Executive Committee and annual and special conferences)	1921–42	1921–2: Maintenance of hospitals. Visit to Industrial Orthopaedic Society, Manor House Hospital (London). 1941–2: Manor House Hospital visit.	Document	Archives and SWML	
MNA/NUM/1/9	Records of the MFGB/NUM (MFGB annual balance sheet)	1941	Distress and Disaster Funds: Colliery Disasters and Manor House Hospital Restoration Fund.	Document	Archives	
MNA/NUM/3/1/1	Minutes of the SWMF Exec Council, and annual and special conferences	1907–40	Hospitals: Caerphilly, Cardiff Infirmary, Manor House, Royal Gwent, Royal Mineral Water Hospital Bath, St John's Auxiliary Hospitals (1917). Duke Fingard Inhalation Clinic (1940).	Document	Archives and SWML	
MNA/NUM/3/3/2	SWMF correspondence bound volume of circulars	1916–27	SWMF contributions to voluntary hospitals: Cardiff Infirmary, Royal Mineral Water Hospital Bath.	Document	Archives	
MNA/NUM/3/5/10	SWMF: Compensation Records (annual reports of silicosis cases)	1935–40	SWMF balance sheets, 1936 and 1938 (including to hospital in Bath).	Document	Archives	Y
MNA/NUM/3/5/22	SWMF: Compensation Records (correspondence re Fatal Accidents Scheme)	1943–7	Reference to air raid on Swansea Hospital, 16 February 1943.	Document	Archives	Y
MNA/NUM/3/8/17	Area No. 2 Council Minutes (register of ordinary accident cases)	1934–52	Reference to tickets for Bath Mineral Hospital. Payments to Cardiff hospitals.	Document	Archives	Y
MNA/NUM/L/1	Abercrave Lodge (annual and general meetings minutes)	1935–57	Hospital contributions. Hospital governors.	Document	Archives	

Reference Code	Collection	Dates	Description	Media	Location	DP
MNA/NUM/L/2/89	Abercynon Lodge (explanatory leaflet on the work of the Cardiff and District Hospital Society)	1942	Benefits. Contributions. Dependants. Privileges. Surgical appliances. Reciprocity between contribution schemes. Municipal hospitals. Hospital vouchers. Non-contributors. Cases where responsibility not accepted, e.g. TB, infectious diseases and the incurable.	Document	Archives	
MNA/NUM/L/3/1	Abergorki Lodge (annual, general and committee meetings minute book)	1913–15	Levies to Cardiff Infirmary and Auxiliary Fund. Appeal for Bath Royal Mineral Hospital, and reference to tickets.	Document	Archives	
MNA/NUM/L/3/7	Abergorki Lodge (Lodge Secretary's correspondence book)	1917–18	Porth Cottage Hospital extension, establishment of Central Hospital for valleys.	Document	Archives	
MNA/NUM/L/3/16	Abergorki Lodge (Lodge Secretary's correspondence book)	1930–1	Operation at Llwynypia Hospital. Payments to Bristol Infirmary. Grant to Pentwyn Hospital. Abergorki Colliery Hospital Fund.	Document	Archives	Y
MNA/NUM/L/6/1	Abertridwr Lodge (meetings minutes, balance sheet, membership lists)	1925–59	Caerphilly Workmen's (Miners') Hospital, building extension, tickets in aid of Hospital, election of delegates.	Document	Archives	
MNA/NUM/L/8/31	Ammanford Lodge (Lodge Secretary's correspondence and papers)	ud	Papers relating to Swansea General and Eye Hospital Contributory Scheme	Document	Archives	
MNA/NUM/L/9/1	Bargoed Housecoal Lodge (committee minutes)	1947–50	Rationing and shortages at hospital. Cardiff District Hospital Fund. Aberbargoed Hospital reports. Cardiff Infirmary. Nominations for Hospital Board.	Document	Archives	
MNA/NUM/L/9/2	Bargoed Housecoal Lodge (account book)	1941–50	Expenditure including hospital attendance, and Hospital Committee.	Document	Archives	

Reference Code	Collection	Dates	Description	Media	Location	DP
MNA/NUM/L/10/1	Bedwas Lodge (annual, general and committee meetings minutes)	1925–33	Contributions to Royal Gwent Hospital. Caerphilly Miners' Hospital delegate reports, extension to Miners' Hospital 1925, radiologist's qualifications and pay. Hospital rules. Hospital report, ENT Department established. Detailed hospital reports; administration, financial. Ambulance car for hospital. Resignation of hospital Matron, 1932.	Document	Archives	
MNA/NUM/L/10/3	Bedwas Lodge (annual, general and committee meetings minutes)	1940–2	Hospital and Medical Board travel expenses. Donations: Cardiff Royal Infirmary, Royal Gwent Hospital, Bath Hospital. Delegate nomination for Royal Gwent Hospital.	Document	Archives	
MNA/NUM/L/10/5	Bedwas Lodge (annual, general and committee meetings minutes)	1944–6	Cardiff Infirmary, reference to scheme of centralization (1945). Hospital scheme; industrial diseases, additional doctors. Caerphilly Miners Hospital scheme reference. Travel expenses to Gloucester Hospital. Hospital Board nominations.	Document	Archives	
MNA/NUM/L/23/160	Coegnant Lodge (Lodge Secretary's correspondence and papers)	1937–44	Maesteg and District General Hospital annual reports: 1937, 1941, and 1944.	Document	Archives	
MNA/NUM/L/31/6–9	Elliot Lodge (financial records)	1933–51	Account books including Hospital Fund accounts, 1935–1947.	Document	Archives	
MNA/NUM/L/32/1	Emlyn Lodge (Lodge account book)	1937–51	Payments to Hospital and Ambulance Account: Swansea Hospital, Ambulance (St John Ambulance), Carmarthen Infirmary.	Document	Archives	
MNA/NUM/L/33/39	Ferndale Lodge (Lodge Secretary's correspondence and papers)	1931	Ferndale Lodge Hospital and Conveyance Fund rules.	Document	Archives	
MNA/NUM/L/33/70	Ferndale Lodge (compensation papers)	1928–44	Accident and compensation records for Ferndale Collieries (1928–37) and register of hospital entrance (1936–44).	Document	Archives	Y

Reference Code	Collection	Dates	Description	Media	Location	DP
MNA/NUM/L/34/1	Fforchaman Lodge (annual, general and committee minutes)	1938–40	References to Medical Boards and Hospital Committee.	Document	Archives	Y
MNA/NUM/L/34/6	Fforchaman Lodge (annual, general and committee minutes)	1947–9	Medical Superintendent at Morriston Emergency Hospital, reference to travel expenses of members. Loss of pay attending Morriston Hospital. Hospital committee, delegates. Hospital grants.	Document	Archives	Y
MNA/NUM/L/35/1	Fochriw No. 1 and Nantwen Lodges (minute books)	1917–34	Hospital Governor appointments (Merthyr General, 1917 on). 1919: re hospital meeting, and Matron handed notice in (after agitation of Labour members).	Document	Archives	
MNA/NUM/L/39/1 and 2	Gellyceidrim Lodge (Lodge account book)	1923–44	Travel expenses to Swansea Hospital.	Document	Archives	
MNA/NUM/L/39/12 and 13	Gellyceidrim Lodge (Lodge Secretary's carbon-copy letter book)	1927–31	Swansea Hospital contributions. References to doctors. Llanbyther Sanatorium expenses.	Document	Archives	Y
MNA/NUM/L/39/14	Gellyceidrim Lodge (general correspondence to Lodge Secretary)	1925–31	Swansea Hospital discharge notice (1929), Doctors' notes requesting ambulance for patients from Swansea Hospital.	Document	Archives	Y
MNA/NUM/L/43/A1	Graig Merthyr Lodge (general and committee minutes)	1937–40	Reference to hospital contributions (Swansea) and deductions. Hospital governors' meeting and workers' representation, request for increased representation on Board of Management.	Document	Archives	Y
MNA/NUM/L/43/A8	Graig Merthyr Lodge (general and committee minutes)	1948	Hospital governors' meeting references. Expenses for hospital travel. Bath Hospital; appearance that wealthy having precedence, so considering using Droitwich instead. Pneumoconiosis cases and admission to Llandough Hospital research department, patients invited, covered financially.	Document	Archives	Y

Reference Code	Collection	Dates	Description	Media	Location	DP
MNA/NUM/L/58/1	Norchard and Princess Royal Lodges (minute book of Norchard Lodge Pit Head Committee Meetings)	1942–9	SWMF letters reference Talygarn rehabilitation centre and list of hospitals working in conjunction. X-ray treatment and loss of bonus for attending hospital.	Document	Archives	
MNA/NUM/L/62/A3	Park and Dare Lodge (minute book for annual, general and committee meetings; also special and colliery workers meetings and subscribers to Pentwyn Cottage Hospital, 1943)	1941–3	Minutes of meeting of subscribers Pentwyn Cottage Hospital; Subscribers' dependents, question relating to coverage by poundage paid to Colliery Office – subscriber only but rule not strictly adhered to. Staff salaries, to enquire if similar to other hospitals. Minutes of meeting of subscribers Pentwyn Cottage Hospital; appointment of workmen's representatives, Ocean Coal Co. granted usual supplies of coal, water and electricity to those who had made donations to hospital funds. Daily papers, supply inadequate, *Daily Worker* to be available. Cost of conveying body to Pentwyn Hospital for post-mortem. Establishment of fund for travel expenses for medical attention. Donation to Cwmparc Allotment Society. Injury case, complaint re lack of ambulance facilities. Possible new Medical Expenses Fund 1942. Men transferring to other doctors. 1942: two children in need of operations, could not be done by Dr Armstrong, Pentwyn Hospital not prepared to bear expense, appeal to Hospital Committee. Porthcawl Rest subscription. Donation request for artificial limb cost.	Document	Archives	
MNA/NUM/L/63/44	Penallta Lodge (Lodge Secretary's correspondence and papers)	1919–65	Miscellaneous papers, including hospital, ambulance and welfare papers, 1927–54.	Document	Archives	
MNA/NUM/L/66/1	Rhos Lodge (account book)	1934–44	Travel expenses to hospital, and Silicosis Board.	Document	Archives	
MNA/POL/1/1	Aberdare Town Ward Labour Party (committee minutes)	1933–42	Maternity Hospital Aberdare, for abnormal cases if home surroundings unsuitable. Discussion relating to hospitals.	Document	Archives	

Reference Code	Collection	Dates	Description	Media	Location	DP
MNA/POL/1/2	Aberdare Town Ward Labour Party (committee minutes)	1943-52	Hospital Committees (Aberdare and Merthyr).	Document	Archives	
MNA/POL/2/1, 2 and 3	Aberdare Trades and Labour Council (annual and monthly meetings minutes)	1925-52	(1) Llwynypia Hospital, General and Maternity. Small Pox Hospital. Aberdare General Hospital. Kennard Clinic Cwmafon. District Council Health and Medical Committee; reference to Isolation Hospital. Prince of Wales Hospital Cardiff; dental clinics, surgical appliances. Election of hospital presidents. (2) Aberdare General Hospital, election of vice-president. General hospital appointments of staff. Provision of Maternity Hospital for Aberdare. Mardy and Merthyr Isolation Hospitals. (3) Hospital scheme, doctors and Board disagreement. Hospital Boards.	Document	Archives	
MNA/POL/2/7	Aberdare Trades and Labour Council (Executive Committee minutes)	1941-51	Hospital Boards; Labour members; Doctors' complaints (5+1 woman) regarding 3 surgeons to do operations at hospital, and improvements needed. Welsh Hospitals Regional Board selections for Hospital Management Committees. Aberdare Medical Scheme. Trade Union Medical Scheme; doctors' charges; nominations. Medical examinations for unemployed. Patients' complaints re preferential treatment and moving hospitals. Aberdare Hospital; patient's bill; visiting day.	Document	Archives	
MNA/POL/2/10	Aberdare Trades and Labour Council (balance sheets with annual reports)	1907-62	1907: references to Infectious Diseases Hospital and improved sanitary appliances.	Document	Archives	

Reference Code	Collection	Dates	Description	Media	Location	DP
MNA/POL/3/1 and 3	Ammanford, Llandebie and District Trades and Labour Council (annual, general and Executive Council minutes)	1931-48	(1) Industrial Orthopaedic Society and its governance of Manor House Hospital. Hospital facilities in Amman Valley requirements. (3) Llandilo – new hospital building, builders' pay and status as 'industrial workers'. 1947: reference to new government. Medical Health Scheme. Refers to Beveridge Report. NHS nominations for Hospital Management Committees. Bus facilities to Morriston Hospital.	Document	Archives	
MNA/POL/3/3/1	Ammanford, Llandebie and District Trades and Labour Council (annual, general and Executive Council minutes)	1938-41	1938: Swansea Hospital contributory scheme and centralization scheme for cottage hospitals.	Document	Archives	
MNA/POL/5	Bedlinog Independent Labour Party, press cuttings (in account book)	1934-6	*Western Mail*; 1934: Lady Windsor Colliery Nursing Fund receipts and disbursements (to Cardiff Royal Infirmary, Pontypridd Cottage Hospital, Porthcawl Rest); 1933: advert for Westminster Hospital Rebuilding Appeal. 1935: article 'Spending £100,000 for Health and Work in the Rhondda', refers to money for a hospital in Glamorgan.	Document	Archives	
MNA/POL/6/1	Caerphilly Labour Party (Executive Committee minutes)	1938-41	UDC: Isolation Hospital, extension, staff working conditions and houses.	Document	Archives	
MNA/POL/6/5	Caerphilly Labour Party (Caerphilly Area Labour Party minutes)	1940-50	Welsh Board of Health, Nuffield Trust, Health Services. List of hospitals in Divisional Group, 1948. Caerphilly and Gelligaer possible joint Maternity Home (part of Miners' Hospital). Small-pox Hospital, evacuees' sick bay for contagious diseases; isolation hospital, staff wages; Church Village County Hospital;Gwaun Hospital; Llwynpia Hospital, blood transfusions. Port Talbot Hospital, US Army request to use part for VD cases.Llwynypia	Document	Archives	

Reference Code	Collection	Dates	Description	Media	Location	DP
			Hospital, nurses' lecture rooms heating. Pontypridd and Caerphilly Joint Hospital for Skin Treatment.			
MNA/POL/6/7	Caerphilly Labour Party (Bargoed Ward Labour Party minutes)	1939–42	1940: TB report comments; King Edward Memorial doctor's research in Denmark – on return, in charge of X-ray department. X-rays at Rhymney Cottage Hospital. 1940: Chester Sanatorium taken over by military authorities for soldiers with bad chests and lung problems. PAC, work relating to artificial limbs and dental treatment. Ambulances. isolation hospital – blood transfusion case. Hospital: staff salary increases; recruitment problems; heating and lights; drainage system overhaul; contracts of supply. References to MOH, Medical Superintendent of Hospital. Isolation hospitals: connection to main water supply; sewerage system. Welsh Board of Health payment to improve hospital sanitary system, 1942. MO reported 2 cases of pneumonia in hospital, 1942 – taking these cases permissible if beds available. Medical Aid. State-run hospitals. Pay for doctors in charge of: isolation hospital; clinics (female doctor); Bargoed Hostel. Gelligau Hospital – resignation of doctor. Smallpox Hospital at Gelligau	Document	Archives	
MNA/POL/6/8	Caerphilly Labour Party (Gelligaer Area Labour Party minutes)	1940–9	Ministry of Health recruitment of maids to hospitals. Shortage of doctors. Reference to training hospitals (e.g. Cardiff Infirmary) Hospital Governors. New Health Committee and Hospital Boards. Church Village County Hospital. Repairs to hospitals. Bedlinog Children's Hospital. Maternity Hospital. Hospital Committee and Hetherington Report 1944 staff wages and conditions.	Document	Archives	

335

Reference Code	Collection	Dates	Description	Media	Location	DP
MNA/POL/8/1	Ebbw Vale Branch Iron and Steel Trades and Labour Council (cash book)	1899–1919	Receipts and expenditure, including Hereford Eye Hospital, Cardiff and Bristol Infirmaries.	Document	Archives	
MNA/POL/14/14/1–2	Newport Trades and Labour Council and Labour Party (annual report and balance sheet for County Borough of Newport)	1929–38	1929: Hospitals; Royal Gwent, Allt-yr-yn (Infectious Diseases). 1938: Hospitals: Allt-yr-yn and Crick House (Infectious Diseases). Woolaston House Institute and Infirmary. Cost of Poor Relief for people in hospital. Out-door Relief costs including medical services	Document	Archives	
MNA/POL/15/1	New Tredegar Trades and Labour Council (minutes)	1938–51	1947: refers to county council report regarding hospitals, and new NHS. 1948: reference to selection of new Regional Hospital Board.	Document	Archives	
MNA/POL/24/1	Ynyshir Ward Labour Party (Rhondda Borough Trades and Labour Council and Labour Party Executive Committee minutes)	1936–8	Church Village Hospital to replace Pontypridd and Llwynypia ready 1941, and reference to builders. Isolation Hospital: provision of car for patients; complaint re child sent home too early and another child infected as result; employment conditions. Porth TB clinic complaint re patients' long wait. Dispenser appointed, Llwynypia Hospital. Porth Hospital model kitchens.	Document	Archives	
MNA/POL/24/2	Ynyshir Ward Labour Party (committee minutes)	1947–51	Regional Hospital Boards' takeover of vaccination, immunization and midwifery. Llwynypia Hospital; patient transfers to Llantwit Fadre; admission of chronic cases from Pontypridd Central Homes; lack of provision for chronic and emergency cases; 30–40 emergency beds; 'fight' for hospital; attendants' uniforms.	Document	Archives	
MNA/PP/9/6	H. W. Currie	1937	Newspaper cuttings relating to voluntary hospitals and nationalization of hospitals.	Document	Archives	

Reference Code	Collection	Dates	Description	Media	Location	DP
MNA/PP/11/16	Bryn Davies	1944	Powell Duffryn Workmen's Cottage Hospital, Aberbargoed; Income and Expenditure account, 1944, including salaries, contributions, supplies, provisions, statistics (patients, X-rays, casualties, treatments, operations, bed costs). Committee attendance by colliery members.	Document	Archives	
MNA/PP/16/7/1	S. O. Davies	1917–49	Newspaper cutting re specialists for Merthyr and Aberdare Hospital.	Document	Archives	
MNA/PP/16/11/1–34	S. O. Davies	1948	*Parliamentary Debates* (Hansard). Written answers re NHS – mental hospitals.	Document	Archives	
MNA/PP/16/50/7/1	S. O. Davies	1945	Constituency correspondence; letter from medical superintendent of Glan Ely TB hospital describing patient's state.	Document	Archives	Y
MNA/PP/16/50/8	S. O. Davies	1946	Constituency correspondence; application for supplementary clothing coupons for patients in hospital and sanatoria; Ministry of Pensions notes on War Pensions re disablement, hospitals and clinics, allowances.	Document	Archives	Y
MNA/PP/16/50/9	S. O. Davies	1947	Constituency correspondence; Sandbrook Rheumatic Hospital School (minutes extracts); letters relating to Merthyr Borough Council and NHS Services Act Executive Council.	Document	Archives	Y
MNA/PP/21/6	D. Evans	1943	Pontypridd Trades Council and Labour Party pamphlet, reference to Pontypridd Cottage Hospital. 1926 General Strike, coal for hospital.	Document	Archives	
MNA/PP/24/1	Edgar Evans (Bedlinog)	1926–7	Bedlinog Council of Action minute book: Merthyr General Hospital scheme for outside contributors.	Document	Archives	

Reference Code	Collection	Dates	Description	Media	Location	DP
MNA/PP/41/2, 4 and 5	David Harris (Glais) (exercise books containing bilingual manuscript reminiscences)	1970s, ref C19th	List of Clydach doctors, and Hospital Matron. Morriston Hospital. Clydach Hospital 1918, brief history, names of matrons and doctor, WWII Swansea Blitz and removal of patients.	Document	Archives	Y
MNA/PP/50/3	W. R. James (Trelewis), Taff Merthyr Lodge minute book	1946–52	Refers to collections for Great Ormond Street Children's Hospital; Cardiff and District Hospital Society and Pneumoconiosis Clinic at Royal Infirmary. Welsh Hospital and Health Services Association. Bath Hospital, Llandrindod Wells and Droitwich Spas.	Document	Archives	
MNA/PP/54/5 and 6	Hubert Jenkins (office diary)	1919–24	Cardiff Infirmary appeal. Medical Scheme (1920). Visits to Aberdare General Hospital and Mountain Ash Cottage Hospital. Royal Gwent Hospital, interview with doctor re X-ray apparatus. Cottage Hospital. Travel expenses to Bristol Infirmary.	Document	Archives	
MNA/PP/67/18	W. Eddie Jones	1932	Cost of Poor Relief including Institutional Relief, Domiciliary Relief, Public Assistance Institutions cost per inmate; Cambrian House (Caerleon), Coed y Gric (Pontypool), Hatherleigh Place (Abergavenny), Hill House (Monmouth), Ty-Bryn (Tredegar).	Document	Archives	
MNA/PP/67/29	W. Eddie Jones (newspaper cutting)	1935	Royal National Orthopaedic Hospital, Dr Arthur Rocyn Jones consultant orthopaedic surgeon, saw cases at Newport clinics.	Document	Archives	
MNA/PP/67/80	W. Eddie Jones (newspaper cuttings)	c.1930s	1933: article re Cardiff Corporation accounts: hospitals, sanatorium and smallpox hospital, Lord Pontypridd Hospital at Dulwich House for children with rheumatic cardiac disease, smallpox hospital at Caerau. Llandough General Hospital near completion. 1933: Cardiff Corporation article: grants Edward Nichol Home (Penylan), Cardiff Royal Infirmary, Hamadryad Seaman's Hospital.	Document	Archives	

Reference Code	Collection	Dates	Description	Media	Location	DP
MNA/PP/73/7	James Lewis (Maesteg) (miscellaneous pamphlets and printed material)	1933-46	Pamphlet: 1936 SWMF balance sheet, refers to grants to Royal Hospital (Bath).	Document	Archives	
MNA/PP/78/1 and 2	Glyn Mathias (Gorseinon)	1933	Bryngwyn Sheet Works payslips, including deductions for Swansea Hospital and Gorseinon Hospital.	Document	Archives	
MNA/PP/113/9	Emlyn Thomas (Maerdy) (SWMF Mardy Lodge, statement of accounts)	1920	Charity and Distress Funds including, King Edward VII Hospital (Cardiff) and Bristol Royal Infirmary.	Document	Archives	
MNA/PP/118/12	John Thomas (Aberavon), 'The Dockers' Record' (24 monthly reports of the DWRGWU)	1901-16	Roll of Honour for members elected to public bodies including Boards of Guardians and Hospital Trustees.	Document	Archives	
MNA/PP/118/107	John Thomas (Aberavon), (D5) South Wales Labour Annual	1902	Borough Districts details including hospitals, sanatorium.	Document	Archives	
MNA/TUG/1/1	Amalgamated Society of Railway Servants (Merthyr) (minute book)	1888-95	Hospital funds. Doctors who attend Merthyr General Hospital, advisability of having all doctors in district attending at hospital as long as 'gratis' and 'for good of suffering humanity'.	Document	Archives	
MNB/COL/16/3	Killan Colliery (Dunvant)	1923	Weekly pay sheet: includes deductions made for hospital.	Document	Archives	
MNB/COL/17/D2-11	Morlais Colliery	1940-4	Weekly wage sheets: lists deductions from wages for hospital (including Swansea and Llanelly).	Document	Archives	
MNB/I/7/1	Mountain Ash and Penrhiwceiber Hospital (statement of accounts for year ending 31 Dec 1924)	1925	2 photographs of hospital. Opened 18 December 24, patients transferred from Cottage Hospital. Lists management board, staff, governors (including collieries, co-op, railwaymen). Statistics relating to patients. References to matron, surgeons from Cardiff Infirmary, X-ray equipment. Balance sheets.	Document	Archives	Y

Reference Code	Collection	Dates	Description	Media	Location	DP
MNB/I/7/2, 4, 5,and 8	Mountain Ash and Penrhiwceiber Hospital (annual report and financial statement)	1933–47	1933: Refers to: hospital admission and tickets; X-ray dept; possible new children's ward. 1938: Reference to temporary children's ward of 8 beds in hospital 'Flat', and need for funding of project. 1939: Appointment of Orthopaedic Surgeon, Dr Nathan Rocyn Jones (of Cardiff). Refers to 'Clear the Hospital' Order received, 1 September 1939, re national emergency, and discharge of all patients. Honorary medical staff including female doctor, Dr Nora Thomas. 1947: Reference to matron (with hospital for 24 years). Children's ward – never achieved. Final report prior to hospital being handed over to the state 5 July 1948.	Document	Archives	
MNB/I/8/17	North's Workmen's Institute (Maesteg) (statements of account and balance sheets)	1929–57	Books, papers and periodicals supplied for Cottage and Isolation Hospitals. Subscriptions and papers for Maesteg and District Hospital.	Document	Archives	
MNB/NUM/I/1/6	Abercynon Lodge (Lodge Secretary's carbon-copy letter book)	1938	Certifying surgeon's fees. Hospital tickets.	Document	Archives	
MNB/NUM/I/2/1-4	Ammanford No. 2 Lodge (minute books)	1924–34	Swansea Hospital, contributions, cases, dispute. Admissions to London Hospital. Brondeg Cottage Hospital Scheme appeal. Llanelly Workmen's Medical Committee grant. Amman Valley Hospital Trustees nominations and committee. Contribution scheme re South West Wales Voluntary Hospital.	Document	Archives	
MNB/NUM/I/2/8	Ammanford No. 2 Lodge (Lodge balance sheet for 1938)	1939	Payments to Swansea Hospital and Amman Valley Hospital.	Document	Archives	

Reference Code	Collection	Dates	Description	Media	Location	DP
MNB/NUM/L/7	Abercynon Lodge (Lodge Secretary's correspondence received)	1938–40	Letter from Merthyr General Hospital (1938) asking for interview with lodge, regarding large number of men and dependants living in hospital area and working Abercynon. Treated at Merthyr but their contributions given to other hospitals.	Document	Archives	
MNB/NUM/L/7/1	Daren Lodge (general account book)	1943–60	Expenditure, including delegates to Swansea Hospital Board.	Document	Archives	
MNB/POL/1/8	Ammanford Trades and Labour Council (balance sheet, annual report, and Stalingrad Hospital account)	1944	Stalingrad Commemoration Hospital – accounts for fund, including donations from Ammanford St John Nursing and Ambulance Division; 7 beds purchased and inscribed.	Document	Archives	
MNB/POL/2/2	Bridgend Trades Council (minute book)	1945–52	Reference to General Hospital workers on Hospital Boards. Nominations for Local Hospital Management Committees.	Document	Archives	
MNB/POL/6/A4	Newport Constituency Labour Party (Executive and General Committee minutes)	1921–5	Woolaston House (Poor Law Institute), appointment of master and matron. Labour Guardians' support of matron for Children's' Homes. Committee representatives for administration of grants to hospitals.	Document	Archives	
MNB/POL/6/A6	Newport Constituency Labour Party (Executive and General Committee minutes)	1930–3	Manor House Hospital contributory scheme. Woolaston House; work hours of nurses and position of OAP inmates including cost.	Document	Archives	
MNB/POL/6/A8	Newport Constituency Labour Party (Executive and General Committee minutes, and Health Committee report)	1938–44	Woolaston House Infirmary: 1942: prosecution of 2 wartime nurses; 1943: report by Social Welfare Committee re diet and treatment of patients; poor treatment of Probationer Nurses; PAC Relieving Officer and admittance note. Royal Gwent Hospital waiting list. Appeal for pillows for military hospitals. Manor House Hospital appeal for funds.	Document	Archives	Y

Reference Code	Collection	Dates	Description	Media	Location	DP
MNB/PP/12/C/1–15	William Henry Davies (Penclawdd) (annual reports: MOH, Gower Rural Sanitary Authority)	1895–7, 1899, 1900, 1902–11	1895 and 1896: Need for isolation hospital. 1897: Isolation hospital, possible establishment of joint hospital with Llangyfelach and Oystermouth. 1903: Swansea Isolation Hospital to receive Gower cases if room. 1908: Site for isolation hospital. 1909: Isolation hospital in conjunction with Mumbles in progress. 1911: Swansea General Hospital admittance of TB cases if space. No provision of dispensary. Phthisis; no sanatorium or hospital accommodation.	Document	Archives	
MNB/PP/53/1	Stan Nind (Machen) (Caerphilly District Miners' Hospital annual report and financial statement)	1924	Committee members. Matron's annual report including statistics relating to beds, admissions and discharges, deaths, operations, X-ray department, massage department, treatment numbers. Income and expenditure for surgery and dispensary, staff, provisions. Capital account to buy and equip 'The Beeches'.	Document	Archives	
MNC/COP/1/1	Aberdare Co-operative Society (minute book)	1929–32	Donations: Cardiff Royal Infirmary, Treloar Cripples Hospital and College, Aberdare and District General Hospital, Seamen's Hospital Greenwich. Sick-room appliances donated to Aberdare General Hospital.	Document	Archives	
MNC/COP/1/3	Aberdare Co-operative Society (minute book)	1937–40	Donations: Cardiff Royal Infirmary, Royal National Hospital for Rheumatic Diseases (Bath), Treloar Cripples Hospital, Seamen's Hospital Greenwich.	Document	Archives	
MNC/COP/1/6	Aberdare Co-operative Society (minute book)	1945–8	Donations: Hospital for Sick Children (Great Ormond Street, London), Seamen's Hospital Greenwich. Specialists at hospitals, refers to enquiry into decision of Aberdare General Hospital re service. Aberdare and Mountain Ash Hospitals, applications for quotas of governors re annual subscriptions. Mountain Ash Hospital prescriptions.	Document	Archives	Y

Reference Code	Collection	Dates	Description	Media	Location	DP
MNC/PP/17/9	Selwyn Jones (*Rhondda Vanguard!* newspaper, Feb 1936 (Rhondda Communist Party))	1930s	Article re Llwynypia Hospital, and treatment of children of unemployed parents refused admission after certified by local doctors as needing operations. Dispute over responsibility for maintenance of these children in hospital (Councils, MOH, Relieving Officers).	Document	Archives	
PHO/PORT/81	Portraits (individual portraits)	c.1914	2 photographs of First World War soldiers recovering in hospital (Onllwyn).	Photographs	Archives	

Asylums

Asylums accommodated a minority of people with mental impairments, the majority of whom lived in the community or occupied workhouses. The confinement of the insane had its roots in the medieval Bethlem Hospital, but private or commercial madhouses had sprung up from the 1650s and in the eighteenth century the charitable impulse had produced not only the renowned Quaker 'Retreat' near York but also the subscription asylum modelled on the voluntary hospital. Following permissive legislation in 1808, the Lunacy Acts of 1845 obliged all counties and boroughs in England and Wales to build asylums for their pauper lunatics, either singly or in combination with neighbouring authorities. (SWCC: MNA/POL/3/3; MNA/POL/24/1–2).

As asylums failed to fulfil their therapeutic promise, anxieties about wrongful detention intensified and the 1890 Lunacy Act brought in a complex system of legal orders and medical certificates to ensure that only the truly mad were admitted. The civil rights of pauper patients, of course, had a less robust defence, as did those of inmates incarcerated under the Mental Deficiency Act of 1913. By the 1920s, however, psychiatry was moving in the direction of prevention and management. Therefore, the 1930 Mental Treatment Act introduced the concept of voluntary patients and endorsed outpatient clinics to lessen the taint of mental illness.

Reference Code	Collection	Dates	Description	Media	Location	DP
MNA/NUM/L/2/89	Abercynon Lodge (explanatory leaflet on the work of the Cardiff and District Hospital Society)	1942	Reference to cases where responsibility not accepted, e.g. mental illness cases.	Document	Archives	
MNA/NUM/L/3/16	Abergorki Lodge (Lodge Secretary's correspondence book)	1930–1	Reference to mental illness case, Pontypridd Homes and Bridgend Institution.	Document	Archives	Y
MNA/POL/2/1	Aberdare Trades and Labour Council (annual and monthly meetings minutes)	1925–52	Transfer of Poor Law matters to county council; mental illness cases moved to Hensol Castle. Reference to councillor's talk re medical examination of school children; Pendine School Camp, Greenhill Occupational Centre for Mentally Defective Children (Aberaman), mental and physical defectives (the Open Air School).	Document	Archives	
MNA/POL/3/3	Ammanford, Llandebie and District Trades and Labour Council (annual, general and Executive Council minutes)	1931–48	Reference to councillor's report on Mental Hospital Committee; care and treatment; changing attitudes; certification only in extreme cases. Joint Counties Mental Defectives Home (Pantglas), patients' pocket money.	Document	Archives	
MNA/POL/6/8	Caerphilly Labour Party (Gelligaer Area Labour Party minutes)	1940–9	Mental health: patient numbers; clinics; voluntary treatment. Mental hospitals.	Document	Archives	
MNA/POL/14/14/1–2	Newport Trades and Labour Council and Labour Party (annual report and balance sheet for County Borough of Newport)	1929–38	1929: Newport Mental Hospital. 1938: Mental Deficiency and Crindau Occupation Centre.	Document	Archives	
MNA/POL/24/1	Ynyshir Ward Labour Party (Rhondda Borough Trades and Labour Council and Labour Party Executive Committee minutes)	1936–8	Bridgend Mental Hospital – introduction of voluntary and temporary patients.	Document	Archives	

Reference Code	Collection	Dates	Description	Media	Location	DP
MNA/POL/24/2	Ynyshir Ward Labour Party (committee minutes)	1947–51	Guardianship of Mental Defectives – level of old Glamorgan scales raised to those of National Assistance (1948); advising parents to allow Glamorgan County Council to take over guardianship – increased benefits and ensured guardianship. Bridgend [Hospital] voluntary patient subjected to 'wrong' conditions.	Document	Archives	
MNA/PP/9/6	H. W. Currie	1937	Newspaper cuttings relating to clinics for mental and nervous diseases.	Document	Archives	
MNA/PP/16/50/9	S. O. Davies	1947	Constituency correspondence; removal of patient from Glamorgan County Mental Hospital.	Document	Archives	Y
MNA/PP/54/5 and 6	Hubert Jenkins (office diary)	1919–24	Meetings attended regarding 'mental defectives', Bridgend Asylum.	Document	Archives	
MNA/PP/67/18	W. Eddie Jones	1932	Cost of Poor Relief including persons in mental hospitals.	Document	Archives	
MNA/PP/118/107	John Thomas (Aberavon), (D5) South Wales Labour Annual	1902	Borough Districts details including asylums.	Document	Archives	
MNB/POL/2/2	Bridgend Trades Council (minute book)	1945–52	Reference to mental hospital workers on hospital boards.	Document	Archives	
MNB/POL/6/A8	Newport Constituency Labour Party (Executive and General Committee minutes, and Health Committee report)	1938–44	Mental Deficiency Committee nomination.	Document	Archives	Y
MNC/COP/27/14	People's Yearbook (Annual of the Co-operative Wholesale Society Ltd)	1933	Women's Co-operative Guild: mental hospitals, grading of patients, accommodation for temporary cases, separate administration buildings and convalescent home.	Document	Archives	

Sanatoria

Isolation hospitals emerged in the late nineteenth century as part of the system for notifying infectious diseases (see Chapter 5; Infectious Diseases). The 1866 Sanitary Act empowered but did not oblige local authorities to build isolation hospitals. After the Isolation Hospitals Act of 1893, however, county councils could demand the construction of institutional facilities because the notification of infectious cases to medical officers of health led to the mandatory isolation of patients.

Tuberculosis patients were placed in specialist sanatoria. The 1911 National Insurance Act required county committees to arrange for the treatment of insured persons with TB, while the 1913 Public Health Act enabled local authorities to treat the uninsured free of charge. The Public Health Act of 1921 abolished the distinction between insured and uninsured persons when it gave county and county borough councils a statutory duty to provide sanatoria for patients with tuberculosis, to remove highly infectious cases to hospital, and to develop care and aftercare services.

On the South Wales Coalfield, local authorities operated their TB policies in close partnership with the King Edward VII Welsh National Memorial Association (SWCC: MNA/POL/14/14/2; RC773 POW).

Reference Code	Collection	Dates	Description	Media	Location	DP
MNA/COP/2/1-11	Ammanford Co-op Society (general and committee meeting minutes)	1900–38	References to tickets for sanatorium.	Document	Archives	
MNA/NUM/LJ/39/12 and 13	Gellyceidrim Lodge Secretary's carbon-copy letter book	1927–31	Reference to Llanybyther Sanatorium expenses.	Document	Archives	Y
MNA/POL/14/14/2	Newport Trades and Labour Council and Labour Party (annual report and balance sheet for County Borough of Newport)	1938	TB and Welsh National Memorial Association, hospitals, sanatoria and centres.	Document	Archives	
MNA/POL/6/7	Caerphilly Labour Party (Bargoed Ward Labour Party minutes)	1939–42	1940: Chester Sanatorium taken over by military authorities for soldiers with chest and lung problems.	Document	Archives	
MNA/PP/118/107	John Thomas (Aberavon), (D5) South Wales Labour Annual	1902	Borough Districts details including sanatorium.	Document	Archives	
MNA/PP/16/50/5, 7/2 and 8	S. O. Davies (constituency correspondence)	1943–6	1943: Serviceman unable to afford clothing for son at TB sanatorium; scheme for treatment of TB in Wales. 1945: Servicemen at Pentsam TB Sanatorium. 1946: Application for supplementary clothing coupons for sanatoria patients.	Document	Archives	Y
MNB/PP/12/C/2/1-15	William Henry Davies (Penclawdd) (annual reports: MOH, Gower Rural Sanitary Authority)	1911	1911: Phthisis and lack of sanatorium or hospital accommodation.	Document	Archives	

Reference Code	Collection	Dates	Description	Media	Location	DP
RA644.T7 NEW	*New Weapons Against Tuberculosis. An explanation of Mass X-ray Examination and the New Financial Allowances*	1943	Pamphlet: refers to home treatment, sanatorium and institutions.	Document	SWML	
RA644.T7 WAR	Socialist Medical Association Pamphlet	1942	The War, Tuberculosis, and the Workers'. Reprint from *Medicine Today and Tomorrow*, June 1941. Financial difficulties, sanatorio.	Document	SWML	

Convalescent Homes

Convalescent homes were complementary to the large and smaller hospitals, enabling patients to recover and recuperate at a more leisurely pace. They were funded by similar means to the hospitals, with donations and subscriptions from charitable organizations, trade unions (including the SWMF), friendly societies, co-operative societies and workplace schemes. Where homes had strong links to local industries or groups, representative members often sat on their boards and influenced policy decisions.

On the South Wales Coalfield, convalescent homes provided an important service for men and women. They were used by men recovering from work-related accidents, as well as women who needed a period of rest. Miners' wives were sometimes admitted for a short holiday (SWCC: AUD/481). There were restrictions on types of patient who were accepted; for example, those with contagious diseases, mental illnesses, or with permanent conditions were not eligible. Admission to the homes was by a ticket system, whereby subscribing organizations were allocated a number of tickets to distribute to their members on application. The locations were rural or coastal, so that patients could benefit from the healthier environment. In south Wales, there were convalescent homes at Porthcawl, Southerndown and Talygarn. Other homes were used at Weston-super-Mare and Bournemouth (SWCC: AUD/301; HD9552.3 MIN; MNA/COP/7/14–15; MNA/NUM/L/34/1; MNA/PP/11/13; PHO/NUM/6/1–9).

In 1943 the Talygarn Convalescent Home was purchased from the South Wales District Committee by the Miners' Welfare Commission for conversion into a rehabilitation centre for injured miners whose labour was essential to the war effort.

Reference Code	Collection	Dates	Description	Media	Location	DP
	The Welsh Housing and Development Year Book	1923–4	1923: Convalescent colonies.	Document	SWML	
AUD/301	Jim Minton	1882–c.1973	Co-operative ticket to Combe Down Rest Home near Bath for Mrs Minton.	Transcript of audio	SWML	Y
AUD/481	Mrs Bessie Webb and Mrs Hannah Katie Evans	1920–75	Porthcawl Rest – miners' wives sent there for holiday (paid for by Miners' Association).	Audio tape	SWML	Y
HD2951.A5	Annual Co-operative Congress Reports (incomplete)	1913–76	1930: Convalescent homes, funds, reports.	Document	SWML	
HD7269.M62.OTH	*The Other Side of the Miner's Life: A Sketch of Welfare Work in the Mining Industry* (pamphlet)	1936	Issued by Philip Gee (Lincoln's Inn) with authority of The Mining Association of Great Britain. Contents include Convalescent homes.	Document	SWML	
HD9550 EBB	*The Ebbw Vale Works Magazine* (Vol. 5, No. 19)	June 1926	Article 'The Miners' Convalescent Home at Talygarn'.	Document	SWML	
HD9552.3 MIN	*The Miner* (Vol. I, No. 1)	Oct 1944	Article: 'Rehabilitation', relating to Talygarn, and orthopaedic injuries.	Document	SWML	
HD9552.3 MIN	*The Miner* (Vol. II, No. 11)	Sept 1946	2 letters relating to Talygarn.	Document	SWML	
HD9552.3 MIN	*The Miner* (Vol. I, No. 9/10)	June/July 1945	Article: 'Welfare Activities in Mining Communities, South Wales Coalfield'; reference to Talygarn Convalescent Home, and Porthcawl Rest Convalescent Home.	Document	SWML	
HD9552.3 MIN	*The Miner* (Vol. I, No. 9/10)	June/July 1945	Article: 'Convalescent Home', referring to Talygarn, and Court Royal Hotel, Bournemouth.	Document	SWML	
HD9552.3 MIN	*The Miner* (Vol. II, No. 10)	Aug 1946	Whole issue – Talygarn Miners' Rehabilitation Centre. Refers to orthopaedics, hospitals, nervous strain/shock, physiotherapy, staff, treatments, cases, illustrations of X-ray photos.	Document	SWML	

Reference Code	Collection	Dates	Description	Media	Location	DP
HD9552.3 MIN	The Miner (Vol.II, No. 9)	July 1946	Editorial relating to new Miners' Rest Home, Bournemouth.	Document	SWML	
HD9552.3 MIN	The Miner (Vol. II, No. 12)	Oct 1946	Article: 'A Patient's Impression of Talygarn Miners' Rehabilitation Centre', referring to orthopaedic injury.	Document	SWML	
HV686.R3	Reports of the MOH, and School MO, Rhondda UDC	1930	Reference to Tygwyn Convalescent Home.	Document	SWML	
MNA/1/16/3	Forest of Dean District Welfare Association (committee minutes)	1929–35	Rest cases to Weston, Porthcawl, Bournemouth, Southerndown. Weston-super-Mare Convalescent Home (1933) accepting patients on similar basis to Porthcawl Rest, and patients to have choice.	Document	Archives	Y
MNA/COL/2/4–38	Clydach Merthyr Colliery (Manager's carbon-copy correspondence books)	1937–48	References to Bournemouth and Talygarn Rest Homes.	Document	Archives	Y
MNA/COP/1/7	Aberdare and District Co-op Society Ltd (general and Board meeting minutes)	1920–2	Western Co-operative Convalescent Fund, lists applicants for benefits and whether or not successful. 1922: argument with Cwmbach Co-op regarding the Fund. Applications for tickets to Rest Homes.	Document	Archives	
MNA/COP/3/1	Briton Ferry and Neath Co-op Society (general and committee meetings minutes)	1944–54	Convalescent treatment requests. Western Co-op Convalescent Fund Committee.	Document	Archives	
MNA/COP/7/1–13	Ton Co-op Society (general and Committee minutes)	1884–1927	Donations and tickets: Porthcawl and Southerndown Rests, Roden and Talygarn Convalescent Homes.	Document	Archives	
MNA/COP/7/14–15	Ton Co-op Society (Board meetings minutes)	1928–48	Western Co-op Convalescent Fund and applications (details). Porthcawl and Southerndown Rests. Roden Convalescent Home. St Athans Miners' Welfare Camp. Subscription to North Devon Convalescent Children's Home.	Document	Archives	

Reference Code	Collection	Dates	Description	Media	Location	DP
MNA/COP/7/69	Ton Co-op Society (constitution and rules of the 'Rest' Convalescent Home, Porthcawl)	1898	Administration. Subscriptions and donations. Medical officers. Admission. Patients cert. Unsuitable cases (e.g. seriously ill, infectious, epileptics, children, mentally ill, immoral).	Document	Archives	
MNA/I/20/A1	Maerdy Workmen's Hall and Institute	1920s	Subscriptions to Porthcawl Rest, and applications for tickets (names).	Document	Archives	
MNA/NUM/3/1/1	Minutes of the SWMF Executive Council, and annual and special conferences	1907–40	Hospitals: Caerphilly, Cardiff Infirmary, Manor House, Royal Gwent, Royal Mineral Water Hospital. Bath, St John's Auxiliary Hosps (1917). Convalescent homes: Porthcawl Rest, Southerndown, Talygarn; Duke Fingard Inhalation Clinic (1940).	Document	Archives and SWML	
MNA/NUM/3/3/14	Correspondence with SWMF No. 1 Area (correspondence (Files 16 and 17))	1931–42	File 16: 1941: Talygarn Tickets.	Document	Archives	Y
MNA/NUM/3/3/18	Correspondence with SWMF No. 5 Area	1934–41	Talygarn audit and tickets.	Document	Archives	
MNA/NUM/3/3/2	Correspondence (bound volume of circulars)	1916–27	Talygarn inspection re purchase.	Document	Archives	
MNA/NUM/3/3/2	Correspondence (bound volume of circulars)	1916–27	SWMF donations, including Porthcawl Rest.	Document	Archives	
MNA/NUM/3/3/21	Correspondence with SWMF No. 8 Area	1934–42	Requests for Southerndown Rest and Talygarn tickets.	Document	Archives	
MNA/NUM/3/3/23	Correspondence with lodges (Files 2–8)	1934–42	Talygarn tickets.	Document	Archives	Y
MNA/NUM/3/3/33/2	Great Western Lodge (correspondence)	1934–42	Talygarn tickets.	Document	Archives	

Reference Code	Collection	Dates	Description	Media	Location	DP
MNA/NUM/3/3/44/2	Waunllwyd Lodge (correspondence with lodges)	1934–41	1938: letter re Porthcawl Rest tickets.	Document	Archives	
MNA/NUM/3/5/10	SWMF: Compensation Records (annual reports of silicosis cases)	1935–40	SWMF balance sheets 1936 and 1938 (including to Porthcawl Rest Home).	Document	Archives	Y
MNA/NUM/3/5/31	SWMF: Compensation Records (register of patients at Talygarn Convalescent Home)	1924–36	Personal details of patients, occupation, colliery where employed, dates at the home, whom nominated and sanctioned by, general remarks.	Document	Archives	Y
MNA/NUM/3/6/23	Records of the SWMF/NUM (South Wales Area) (Conciliation Board minutes)	1944	Rehabilitation and Talygarn. Payment of wages to workmen who attend at rehabilitation or other centres for re-examination.	Document	Archives	
MNA/NUM/3/8/17 (A)	Area No. 2 Council Minutes (register of ordinary accident Cases)	1934–52	Reference to tickets for Talygarn Convalescent Home and Porthcawl Rest Home. Convalescent home in Bournemouth.	Document	Archives	Y
MNA/NUM/3/8/7b	Maesteg District/Area (balance sheets)	1915–29	Talygarn Convalescent Home, Porthcawl Rest.	Document	Archives	
MNA/NUM/L/1	Abercrave Lodge (annual and general meetings minutes)	1935–57	Talygarn Convalescent Home.	Document	Archives	
MNA/NUM/L/10/3	Bedwas Lodge (annual, general and committee meetings minutes)	1940–2	Donations to Porthcawl Rest and other references. Talygarn tickets.	Document	Archives	
MNA/NUM/L/10/5	Bedwas Lodge (annual, general and committee meetings minutes)	1944–6	Porthcawl Rest, tickets and donations.	Document	Archives	
MNA/NUM/L/13/1	Blaengwrach Lodge (annual and committee meetings minute book)	1946–8	Bournemouth Convalescent Home for Miners to open 1947, tickets allocation to lodges.	Document	Archives	
MNA/NUM/L/19/116	Caerau Lodge (Lodge Secretary's correspondence and papers)	1909–33	Medical certificates for admission to Porthcawl and Talygarn Rest Homes.	Document	Archives	Y

Reference Code	Collection	Dates	Description	Media	Location	DP
MNA/NUM/L25/1	Cwmcynon Lodge (account book)	1943–8	References to grants to Porthcawl (to send miners to the 'Rest' Convalescent Home).	Document	Archives	
MNA/NUM/L28/17	Deep Duffryn Lodge (financial records)	1934–47	Account book (including accounts for Convalescent and Auxiliary Fund).	Document	Archives	
MNA/NUM/L3/1	Abergorki Lodge (annual, general and committee meetings minute book)	1913–15	Refers to Doctors' Committee and Institutions – Porthcawl Rest, Cardiff, Bristol and Bath Mineral Waters, funds.	Document	Archives	
MNA/NUM/L3/1	Abergorki Lodge (annual, general and committee meetings minute book)	1913–15	'Rest' tickets.	Document	Archives	
MNA/NUM/L3/12	Abergorki Lodge (Lodge Secretary's correspondence book)	1924–5	Talygarn tickets.	Document	Archives	Y
MNA/NUM/L3/16	Abergorki Lodge (Lodge Secretary's correspondence book)	1930–1	Talygarn tickets.	Document	Archives	Y
MNA/NUM/L3/18	Abergorki Lodge (correspondence re compensation cases)	1926–39	Reference to Talygarn and disturbance by resident who had been subsequently discharged.	Document	Archives	Y
MNA/NUM/L34/1	Fforchaman Lodge (annual, general and committee minutes)	1938–40	Porthcawl Rest, tickets for women, 1939 – discussion re issue to women as not injured or recovering workmen, to be discussed the year after.	Document	Archives	Y
MNA/NUM/L34/1	Fforchaman Lodge (annual, general and committee minutes)	1938–40	Porthcawl Rest levy and tickets (including to women). Tickets for Southerndown Rest and Talygarn.	Document	Archives	Y
MNA/NUM/L34/6	Fforchaman Lodge (annual, general and committee minutes)	1947–9	Porthcawl Rest, tickets, levy, 2 tickets for wives, 1948.	Document	Archives	Y
MNA/NUM/L34/6	Fforchaman Lodge (annual, general and committee minutes)	1947–9	Applications for Bournemouth Convalescent Home.	Document	Archives	Y

Reference Code	Collection	Dates	Description	Media	Location	DP
MNA/NUM/L/39/12 and 13	Gellyceidrim Lodge (Lodge Secretary's carbon-copy letter book)	1927–31	References to applications for Talygarn tickets.	Document	Archives	Y
MNA/NUM/L/43/A1	Graig Merthyr Lodge (general and committee minutes)	1937–40	Applications for Talygarn Convalescent Home.	Document	Archives	Y
MNA/NUM/L/43/A8	Graig Merthyr Lodge (general and committee minutes)	1948	Miskin Manor Convalescent Home availability for miners' wives.	Document	Archives	Y
MNA/NUM/L/43/A8	Graig Merthyr Lodge (general and committee minutes)	1948	Bournemouth Convalescent Home (Court Royal) levy, rules regarding the fund (9 listed, started 1948), list of people sent there 1947–8, ref to sending the 'old men' there. Talygarn.	Document	Archives	Y
MNA/NUM/L/52/2 and 3	Morlais Lodge (Lodge Secretary's carbon-copy letter book)	1931–4	Talygarn forms.	Document	Archives	
MNA/NUM/L/58/1	Norchard and Princess Royal Lodges (minute book of Norchard Lodge Pit Head committee meetings)	1942–9	SWMF letters including references to Talygarn rehabilitation centre and list of hospitals working in conjunction. Circular referring to new Convalescent Home at Bournemouth. Rest Home tickets.	Document	Archives	
MNA/NUM/L/6/1	Abertridwr Lodge (meetings minutes, balance sheet, membership lists)	1925–59	Talygarn Convalescent Home – letter of apology regarding conduct of member staying there. Reference to ticket for Court Royal, Bournemouth.	Document	Archives	
MNA/POL/5	Bedlinog Independent Labour Party (press cuttings (in account book)	1934–6	*Western Mail* cuttings; 1934: Lady Windsor Colliery Nursing Fund receipts and disbursements (to Cardiff Royal Infirmary, Pontypridd Cottage Hospital, Porthcawl Rest).	Document	Archives	
MNA/POL/6/5	Caerphilly Labour Party (Caerphilly Area Labour Party minutes)	1940–50	References to tickets for Porthcawl Rest.	Document	Archives	

Reference Code	Collection	Dates	Description	Media	Location	DP
MNA/POL/8/1	Ebbw Vale Branch Iron and Steel Trades and Labour Council (cash book)	1899–1919	Receipts and expenditure, including Porthcawl Rest.	Document	Archives	
MNA/PP/11/13	Bryn Davies	1932–49	The 'Rest' (Sea-Side) Convalescent Homes, Porthcawl and Southerndown; letters regarding meetings and form for admission (including list of 18 rules for patients).	Document	Archives	
MNA/PP/118/25	John Thomas (Aberavon) (minutes of TGWU Tinplate Section Annual Conference)	1930	Swansea Conference, TGWU Area 4, 20 April 1929 (Tinplate Section): Reference payment to Convalescent Home of the union.	Document	Archives	
MNA/PP/50/3	W. R. James (Trelewis) (Taff Merthyr Lodge minute book)	1946–52	Porthcawl and Southerndown Rests applications. Bournemouth Home.	Document	Archives	
MNA/PP/73/1	James Lewis (Maesteg) (Maesteg Medical Fund committee minute book)	1929–39	Porthcawl Rest grant.	Document	Archives	
MNA/PP/73/6	James Lewis (Maesteg)	1930–47	(Papers re James Lewis's tenure of office as secretary of Llynfi Sundries Lodge) Talygarn tickets reference.	Document	Archives	
MNA/PP/73/7	James Lewis (Maesteg) (Misc. pamphlets and printed material)	1933–46	1936: SWMF balance sheet, including ref grants to Porthcawl Rest.	Document	Archives	
MNA/TUG/7/1/C/1-2	Iron and Steel Trades Confederation (reports, circulars, minutes and papers)	1934–48	1944: Convalescent Home, Conway, north Wales.	Document	Archives	
MNA/TUG/7/1/C/1-2	Iron and Steel Trades Confederation (reports, circulars, minutes and papers)	1934–48	1948: Letter; Convalescent Home facilities for women members. 1946 and 1948: letters re Lark Hill Convalescent Home (and application form), Conway, north Wales.	Document	Archives	

Reference Code	Collection	Dates	Description	Media	Location	DP
MNB/COL/17/C25B	Morlais Colliery (Secretarial Dept circulars)	1925–7	Letters: Talygarn Convalescent Home and admission tickets.	Document	Archives	
MNB/COL/17/C25G	Morlais Colliery (Secretarial Dept circulars)	1931–7	Talygarn regulations for admission.	Document	Archives	
MNB/COL/17/C33A	Morlais Colliery (welfare and safety circulars)	1922–79	Convalescent Home Rules, 1927. Talygarn regulations for admission.	Document	Archives	
MNB/I/1/1	Abercrave Colliery Sick Fund (minute book)	1909–52	Porthcawl, Talygarn, Southerndown Rest Homes and tickets.	Document	Archives	Y
MNB/I/13/1	Yniscedwyn Sick Fund (general and committee minute book)	1930–58	Porthcawl Rest donation. Refers to Talygarn and Bournemouth Convalescent Homes.	Document	Archives	Y
MNB/I/3/C12	Abergorki Workmen's Hall and Institute (Secretary's carbon-copy letter book)	1948–9	Rest Home facilities for women with (miners' relatives) at convalescent homes.	Document	Archives	Y
MNB/I/3/C28–32	Abergorki Workmen's Hall and Institute (Secretary's carbon-copy letter book)	1945–8	South-Western Divisional Welfare Convalescent Home facilities for women – applications for Hafod, Boverton or Arosfa Porthcawl, and scheme for miners' wives and Dependants.	Document	Archives	
MNB/NUM/L/1/6	Abercynon Lodge (Lodge Secretary's carbon-copy letter book)	1938	Talygarn admissions. Porthcawl Rest.	Document	Archives	
MNB/NUM/L/2/1–4	Ammanford No. 2 Lodge (minute books)	1924–34	References to tickets for Talygarn and Porthcawl Rest.	Document	Archives	
MNB/NUM/L/2/17	Ammanford No. 2 Lodge (regulations for admission of patients to Talygarn Convalescent Home)	c.1930	Single page of regulations for admission to Talygarn Convalescent Home. Reference to 'Priority' and 'Ordinary' admissions.	Document	Archives	

Reference Code	Collection	Dates	Description	Media	Location	DP
MNB/NUM/L/3/1	Blaenserchan Lodge (account book)	1918–63	Expenditure: donations for Porthcawl Rest.	Document	Archives	
MNB/NUM/L/4/1	Caerau Lodge (statement of accounts)	1929	Expenditure: Porthcawl Rest Tickets.	Document	Archives	
MNB/NUM/Misc/ 18	Circulars (NUM Miscellanea)	1946–66	Circulars re convalescent homes and holiday villages.	Document	Archives	
MNC/COP/1/1	Aberdare Co-operative Society (minute book)	1929–32	Donations: Western Co-op Convalescent Fund. Southerndown Rest, and Roden Convalescent Home applications. Western Co-op Convalescent Fund – applications for benefit.	Document	Archives	
MNC/COP/1/3	Aberdare Co-operative Society (minute book)	1937–40	Staff member sent to Roden House. Convalescent Benefit and ticket applications.	Document	Archives	
MNC/COP/1/6	Aberdare Co-operative Society (minute book)	1945–8	Convalescent Benefit applications. Convalescent Fund and silicosis and pneumoconiosis.	Document	Archives	Y
MNC/COP/11/1	Garndiffaith Co-op Society (minute book)	1928–30	Applications for Porthcawl Rest and Southerndown. Refers to Convalescent Benefit and Sick Visiting.	Document	Archives	
MNC/COP/13/1	Mid-Rhondda Co-op Society (minute book)	1920–6	Nominations for Board of Western Convalescent Fund and applications for benefits.	Document	Archives	
MNC/COP/13/1	Mid-Rhondda Co-op Society (minute book)	1920–6	1923: appeal relating to Porthcawl and Southerndown Rests and liquidation of debts.	Document	Archives	
MNC/COP/15/1	Penarth Co-op Society (minute book)	1922–39	Donations to Western Section Convalescent Fund.	Document	Archives	
MNC/COP/15/2	Penarth Co-op Society (minute book)	1937–9	Donations: Western Section Convalescent Fund. Applications for Southerndown.	Document	Archives	

Reference Code	Collection	Dates	Description	Media	Location	DP
MNC/COP/16/1	Penygraig Co-op Society (minute book)	1912–16	1913: Convalescent Fund set up, and Convalescent Home (1915). Convalescent applications (TB excluded), Porthcawl Rest tickets.	Document	Archives	
MNC/COP/3/1	Abersychan Co-op Society (minute book)	1908–12	Donations: Porthcawl Rest. Porthcawl Rest tickets.	Document	Archives	
MNC/COP/3/3	Abersychan Co-op Society (minute book)	1924–31	Porthcawl Rest donations and tickets. Convalescent homes.	Document	Archives	
MNC/COP/3/3	Abersychan Co-op Society (minute book)	1924–31	Western Section Convalescence Fund references.	Document	Archives	
MNC/COP/3/4	Abersychan Co-op Society (minute book)	1945–9	Western Co-op Convalescent Fund Committee.	Document	Archives	
MNC/COP/3/5	Abersychan Co-op Society (Accounts (reports and balance sheets))	1906–7	Working expenses including hospital (1906), Porthcawl Rest and insurance.	Document	Archives	
MNC/COP/5/1	Alltwen and Pontardawe Co-op (minute book (Welsh))	1914–17	Subscriptions to Co-op and Western Convalescent Funds.	Document	Archives	
MNC/COP/6/1	Blaenavon Co-op Society (minute book)	1915–18	Applications for Convalescent Fund.	Document	Archives	
MNC/COP/6/3	Blaenavon Co-op Society (minute book)	1922–5	Convalescent Fund application and payment to fund.	Document	Archives	
MNC/COP/6/5	Blaenavon Co-op Society (minute book)	1937–54	Western Section Convalescent Fund invitation for affiliation.	Document	Archives	
MNC/COP/9/1	Cardiff Co-op Retail Society (minute book)	1933–4	Donations: Western Convalescent Fund (and committee nominations, and applications).	Document	Archives	

Reference Code	Collection	Dates	Description	Media	Location	DP
MNC/ISTC/1/1	National Union of Blastfurnacemen, Ore Miners, Coke Workers and Kindred Trades (Annual Conference reports)	1919–25	Convalescent Home Benefit. Union accounts including expenditure on convalescent homes.	Document	Archives	Y
MNC/ISTC/3/1	National Union of Blastfurnacemen, Ore Miners, Coke Workers and Kindred Trades (Delegate Board minutes)	1922–31	Convalescent Homes section; reports on Convalescent Home Benefit Fund, National Convalescent Benefit. Medical certificate example and details (for convalescent homes), Cleveland Convalescent Home Fund details.	Document	Archives	
MNC/ISTC/4/1	National Union of Blastfurnacemen, Ore Miners, Coke Workers and Kindred Trades (Annual General Meeting reports)	1938–41	Accounts for union including benefits such as convalescent homes. Cleveland District Convalescent Home Fund details (for members, wives, children).	Document	Archives	
PHO/NUM/6/10–15	NUM Miscellaneous (NUM Miners Rest Homes)	1923–c.1964	Talygarn Miners' Rest Home; 21 photographs including postcards of exterior and interior views of building and group of entertainers. Miners in gardens, playing bowls and exercising in gym. Men attending celebratory dinners.	Photographs	Archives	Y
PHO/NUM/6/1–5	NUM Miscellaneous (NUM Miners Rest Homes)	c.1958–61	Bournemouth Miners' Rest Home; 9 photographs including matron, staff and miners. Views of exterior and interior of building and gardens.	Photographs	Archives	Y
PHO/NUM/6/6–9	NUM Miscellaneous (NUM Miners Rest Homes)	1920–50	Porthcawl Miners' Rest Home; 10 photographs including matron, staff, and patients (including amputees). Views of exterior and interior of buildings.	Photographs	Archives	Y
RA973 CON	Talygarn souvenir	ud	Photocopy of souvenir from Talygarn Convalescent Home for the South Wales Mining Industry, Pontyclun. Includes photos.	Document	SWML	

Reference Code	Collection	Dates	Description	Media	Location	DP
RA973 RAI	Photocopy of newspaper article from *The Daily Echo*	1997	Photocopy of newspaper article from *The Daily Echo*, 8 November 1997 re Court Royal Miners' Convalescent Home, Bournemouth (50th anniversary).	Document	SWML	
	Scrapbooks of newspaper cuttings (labelled 'Cuttings Book, 1945–1947'.)	1945–7	Talygarn, South Wales Miners' Rehabilitation Centre.	Document	SWML	

Appendix A

How to use the South Wales Coalfield Collection

Manuscript sources in the South Wales Coalfield Collection consist mainly of official records (such as minute books, annual reports and financial accounts), correspondence (such as letters or notes to be read by others) and personal diaries. The official records were produced by organizations such as trade unions, collieries and welfare or co-operative societies. Printed records such as annual reports, handbooks and pamphlets were published for mass distribution and they are therefore more legible. Many other records are handwritten, in ledgers, notebooks and diaries. Minutes and business correspondence are relatively legible, while personal correspondence can be less so because the quality of handwriting can vary greatly.

The oral history and video collections record the living memory of all kinds of people. They talk about their own experiences as well as those of their families and their communities. The recordings provide an important research tool for understanding our shared history and can potentially fill in some of the gaps that manuscripts and books inevitably leave.

There can be limitations on access to material, especially where it contains sensitive personal information relating to people who are still alive. This is because the Data Protection Act sets out strict conditions for access to such information. Sensitive information includes details of medical conditions, compensation details or information about trade union membership. Restrictions are placed on access to such material and a lifespan of 100 years is generally assumed. Staff are able to give further advice on this matter. Further information about the Data Protection Act and the Freedom of Information Act may be found on the Information Commissioner's website at http://www.information commissioner.gov.uk.

Before beginning a search of the SWCC, decide on the theme or topic to be researched. Once this has been decided, select a few descriptive words or phrases and use these to search the catalogues. Discuss the research with the archivist or librarian as there may be other relevant material. Start with the most relevant material and decide how to record and store any notes taken. It may be necessary to book a seat before visiting, and ordering material in advance will give extra time for studying the material on arrival. If using a laptop computer, mention this in advance to staff to ensure seating close to a power point. Only pencil should be used for handwritten notes.

Ensure that a record is kept of the catalogue reference and description of the material being used, in case it is needed for citations, or future reference. Once the most obviously relevant material has been consulted, it is worth searching the catalogues again to ensure nothing has been missed. Then sample some other material which may not appear to be so relevant, as there may be something useful there which will make it worthwhile searching more thoroughly. If researching a topic which relates to particular dates, or legislation, check that the dates of material ordered are relevant before spending much time reading it. Remember that it may be necessary to anonymize personal information relating to living individuals which is covered by the Data Protection Act.

Appendix B

Medical Records beyond the South Wales Coalfield Collection

Medical records for the South Wales Coalfield are, of course, not only to be found in the South Wales Coalfield Collection (SWCC); they are also housed in repositories serving the UK as a whole, and in local archives and libraries. However, these materials are difficult to identify because the south Wales region is not a searchable category. Therefore, this appendix is not a systematic review of all the resources available but merely a selection from the British Library, the National Archives, the Wellcome Library for the History and Understanding of Medicine, the National Library of Wales, and four record offices and four public libraries that serve the coalfield area.

The British Library

The British Library (BL) – the national library of the United Kingdom with 150 million items – is based at St Pancras in central London. Though it has a number of different catalogues, three are most relevant to the SWCC: the catalogue of Western language manuscripts, private papers and archives, which have been acquired since 1753; the integrated catalogue of books, serials, printed music and maps; and the catalogue for the National Sound Archive (NSA). Looking for 'south Wales' in the manuscript catalogue throws up just one reference – to *New* South Wales in Australia where among the Nightingale Papers there is a discussion of nursing practice (BL: Add 47757). Similarly, the integrated catalogue yields references to education, religion, industrial unrest, colliery companies and above all the geological conditions of the region, but nothing of direct relevance to the history of health care. Even the oral history holdings within the sound archive – important collateral for the audio-visual media at the Miners' Library – offers only one title under 'south Wales' of potential interest: an interview in the George Ewart Evans Collection with Howell Jeffries (born 1903), who reminisces about living and working conditions during the 1920s (NSA: T1429WR C1).

In the absence of a regional dimension, catalogues in the British Library have to be interrogated by theme or by place name. In the manuscript catalogue, medical materials for the late modern period are not greatly in evidence, Marie Stopes's papers, including the establishment of family planning clinics in Cardiff and Swansea, being a notable exception (BL: Add 58624–58626, Add 58632–58633). Similarly, there are fascinating oral histories in the sound archive. Dr Samuel Isaacs, for instance, was born in Merthyr in 1913, went to Cardiff to qualify, and returned to work in the town as a GP between 1936 and 1947. His testimony forms part of 'The Oral History of General Practice' project (NSA: C648/59). Overall, however, the archive contains comparatively few titles for medicine and health before 1948. With the integrated catalogue, on the other hand, regional invisibility breeds profusion rather than scarcity because searching by themes (such as industrial diseases, mining accidents, sanitation, nutrition, hospitals and nurses) produces a mass of references, which are undifferentiated by location. Only by pairing each theme with each significant place name in the region, and keying in every couplet separately, is it possible to build up a comprehensive picture of medical records relevant to the South Wales Coalfield. Undoubtedly, there are many items of interest – from *The Hospitals of Wales* by G. Arbour Stephens (1912) (BL: B.68.a.15 DSC) to *The Pit of Death* by M. Davis, one of the twenty-four survivors of the Pontypridd Pit Disaster at the turn of the nineteenth century where 276 lives were lost (BL: RB.31.b.151/28). Finding them, however, is a little like looking for the proverbial needle in a haystack.

The National Archives

The catalogue for the National Archives (TNA) – previously the Public Record Office – at Kew in West London 'contains 9.5 million searchable descriptions of records from central government, courts of law and other UK national bodies' (http://www.bl.uk). Since the records are organized according to the government departments that originated them, resources for medicine and health are more readily accessible. General material relating to occupational health and welfare is to be found among the Home Office and Ministry of Labour papers, while the Ministry of Power has items of regional as well as national significance – like the 1946/7 amendment to the regulation of dust in coal mines, which followed a report by the South Wales Pneumoconiosis Joint Committee (TNA: POWE8/1043). Occupational health was also covered in the work of the Ministry of Health; in 1945, for instance, a deputation from the South Wales Miners' Federation was received to argue for an increase in the number of doctors who sat on medical boards under the pneumonoconiosis compensation scheme (TNA: MH55/1060).

Community health was also a responsibility shared between government departments. Thus the School Medical Service fell within the orbit of the Ministry of Education whose archive houses an 'Investigation into the Physical Condition of Children in Coalmining Areas of South Wales' (1928–31) (TNA: ED 50/83). Nevertheless, most holdings for community health are lodged with the Ministry of Health. Public health features strongly and there are sanitary papers for the principal towns in south Wales during the 1890s (see, for example, TNA: MH12/8029, MH12/8184, MH12/16475). Outbreaks of infectious diseases are likewise recorded – smallpox in Swansea (1921–9) (TNA: MH96/395) and diphtheria in Neath (1922–37) (TNA: MH96/443). The arrangements for isolation facilities are documented, including the loan to the Cardiff authorities of the Cholera Hospital on the island of Flat Holm in the Bristol Channel (1894–6) (TNA: MH48/485). The treatment of tuberculosis during the 1920s is also mentioned for Cardiff, Carmarthen,

Merthyr and Newport (TNA: MH96/1094, MH96/1074, MH96/1097, MH96/1099), along with the development of the Sully Hospital after 1928 (TNA: MH96/1040-1043).

But the ministry's role was extending beyond the traditional public health agenda. Some of these new functions were routine: such as regularly approving the activities of institutions for blind people under legislation of 1920, which the major local authorities in south Wales undertook (see, for example, TNA: MH96/11-13, MH96/60-63, MH96/65-70). Other tasks leaving an archive trail were a response to priorities in national health policy. In Rhondda, for example, a model infant welfare centre was built with a grant from the Carnegie Trust in an effort to prevent the death of small children (TNA: MH96/854); while the papers of the Welsh Consultative Council on Maternal Mortality, which conducted enquiries in Carmarthenshire, Newport, Pontypridd, Swansea and Cardiff during the 1920s, reflected anxieties about the unnecessary fatalities of childbirth (TNA: MH96/907).

The Ministry of Health also engaged with the delivery of local health care. Therefore, its records concern themselves with the implementation of policies like the 1936 Midwives Act in Merthyr (TNA: MH96/848) and the management of maternity homes in Cardiff (1934) (TNA: MH96/847), Newport (1925-52) (TNA: MH96/842-843) and Swansea (1919-34) (TNA: MH96/849). In addition, the medical aid societies are in evidence in Ebbw Vale (1912-47) (TNA: MH49/19-20), Neath (1913-48) (TNA: MH49/28-29) and Tredegar (1912-48) (TNA: MH49/24-27), their records revealing not only the annual accounts but also episodic disputes around the dispensation of drugs and the fraudulent use of medical certificates.

Bricks and mortar as well as personnel appear. Thus the proposals for the Joint Counties Asylum at Carmarthen (1858-66) (TNA: MH83/335), and the records for the St David's Hospital that it became (1852-1960) (TNA: MH96/1862), are extant, together with material for the Whitchurch Mental Hospital that opened in Cardiff at the beginning of the twentieth century (1900-13) (TNA: MH96/ 296). There are also papers for institutions like the Prince of Wales Orthopaedic Hospital in Cardiff (1921-4)

(TNA: MH96/845), the Caerphilly District Miners' Hospital during the 1940s (TNA: MH96/1670) and the Ebbw Vale General Hospital, which in the 1930s submitted an application for assistance under the Special Areas Fund (TNA: MH96/286–87). The role of hospitals in wartime is also well documented. At the outbreak of the Second World War, for instance, emergency hospital accommodation was organized for military, sick and casualty patients in Newport and Monmouthshire (TNA: MH96/120) and in Cardiff and East Glamorganshire (TNA: MH96/121), and permanent premises for cancer treatment were built when the blitzed wards at Swansea Hospital were replaced between 1946 and 1948 (TNA: MH96/297). Even the patient's perspective is occasionally represented in hospital material. In 1946 an inquiry was requested into the treatment at Tydfil Lodge Infirmary of Mrs Margaret Lewis (deceased) (TNA: MH96/938).

The accessibility of all hospital records is greatly enhanced by the UK Hospital Records Database (http://www.national archives.gov.uk/hospitalrecords): a joint venture between the former Public Record Office and the Wellcome Trust, which enables online searching by name and place with entries charting changes of title, dates of foundation and closure, status (for example, voluntary, NHS), type (for example, general, acute, mental, geriatric, war) and the location and nature of surviving records, plus the existence of any finding aids.

The Wellcome Library for the History and Understanding of Medicine

The Wellcome Trust's own specialist Library for the History and Understanding of Medicine (WL) is a rich resource for the history of medicine. Though hunting for the term 'south Wales' is unfruitful, looking up the main towns in the region produces an array of references. The manuscript collection includes correspondence relating to the establishment of a family planning clinic in Pontypridd (1930) (WL: SA/FPA/SR22/4) and papers for the Cardiff branch of the Glamorgan County Nursing Association and the Queen's

Institute of District Nurses (1938) (WL: SA/QNI/X.24). The printed holdings for south Wales are more extensive. Over and above the episodic runs of medical officer of health annual reports for all the principal local authorities, there are hospital reports, books and government papers with a south Wales orientation. The annual reports for hospitals cover the Caerphilly District Miners' Hospital for 1927 and 1928 (WL: WX28. BW3 C12C12); Pontypridd and District Cottage Hospital, also for 1927 and 1928 (WL: WX28.BW3 P81P81); the County Infirmary, Carmarthen for 1937 and 1939 (WL: WX28. BW3 C28C28); and the Cardiff City Mental Hospital for 1944, 1947 and 1948 (WL: WLM28. B3 C261947).

Among the books are *A Sanitary Survey of Glamorganshire* by William Williams (1895) (WL: WA670. BW3 1895W72s); *Miners' Nystagmus, Parts I–X*, by Frederick Robson (1923) (WL: WW505 1923R66p); *The Health of Old and Retired Coalminers in South Wales* by Enid M. Williams (1933) (WL: XWF); *The Cardiff Medical Society* by A. W. Sheen (1939) (WL: CAG.41\BRI); and a *Description of Mount Stuart, Bute, as an Hospital: with full report of the life and work there during the Great War 1914–1918*, which was probably published in 1920 (WL: LNJY. 4682). Government papers include *Dr S. W. Wheaton's Report to the Local Government Board on the Sanitary Circumstances and Administration of the Neath Rural District* (1911) (WL: XWA); the *Report of an Inquiry into an Obscure Disease, Encephalitis Lethargica*, with extracts from a report by Dr Carnwath of Tredegar (1918) (WL: XWA); and *Studies in Nutrition: An Inquiry into the Diet of Families in Cardiff and Reading* by E. P. Cathcart and A. M. T. Murray, with assistance by M. Shanks (1932) (WL: WB100 1932M48s).

The National Library of Wales

Complementing the resources of the British Library, the National Archives and the Wellcome Library are the repositories located in Wales, namely the National Library of Wales at Aberystwyth in Ceredigion and the record offices and local libraries in the coalfield area. The National Library of Wales (NLW) has a vast collection in a variety of media. There are three relevant catalogues: books, periodicals and newspapers, plus maps and photographs; archives and manuscripts, split into those listed before and after 1999; and the National Screen and Sound Archive of Wales. Again, combing these catalogues for 'south Wales' throws up a list of references dominated by geological structure and industrial strife. Given the geographical coverage of the National Library, however, tapping into its holdings for medicine and health poses similar problems to exploiting the British Library.

The National Library has enjoyed copyright status since 1911 and so, in theory, it has received every printed work published in Britain and Ireland since that date. Interrogating the catalogue for items of relevance to medical history throws up a range of titles for the South Wales Coalfield, over and above the ubiquitous annual reports of medical officers of health: *Chronic Pulmonary Disease in South Wales Coalminers*, by the Medical Research Council (1945), for instance (NLW: XRC756. C55); a report on *Scavenging and Street Cleansing Work*, by the Surveyor for the County Borough of Swansea (1912) (NLW: TAWE WCOLLSWA); *The Regional Treatment of Housing and Development Problems in South Wales*, published by the Welsh Housing and Development Association (1919) (NLW: CAER WCOLLCA); and the inaugural proceedings of the Welsh National School of Medicine, published by the *Western Mail* newspaper (1915) (NLW: BAN WCOLLBA).

Non-published medical records at the National Library are frequently buried within the collections around which the archives and manuscripts are organized. These collections cover key political figures in Welsh society such as James Griffiths (1890–1975), who served as Minister of National Insurance in the 1945 Labour government and played a major role in policy development (NLW: James Griffiths Papers). There are collections for organizations as well as individuals. The archive of the Labour Party of Wales, for example, may shed light on a broad spectrum of health issues (NLW: C1985/35, C1987/52, C1992/49, C1996/32, C1998/8); while the papers of the Coalowners' Association

(NLW: Mons. and S. Wales Coalowners' Assoc. Records), and those for individual businesses – the Evans and Bevan group of anthracite collieries in the Vale of Neath (1867–1912), or the Nevill family's copper works at Swansea and Llanelly (1797–1910) (NLW, 1996, pp. 87, 117, 144) – may offer insight into the attitudes of employers to safety at work.

The manuscript collections also contain material with a direct bearing on medicine and health. The account book for the Llandybie Colliery shows the record of contributions to the medical fund between 1920 and 1922 (NLW: Misc. Vol. 102). There are the papers of Dr Griffith Evans (1835–1935), the bacteriologist who pioneered protozoon pathology (or the study of disease-causing parasites) (NLW: Griffith Evans Papers) and of Dr David G. Morgan (1903–65), a medical administrator in the Cardiff area (NLW: D. G. Morgan Papers). The scrapbooks of Sir John Lynn Thomas, a surgeon at the Prince of Wales Orthopaedic Hospital, have been deposited, which include offprints, questionnaires and letters relating to Colles' fracture of the wrist (NLW: MSS 13723–36). And the R. J. Rees Manuscripts contain two volumes of reports, correspondence and statistics – dealing with public health, infectious diseases, sanitation and housing – that were compiled by Morgan James Rees when he was Medical Officer of Health in Aberdare and later employed by the Local Government Board (NLW: MSS 4779–91). However, one of the medical holdings of most significance is the archive of the King Edward VII Welsh National Memorial Association (1910–48), which played a major role in the management of tuberculosis (NLW: W.N. M. A. Records).

In addition to printed and manuscript records, the National Library is home to the National Screen and Sound Archive of Wales (NSSAW). Needless to say, a copy of *The Citadel* (1938) is in its possession (NSSAW: 1262). Based on the famous novel by A. J. Cronin, this feature film is one of several health-related items from the interwar period. The others are documentaries. *Ocean Collieries Recreational Union* (*c*.1934) is an incomplete, six-minute film, which considers improvements to the working conditions of miners, including the installation of pithead baths and first aid rooms (NSSAW: 361). With *Operation for Appendicitis* (1933), the focus is the medical profession (NSSAW: 2241). In just over two minutes, Dr James Wade is shown removing an inflamed appendix at the Pontypridd and District Hospital. Two years later he retired as honorary consulting surgeon: an event that the hospital governors marked with a presentation and a celebratory tea in which the patients also participated. A member of the family captured the occasion in a short home movie (NSSAW: 2240).

Local Record Offices and Libraries

The South Wales Coalfield is itself dotted with a host of small local history collections. However, eight main repositories span the coalfield from east to west: Gwent Record Office in Cwmbran (GwRO) and the Newport Library and Information Service; Glamorgan Record Office (GlamRO) and the Central Library in Cardiff; the West Glamorgan Archive Service (WGAS) and the Central Library in Swansea; and Carmarthenshire Archives Service in Carmarthen (CAS) and the Public Library in Llanelly. Whereas the record offices have developed finding aids to help researchers, the libraries are geared to the general reader and have search engines of varying sophistication for academic study. Nevertheless, there is little doubt that these scattered repositories contain an abundance of records for the medical history of the coalfield.

The four record offices hold an extensive range of Poor Law and local government papers with which to investigate the grass-roots provision of statutory health care (see, for example, T. G. H. Davies, 1995). In addition, each of the four libraries has a spread of local newspapers. At Swansea, exploring medical matters is facilitated by an online index to *The Cambrian*: the first English-language newspaper in Wales, which started in 1804 and ceased publication in 1930 (http://www.swansea.gov.uk/cambrian). Although articles tackle a comprehensive spread of subjects, *The Cambrian* is particularly useful for the reporting of mining accidents and the hazards of copper smoke.

The industrial heritage of south Wales is prominent throughout the local collections with record offices and libraries possessing impressive archives for commercial

373

companies (see, for example, WGAS: D/D SB 15, D/D MC, D/D Yc, D/D Xhw, D/D CV 4, D/D Gil) as well as for the friendly societies and co-operative societies (see, for example, CAS: DSO 38, DSO 74; GlamRO: D/D X 769/1–32, D/D X 600/1), trades unions and trades councils (see, for example, GlamRO: D/D ISTC 1/1–65, D/D NUR 3/1–2, D/D X 749) that are so significant in the South Wales Coalfield Collection. Equally valuable are sets of personal papers like the correspondence, minute books, accounts, newspapers and pamphlets of Stephen Owen Davies – a miners' agent for the Dowlais district of the South Wales Miners' Federation – that cover the period 1912 to 1961 (GlamRO: D/D Xhv 1–141). References to occupational health are not immediately obvious but, as experience of the SWCC shows, trawling this material in a hands-on way fleshes out the dynamics of workplace welfare and mutual aid. Therefore, these sources are no less important than official documents like the annual reports of HM Inspector of Mines (1888–1938) (GlamRO: D/D NCB 67/2), or the coroner's report on the Senghenydd Colliery Disaster (1914) (GlamRO: D/D X gj). Nor should they be overshadowed by material of specific medical relevance like the papers of the Rhondda Colliery Rescue Association (1907–55) (GlamRO: D/D NCB 37/16–23), or the sick pay account book of the Order of Sons of Temperance at Merthyr (1898–1938) (GlamRO: D/D X 73/3/1–7).

The papers of trades unions, trades councils, friendly societies and co-operative societies are not only pertinent to the occupational health of the coalfield; they also conceal evidence of many aspects of community health but especially diet, nutrition and food policy. Other holdings are explicitly relevant. The ever-present annual reports of medical officers of health turn up in local record offices as they do in the national repositories (see, for example, Cohen, 1991), but they are joined by the annual reports of the port sanitary authorities, the run for Swansea (1895–2003) being particularly impressive (WGAS: PH1). Records also survive for public health institutions like the County Isolation Hospital at Tumble in Carmarthenshire (1937–48) (CAS: currently unreferenced). However, efforts to construct a healthier urban environment are particularly well represented with archives for Burry Port Garden Suburb Ltd (1917–72) (CAS: DB 3) and the Great Western Garden Village Society Ltd at Caerphilly (1925–72) (GlamRO: DGS/C/1–16).

Poor living and working conditions in the coalfield exposed its population to illness and disability. Cardiff Central Library has a copy of the Ministry of Health's *Report of the Committee of Inquiry into the Anti-tuberculosis Service in Wales and Monmouthshire*, published by HMSO in 1939. At local level, the vulnerability of children was addressed through bodies like the Newport Infantile Health Central Committee – set up by the local authority – whose annual reports are extant between 1909 and 1931 (GwRO: M160 614). Children and adults alike were prone to disability, which prior to the National Health Service was primarily managed via the charitable sector. Its records are numerous. There are, for instance, minute books for the Cardiff Poor Cripples' Aid Society (1908–49) (GlamRO: DPC 1/1, 2) and annual reports for the Newport Poor Cripples' Aid Society (1932–46) (GwRO: pqM160 362.78); whilst both the Swansea and South Wales Institution for the Blind (WGAS: D/D PRO/Ch/82/20) and the Cambrian Institution for the Deaf and Dumb (WGAS: E/Cam 1–6) have extensive records.

Cardiff University is concentrating its archival efforts on two particular areas of medical knowledge and practice: 'the history of genetics in medicine and the history of evaluative approaches to health care' (Kelly, 2004). The holdings of the coalfield record offices and libraries bring a different focus to the activities of practitioners. Minute books survive for the Swansea Division of the South Wales and Monmouthshire Branch of the British Medical Association (1903–1979) (WGAS: D/D BMA/S), as do those for the Cardiff Medical Society (1877–1978), established in 1871 to promote the advancement of medical knowledge and the welfare of the medical profession (GlamRO: DCMS/1–14). Individual practitioners as well as professional organizations are in evidence: the general practice records of the Cresswell family of Dulais (1867–1967), (GlamRO: D/D X 83/1–14); prescription books for a firm of chemists in Llanelly (1891–1979) (CAS: DB 111); and the medical records,

pamphlets, lecture notes and books of a midwife called Mrs
Ann Evans (1914–39) (GlamRO: D/D X 236/1–25). Hospital
nursing is depicted in the Nursing Committee Minutes of the
Cardiff Royal Infirmary (1885–1920) (GlamRO: DHC
39–41). Community nursing, on the other hand, is displayed
in the records of charitable bodies like the Aberavon and Port
Talbot District Nursing Association (1898–1959) (WGAS:
PTL PTNA 1–3), the Newport Nursing Institute (1900, 1901
and 1916) (GwRO: PM160 361.1) and the Newport Home
Nursing Association (1928–48) (GwRO: M160. 362).

Institutionalized health care is the most visible element of
the medical history of the coalfield. Substantial records
(notably, annual reports, minute books, financial statements
and registers of patients) thus survive for the main general
hospitals in the region: the Cardiff Royal Infirmary
(1822–1944) (GlamRO: DHC/1–115); Swansea Hospital
(1817–1948) (WGAS: D 177); the Royal Gwent Hospital,
Newport (1902–47) (GwRO: M160 362.1); and the
Carmarthen Infirmary (1846–1972) (CAS: T/HOS/1). Local
general and specialist hospitals are also covered. In the
Swansea area, for instance, there are miscellaneous papers for
Clydach Cottage Hospital (1922–48) (WGAS: D/D H/Cly),
Gorseinon Hospital (c.1930–70) (WGAS: D/D H/Gor), Craig
House Maternity Hospital (1920–42) (WGAS: D/D H/Gra),
Mount Pleasant Hospital (1929–80) (WGAS: D/D H/MP),
Rheanfa House Maternity Hospital (1931–40) (WGAS: D/D
X 192) and Stouthall Hospital, Reynoldston (1942–54)
(WGAS: D/D H/Sto). Records for psychiatric hospitals are
likewise numerous with comprehensive sets of papers for the
Glamorgan County Lunatic Asylum, Bridgend (1856–1904)
(GlamRO: DXGC 290), the United Counties Lunatic Asylum
Carmarthen (1876–1940) (CAS: SDH), the City of Cardiff
Mental Hospital (1905–48) (GlamRO: D/D HWH 1–57),
Newport County Borough Asylum, Caerleon (1921–42)
(GwRO: M160 362.2) and Cefn Coed Psychiatric Hospital,
Swansea (1932–63) (WGAS: D/D Z 64). Finally, there are
papers for Sully Sanatorium (1932–93) (GlamRO: HSU 1–14)
and The Rest, a convalescent home in Porthcawl (1862 and
1974) (GlamRO: D/D Xel 1–17), both situated on the Vale of
Glamorgan.

This brief tour of medical records for the South Wales Coalfield outside the South Wales Coalfield Collection has scratched the surface. Only a more thorough appraisal of the British Library, the National Archives and the Wellcome Library, and a comprehensive survey of local record offices and libraries, will bring fully to light the wealth of material that is available for teasing out the complex relationships between medicine, health and industrialization in the region.

Appendix C
Libraries and Archives: Contact Details

National Repositories

The British Library
St Pancras,
96 Euston Road,
London, NWl 2DB.

Tel: +44 (0) 870 444 1500
E-mail: *visitor-services@bl.uk*
Web page: *http://www.bl.uk*

The National Archives
Kew,
Richmond,
Surrey,
TW9 4DU.

Tel: +44 (0) 20 8876 3444
E-Mail: *enquiry@nationalarchives.gov.uk*
Web page: *http://www.nationalarchives.gov.uk*

The Wellcome Library
210 Euston Road,
London, NW1 2BE.

Tel: +44 (0) 20 7611 8722
Fax: +44 (0) 207611 8369
E-mail: *library@wellcome.ac.uk*
Web page: *http://library.wellcome.ac.uk*

Welsh Repositories

The National Library of Wales
Penglais,
Aberystwyth,
Ceredigion,
Wales, SY23 3BU.

Tel: +44 (0) 1970 632 800
Fax: +44 (0) 1970 615 709
E-mail: *holi@llgc.org.uk*
Web page: *http://www.llgc.org.uk*

South Wales Coalfield Archive
Library and Information Centre,
Swansea University,
Singleton Park,
Swansea, SA2 8PP.

Tel: +44 (0) 1792 295021
E-mail: *archives@swan.ac.uk*
Web page: *http://www.swan.ac.uk/swcc*
Archivist: Elisabeth Bennett

The South Wales Miners' Library
Hendrefoelan House,
Hendrefoelan,
Gower Road,
Swansea, SA2 7NB.

Tel: +44 (0) 1792 518603/518693
Fax: +44 (0) 1792 518694
E-mail: *miners@swansea.ac.uk*
Web page: *http://www.swan.ac.uk/lis/library_services/
swml.asp*
Librarian: Siân Williams

Carmarthenshire Archive Service
Parc Myrddin,
Richmond Terrace,
Carmarthen, SA31 IDS.

Tel: +44 (0) 1267 228232
Fax: +44 (0) 1267 228237
E-mail: *Archives@carmarthenshire.gov.uk*
Web page: *http://www.carmarthenshire. gov.uk*

Glamorgan Record Office
The Glamorgan Building,
King Edward VII Avenue,
Cathays Park,
Cardiff, CF 10 3NE.

Tel: +44 (0) 29 2078 0282
Fax: +44 (0) 29 2078 0284
E-mail: *glamro@cardiff.ac.uk*
Web page: *http://www.glamro.gov.uk*

Gwent Record Office
County Hall,
Cwmbran,
Gwent, NP44 2XH.

Tel: +44 (0) 1633 644886 or 1633 644888
Fax: +44 (0) 1633 648382
E-mail: *gwent.records@torfaen.gov.uk*
Web page: *http://www.llgc.org.uk/cac/cac0004.htm*

West Glamorgan Archive Service
County Hall,
Oystermouth Road,
Swansea, SA1 3SN.

Tel: +44 (0) 1792 636589
Fax: +44 (0) 1792 637130
E-mail: *Westglam.archives@swansea.gov.uk*
Web page: *http://www.swansea.gov.uk/
westglamorganarchives*

Cardiff Central Library
(*Temporary address*)
John Street,
Cardiff, CF10 5BA.

Tel: +44 (0) 2038 2116
E-mail: *centrallibrary@cardiff.gov.uk*
Web page: *http://www.cardiff.gov.uk*

Llanelli Library
Vaughan Street,
Llanelli, SA15 3AS.

Tel: +44 (0) 1554 773538
Fax: +44 (0) 1554 750125
E-mail: *mjewell@sirgar.gov.uk*
Web page: *www.carmarthen.gov.uk*

Newport Central Library
John Frost Square,
Newport, NP20 1PA.

Tel: +44 (0) 1633 656656
E-mail: *central.library@newport.gov.uk*
Web page: *http://www.newport.gov.uk*

Swansea Central Library
Alexandra Road,
Swansea, SA1 5DX.

Tel: +44 (0) 1792 516750
E-mail: *central.library@swansea.gov.uk*
Web page: *http://www.swansea.gov.uk*

Bibliography

Printed Resources

Wales and the South Wales Coalfield

Adamson, D. (1999). 'The intellectual and the national movement in Wales', in R. Fevre and A. Thompson (eds), *Nation, Identity and Social Theory: Perspectives from Wales*, Cardiff, University of Wales Press.

Berger, S., Croll, A. and LaPorte, N. (eds) (2005). *Towards a Comparative History of Coalfield Societies*, Aldershot, Ashgate.

Daunton, M. (1977). *Coal Metropolis Cardiff 1870–1914*, Leicester, Leicester University Press.

Davies, B. (1983). *The Iron Industry in Wales 1750–1850*, Treforest, Welsh History Resources Unit.

Edwards, N. (1926). *The History of the South Wales Miners*, London, Labour Publishing Company.

—— (1938). *The History of the South Wales Miners' Federation*, London, Lawrence and Wishart.

Evans, D. G. (1989). *A History of Wales 1815–1906*, Cardiff, University of Wales Press.

—— (2000). *A History of Wales 1906–2000*, Cardiff, University of Wales Press.

Francis, H. (1976). 'The origins of the South Wales Miners' Library', *History Workshop Journal*, 2, 183–205.

—— (1984). *Miners Against Fascism: Wales and the Spanish Civil War*, London, Lawrence and Wishart.

Francis, H. and Smith, D. (1980). *The Fed: A History of the South Wales Miners in the Twentieth century*, London, Lawrence and Wishart.

John, A. H. (1950). *The Industrial Development of South Wales 1750–1850*, Cardiff, University of Wales Press.

Lawrence, R. (2005). *The Miners of the South Wales Coalfield*, Blackwood, Ray Lawrence.

Morgan, K. O. (1981). *Rebirth of a Nation: Wales 1880–1980*, Oxford, Clarendon Press.

Page Arnot, R. (1967). *South Wales Miners*, vol. I, *1898–1914*, London, Allen and Unwin.

Page Arnot, R. (1975). *South Wales Miners*, Vol. II, *1914–1926*, Cardiff, Cymric Federation Press.

Pope, R. (1998). *Building Jerusalem: Nonconformity, Labour and the Social Question in Wales 1906–1939*, Cardiff, University of Wales Press.

Rees, R. (2000). *King Copper: South Wales and the Copper Trade 1584–1895*, Cardiff, University of Wales Press.

Smith, D. and Williams, G. (1980). *Fields of Praise: The Official History of the Welsh Rugby Union 1881–1981*, Cardiff: University of Wales Press.

Strange, K. (1983). *Merthyr Tydfil, Iron Community*, Treforest, Welsh History Resources Unit.

Toomey, R. R. (1985). *Vivian and Sons 1809–1924: A Study of the Firm in the Copper and Related Industries*, New York, Garland.

Williams, C. (1996). *Democratic Rhondda: Politics and Society, 1885–1951*, Cardiff, University of Wales Press.

—— (1998). *Capitalism, Community and Conflict: The South Wales Coalfield, 1898–1947*, Cardiff, University of Wales Press.

Williams, J. (1988). 'The move from the land', in T. Herbert and G. Elwyn Jones (eds), *Wales 1800–1914*, Cardiff, University of Wales Press.

Health, Medicine and Social Welfare

Borsay, A. (ed.) (2003). *Medicine in Wales c.1800–2000: Public Service or Private Commodity*, Cardiff, University of Wales Press.

Bruce, M. (1970). *The Coming of the Welfare State*, London, Batsford.

Brunton, D. (2004). *Medicine Transformed: Health, Disease and Society in Europe 1800–1930*, Manchester, Manchester University Press.

Bynum, W. F. and Porter, R. (eds.) (1993). *Companion Encyclopaedia of the History of Medicine*, London, Routledge.

Cooter, R. and Pickstone, J. (eds) (2000). *Companion to Medicine in the Twentieth Century*, London, Routledge.

Finlayson, G. (1994). *Citizen, State and Social Welfare in Britain 1830–1990*, Oxford, Clarendon Press.

Fraser, D. (1973). *The Evolution of the British Welfare State*, London, Macmillan.

Gazeley, I. (2003). *Poverty in Britain 1900–1965*, Basingstoke, Palgrave Macmillan.

Gilbert, B. B. (1970). *British Social Policy 1914–1939*, London, Batsford.

Hardy, A. (2000). *Health and Medicine in Britain since 1860*, Basingstoke, Macmillan.

Harris, B. (2004). *The Origins of the British Welfare State: Social Welfare in England and Wales, 1800–1945*, Basingstoke, Palgrave Macmillan.

Harrison, M. (2004). *Disease and the Modern World: 1500 to the Present Day*, Cambridge, Polity.

Jones, H. (1994). *Health and Society in Twentieth-century Britain*, London, Longman.

Kidd, A. (1999). *State, Society and the Poor in Nineteenth-century England*, Basingstoke, Macmillan.

Kiple, K. F. (ed.) (2003). *The Cambridge Historical Dictionary of Disease*, Cambridge, Cambridge University Press.

Lawrence, C. (1994). *Medicine in the Making of Modern Britain, 1700–1920*, London, Routledge.

Linehan, D. and Gruffudd, P. (2001). 'Bodies and souls: psychogeographical collisions in the South Wales coalfield, 1926–1939', *Journal of Historical Geography*, 27, 377–94.

Loudon, Irvine (ed.) (1997). *Western Medicine: An Illustrated History*, Oxford, Oxford University Press.

Michael, P. and Webster, C. (eds) (2006). *Medicine and Society in Twentieth-Century Wales*, Cardiff, University of Wales Press.

Porter, R. (1999). *The Greatest Benefit to Mankind: A Medical History of Humanity from Antiquity to the Present*, London, Fontana.

Thompson, S. (2006). *Unemployment, Poverty and Health in Interwar South Wales*, Cardiff, University of Wales Press.

Wear, Andrew (ed.) (1992). *Medicine in Society: Historical Essays*, Cambridge, Cambridge University Press.

Occupational Health

Bartrip, P. W. J. and Burman, S. (1983). *The Wounded Soldiers of Industry*, Oxford, Oxford University Press.

Bartrip, P. W. J. (1987) *Workmen's Compensation in Twentieth-Century Britain*, Aldershot, Avebury.

Bloor, M. (2000). 'The South Wales Miners Federation, miners' lung and the instrumental use of expertise, 1900–1950', *Social Studies of Science*, 30, 1, 125–140.

Bufton, M. W. and Melling, J. (2005). '"A mere matter of rock": organized labour, scientific evidence and British government

385

schemes for compensation of silicosis and pneumoconiosis among coalminers, 1926–1940', *Medical History*, 49, 2, 155–78.

Cooter, R. (1993). *Surgery and Society in Peace and War: Orthopaedics and the Organization of Modern Medicine, 1880–1948*, Basingstoke, Macmillan.

D'Arcy Hart, P. (with E. M. Tansey) (1998). 'Chronic pulmonary disease in South Wales coal mines: an eye-witness account of the MRC surveys (1937–1942), *Social History of Medicine*, 11, 3, *459–68*.

Dennis, V. S. (2005). *Discovering Friendly and Fraternal Societies: Their Badges and Regalia*, Princes Risborough, Shire Publications.

Earwicker, R. (1981). 'Miners' medical services before the First World War: the South Wales Coalfield', *Llafur*, 3, 2, 39–52.

Edwards, H. (1997). *Follow the Banner: An Illustrated Catalogue of the Northumberland Miners' Banners*, Manchester, Carcanet Press.

Evans, N. and Jones, D. (1994). '"A blessing for the miner's wife": the campaign for pithead baths in the South Wales Coalfield', *Llafur*, 6, 3, 5–28.

Green, D. H. (1985). *Working-Class Patients and the Medical Establishment: Self-Help in Britain from the Mid-nineteenth Century to 1948*, Aldershot, Gower.

Jones, D. (1984–5). 'Did friendly societies matter?: a study of friendly societies in Glamorgan 1794–1910', *Welsh History Review*, 12, 324–49.

McIvor, A. J. (2001). *A History of Work in Britain, 1880–1950*, Basingstoke, Palgrave.

McIvor, A. and Johnson, R. (eds) (2006). *Miners' Lung: A History of Dust Disease in British Coal Mining*, Aldershot, Ashgate.

Nash, G. D. Davies, T. A. and Thomas, B. (1995). *Workmen's Halls and Institutes: Oakdale Workmen's Institute*, Cardiff, National Museums and Galleries of Wales.

Ness A. R., Reynolds L. A. and Tansey E. M. (2002). *Population-based Research in South Wales: The MRC Pneumoconiosis Research Unit and the MRC Epidemiology Unit*, London, Wellcome Witness Seminar Transcript Series.

Riley, J. C. (1997). *Sick, Not Dead: The Health of the British Workingmen during the Mortality Decline*, Baltimore, John Hopkins University Press.

Rosner, D. and Markowitz, G. (1993). *Deadly Dust*, Princeton, Princeton University Press.

Salway, G. (2005). *The Architecture of Cleanliness: Miners Welfare and the Pithead Baths at Penallta Colliery*, Caerphilly, Groundwork.

Sellers, C. (1997) *Hazards of the Job: From Industrial Disease to Environmental Health Science*, Chapel Hill, University of North Carolina Press.

Tweedale, G. (2000). *Magic Mineral to Deadly Dust*, Oxford, Oxford University Press, 2000.

Weindling, Paul (ed.) (1985). *The Social History of Occupational Health*, London, Croom Helm.

Williams, M. A. (2002). *A Forgotten Army: Female Munitions Workers of South Wales, 1939–1945*, Cardiff, University of Wales Press.

Community Health

Borsay, A. (2005). *Disability and Social Policy in Britain since 1750: A History of Exclusion*, Basingstoke, Palgrave Macmillan.

Bryder, L. (1988). *Below the Magic Mountain: A Social History of Tuberculosis in Twentieth-century Britain*, Oxford, Clarendon Press.

Burnett, J. (1989). *Plenty and Want: A Social History of Food in England from 1815 to the Present Day*, London, Routledge.

—— (1993). *A Social History of Housing, 1815–1895*, London, Routledge.

Cunningham, H. (1995). *Children and Childhood in Western Society since 1500*, London, Longman.

Davies, T. G. (1995–6). 'Judging the sanity of an individual: some south Wales civil legal actions of psychiatric interest', *National Library of Wales Journal*, 29, 455–67.

—— (1996). 'Wales' contribution to mental health legislation in the nineteenth century', *Welsh History Review*, 18, 1, 40–62.

Dormandy, T. (2001). *The White Death: A History of Tuberculosis*, London, Hambledon and London.

Glynn, I. (2004). *The Life and Death of Smallpox*, London, Profile.

Gruffydd, P. (1995). '"A crusade against consumption": environment, health and social reform in Wales, 1900–1939', *Journal of Historical Geography*, 21, 1, 39–54.

Fisk, M. J. (1996). *Housing in the Rhondda 1800–1940*, Cardiff, Merton Priory Press.

Heywood, C. (2001). *A History of Childhood: Children and Childhood in the West from Medieval to Modern Times*, Cambridge, Polity.

Howett Research Institute (1955). *Family Diet and Health in Pre-war Britain: A Dietary and Clinical Survey*, Report to the Carnegie United Kingdom Trust, Dunfermline, Carnegie United Kingdom Trust.

Jones, P. N. (1969). *Colliery Settlement in the South Wales Coalfield 1850 to 1926*, Hull, Occasional Papers in Geography No. 14, University of Hull Publications.

Lowe, J. (1985). *Welsh Industrial Workers Housing, 1775–1875*, Cardiff, National Museum of Wales.

Phillips, J. and Smith, D. F. (eds.) (2000). *Food Science, Policy and Regulation in the Twentieth Century: International and Comparative Perspectives*, London, Routledge.

Porter, D. (1999). *Health, Civilization and the State: A History of Public Health from Ancient to Modern Times*, London, Routledge.

Smith, D. (ed.) (1996). *Nutrition in Britain: Science, Scientists and Politics in the Twentieth Century*, London, Routledge.

Wohl, A. S. (1984). *Endangered Lives: Public Health in Victorian Britain*, London, Methuen.

Women's Health

Aaron, J., Rees, T., Betts, S. and Vincentelli, M. (eds) (1994). *Our Sisters' Land: The Changing Identities of Women in Wales*, Cardiff, University of Wales Press.

Andrews, E. (2006). *A Woman's Work is Never Done*, Aberystwyth, Honno.

Beddoe, D. (1989). *Back to Home and Duty: Women Between the Wars, 1919–1939*, London, Pandora.

—— (1991). 'Munitionettes, maids and mams: women in Wales 1914–1939', in A. V. John (ed.), *Our Mothers' Land: Chapters in Welsh Women's History, 1830–1939*, Cardiff, University of Wales Press.

—— (2000). *Out of the Shadows : A History of Women in Twentieth-century Wales*, Cardiff, University of Wales Press.

Evans, N. and Jones, D. (1994). '"A blessing for the miner's wife: the campaign for pit-head baths in the South Wales Coalfield 1908–50', *Llafur*, 6, 3, 5–28.

Jones, D. (1991). 'Counting the cost of coal: women's lives in the Rhondda 1881–1911', in A. V. John (ed.), *Our Mothers' Land:*

Chapters in Welsh Women's History, 1830–1939, Cardiff, University of Wales Press.

Jones, O. S. (1987). 'Women in the tinplate industry in Llanelli 1930–50', *Oral History Journal*, 15,1, 72–90.

Mercier, L. and Gier-Viskovatoff, J. J. (2006). *Mining Women: Gender in the Development of a Global Industry, 1670–2000*, Basingstoke, Palgrave Macmillan.

Oakley, A. (1984). *The Captured Womb: A History of the Medical Care of Pregnant Women*, Oxford, Blackwell.

Tew, M. (1998). *Safer Childbirth: A Critical History of Maternity Care*, 3rd edn, London, Free Association.

White, C. and Williams, S. R. (1997). *Struggle or Starve: Women's Lives in the South Wales Valleys between the Wars*, Dinas Powys, Honno.

Williams, A. S. (1997). *Women and Childbirth in the Twentieth Century: A History of the National Birthday Trust Fund, 1928–1993*, Stroud, Sutton.

Health Care Personnel

Anderson, S. (ed.) (2005). *Making Medicines: A Brief History of Pharmacy and Pharmaceuticals*, London, Pharmaceutical Press.

Baly, M. (1987). *A History of the Queen's Institute: 100 Years, 1887–1987*, London, Croom Helm.

—— (1995). *Nursing and Social Change*, London, Routledge.

Cronin, A. J. (1937). *The Citadel*, London, Victor Gollancz.

Digby, A. (1994). *Making a Medical Living: Doctors and Patients in the English Market for Medicine, 1720–1911*, Cambridge, Cambridge University Press.

—— (1999). *British General Practice, 1850–1948*, Oxford, Oxford University Press.

Dingwall, R., Rafferty, A.-M. and Webster, C. (1988). *An Introduction to the Social History of Nursing*, London, Routledge.

Fox, E. (1994). 'District nursing in England and Wales before the National Health Service: the neglected evidence', *Medical History*, 38, 3, 303–21.

Honigsbaum, F. (1979). *The Division of British Medicine: A History of the Separation of General Practice from Hospital Care, 1911–1968*, London, Kogan Page.

Kremers, E. and Urdang, G. (1951). *History of Pharmacy: A Guide and Survey*, Philadelphia, Lippinott.

Loudon, I. (1986). *Medical Care and the General Practitioner, 1750–1850*, Oxford, Clarendon Press.

Salwak, D. (1985). *A. J. Cronin*, Boston, Twayne Books.

Stocks, M. (1960). *A Hundred Years of District Nursing*, London, Allen and Unwin.

Medical Institutions

Aldis, A. S. (1984). *Cardiff Royal Infirmary, 1883–1983*, Cardiff, University of Wales Press.

Arbour Stephens, G. (1912). *The Hospitals of Wales*, Swansea, Lewis Evans.

Bartlett, P. and Wright, D. (eds) (1999). *Outside the Walls of the Asylum: The History of Care in the Community, 1750–2000*, London, Athlone.

Bolwell, J. and Evans, A. (2005). *A History of the County Infirmary, Carmarthen 1847–1948*, Carmarthen, Noon Books.

Cherry, S. (1996). *Medical Services and the Hospitals in Britain, 1860–1939*, Cambridge, Cambridge University Press.

Davies, K. (1996). '"Sexing the mind": gender and madness in nineteenth-century Welsh asylums', *Llafur*, 7, 1, 29–40.

Davies, T. G. (1988). *Deeds Not Words: A History of the Swansea General and Eye Hospital, 1817–1948*, Cardiff, University of Wales Press.

Jones, G. (1998). *The Aneurin Bevan Inheritance: The Story of the Nevill Hall and District NHS Trust*, Abertillery, Gwent, Old Bakehouse Publications.

Melling, J. and Forsythe, B. (eds) (1999). *Insanity, Institutions and Society, 1800–1914: A Social History of Madness in Comparative Perspective*, London, Routledge.

Michael, P. (2003). *Care and Treatment of the Mentally Ill in North Wales, 1800–2000*, Cardiff, University of Wales Press.

Pinker, R. (1966). *English Hospital Statistics, 1861–1938*, London, Heinemann.

Thompson, S. (2003). 'To relieve the sufferings of humanity, irrespective of party, politics or creed?: conflict, consensus and voluntary hospital provision in Edwardian South Wales', *Social History of Medicine*, 16, 2, 247–62.

Williams, D. G. (1993). *Morriston Hospital: The Early Years*, Swansea, Morriston Hospital Golden Jubilee Appeal Fund.

Historical Sources and Methods

Burke, P. (ed.) (1991). *New Perspectives on Historical Writing*, Cambridge, Polity.

—— (2001). *Eyewitnessing: The Uses of Images as Historical Evidence*, London, Reaktion.

Cohen, S. (1991). *A Guide to the Annual Reports of the Medical Officer of Health for Swansea*, Swansea, City Archives Office.

Cule, J. (1980). *Wales and Medicine: A Source-list of Printed Books and Papers Showing the History of Medicine in relation to Wales and Welshmen*, Aberystwyth, National Library of Wales.

Davies, T. G. H. (1995). *Guide to the Committees of the County Borough of Swansea*, Swansea, City Archives Office.

Hey, D. (ed.) (2002). *The Oxford Companion to Local and Family History*, Oxford, Oxford University Press.

Hudson, P. (2000). *History By Numbers: An Introduction to Quantitative Approaches*, London, Arnold.

Jordanova, L. (2000). *History in Practice*, London, Arnold.

Kelly, E. (2004). 'Looking forward to the past: refocusing on the history of medicine at Cardiff University', *SCONUL Focus*, 33, 47–9.

Lambert, P. and Schofield, P. (eds) (2004). *Making History: An Introduction to the History and Practices of a Discipline*, Abingdon, Routledge.

Lord, E. (1999). *Investigating the Twentieth Century: Sources for Local Historians*, Stroud, Tempus.

Munby, L. M. (1997). *Dates and Time: A Handbook for Local Historians*, Salisbury, British Association for Local History.

Murphy, M. (1991). *Newspapers and Local History*, Chichester, Phillimore for British Association for Local History.

National Library of Wales [NLW] (1996). *Guide to the Department of Manuscripts and Records*, Aberystwyth, National Library of Wales.

Oliver, G. (1989). *Photographs and Local History*, London, Batsford.

Perks, R. and Thomson, A. (1998). *The Oral History Reader*, London Routledge.

Plummer, K. (1983). *Documents of Life: An Introduction to the Problems and Literature of a Humanistic Method*, London, Unwin Hyman.

Tagg, J. (1988). *The Burden of Representation: Essays on Photographs and Histories*, London, Macmillan.

Thompson, P. with Perks, R. (1993). *An Introduction to the Use of Oral History in the History of Medicine*, The National Life Story Collection, London, British Library National Sound Archive.

Tosh, J. (1991). *The Pursuit of History: Aims, Methods and New Directions in the Study of Modern History*, London, Longman.

Your V. R. (2005). *Recording Oral History: A Guide for the Humanities and Social Sciences*, 2nd edn, Walnut Creek, California, AltaMira.

Web Resources

History

British History Online
http://www.british-history.ac.uk

Institute of Historical Research
http://www.history.ac.uk

Royal Historical Society Bibliography
http://www.rhs.ac.uk/bibl/ bibwel.asp

Medicine and Health

Avery Historical Museum
http://www.averyweight-tronix.com

Bethlem Royal Hospital Archives and Museum
http://www.bethlemheritage.org.uk/archcat.html

Chronology of state medicine, public health and welfare in Britain
http://www.chronology.org.uk

Coalfield Web Materials: South Wales Coalfield Collection – Medicine and Health
http://www.agor.org.uk/cwm

Gathering the Jewels: The Website for Welsh Cultural History – Health, Welfare and Charity
http:www.gtj.org.uk

History of Medicine On-line
http://www.priory.co.uk/homol.htm

Milestones in Welsh Medicine
http://www.cardiff.ac.uk/schoolsanddivisions/divisions/insrv/library services/scolar/ special/mil

NHS History
http://www.nhshistory.com

Rossbret Institutions: Hospitals
http://www.institutions.org.uk/ hospitals/index.htn?

Health Care Practitioners

Archie Cochrane Archive
http://www.cardiff.ac.uk/schoolsanddivisions/divisions/insrv/library
services/scolar/ archives/cochrane

British Society for the History of Pharmacy
http://www.bshp.org

Finding the Right Clinical Notes: Improving Research Access to
Personal Health Records in Scotland 1600–1994
http://www.clinicalnotes.ac.uk

History of Dentistry Research Group
http://www.rcpsglasg.ac.uk/ hdrg

Royal Pharmaceutical Society of Great Britain
http://www.rpsgb.org.uk

Tredegar Medical Aid Society
http://www.cradleofnhs.org.uk

UK Centre for the History of Nursing and Midwifery
http://www.ukchnm.org

Museums

Big Pit: National Coal Museum
http://www.museumwales.ac.uk/ en/bigpit

British Dental Association Museum
http://www.bda-dentistry. org.uk/museum

Florence Nightingale Museum
http://www.florence-nightingale. co.uk

Glenside Hospital Museum, Bristol
http://www.glensidemuseum. pwp.blueyonder.co.uk

London's Museums of Health and Medicine
http://www.medicalmuseums.org/index.html

National Waterfront Museum, Swansea: Wales' Story of Industry
and Innovation
http://www.museumwales.ac.uk/swansea

Old Operating Theatre Museum and Herb Garden
http://www.thegarret.org.uk/oot.htm

Rochdale Pioneers Museum
http://www.museum.co-op.ac.uk

Historical Sources

Access to Archives: The English Strand of the UK Archives Network
http://www.a2a.org.uk

Archives Network Wales
http://www.archivesnetworkwales

BOPCRIS: Unlocking Key British Government Publications
http://www.bopcris.ac.uk

Cambrian newspaper
http://www.swansea.gov.uk/cambrian

Cardiff: The Building of a Capital
http://www.glamro.gov.uk

Hospital Records Database
http://www.nationalarchives.gov.uk/ hospitalrecords

Medical History Gateway to Internet Resources
http://medhist.ac.uk

SCAN: The Scottish Archive Network
http://www.scan.org.uk

Women's Archive of Wales
http://www.womensarchivewales.org/ en/index.html

Index of Names

Index of Places

Index of Organisations

Index of Subjects

The Index of Subjects relates to the introductions for each chapter and not to the tables